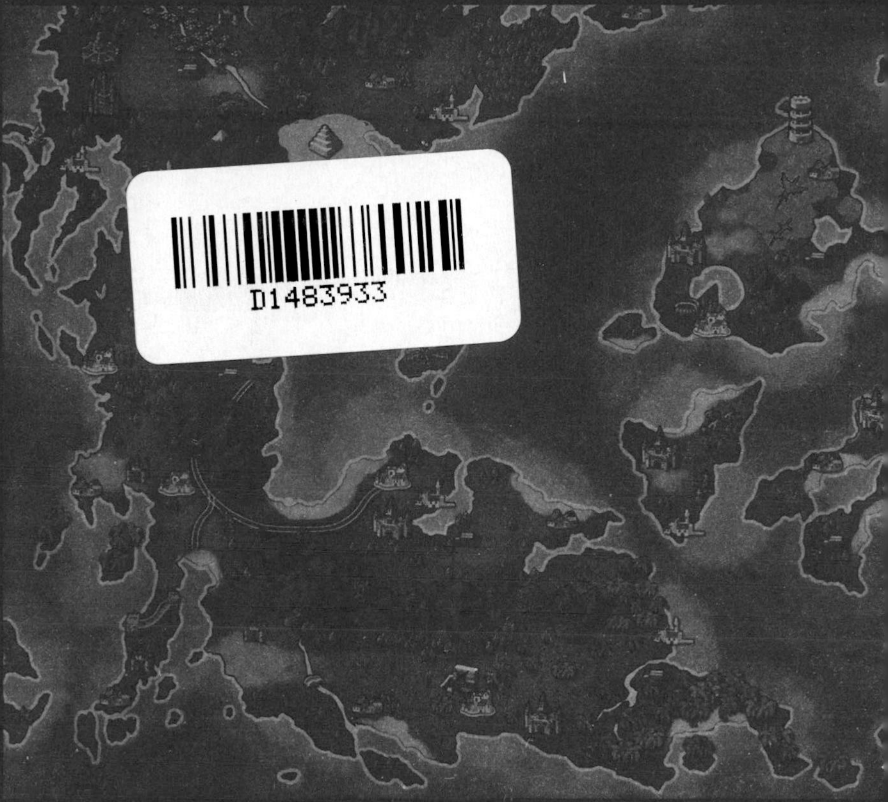



## THE STORY SO FAR

The continent of Consume is plagued by an endless war for domination between the blue-eyed Kingdom of Segua and the red-eyed Ninteldo Empire.

After returning from Decoran, Gear and his companions come home to find Segua Castle in ruins. While Gear and Opal searched for survivors they were attacked by assassins from Decoran. After beating these assassins they learned the name of the person behind the destruction of the castle: Opal's father, Koil. Shattered by the news, Opal wanted to go face her father on her own but Gear managed to persuade her to let him help.

After reaching Koil's hideout, Opal had to face four bosses of her father's elite forces. Defeating them and her father who led them would be the only way for Opal to free herself from the chains of past.

Part 2

# CHAPTER 12

# OPAL'S TEARS

DISC 2

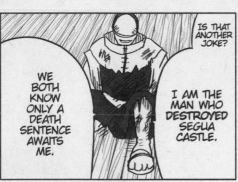

YOU...
YOU'VE DONE HORRIBLE THINGS.
WE'RE TAKING YOU BACK TO SEGUA TO STAND TRIAL FOR YOUR CRIMES.
IS THAT ANOTHER JOKE?
I AM THE MAN WHO DESTROYED SEGUA CASTLE.
WE BOTH KNOW ONLY A DEATH SENTENCE AWAITS ME.
RATHER THAN DIE AT THE HANDS OF THOSE SEGUA PIGS...
I'LL DIE BY MY OWN HAND.

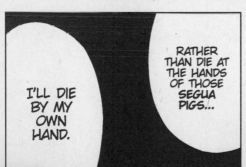

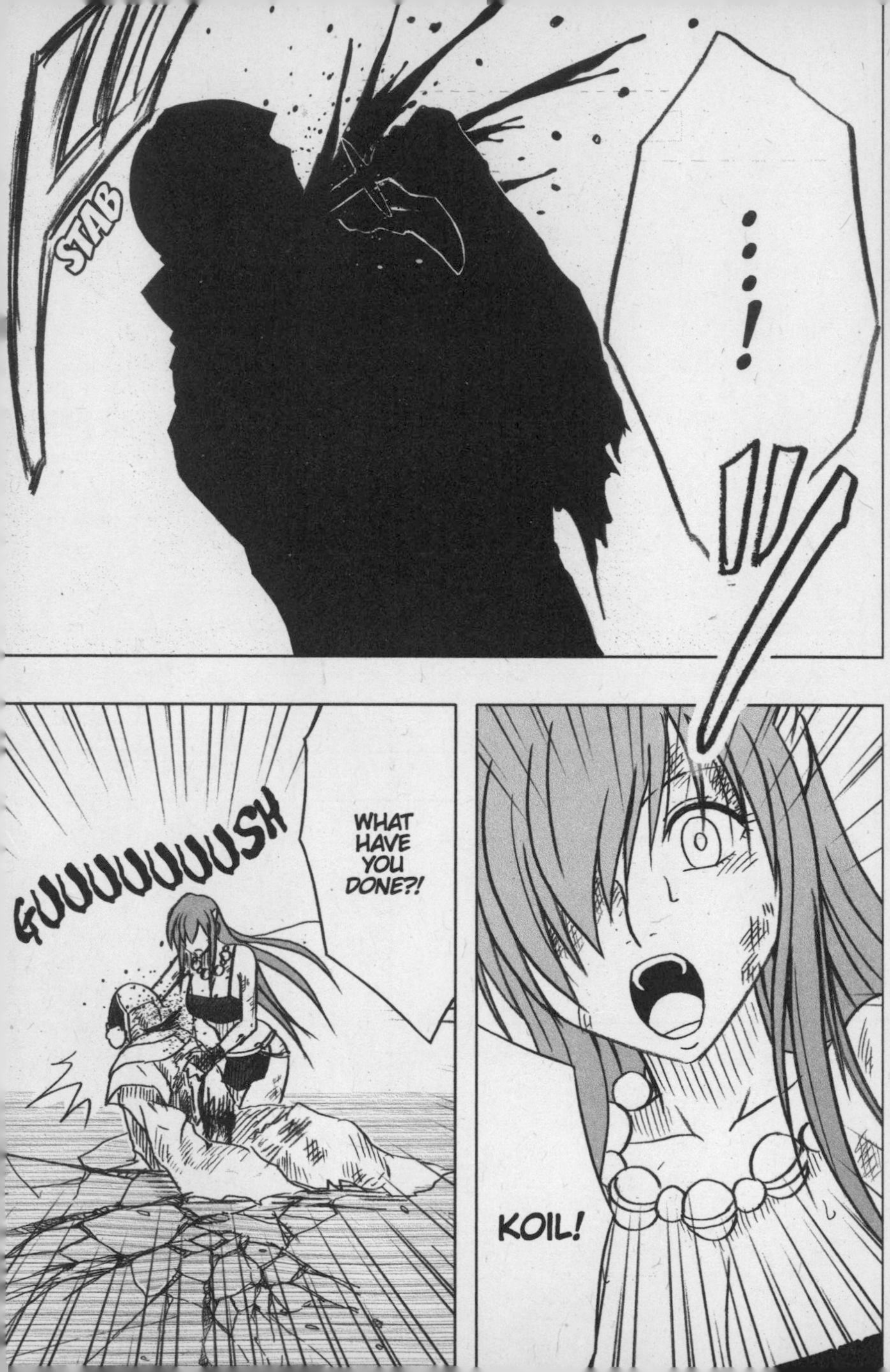
...!
STAB
KOIL!
WHAT HAVE YOU DONE?!
GUUUUUUUSH

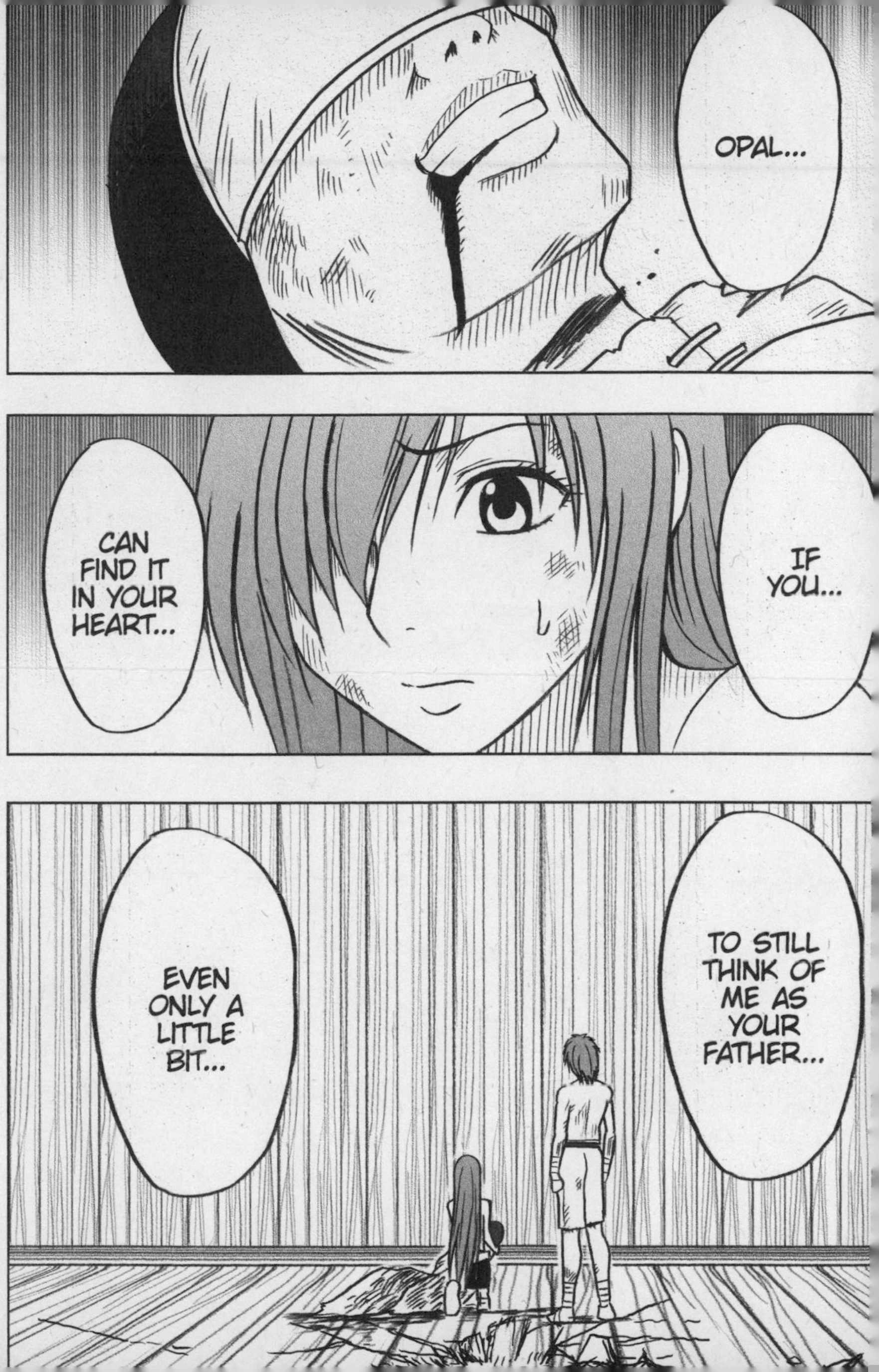
OPAL...
IF YOU...
CAN FIND IT IN YOUR HEART...
TO STILL THINK OF ME AS YOUR FATHER...
EVEN ONLY A LITTLE BIT...

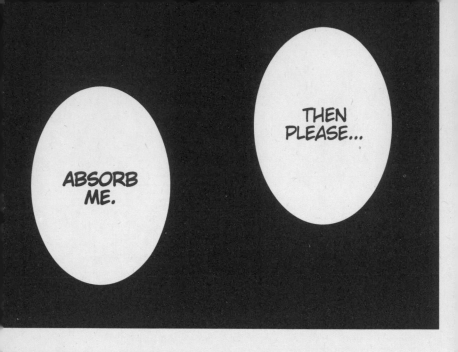

THEN PLEASE...

ABSORB ME.

THIS IS...

MY FINAL ORDER FOR YOU.

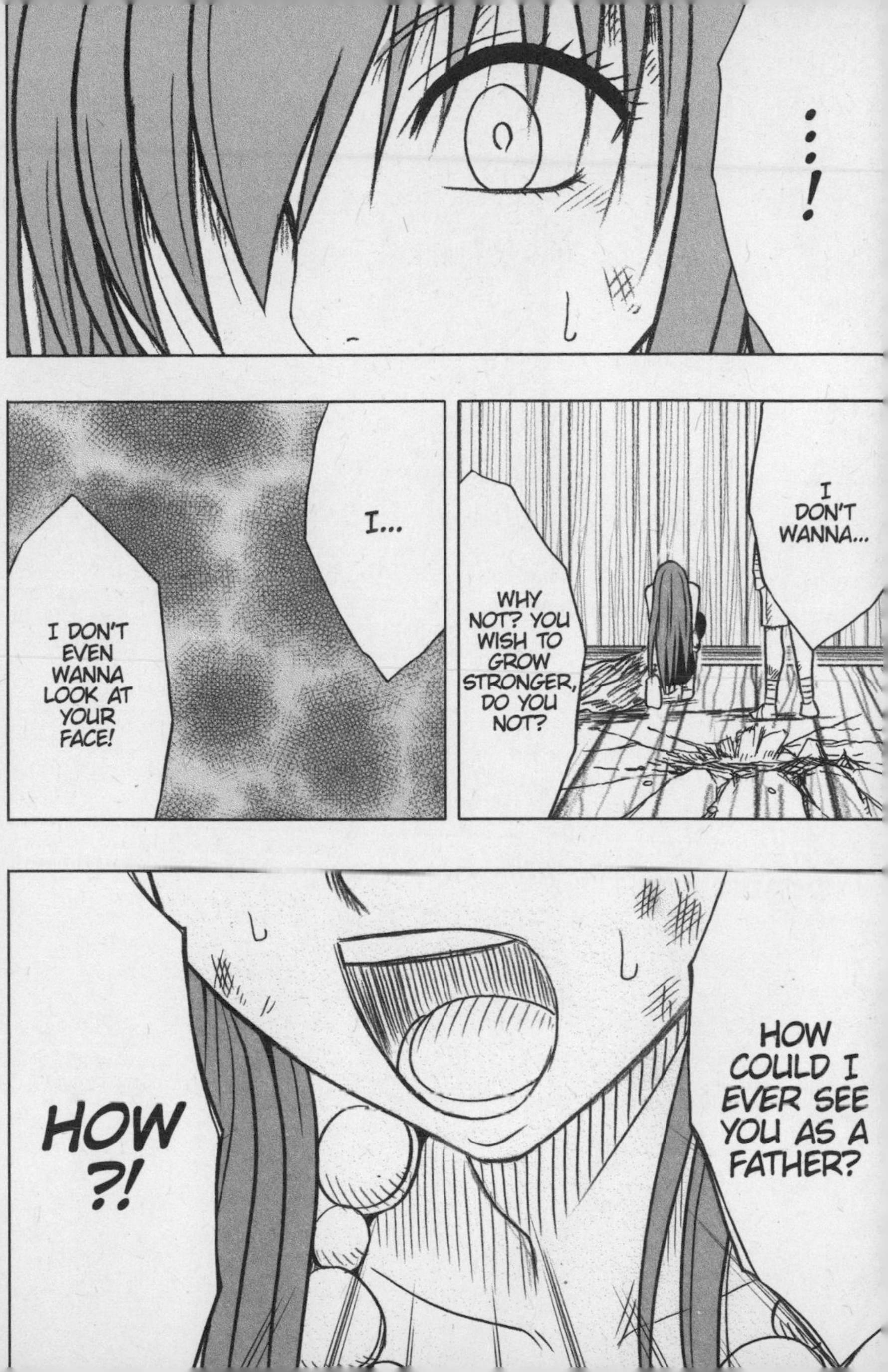
...!
I DON'T WANNA...
WHY NOT? YOU WISH TO GROW STRONGER, DO YOU NOT?
I...
I DON'T EVEN WANNA LOOK AT YOUR FACE!
HOW COULD I EVER SEE YOU AS A FATHER?
HOW?!

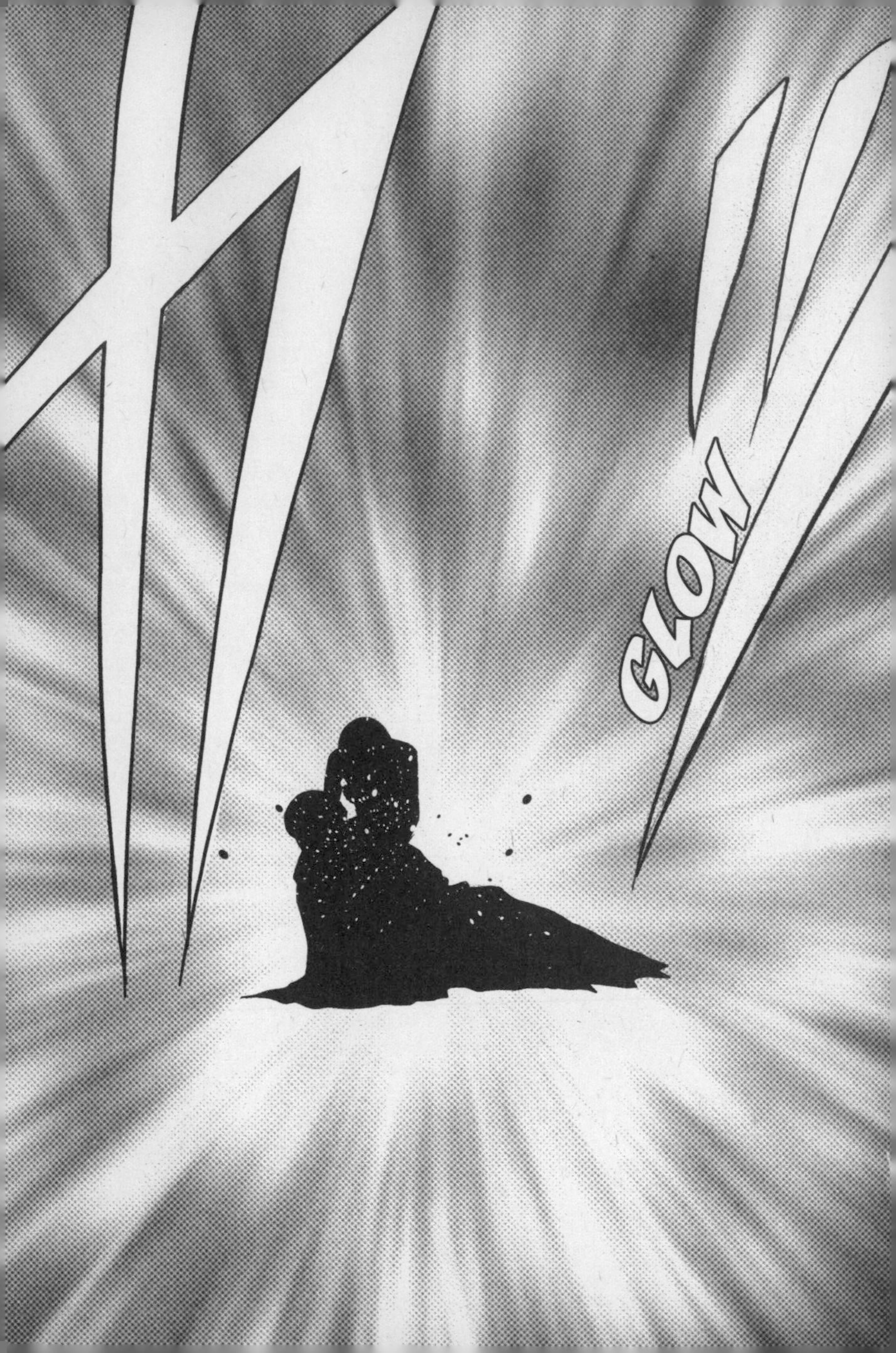
GLOW

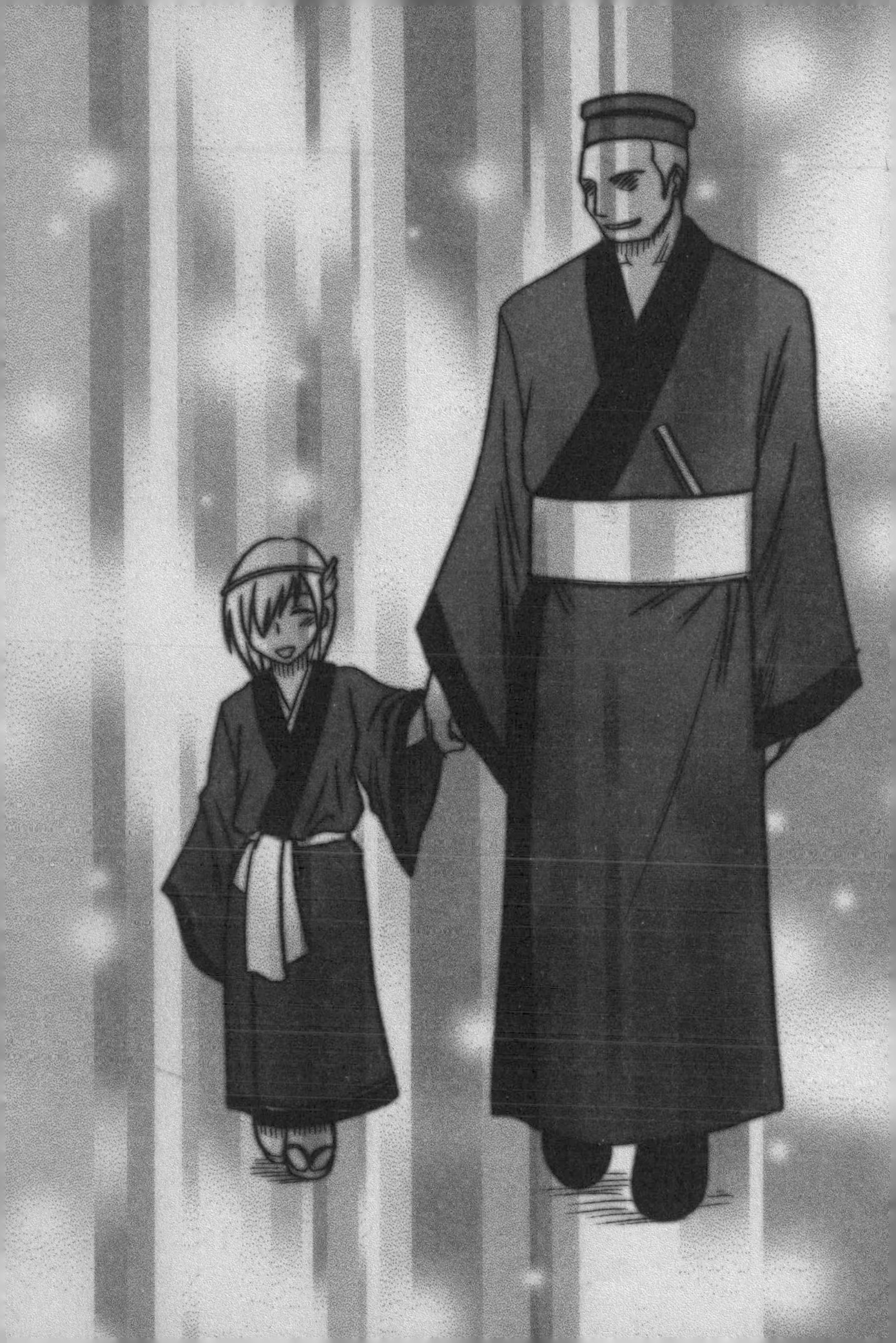

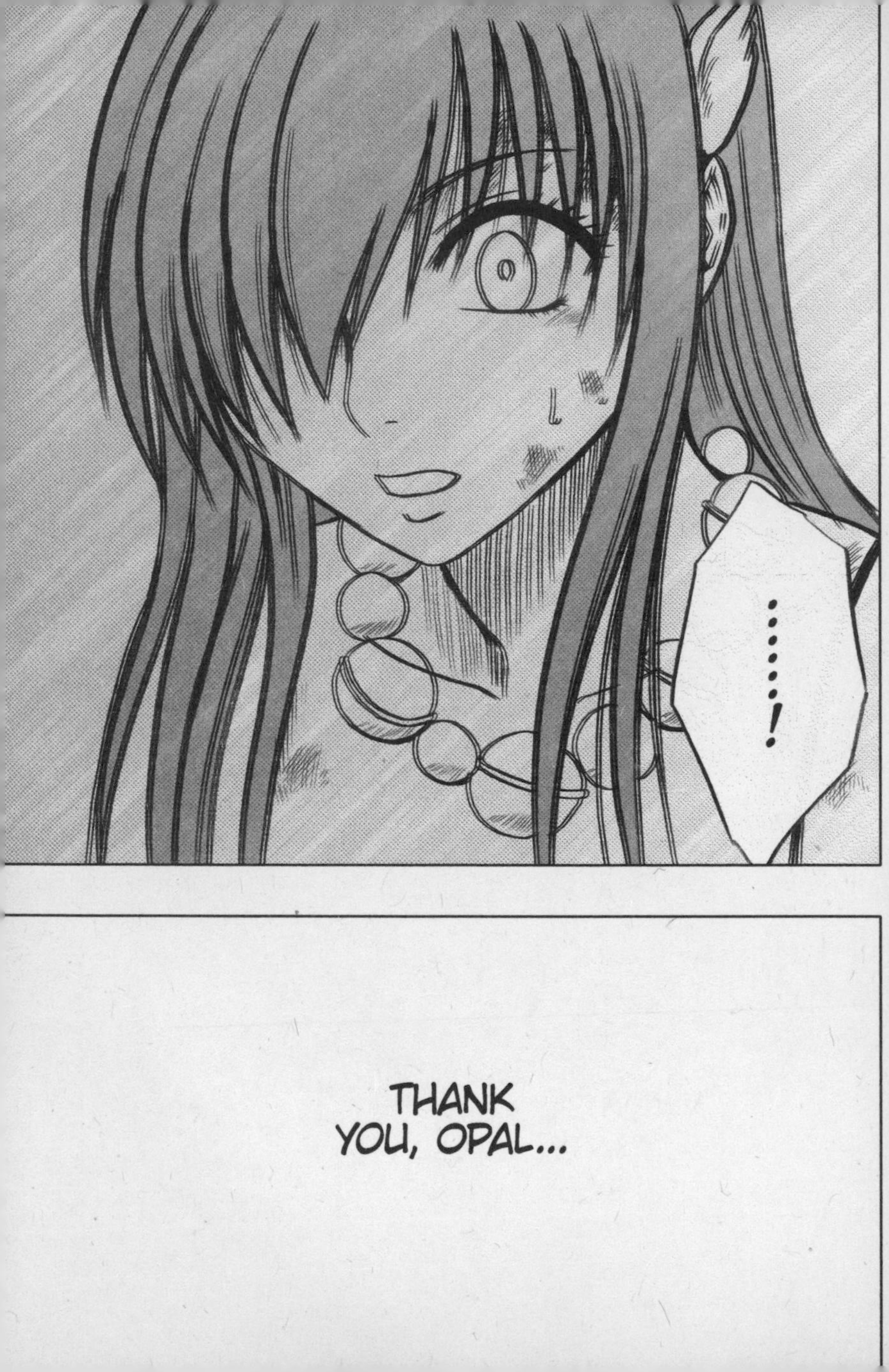
......!
THANK YOU, OPAL...

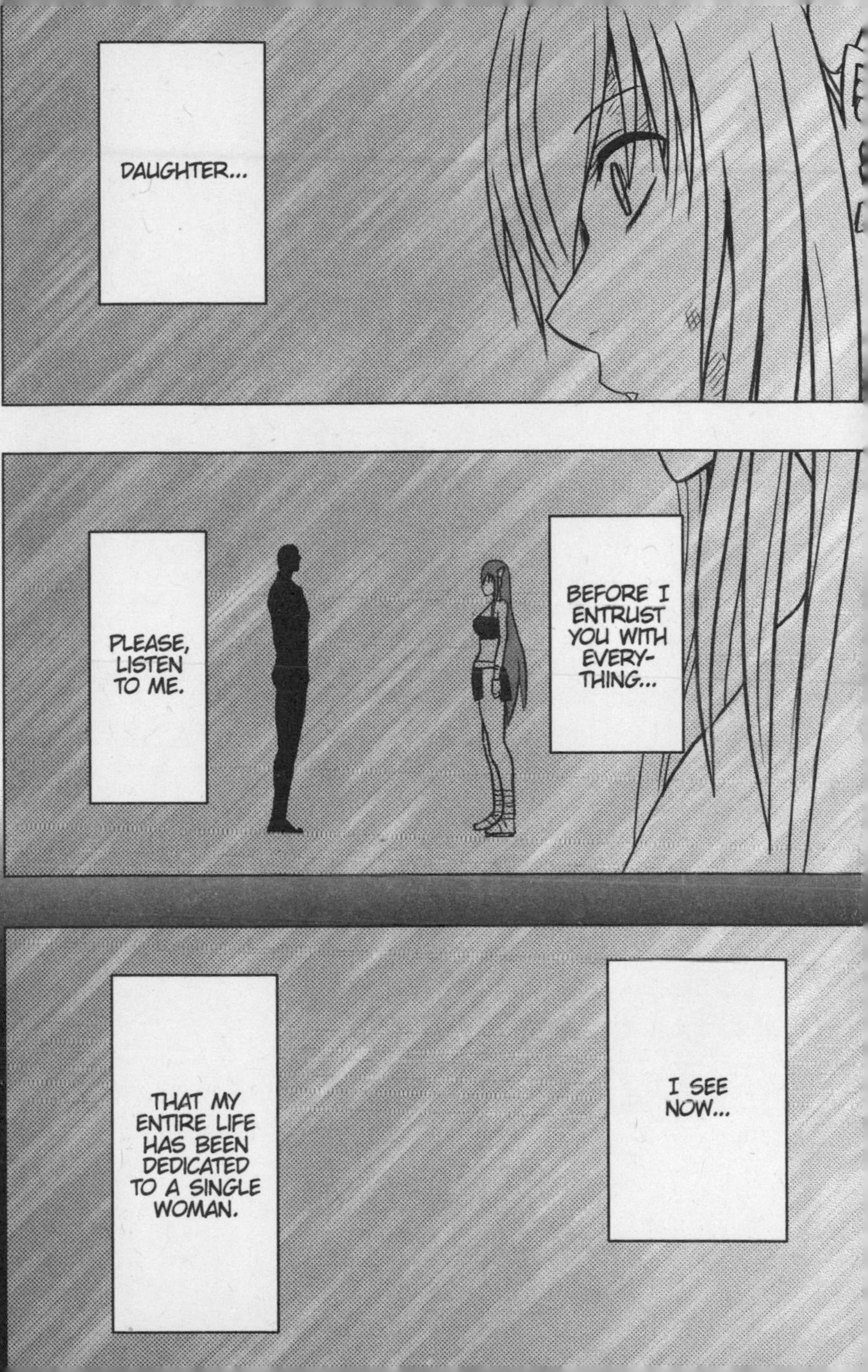
DAUGHTER...
BEFORE I ENTRUST YOU WITH EVERY-THING...
PLEASE, LISTEN TO ME.
I SEE NOW...
THAT MY ENTIRE LIFE HAS BEEN DEDICATED TO A SINGLE WOMAN.

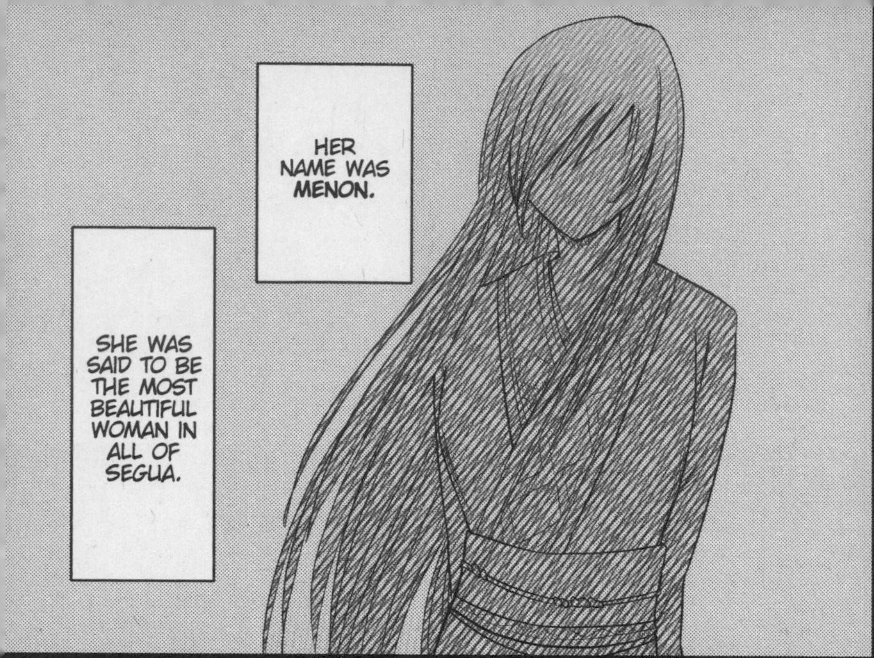
HER NAME WAS MENON.
SHE WAS SAID TO BE THE MOST BEAUTIFUL WOMAN IN ALL OF SEGUA.
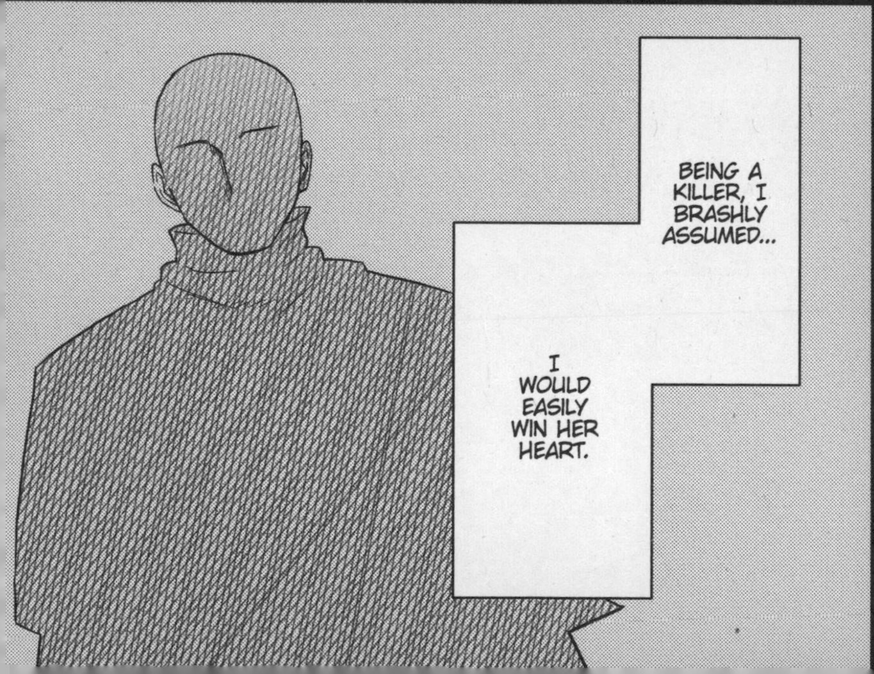
BEING A KILLER, I BRASHLY ASSUMED...
I WOULD EASILY WIN HER HEART.

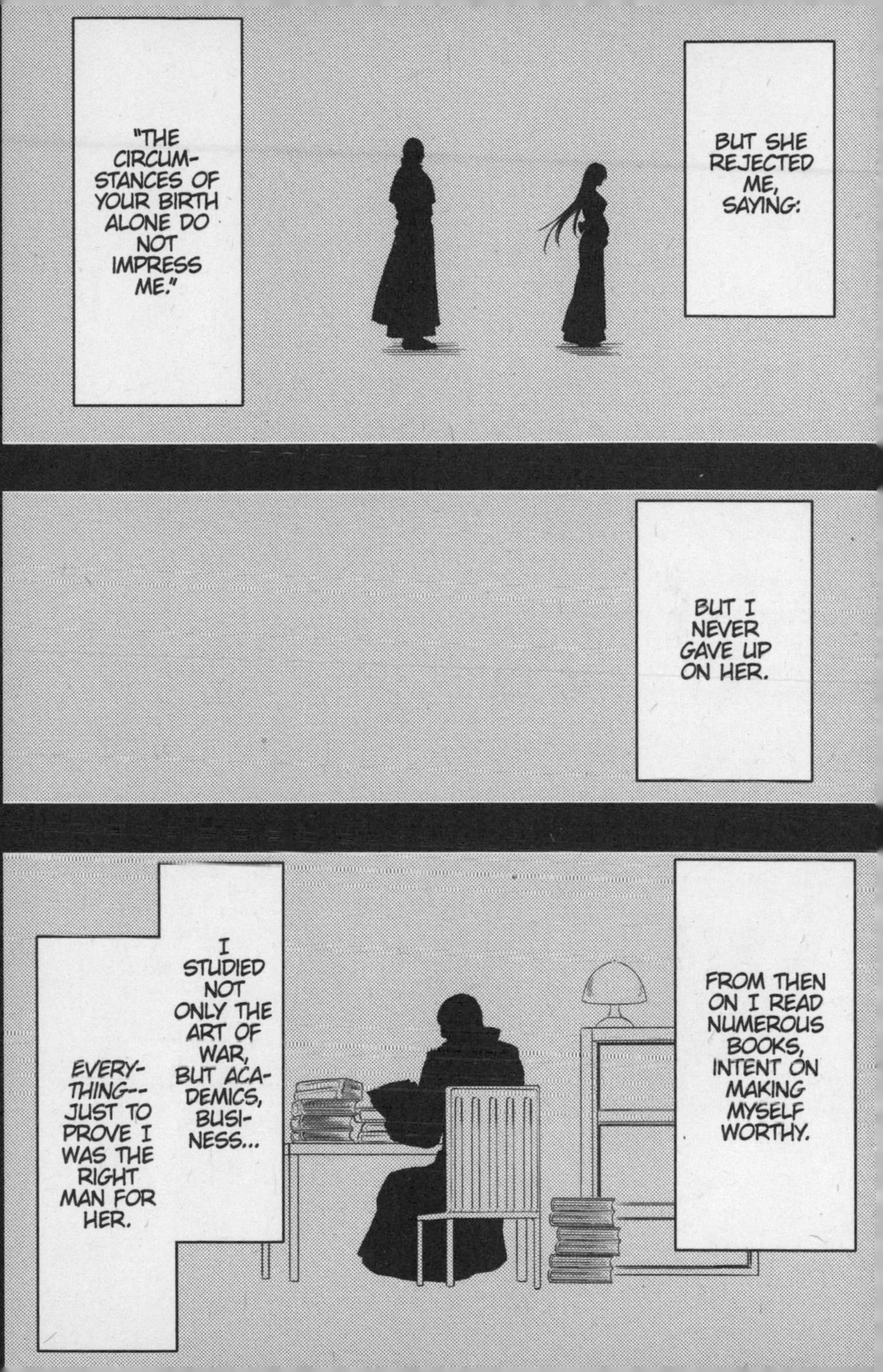
BUT SHE REJECTED ME, SAYING:
"THE CIRCUM-STANCES OF YOUR BIRTH ALONE DO NOT IMPRESS ME."
BUT I NEVER GAVE UP ON HER.
FROM THEN ON I READ NUMEROUS BOOKS, INTENT ON MAKING MYSELF WORTHY.
I STUDIED NOT ONLY THE ART OF WAR, BUT ACA-DEMICS, BUSI-NESS...
EVERY-THING--JUST TO PROVE I WAS THE RIGHT MAN FOR HER.

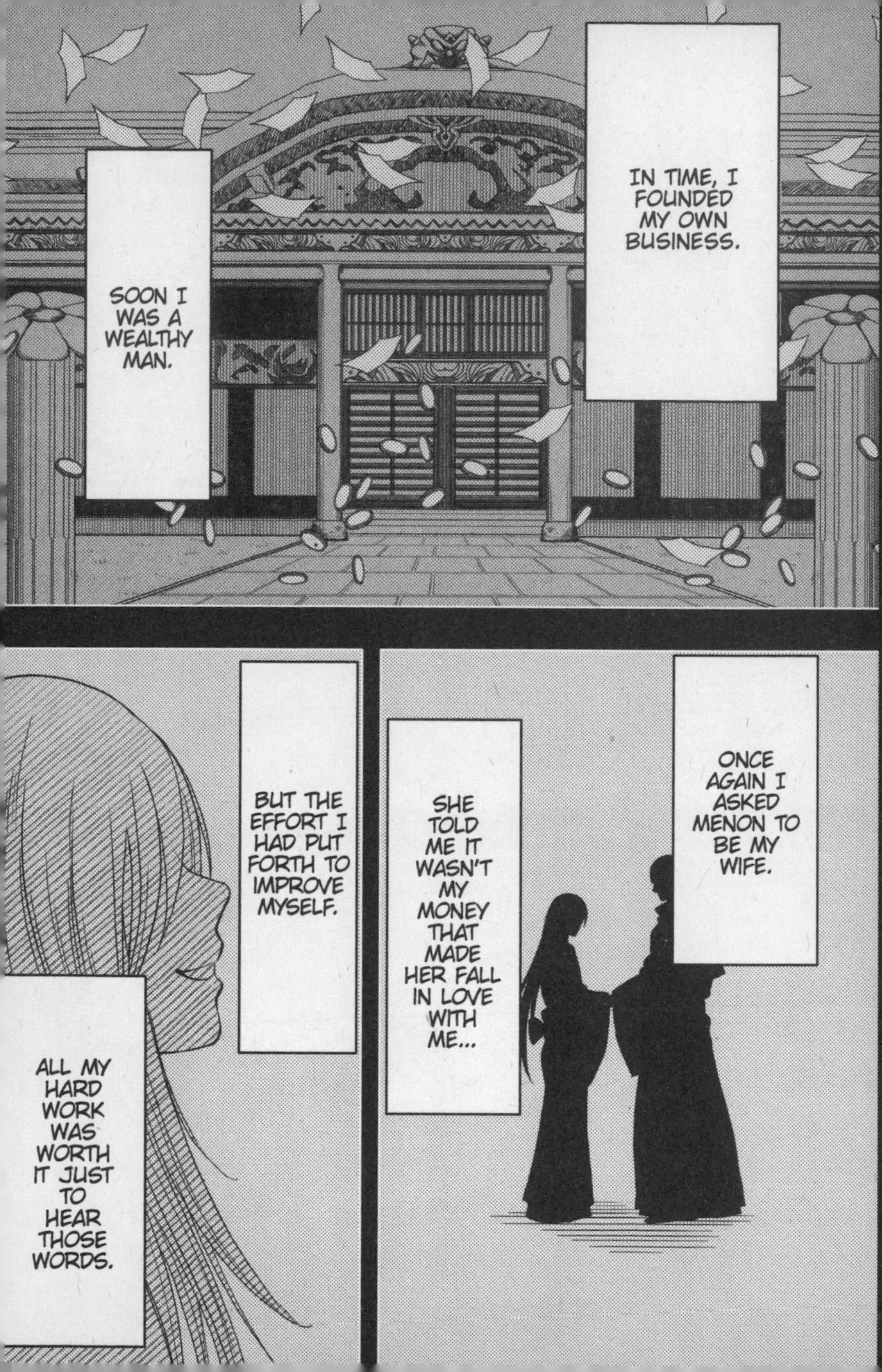
IN TIME, I FOUNDED MY OWN BUSINESS.
SOON I WAS A WEALTHY MAN.
ONCE AGAIN I ASKED MENON TO BE MY WIFE.
SHE TOLD ME IT WASN'T MY MONEY THAT MADE HER FALL IN LOVE WITH ME...
BUT THE EFFORT I HAD PUT FORTH TO IMPROVE MYSELF.
ALL MY HARD WORK WAS WORTH IT JUST TO HEAR THOSE WORDS.

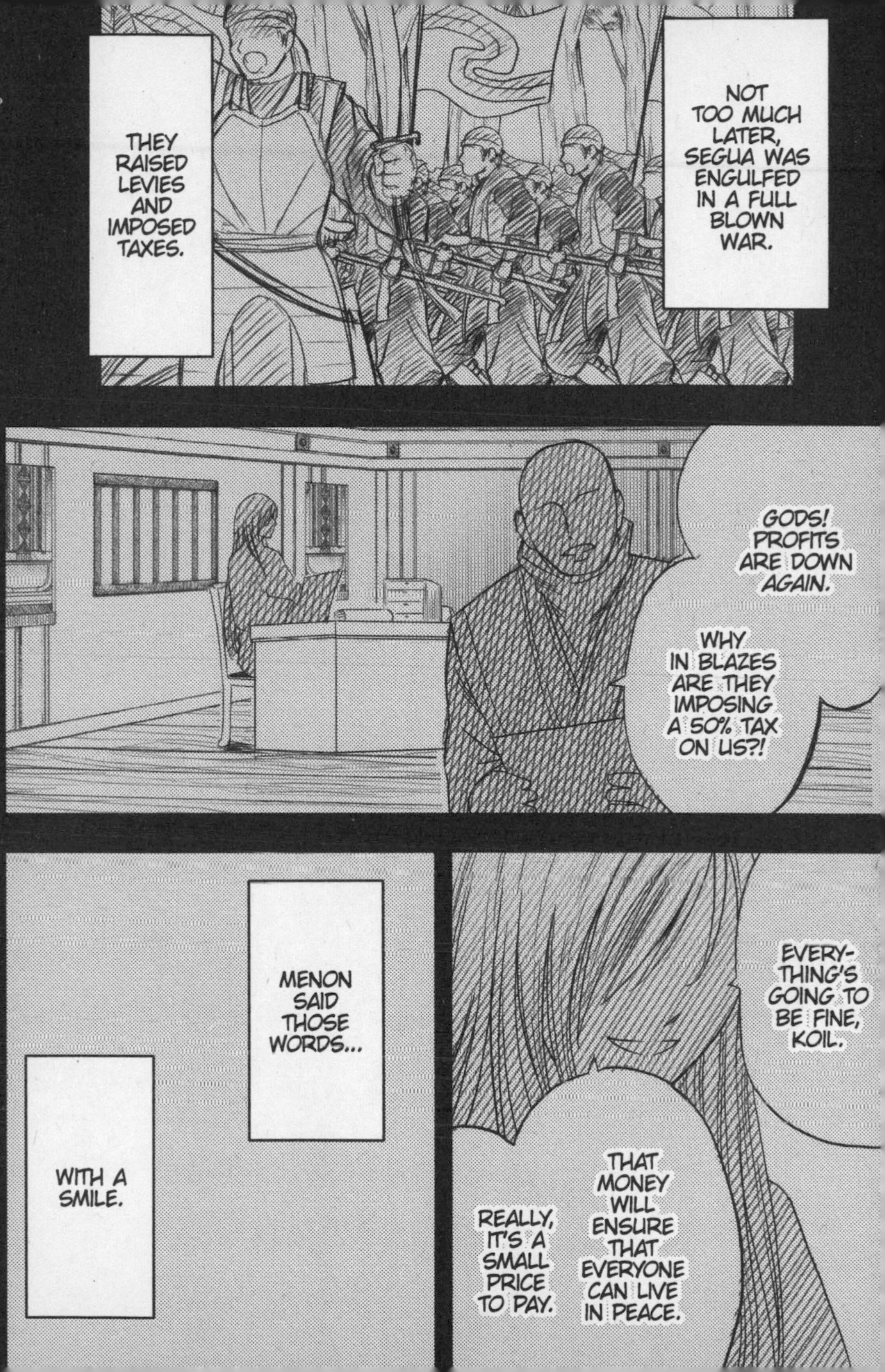
NOT TOO MUCH LATER, SEGUA WAS ENGULFED IN A FULL BLOWN WAR.
THEY RAISED LEVIES AND IMPOSED TAXES.
GODS! PROFITS ARE DOWN AGAIN.
WHY IN BLAZES ARE THEY IMPOSING A 50% TAX ON US?!
EVERY-THING'S GOING TO BE FINE, KOIL.
THAT MONEY WILL ENSURE THAT EVERYONE CAN LIVE IN PEACE.
REALLY, IT'S A SMALL PRICE TO PAY.
MENON SAID THOSE WORDS...
WITH A SMILE.

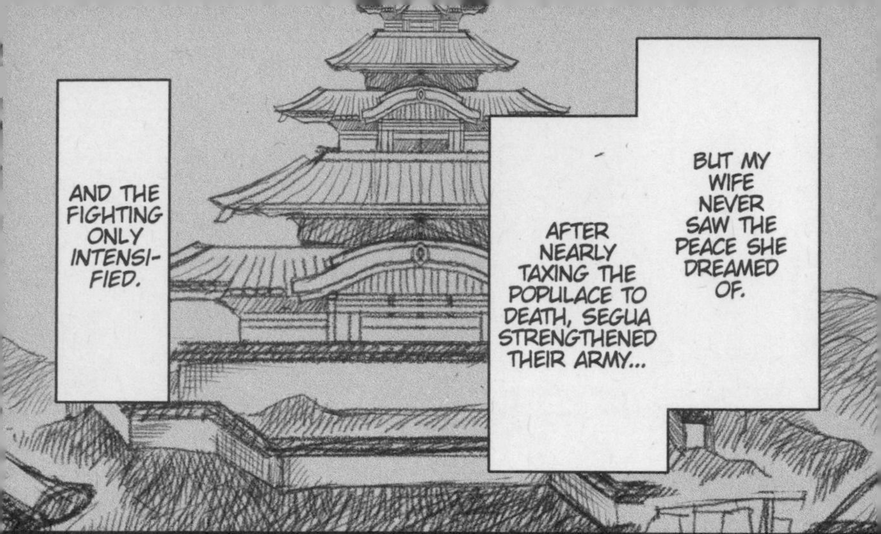
BUT MY WIFE NEVER SAW THE PEACE SHE DREAMED OF.
AFTER NEARLY TAXING THE POPULACE TO DEATH, SEGUA STRENGTHENED THEIR ARMY...
AND THE FIGHTING ONLY INTENSIFIED.
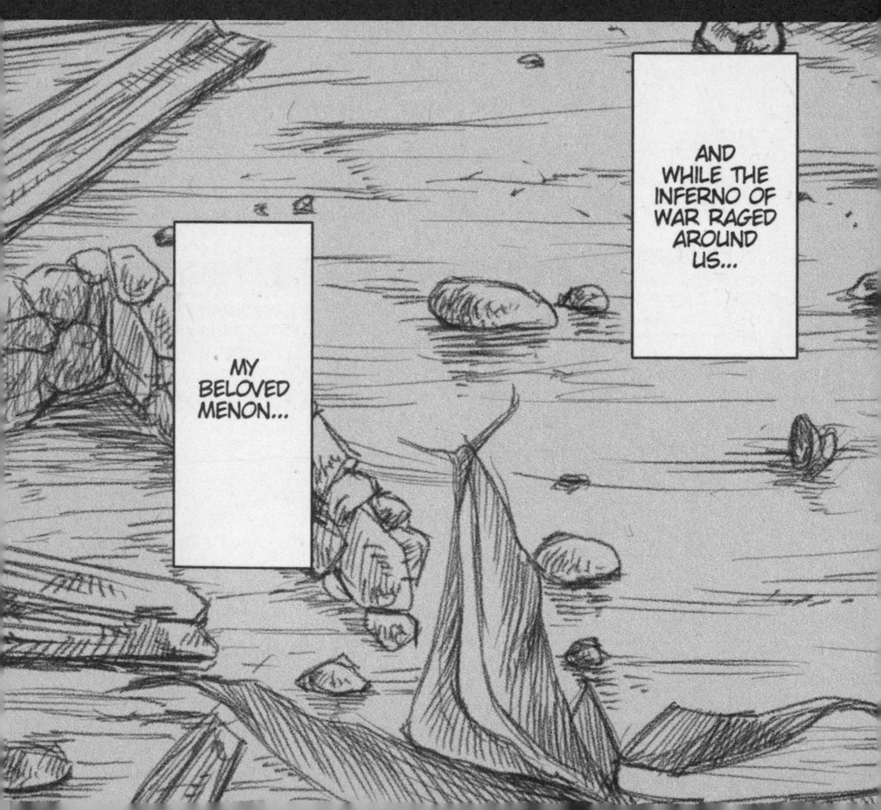
AND WHILE THE INFERNO OF WAR RAGED AROUND US...
MY BELOVED MENON...

DIED.

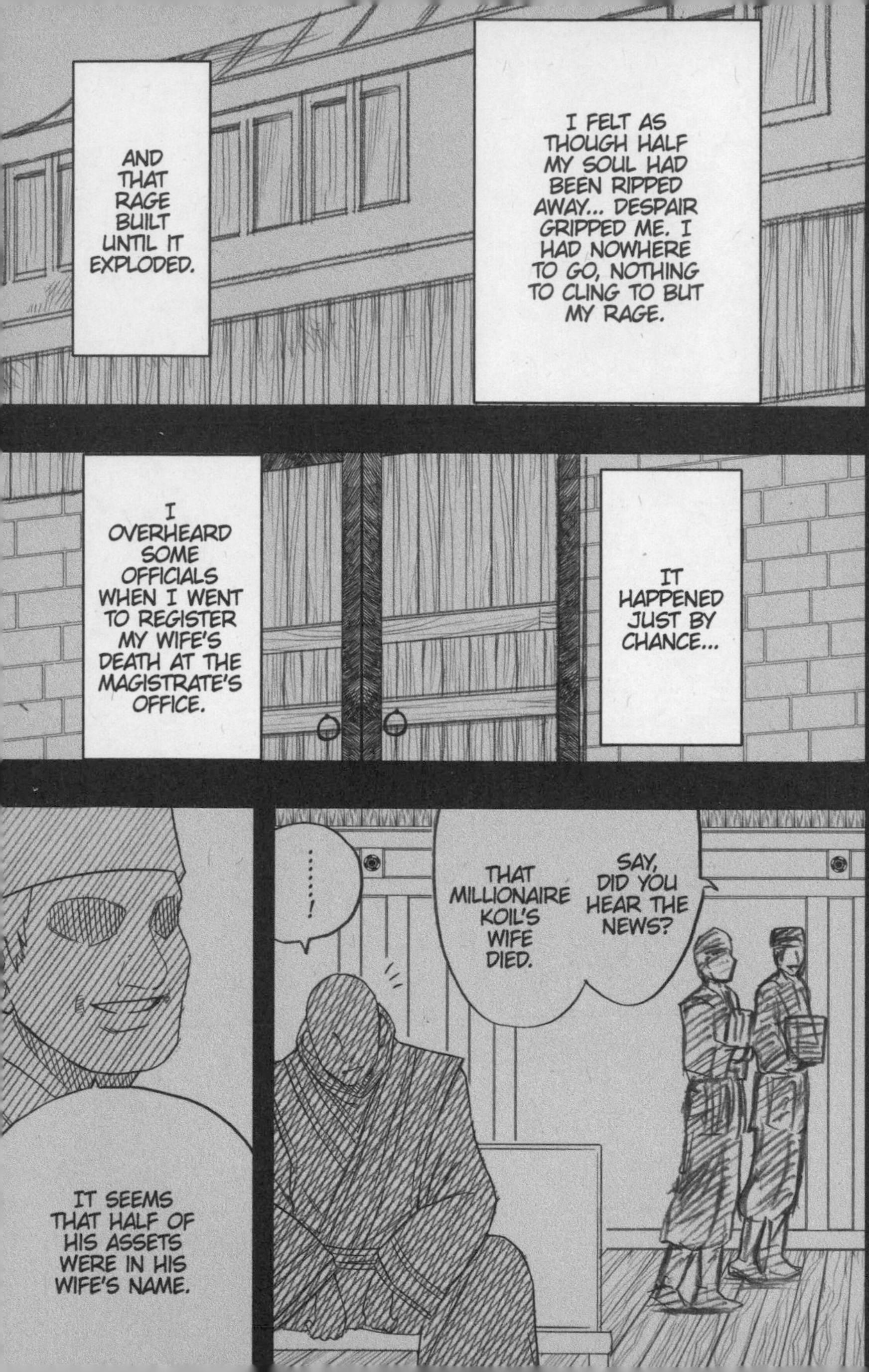
I FELT AS THOUGH HALF MY SOUL HAD BEEN RIPPED AWAY... DESPAIR GRIPPED ME. I HAD NOWHERE TO GO, NOTHING TO CLING TO BUT MY RAGE.
AND THAT RAGE BUILT UNTIL IT EXPLODED.
IT HAPPENED JUST BY CHANCE...
I OVERHEARD SOME OFFICIALS WHEN I WENT TO REGISTER MY WIFE'S DEATH AT THE MAGISTRATE'S OFFICE.
SAY, DID YOU HEAR THE NEWS? THAT MILLIONAIRE KOIL'S WIFE DIED.
......!
IT SEEMS THAT HALF OF HIS ASSETS WERE IN HIS WIFE'S NAME.

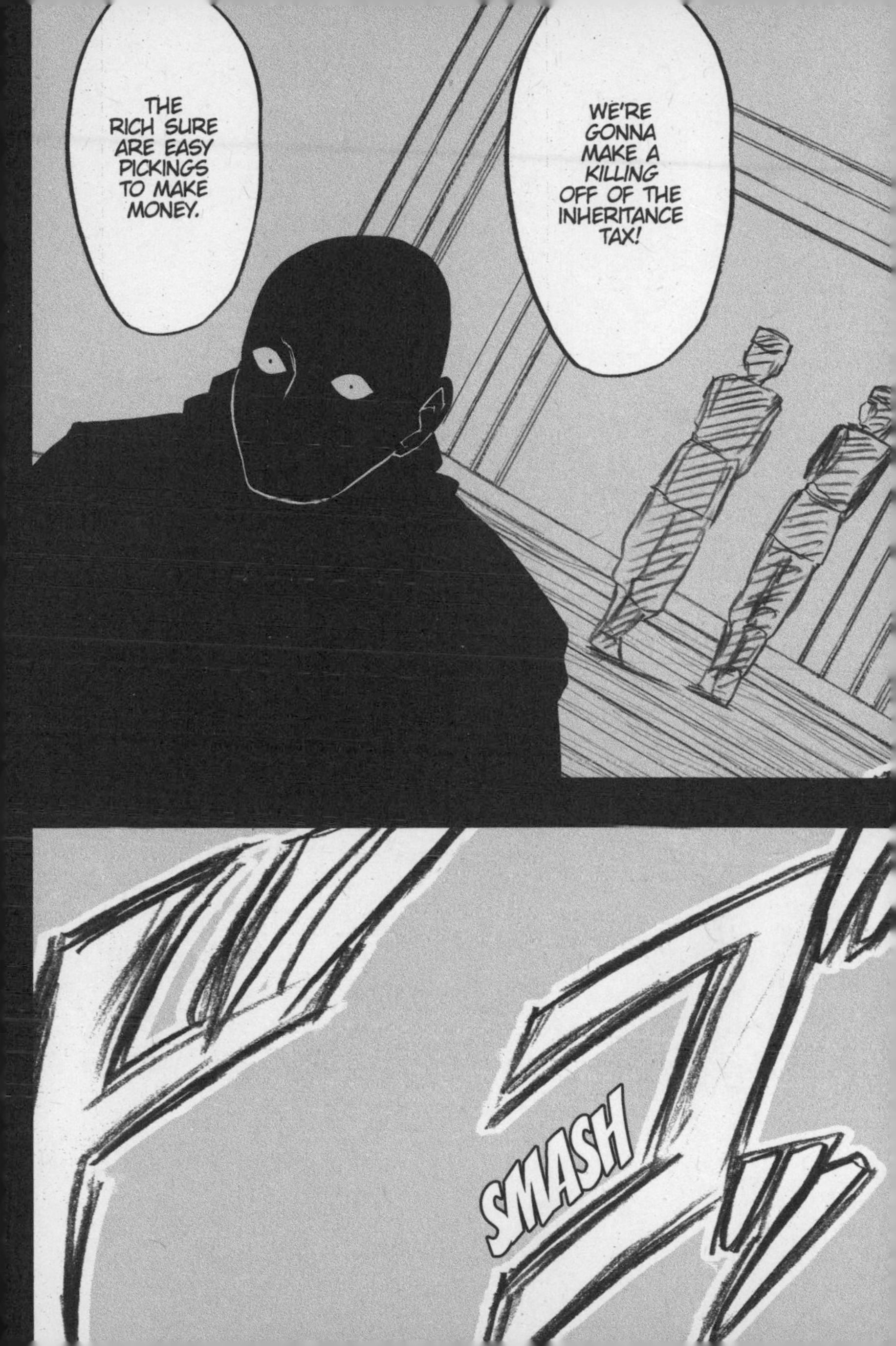
WE'RE GONNA MAKE A KILLING OFF OF THE INHERITANCE TAX!
THE RICH SURE ARE EASY PICKINGS TO MAKE MONEY.
SMASH

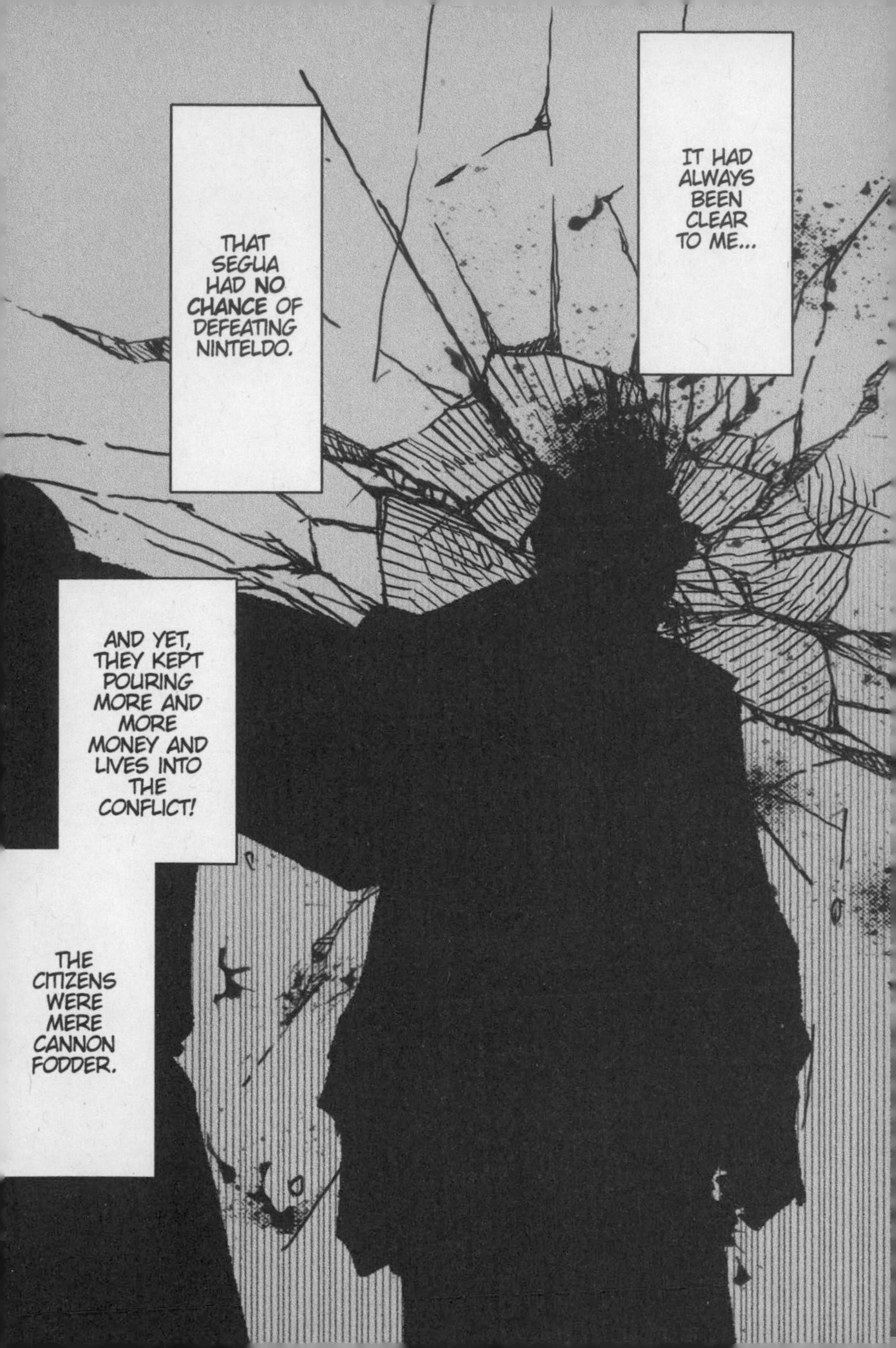
IT HAD ALWAYS BEEN CLEAR TO ME...
THAT SEGUA HAD NO CHANCE OF DEFEATING NINTELDO.
AND YET, THEY KEPT POURING MORE AND MORE MONEY AND LIVES INTO THE CONFLICT!
THE CITIZENS WERE MERE CANNON FODDER.

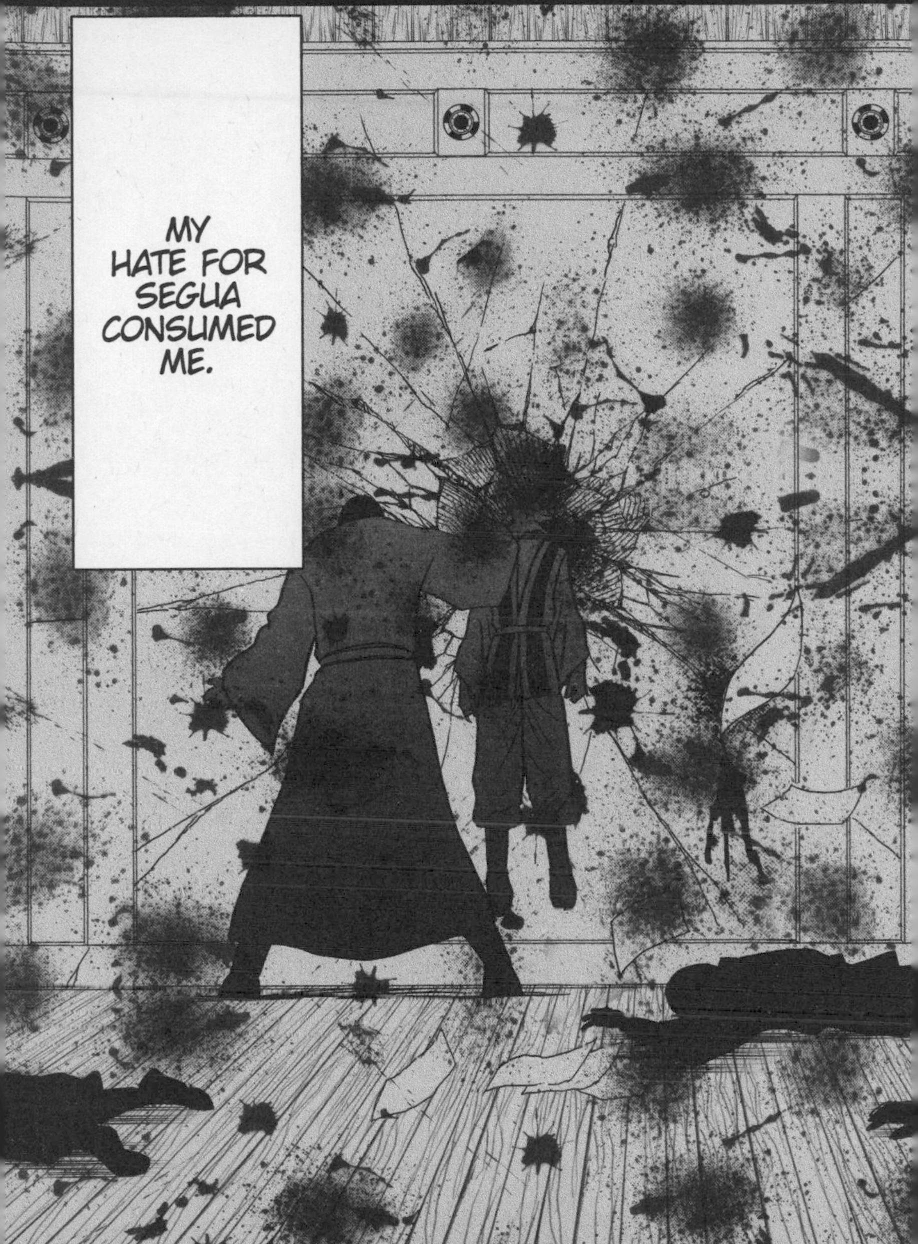
MY HATE FOR SEGUA CONSUMED ME.

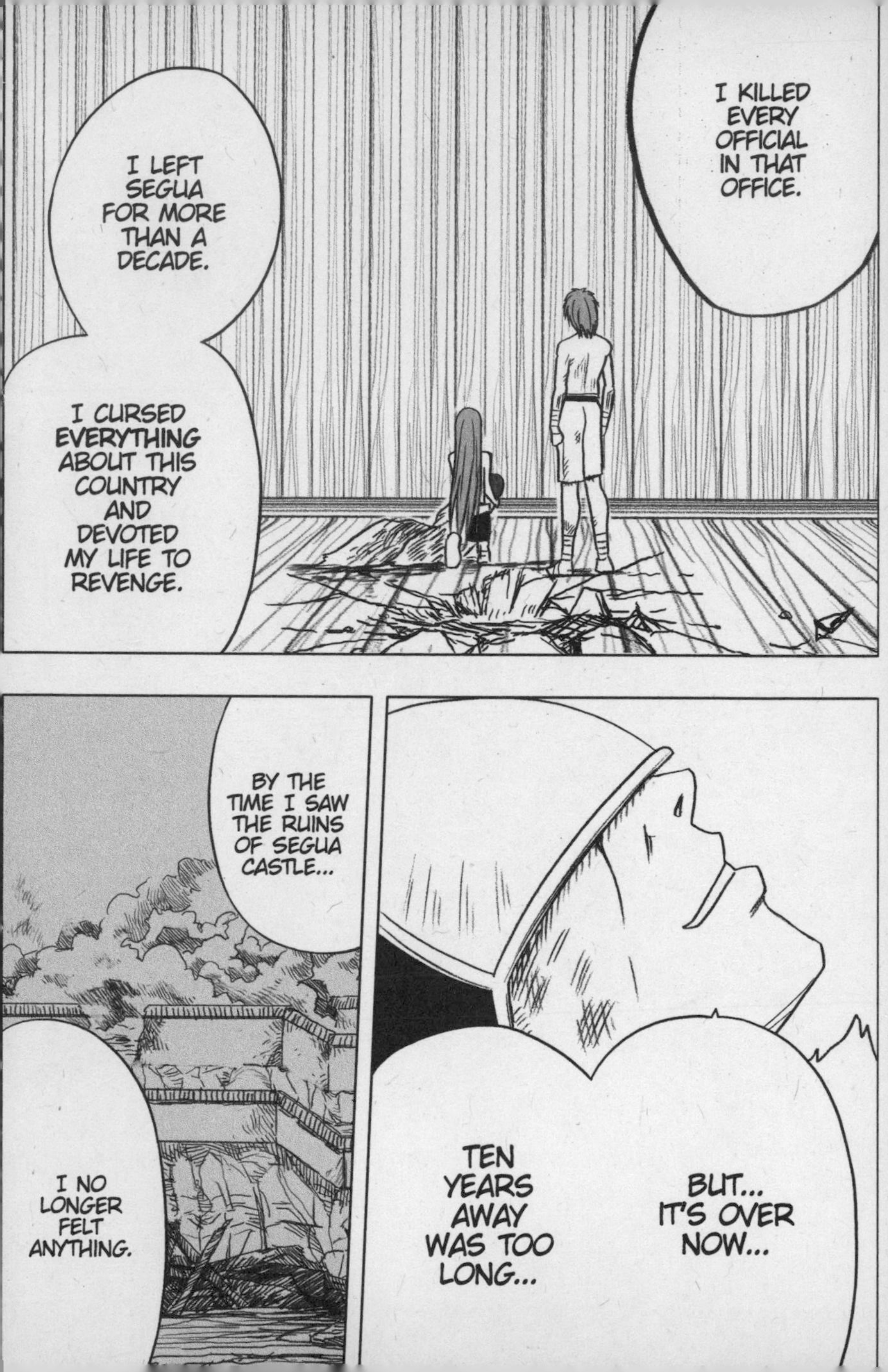
I LEFT SEGUA FOR MORE THAN A DECADE.
I CURSED EVERYTHING ABOUT THIS COUNTRY AND DEVOTED MY LIFE TO REVENGE.
I KILLED EVERY OFFICIAL IN THAT OFFICE.
BY THE TIME I SAW THE RUINS OF SEGUA CASTLE...
I NO LONGER FELT ANYTHING.
TEN YEARS AWAY WAS TOO LONG...
BUT... IT'S OVER NOW...

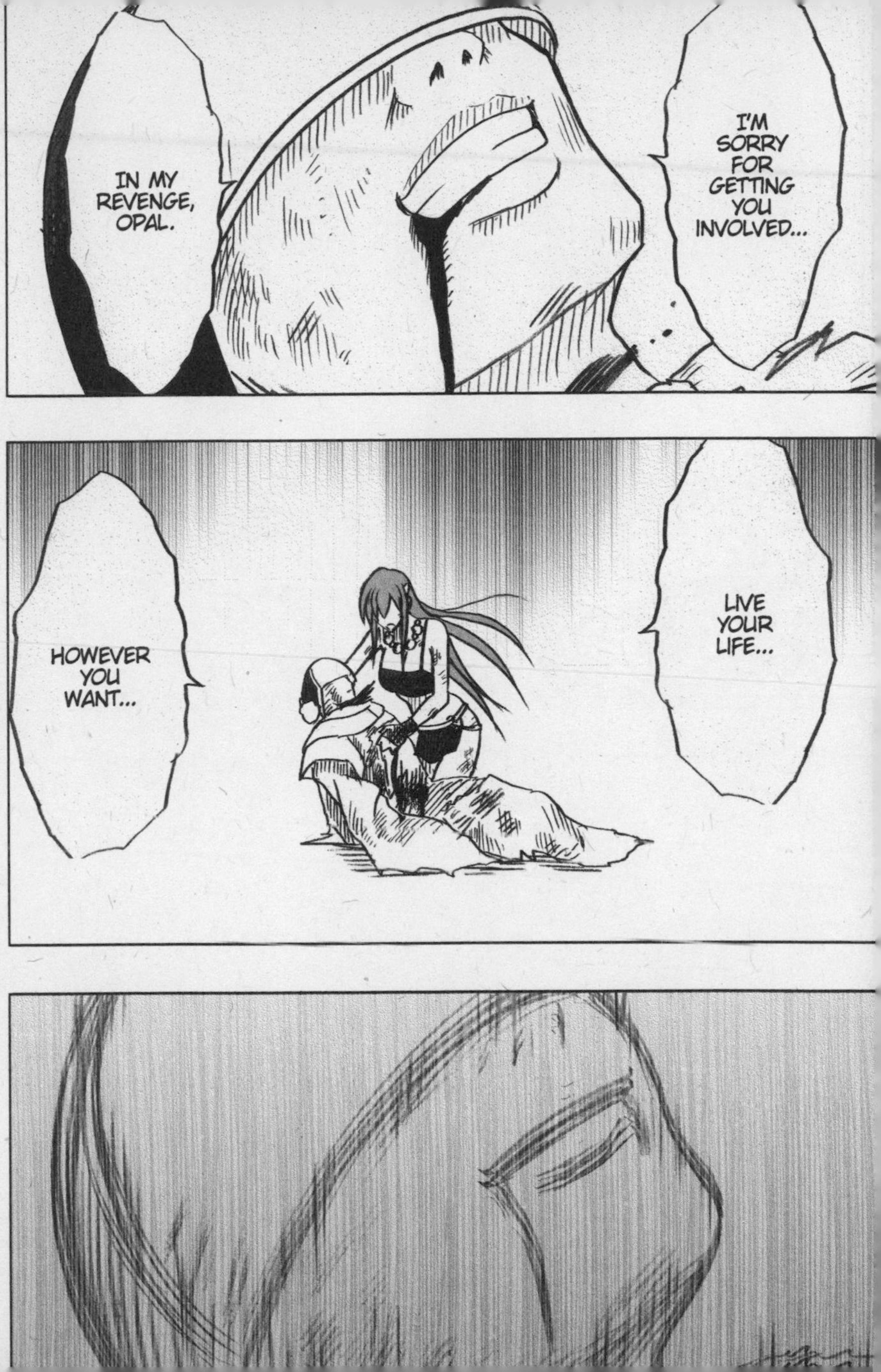
I'M SORRY FOR GETTING YOU INVOLVED...
IN MY REVENGE, OPAL.
LIVE YOUR LIFE...
HOWEVER YOU WANT...

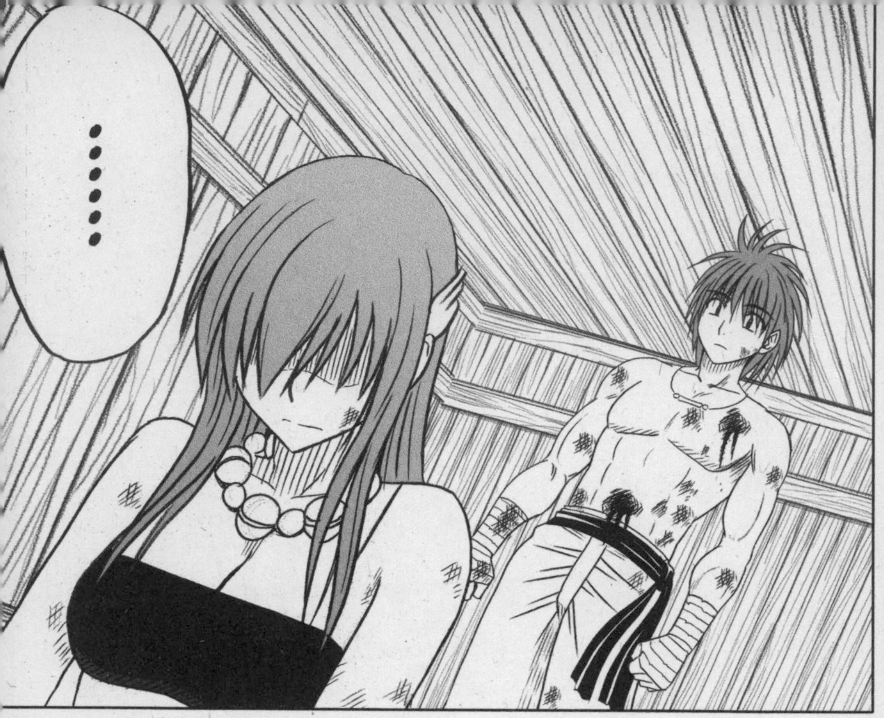
......

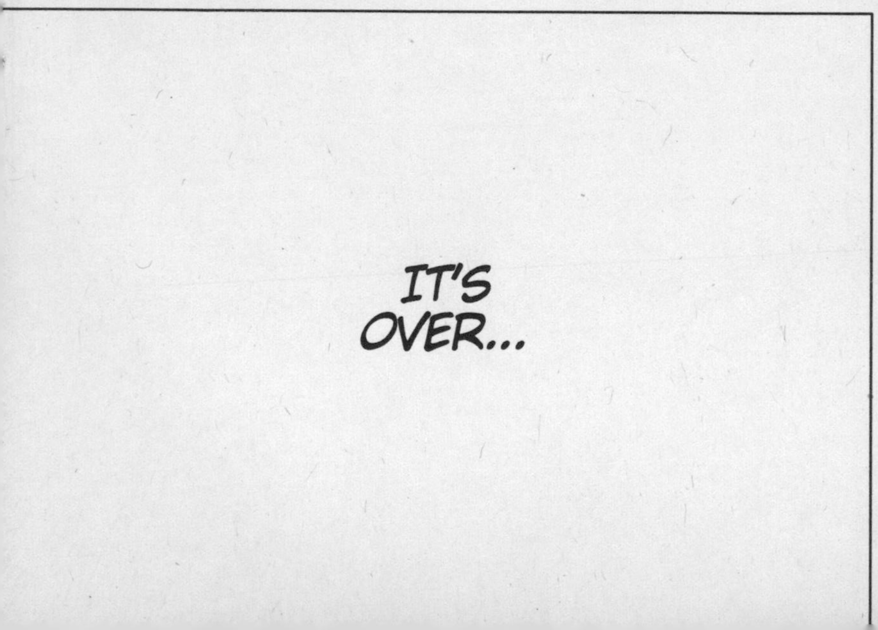
IT'S OVER...

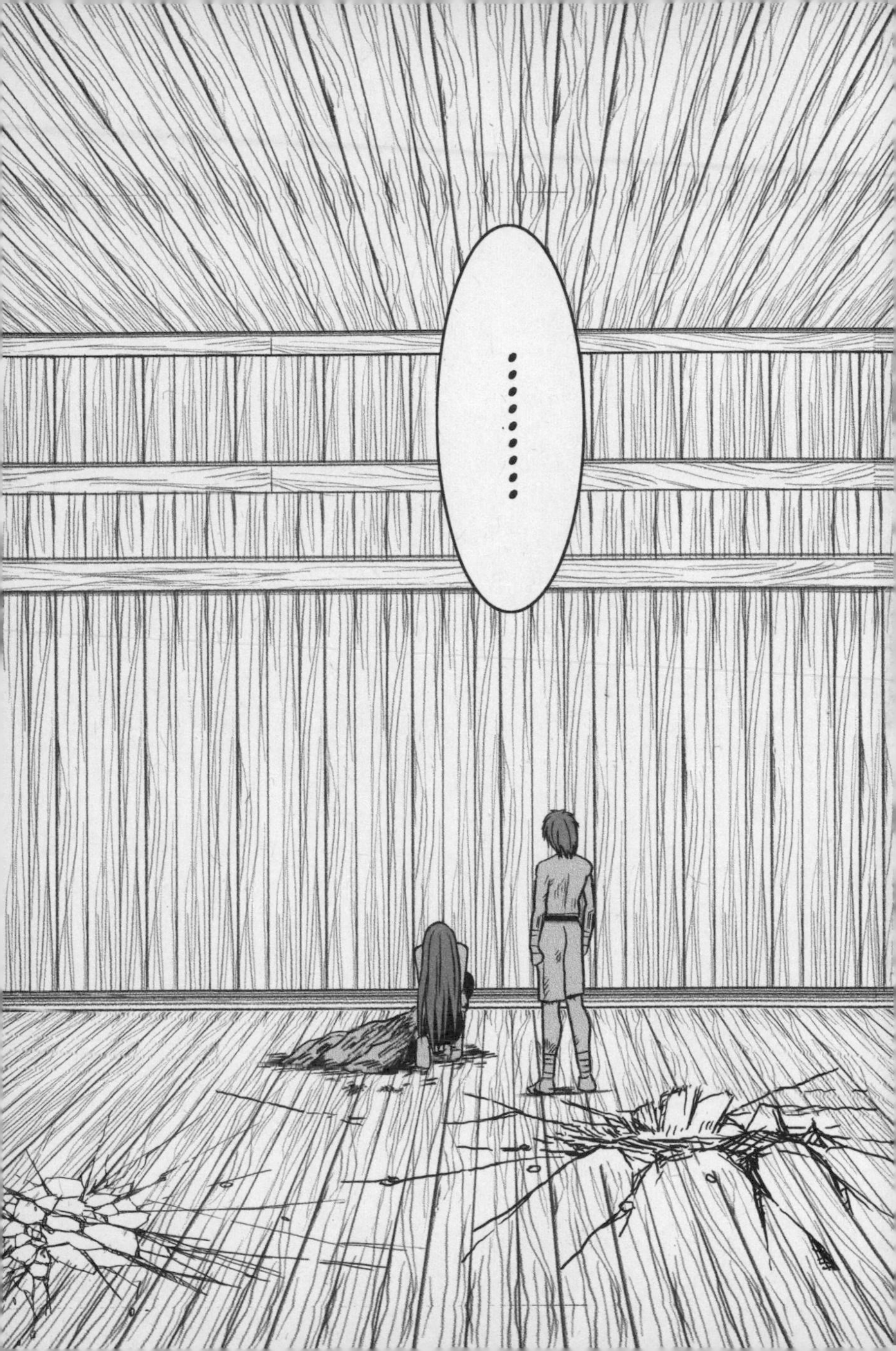
……

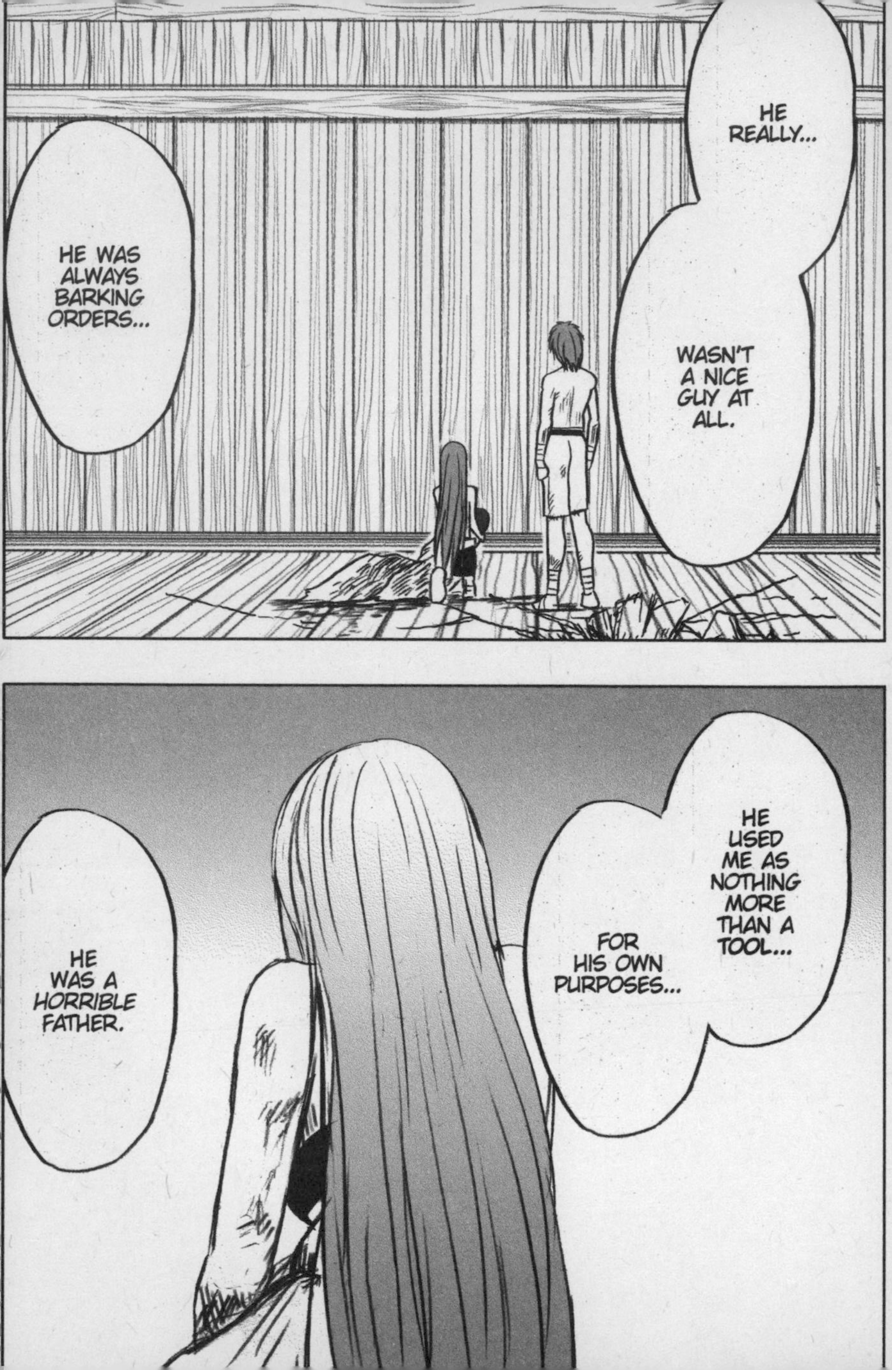
HE REALLY...
WASN'T A NICE GUY AT ALL.
HE WAS ALWAYS BARKING ORDERS...
HE USED ME AS NOTHING MORE THAN A TOOL...
FOR HIS OWN PURPOSES...
HE WAS A HORRIBLE FATHER.

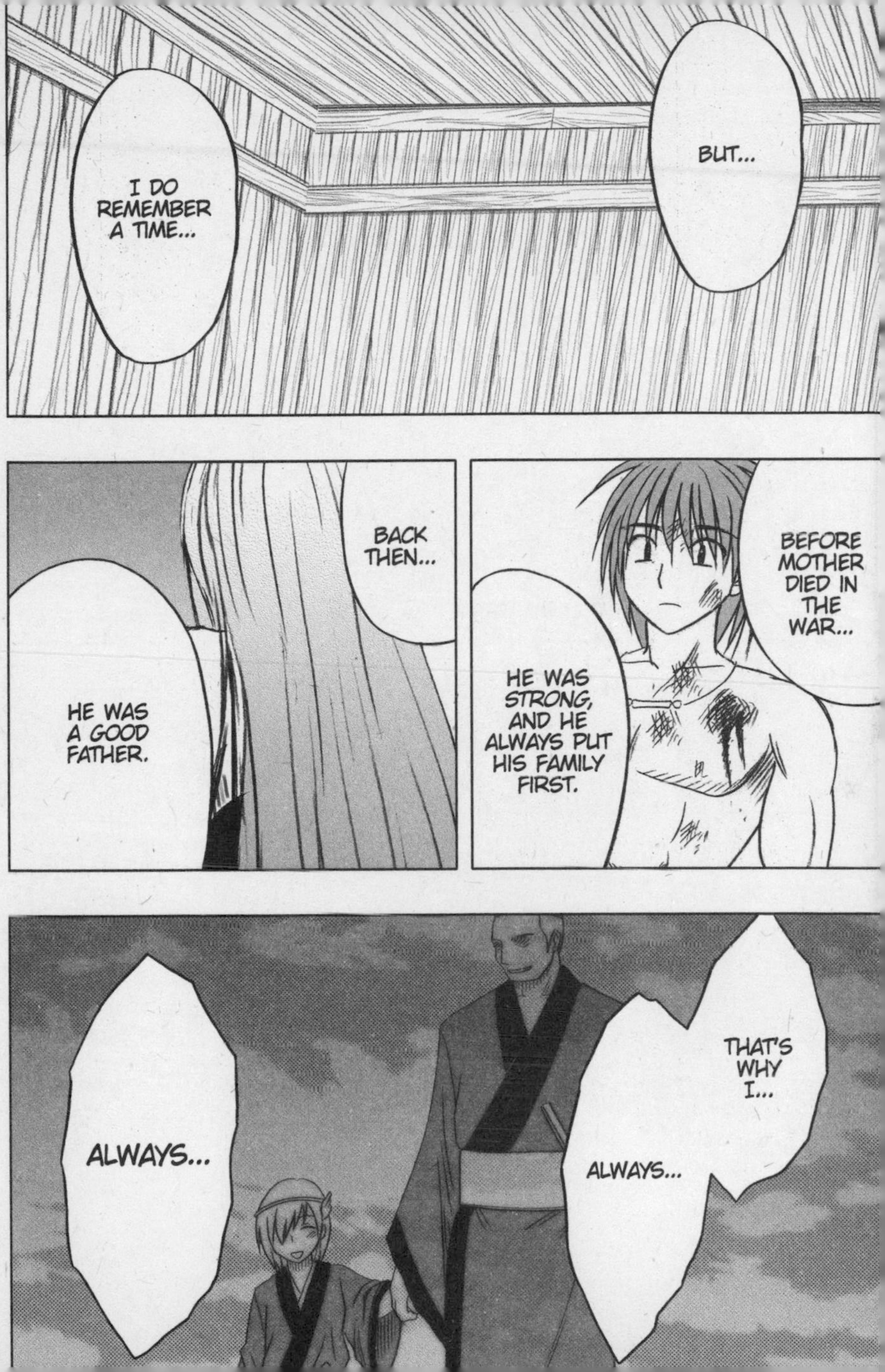
BUT...
I DO REMEMBER A TIME...
BEFORE MOTHER DIED IN THE WAR...
HE WAS STRONG, AND HE ALWAYS PUT HIS FAMILY FIRST.
BACK THEN...
HE WAS A GOOD FATHER.
THAT'S WHY I...
ALWAYS...
ALWAYS...

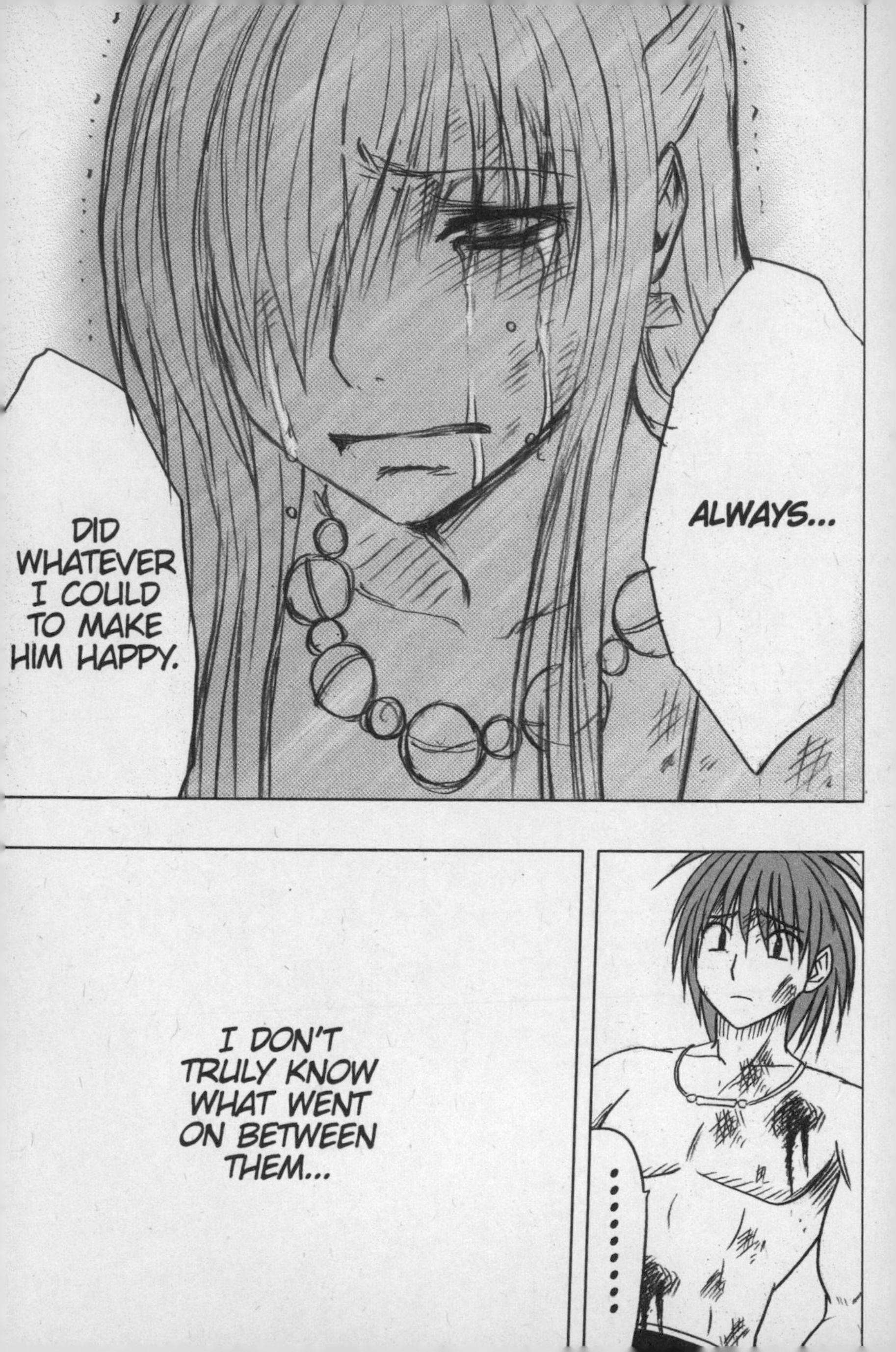
ALWAYS...
DID WHATEVER I COULD TO MAKE HIM HAPPY.
........
I DON'T TRULY KNOW WHAT WENT ON BETWEEN THEM...

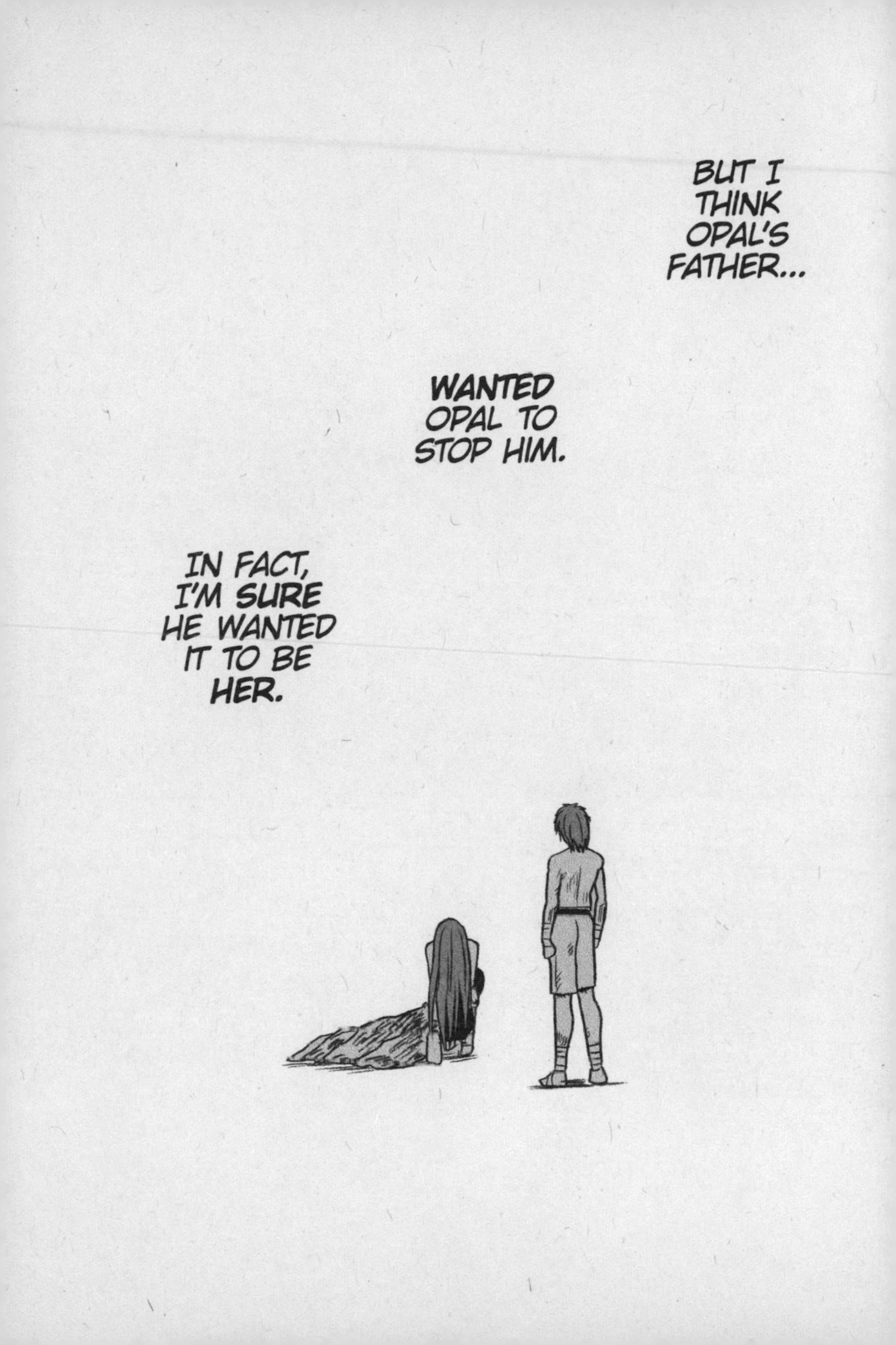
BUT I THINK OPAL'S FATHER...
WANTED OPAL TO STOP HIM.
IN FACT, I'M SURE HE WANTED IT TO BE HER.

SO EVERYTHING TURNED OUT FOR THE BEST...

OR AT LEAST, AS WELL AS IT COULD.

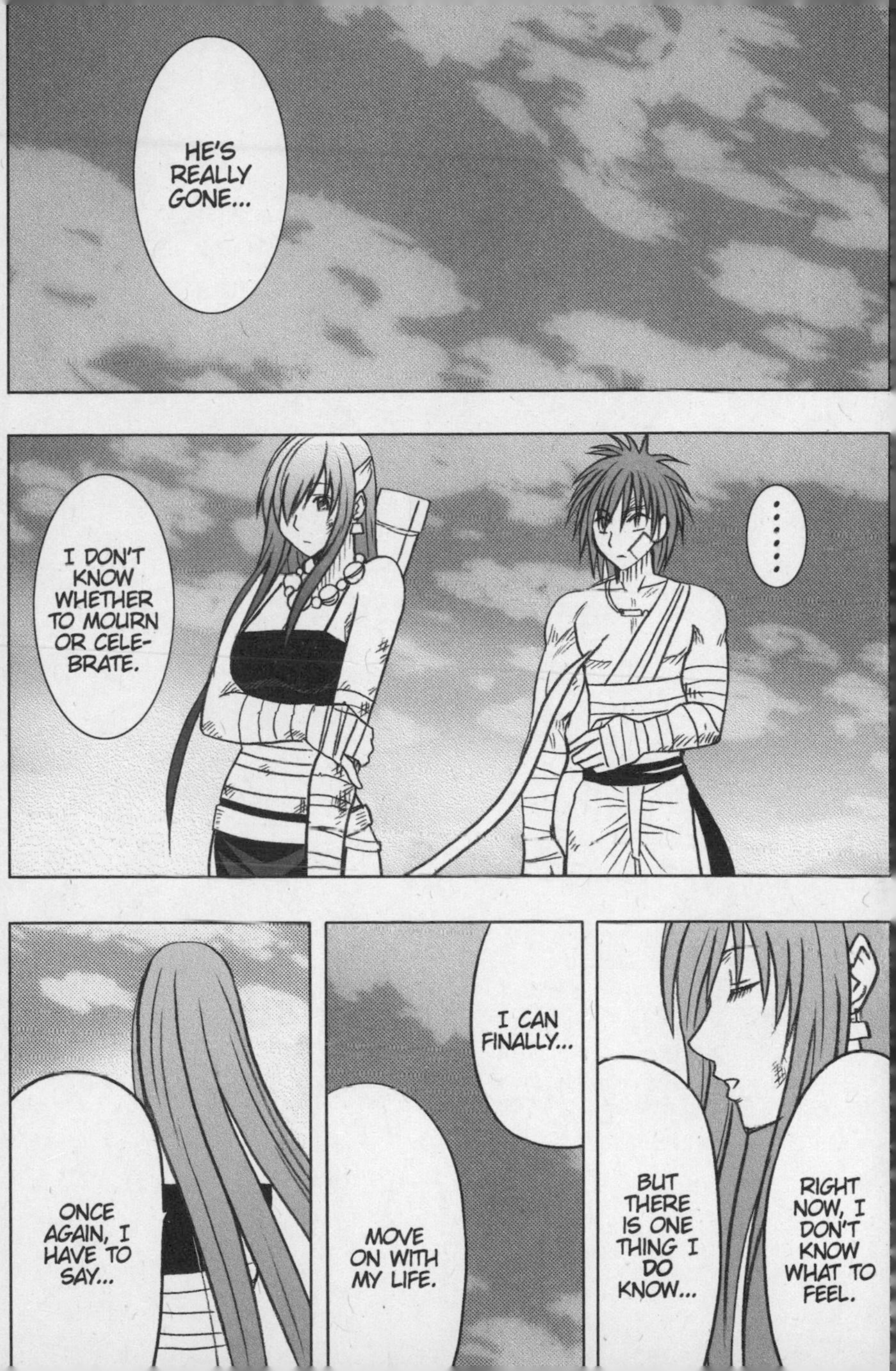
HE'S REALLY GONE...
......
I DON'T KNOW WHETHER TO MOURN OR CELE-BRATE.
RIGHT NOW, I DON'T KNOW WHAT TO FEEL.
BUT THERE IS ONE THING I DO KNOW...
I CAN FINALLY...
MOVE ON WITH MY LIFE.
ONCE AGAIN, I HAVE TO SAY...

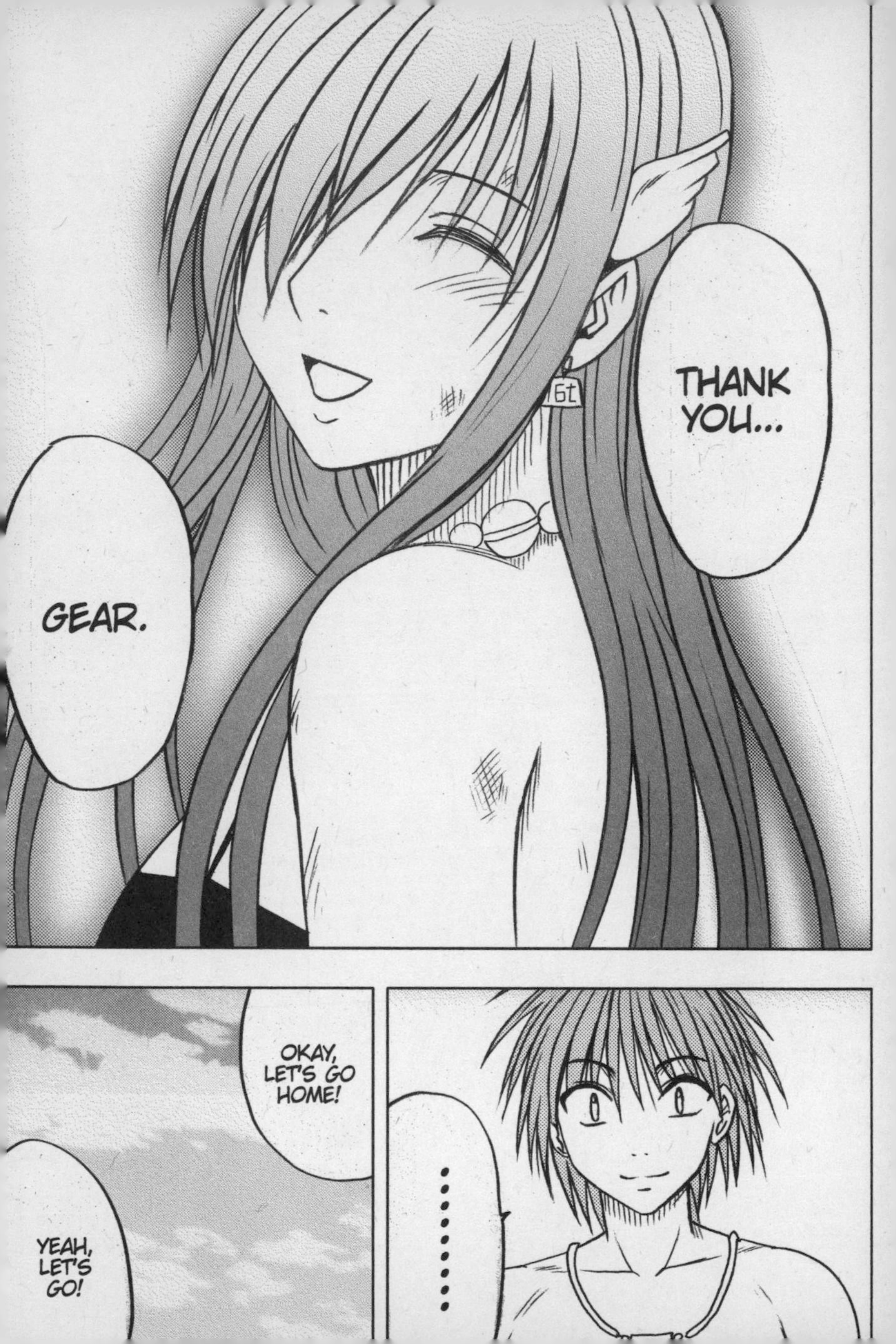
THANK YOU...
GEAR.
......
OKAY, LET'S GO HOME!
YEAH, LET'S GO!

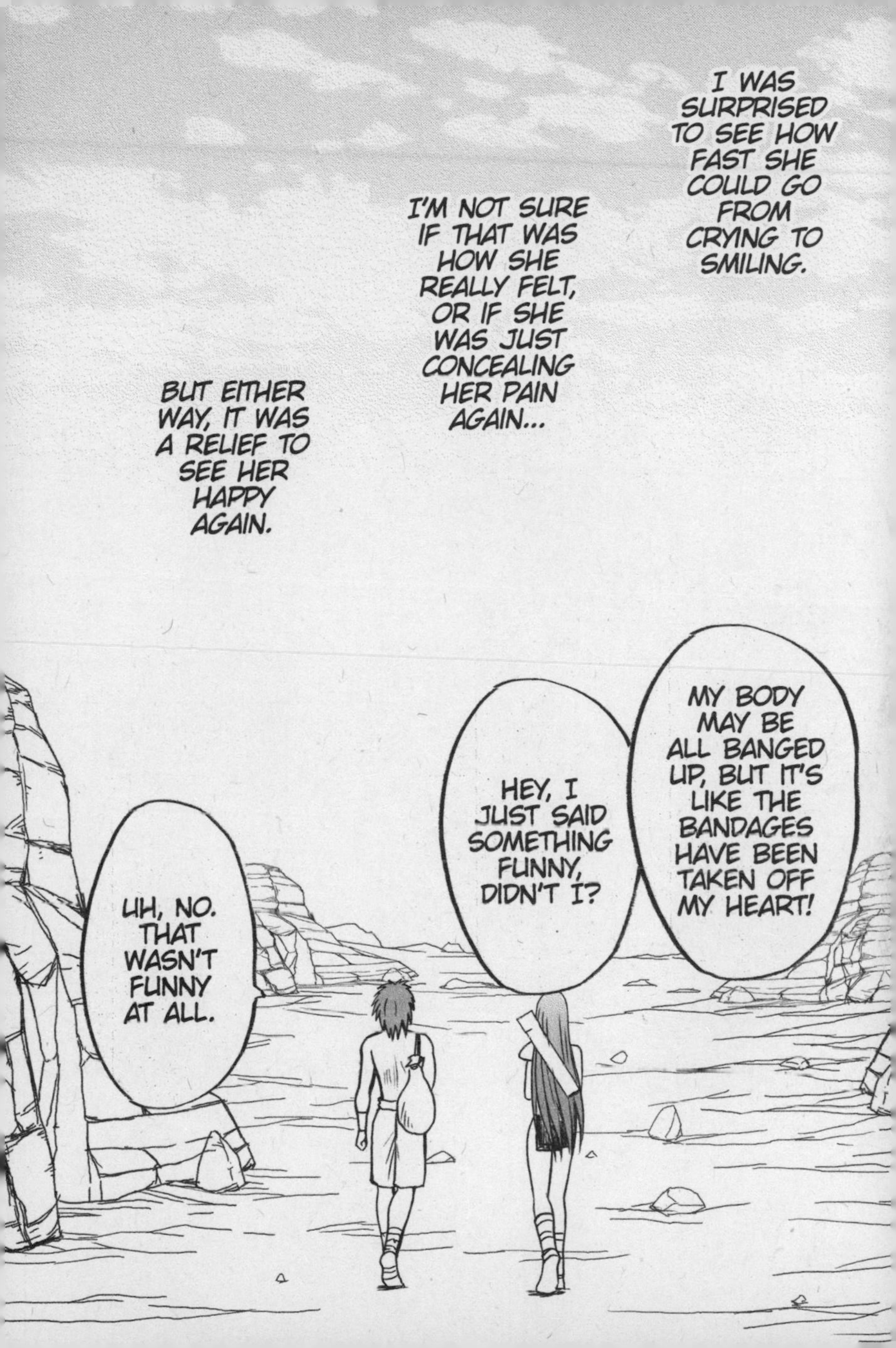
I WAS SURPRISED TO SEE HOW FAST SHE COULD GO FROM CRYING TO SMILING.
I'M NOT SURE IF THAT WAS HOW SHE REALLY FELT, OR IF SHE WAS JUST CONCEALING HER PAIN AGAIN...
BUT EITHER WAY, IT WAS A RELIEF TO SEE HER HAPPY AGAIN.
MY BODY MAY BE ALL BANGED UP, BUT IT'S LIKE THE BANDAGES HAVE BEEN TAKEN OFF MY HEART!
HEY, I JUST SAID SOMETHING FUNNY, DIDN'T I?
UH, NO. THAT WASN'T FUNNY AT ALL.

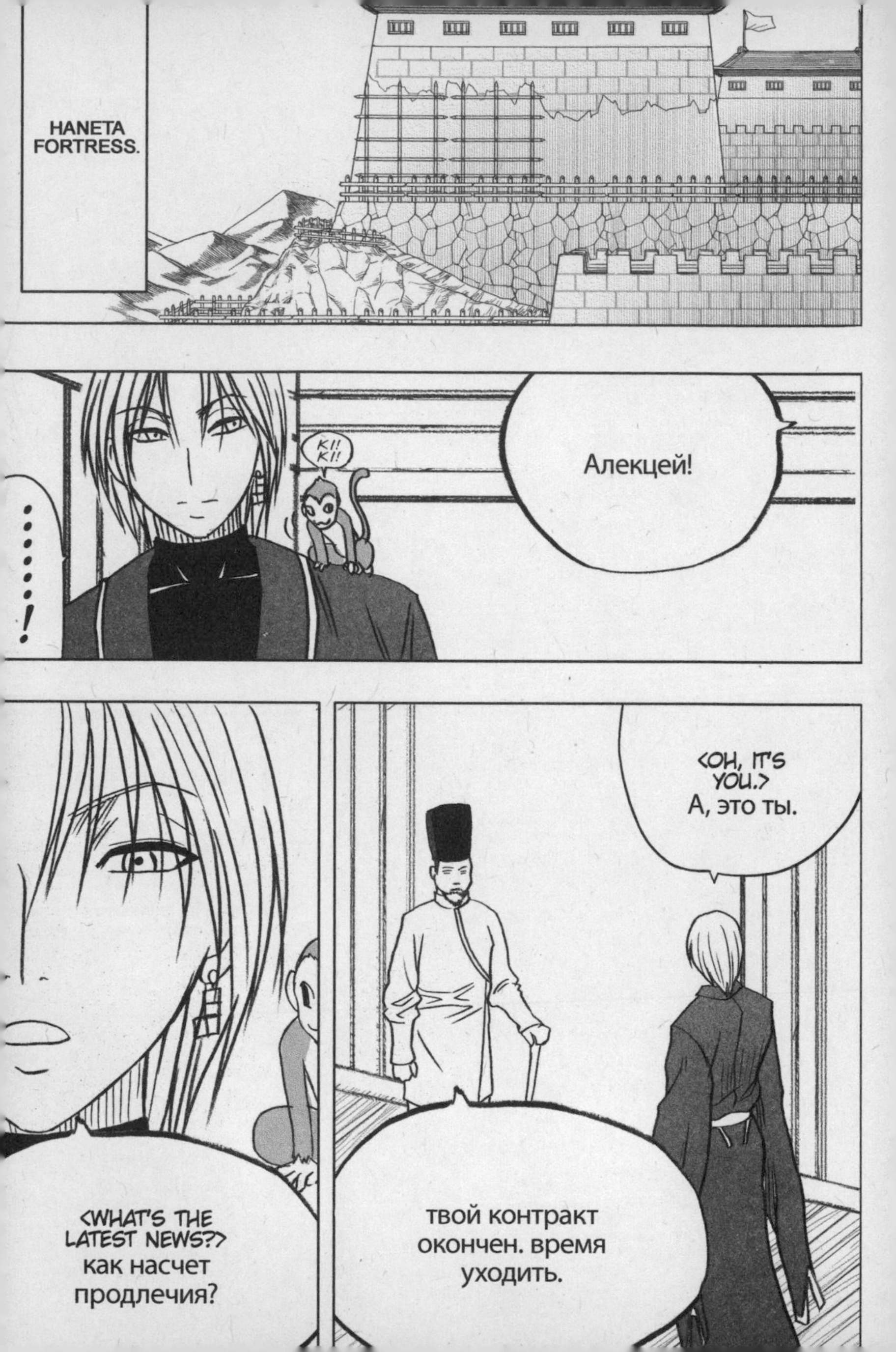
HANETA FORTRESS.
Алекцей!
KI! KI!
......!
<OH, IT'S YOU.> А, это ты.
твой контракт окончен. время уходить.
<WHAT'S THE LATEST NEWS?> как насчет продлечия?

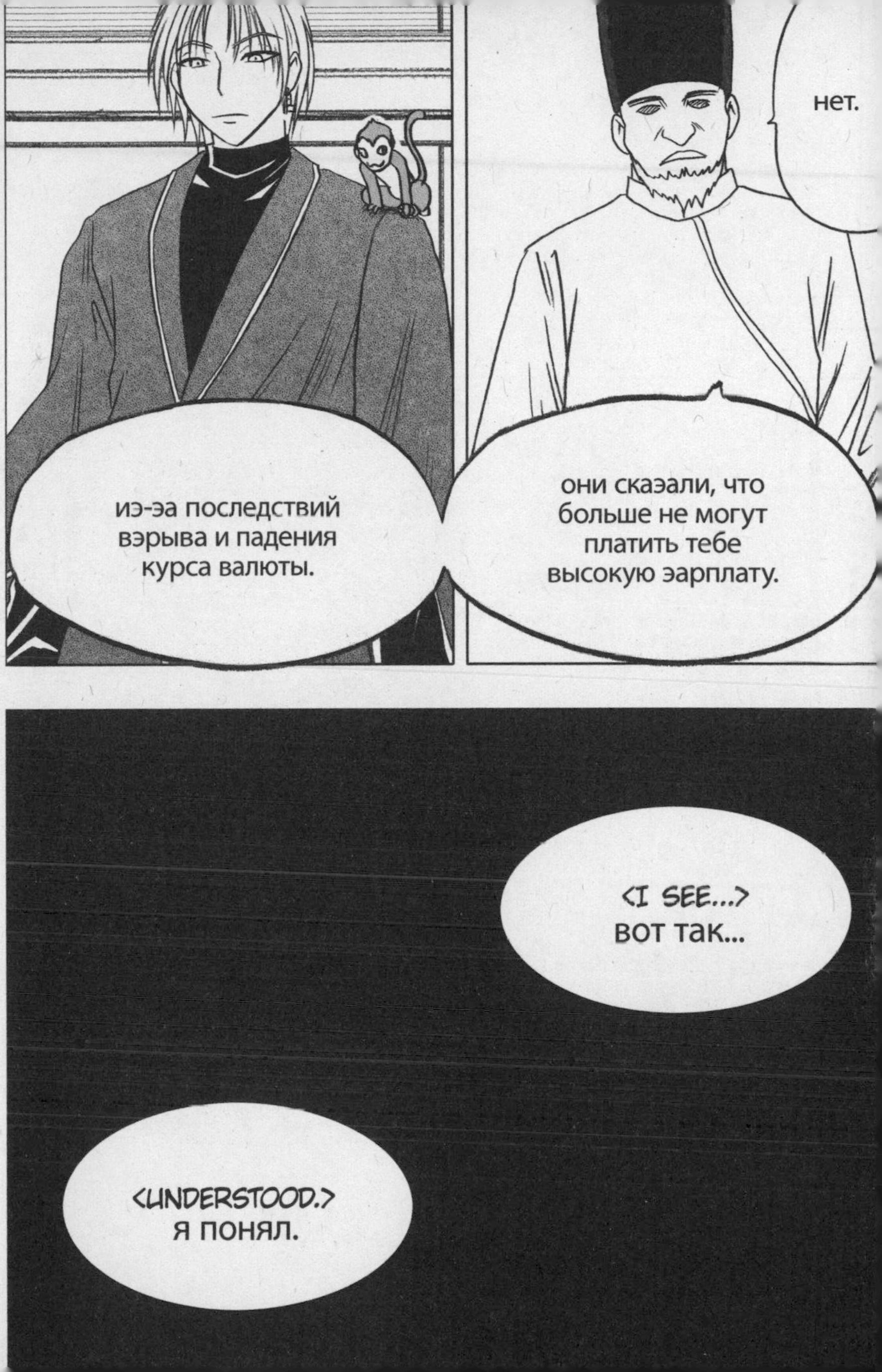
нет.
они скаэали, что больше не могут платить тебе высокую эарплату.
иэ-эа последствий вэрыва и падения курса валюты.
<I SEE...> вот так...
<UNDERSTOOD.> я понял.

Perusing Video Game History

# ON THE EDGE OF THE BLUE WORLD

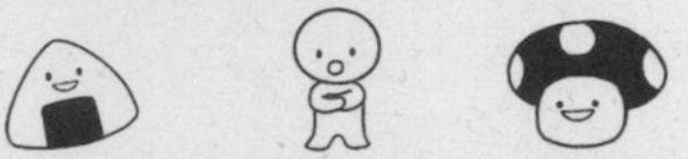

Dr. Onigiri Mr. Why Prof. Mushroom

Today's Topic

## FANTASY ZONE 4

**Mr. Why:** Hello, everyone! Just like in previous volumes, the Doctor, the Professor and I are going to chat a little bit about video games and their history. As always, please keep in mind that this has nothing to do with the main story of the manga in any way. That might be important for those out there who want to throw rotten tomatoes at us.

**Prof. Mushroom**: Hello everyone, I'm Professor Mushroom. I'm quite interested in the latest "3D Televisions" that people are whispering about.

**Dr. Onigiri**: I'm Doctor Onigiri. My dream is to go to Jupiter one day.

**Mr. Why**: In Volume 4, we talked a great deal about *Fantasy Zone*, didn't we?

**Dr. Onigiri**: I actually wanted to talk a bit more about it.

**Mr. Why**: What else did you want to say about *Fantasy Zone?*

**Dr. Onigiri**: Oh, are you interested? It has quite a bit of back story to it.

**Mr. Why**: Oh! Do tell!

**Dr. Onigiri**: In Space Year 6216, the interplanetary monetary system collapsed, causing a mass panic in the Fantasy Zone. During an investigation into the matter, it was discovered that someone had taken control over the population of Menon, stolen money from other systems, and used it to construct a massive fortress.

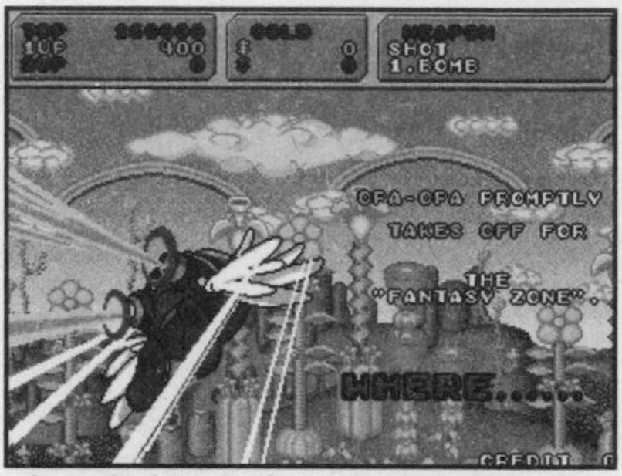
GOLD
WEAPON
SHOT
1.BOMB
OPA-OPA PROMPTLY
TAKES OFF FOR
THE
"FANTASY ZONE".
WHERE......
CREDIT

**Opa-Opa traveling between rounds. The fight will be long and trying...**

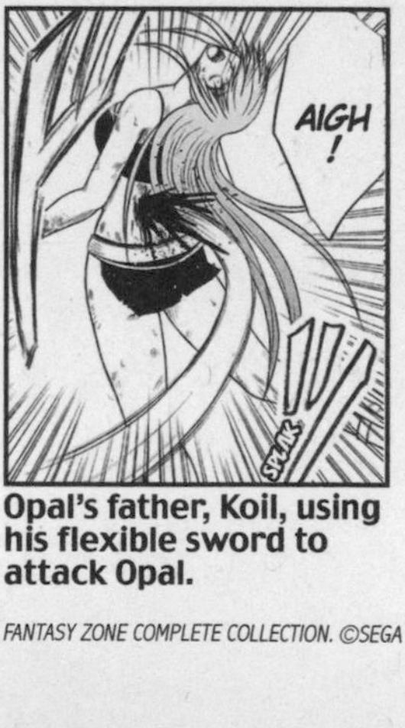
AIGH
!

**Opal's father, Koil, using his flexible sword to attack Opal.**

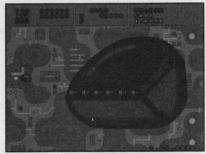

The final round, Round 8, where you face Opa-Opa's father. It's a harsh reality, but you've got no choice but to fight.

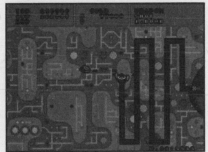

The aliens the boss sends out at you have erratic movements, which makes them difficult to hit.

NO...!
YOU NEED ONLY TO LISTEN TO WHAT I SAY.
DO EVERYTHING I TELL YOU TO, WITHOUT FAIL.
I DON'T WANNA!!
YOU MUST.

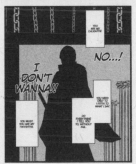

Opal as she severs the chains that bound her to Koil. The day when she can smile once again is sure to follow soon.

It's the story of how the hero, Opa-Opa, decided to stand against this mysterious villain and his wave of destruction.

**Mr. Why**: Hey! That's the final boss that we were discussing in volume 4! What kind of enemy is he?

**Dr. Onigiri**: After defeating 7 bosses, you finally face the final boss in Round 8, Salfar, only to discover that the enemy waiting for you was your own father.

**Mr. Why**: *Whaaat?!*

**Prof. Mushroom**: That's quite a big spoiler. Everyone, keep it hush-hush, okay?

**Dr. Onigiri**: The aliens that the boss sends out follow you around and attack you from behind, so they were rather difficult to avoid. And, as I mentioned in our segment from way back in volume 1, the song has lyrics to it.

**Mr. Why**: You mean the one with the "Yadayo" lyrics?

**Dr. Onigiri**: Quite right. ♫ *"Yadayo Yadayo Iyadayo Iyadayo Kao mo mitakunai yo. Yadayo Yadayo Iyadayo Omae nanka kirainanda yo."* ♫ Which translates to... "No! No! I don't wanna! I don't wanna! I don't even wanna to look at your face! No! No! I don't wanna! I hate your guts!" Those lyrics, along with the final boss fight, left an extremely strong impression on the player.

To be continued...

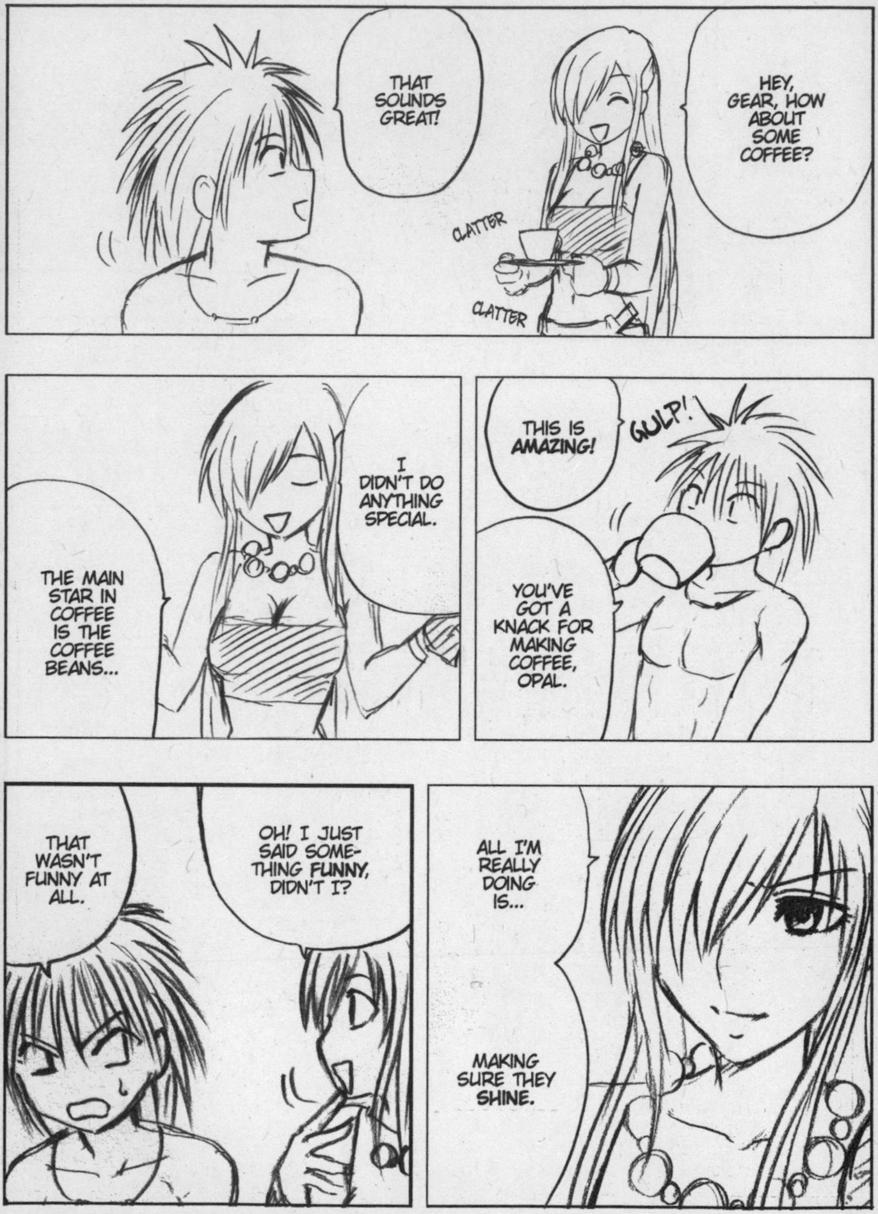
HEY, GEAR, HOW ABOUT SOME COFFEE?
CLATTER
CLATTER
THAT SOUNDS GREAT!
THIS IS AMAZING!
GULP!
YOU'VE GOT A KNACK FOR MAKING COFFEE, OPAL.
I DIDN'T DO ANYTHING SPECIAL.
THE MAIN STAR IN COFFEE IS THE COFFEE BEANS...
ALL I'M REALLY DOING IS...
MAKING SURE THEY SHINE.
OH! I JUST SAID SOME-THING FUNNY, DIDN'T I?
THAT WASN'T FUNNY AT ALL.

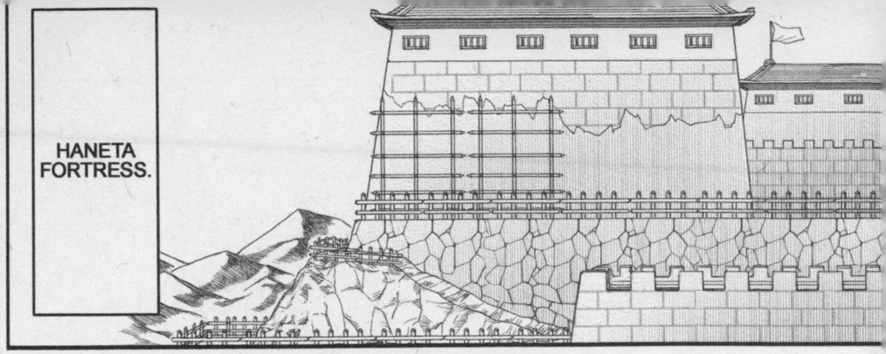
HANETA FORTRESS.

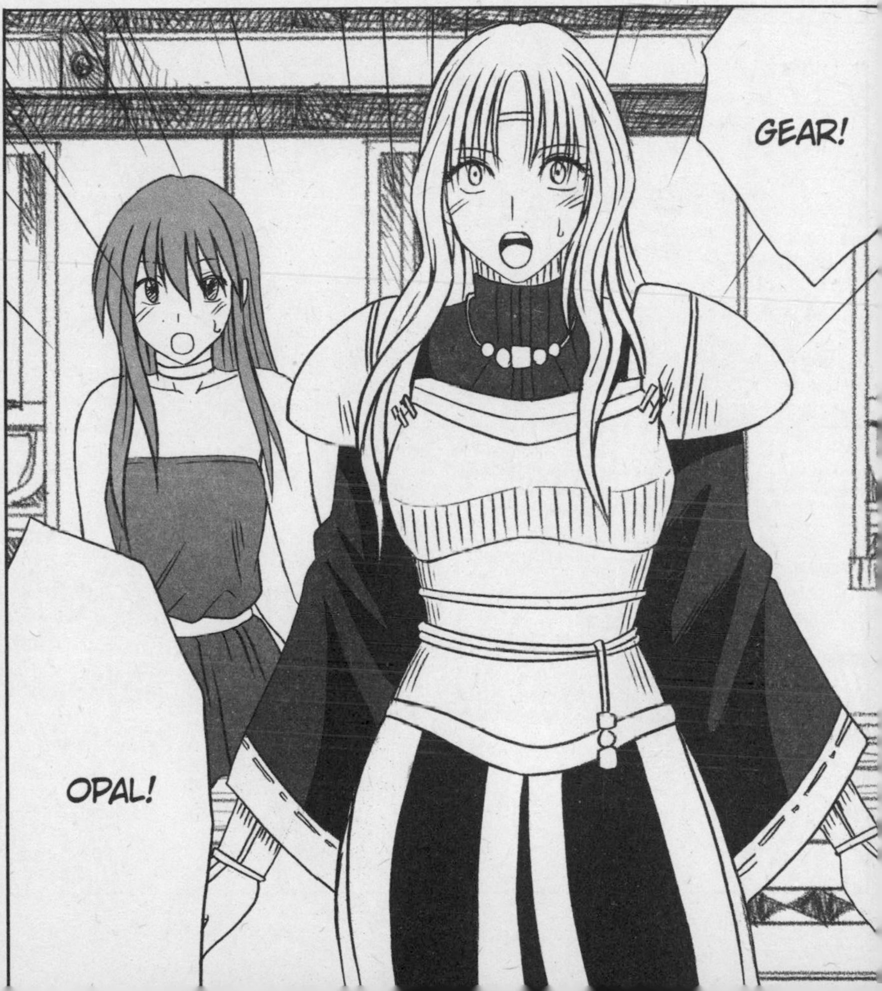
GEAR!
OPAL!

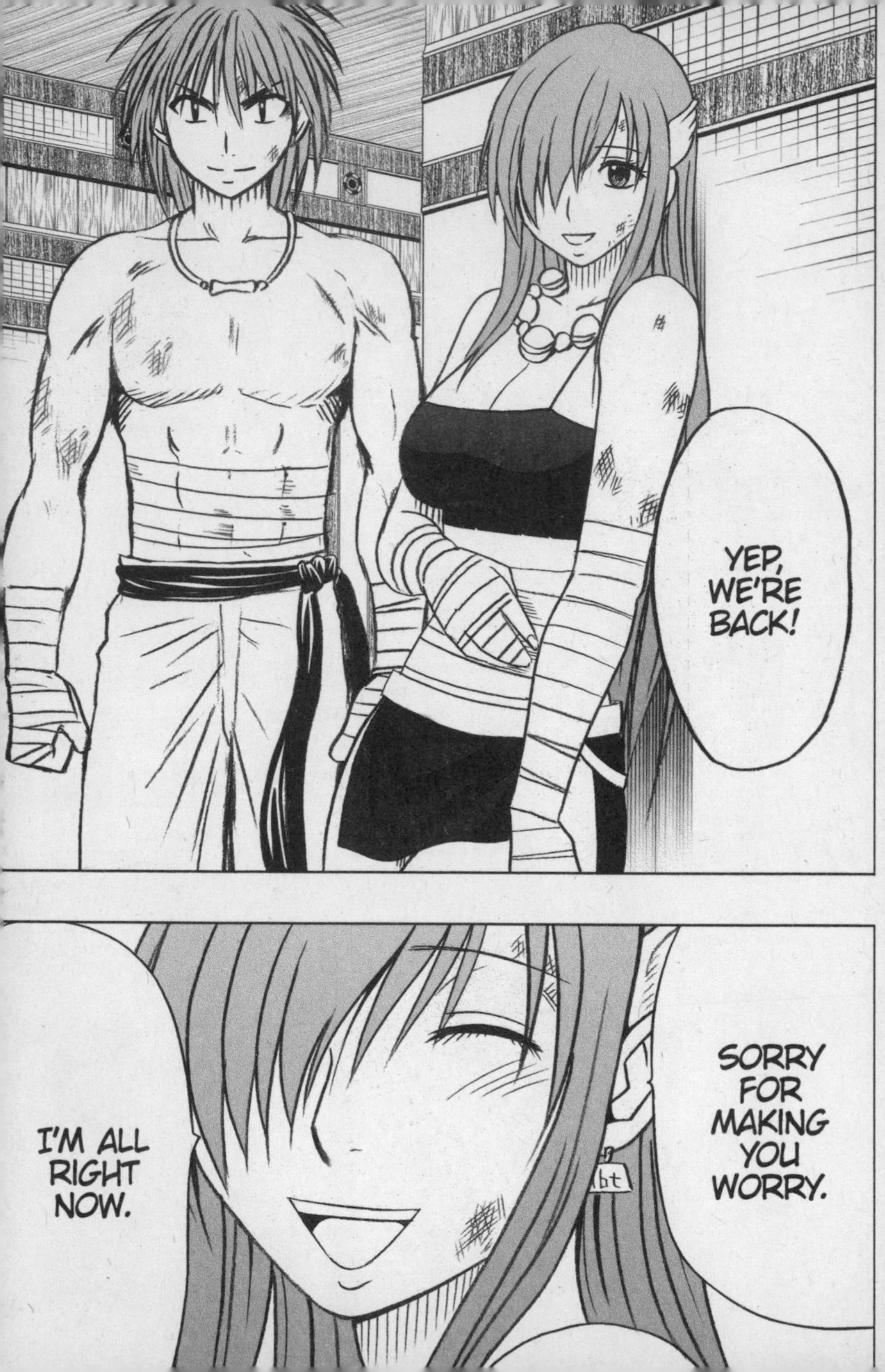
YEP, WE'RE BACK!
SORRY FOR MAKING YOU WORRY.
I'M ALL RIGHT NOW.

Part 2

# CHAPTER 13

# HEAVEN'S LOST GENIUS

## DISC 1

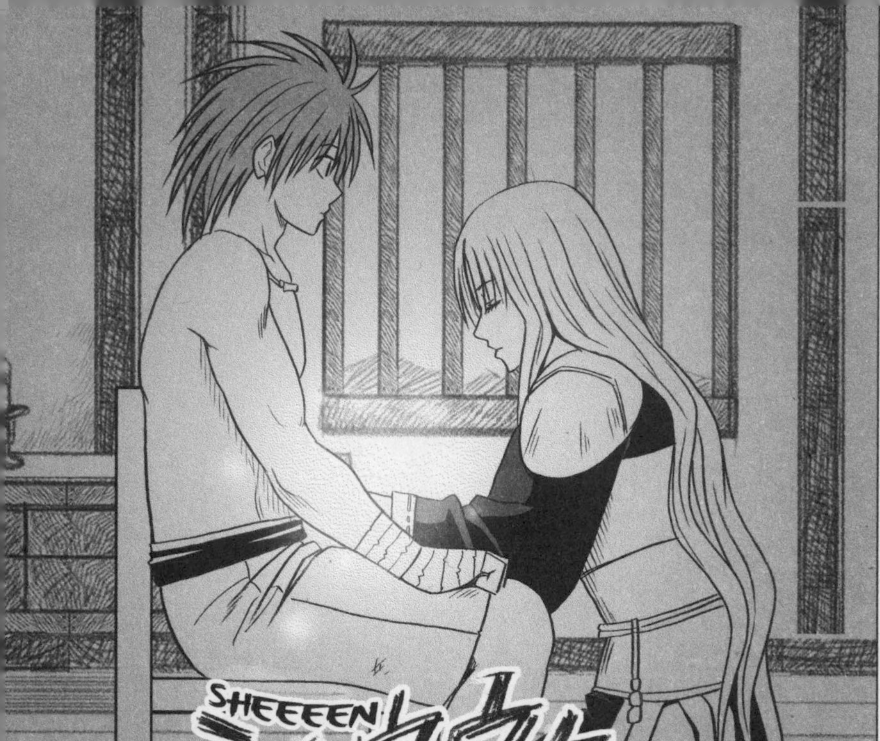
SHEEEEN
シュウウウ
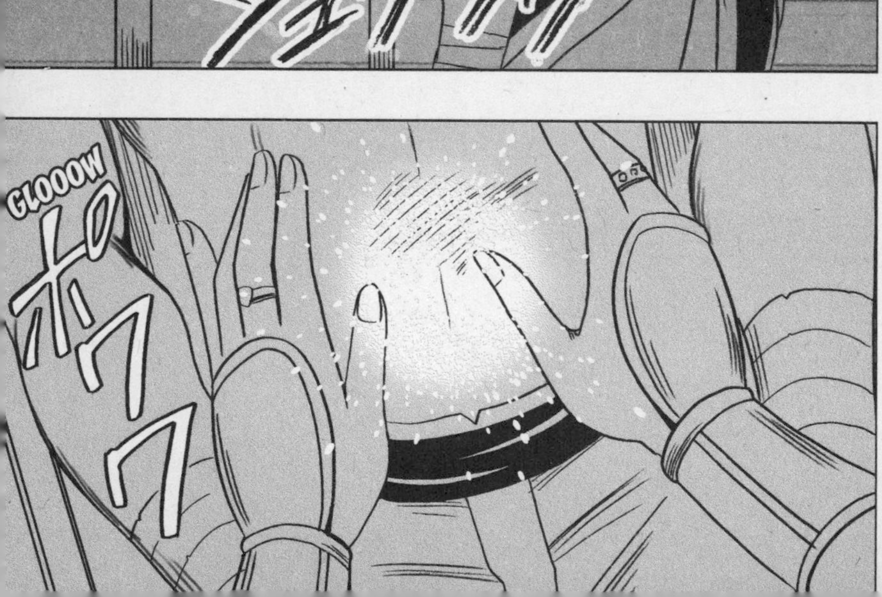
GLOOOW
ホワワ

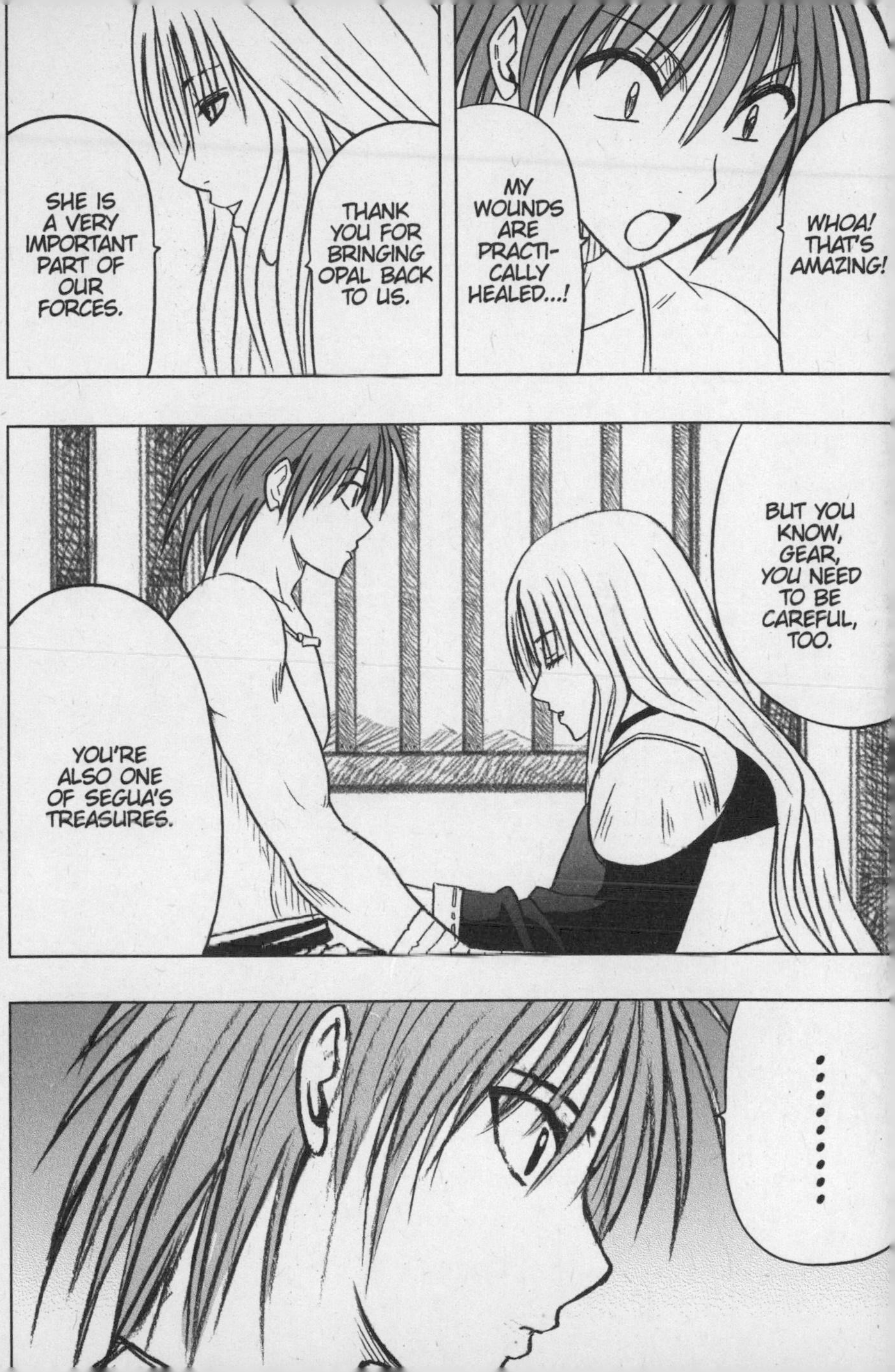
WHOA! THAT'S AMAZING!
MY WOUNDS ARE PRACTI-CALLY HEALED...!
THANK YOU FOR BRINGING OPAL BACK TO US.
SHE IS A VERY IMPORTANT PART OF OUR FORCES.
BUT YOU KNOW, GEAR, YOU NEED TO BE CAREFUL, TOO.
YOU'RE ALSO ONE OF SEGUA'S TREASURES.
.........

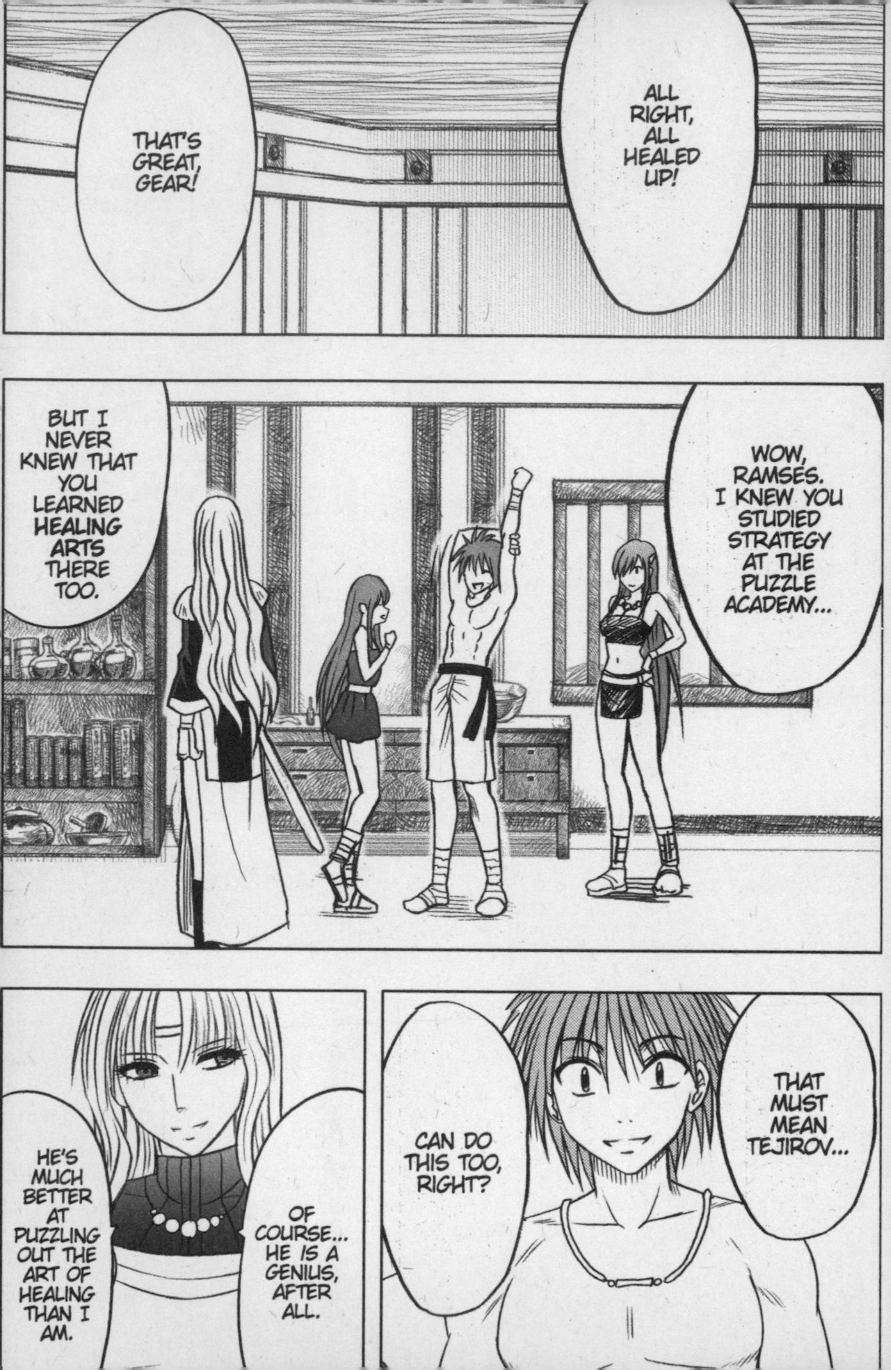
ALL RIGHT, ALL HEALED UP!
THAT'S GREAT, GEAR!
WOW, RAMSES. I KNEW YOU STUDIED STRATEGY AT THE PUZZLE ACADEMY...
BUT I NEVER KNEW THAT YOU LEARNED HEALING ARTS THERE TOO.
THAT MUST MEAN TEJIROV...
CAN DO THIS TOO, RIGHT?
OF COURSE... HE IS A GENIUS, AFTER ALL.
HE'S MUCH BETTER AT PUZZLING OUT THE ART OF HEALING THAN I AM.

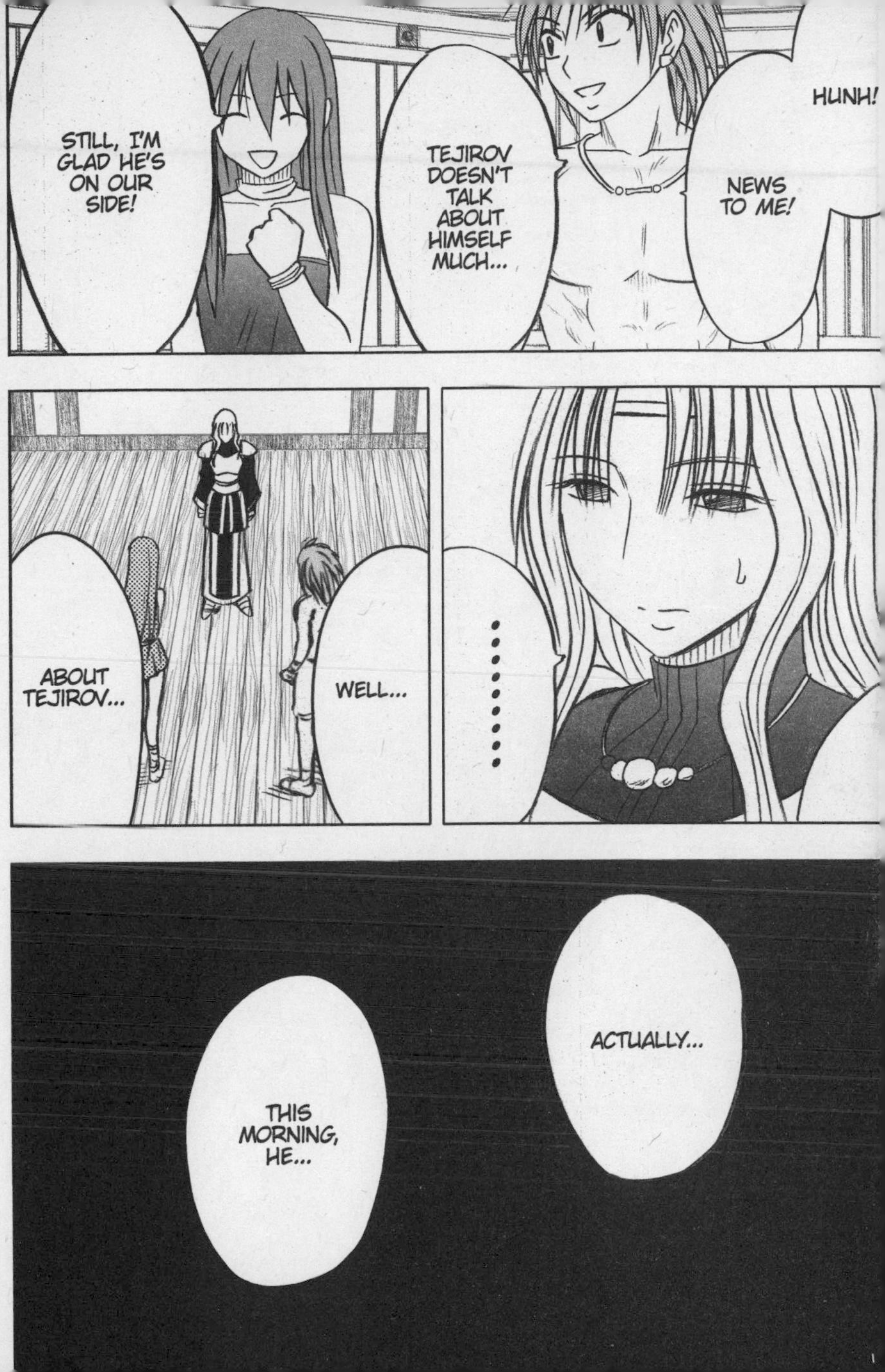
HUNH!
NEWS TO ME!
TEJIROV DOESN'T TALK ABOUT HIMSELF MUCH...
STILL, I'M GLAD HE'S ON OUR SIDE!
........
WELL...
ABOUT TEJIROV...
ACTUALLY...
THIS MORNING, HE...

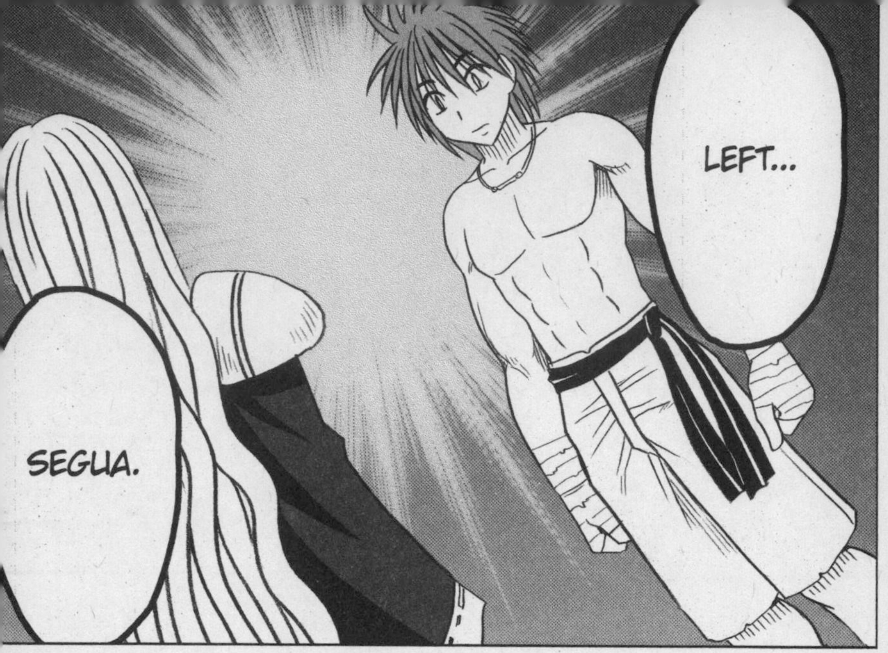
LEFT...
SEGUA.
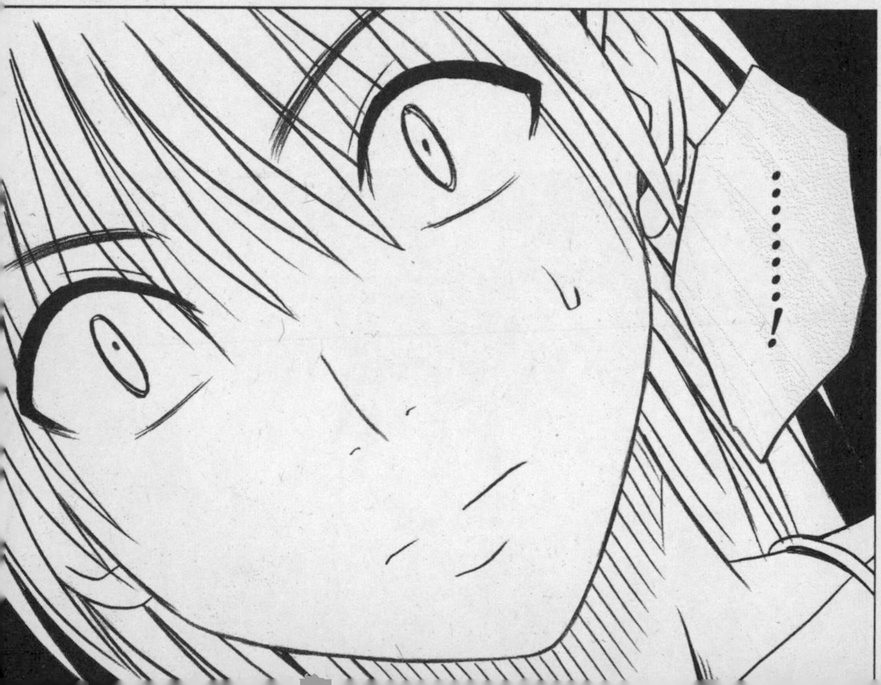
......!

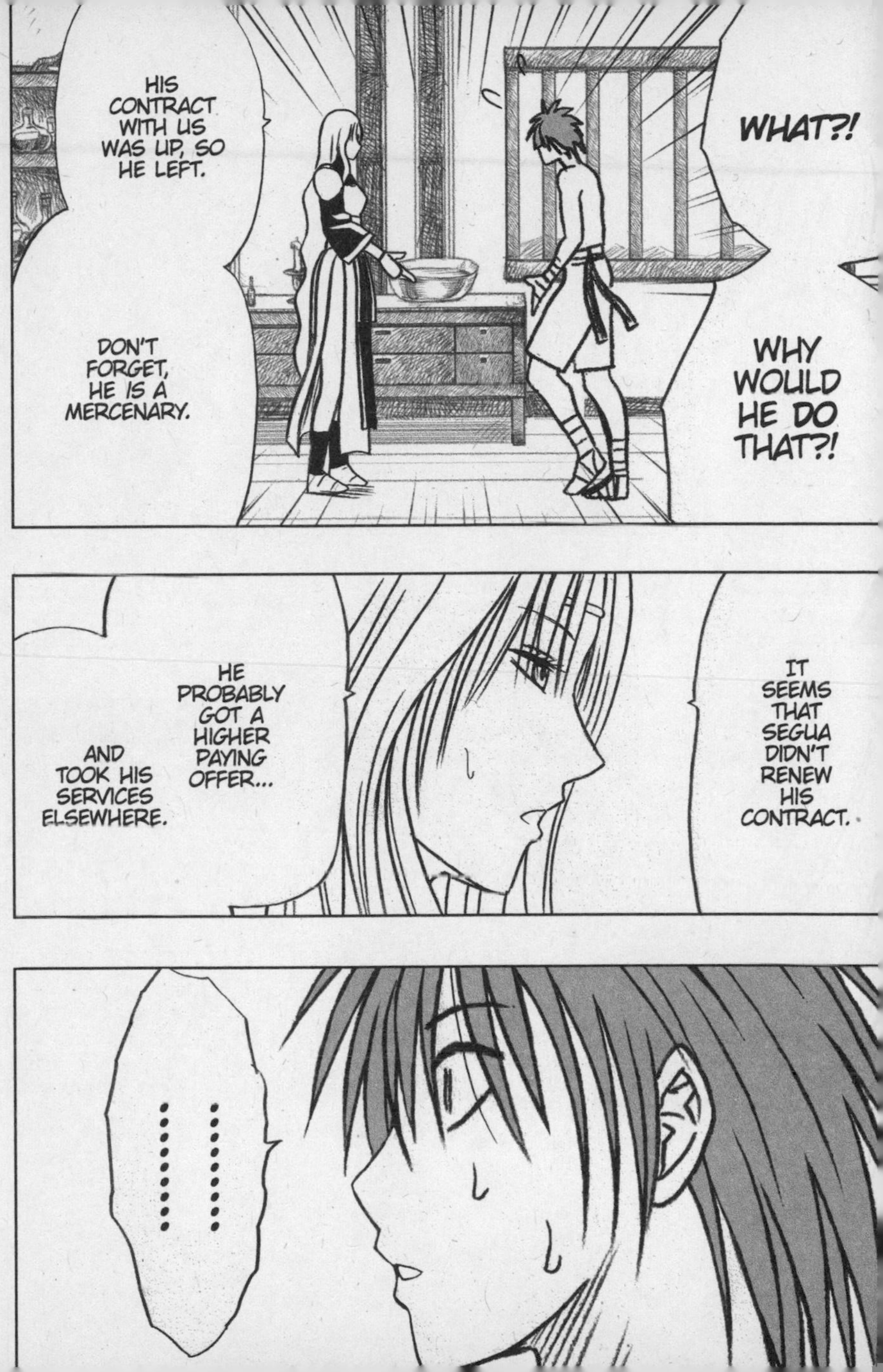
WHAT?!
WHY WOULD HE DO THAT?!
HIS CONTRACT WITH US WAS UP, SO HE LEFT.
DON'T FORGET, HE IS A MERCENARY.
IT SEEMS THAT SEGUA DIDN'T RENEW HIS CONTRACT.
HE PROBABLY GOT A HIGHER PAYING OFFER...
AND TOOK HIS SERVICES ELSEWHERE.
......
......

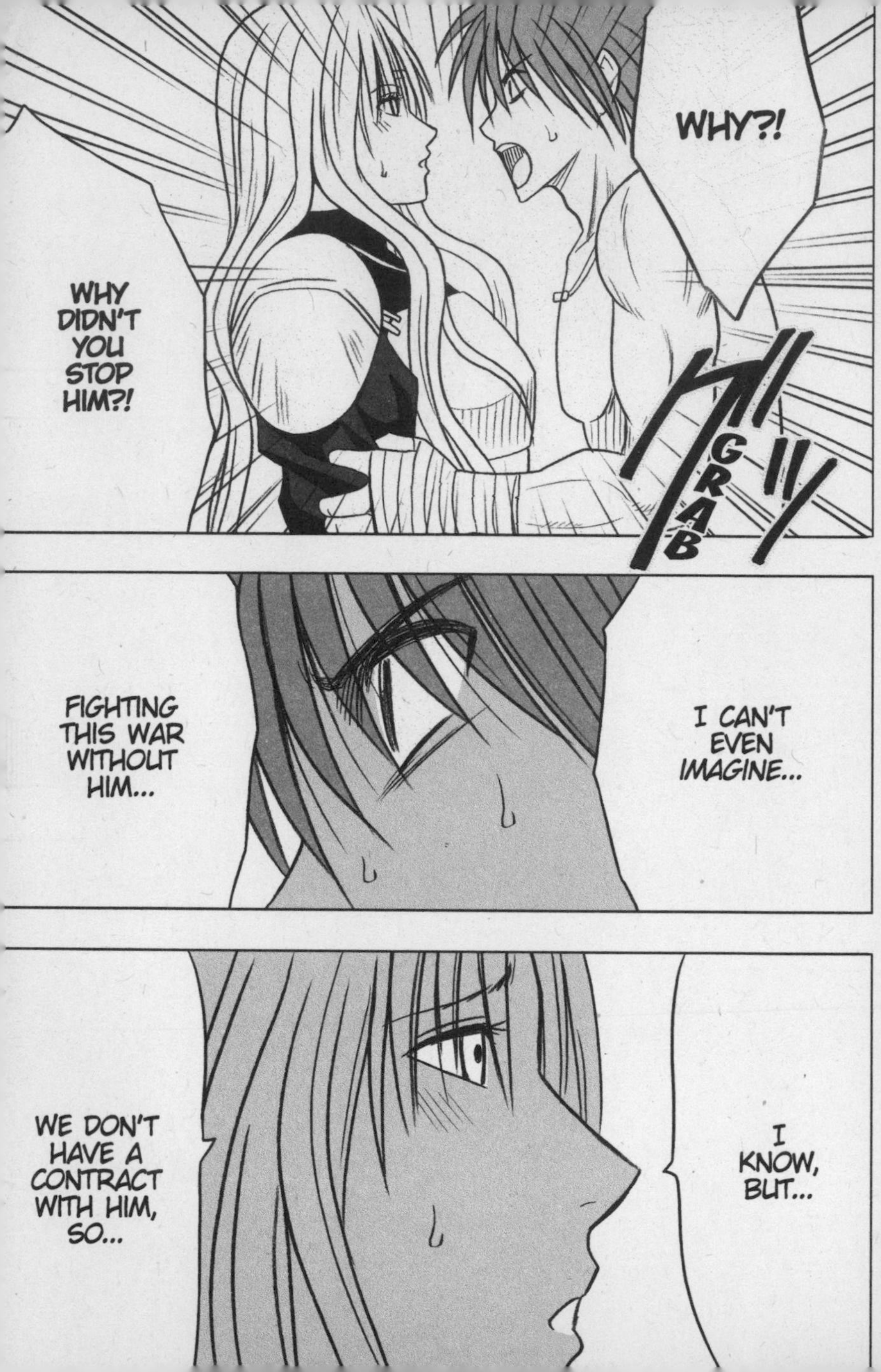
WHY?!
WHY DIDN'T YOU STOP HIM?!
GRAB
I CAN'T EVEN IMAGINE...
FIGHTING THIS WAR WITHOUT HIM...
I KNOW, BUT...
WE DON'T HAVE A CONTRACT WITH HIM, SO...

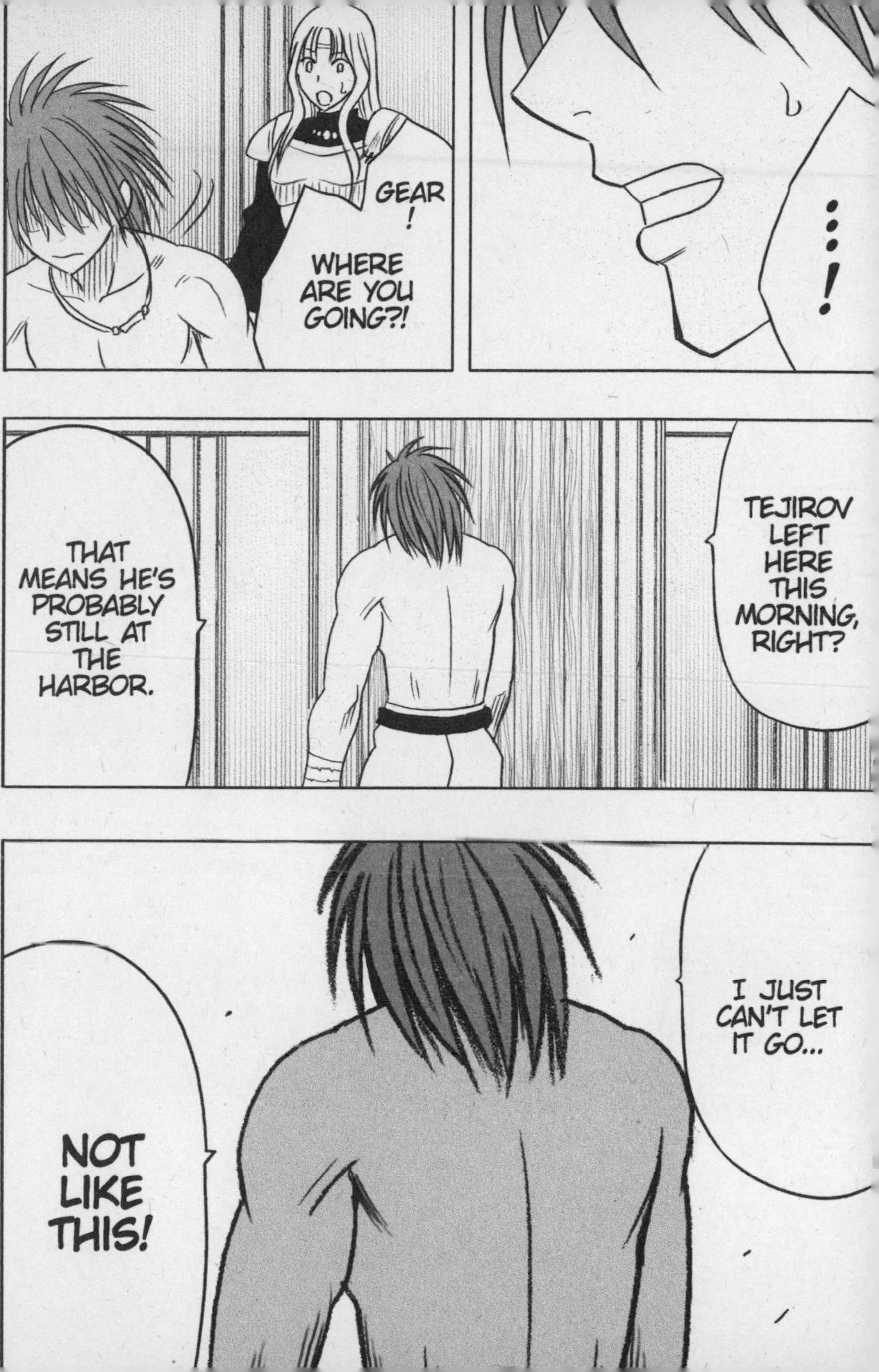
...!
GEAR! WHERE ARE YOU GOING?!
TEJIROV LEFT HERE THIS MORNING, RIGHT?
THAT MEANS HE'S PROBABLY STILL AT THE HARBOR.
I JUST CAN'T LET IT GO...
NOT LIKE THIS!

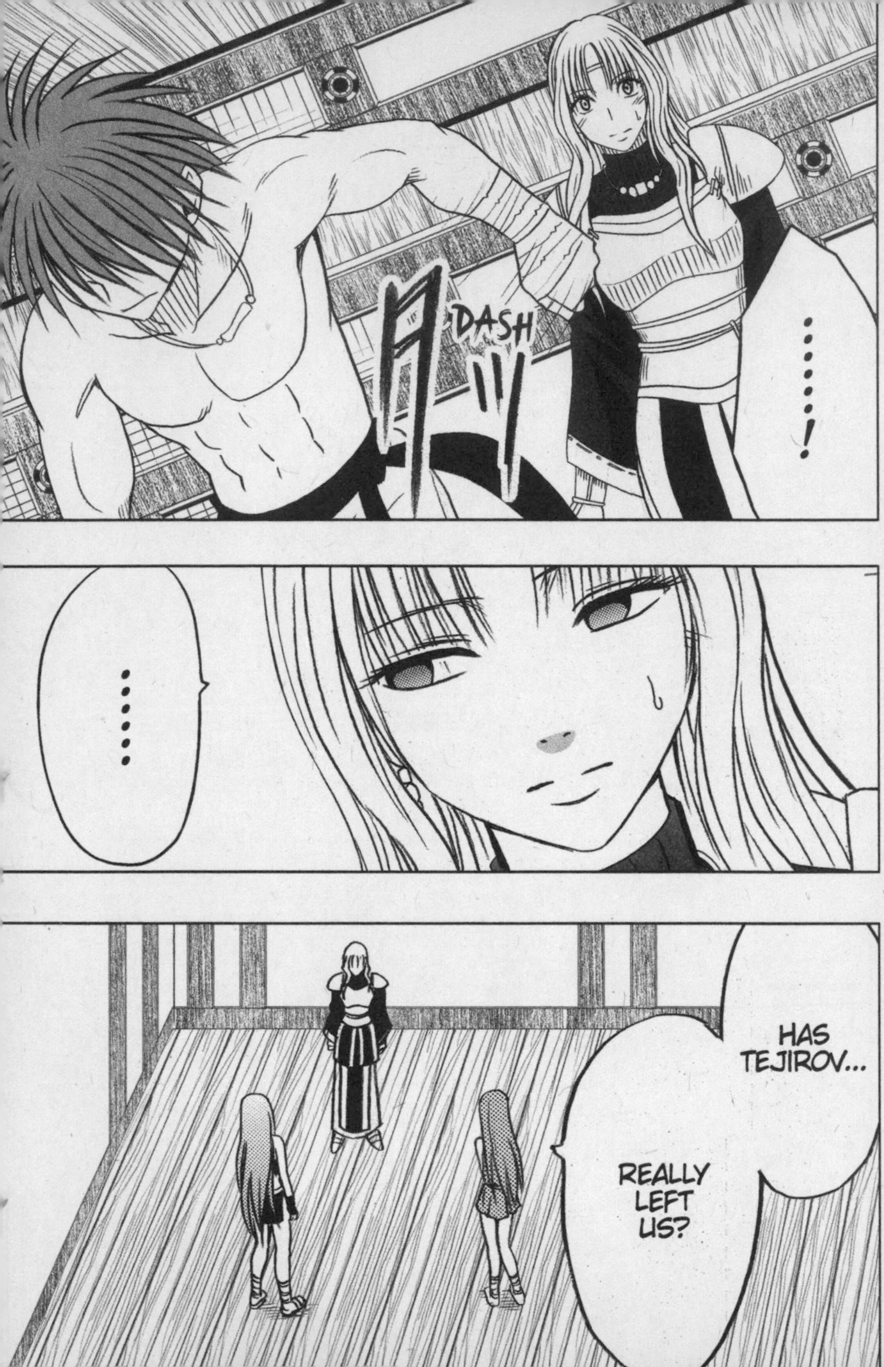

......!
DASH
......
HAS TEJIROV...
REALLY LEFT US?

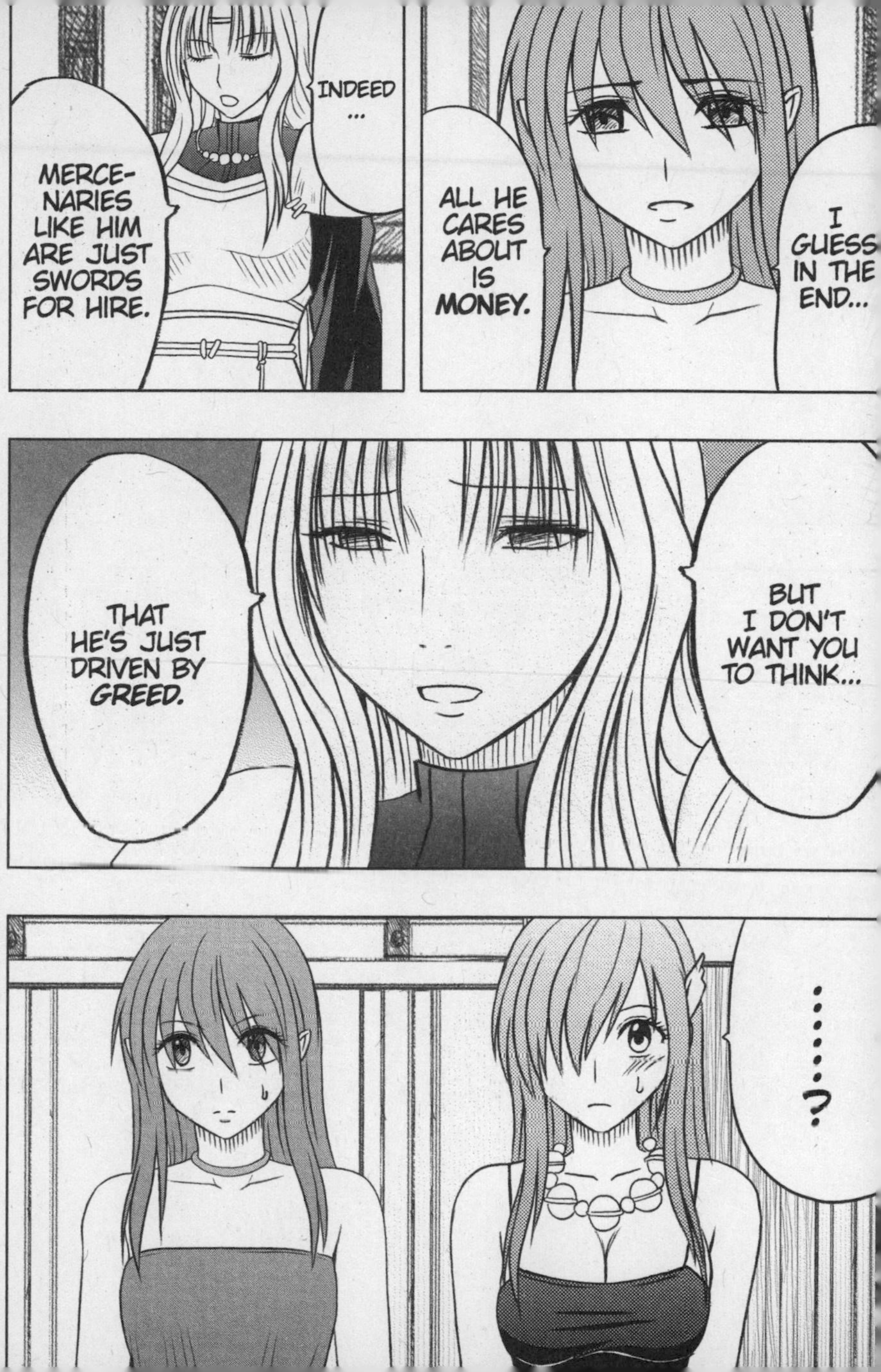
I GUESS IN THE END...
ALL HE CARES ABOUT IS MONEY.
INDEED...
MERCENARIES LIKE HIM ARE JUST SWORDS FOR HIRE.
BUT I DON'T WANT YOU TO THINK...
THAT HE'S JUST DRIVEN BY GREED.
......?

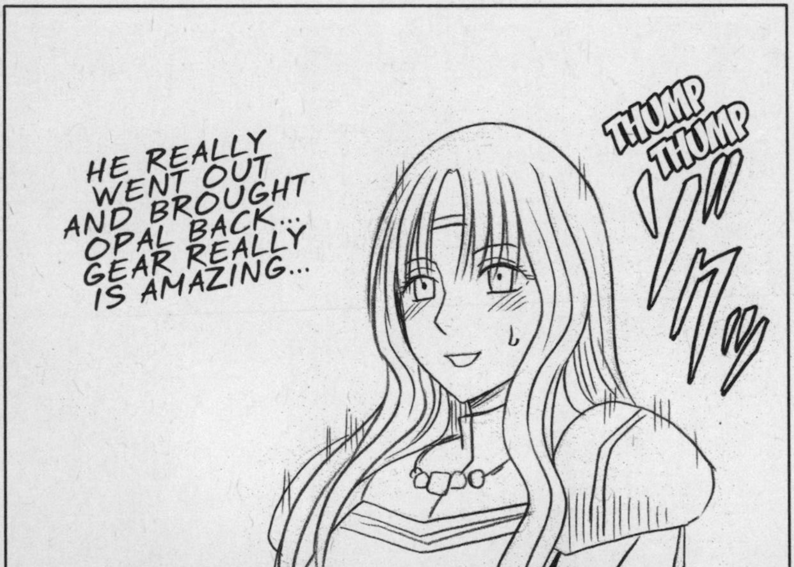
THUMP THUMP
HE REALLY WENT OUT AND BROUGHT OPAL BACK... GEAR REALLY IS AMAZING...

# HEAVEN'S LOST GENIUS

## DISC 2

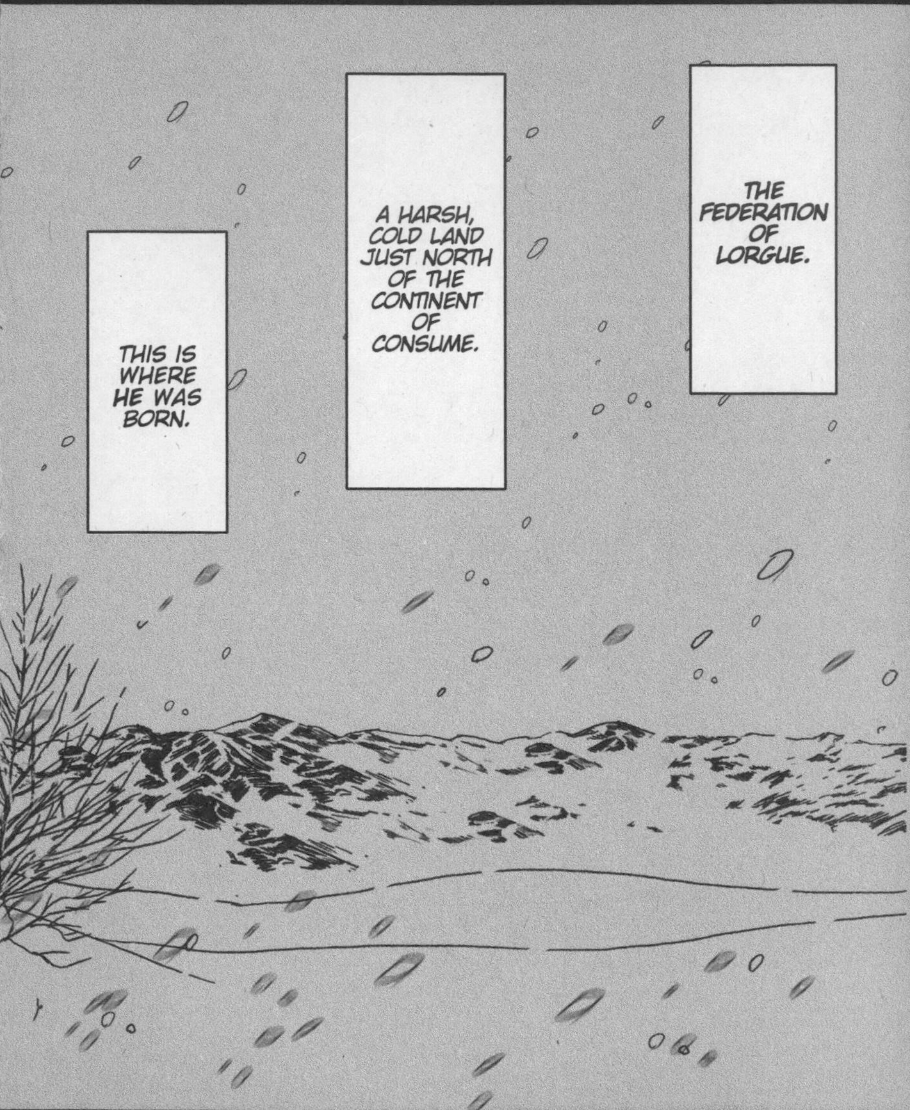
THE FEDERATION OF LORGUE.
A HARSH, COLD LAND JUST NORTH OF THE CONTINENT OF CONSUME.
THIS IS WHERE HE WAS BORN.

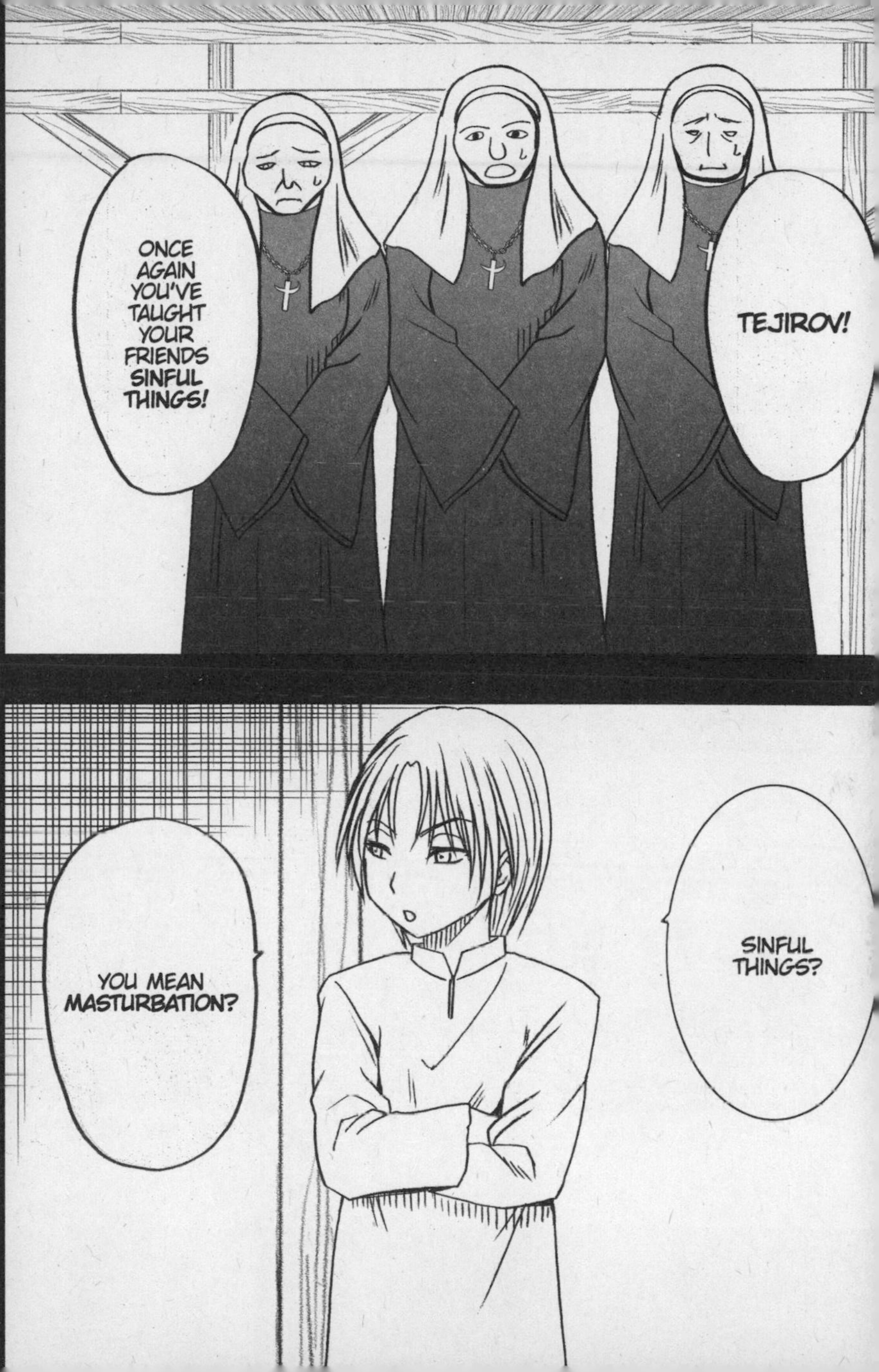
TEJIROV!
ONCE AGAIN YOU'VE TAUGHT YOUR FRIENDS SINFUL THINGS!
SINFUL THINGS?
YOU MEAN MASTURBATION?

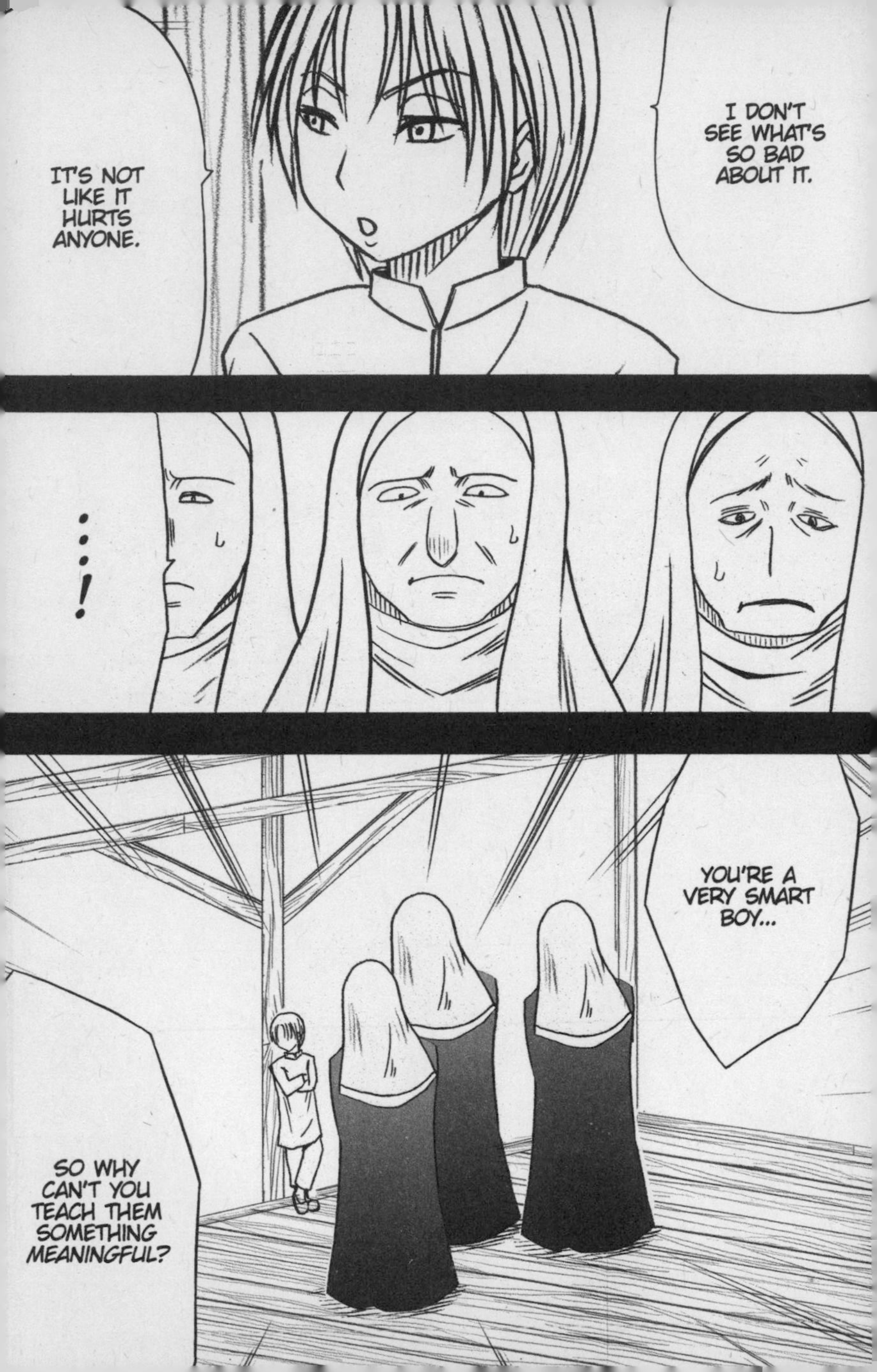
I DON'T SEE WHAT'S SO BAD ABOUT IT.
IT'S NOT LIKE IT HURTS ANYONE.
...!
YOU'RE A VERY SMART BOY...
SO WHY CAN'T YOU TEACH THEM SOMETHING MEANINGFUL?

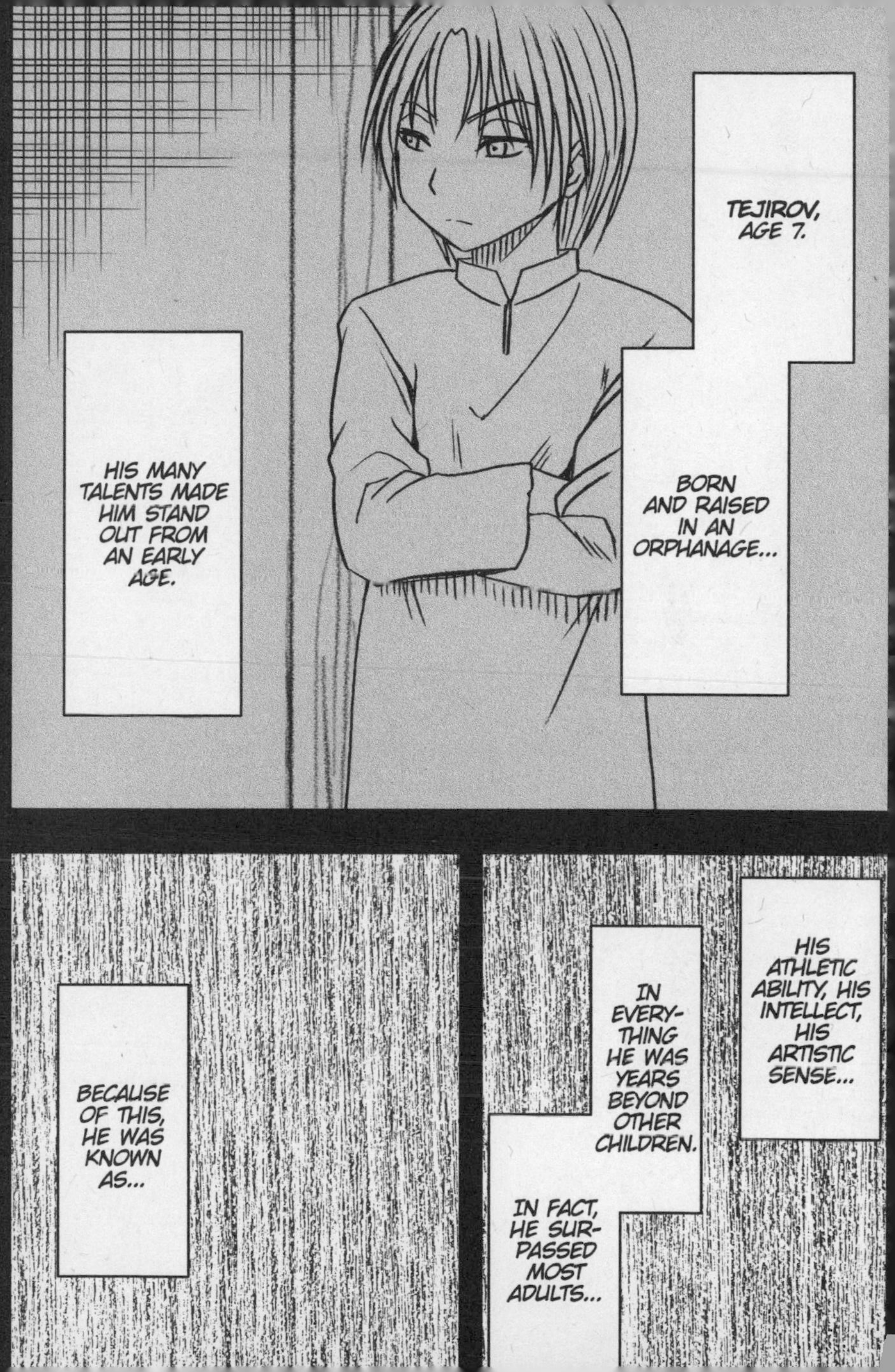
TEJIROV, AGE 7.
BORN AND RAISED IN AN ORPHANAGE...
HIS MANY TALENTS MADE HIM STAND OUT FROM AN EARLY AGE.
HIS ATHLETIC ABILITY, HIS INTELLECT, HIS ARTISTIC SENSE...
IN EVERY-THING HE WAS YEARS BEYOND OTHER CHILDREN.
IN FACT, HE SUR-PASSED MOST ADULTS...
BECAUSE OF THIS, HE WAS KNOWN AS...

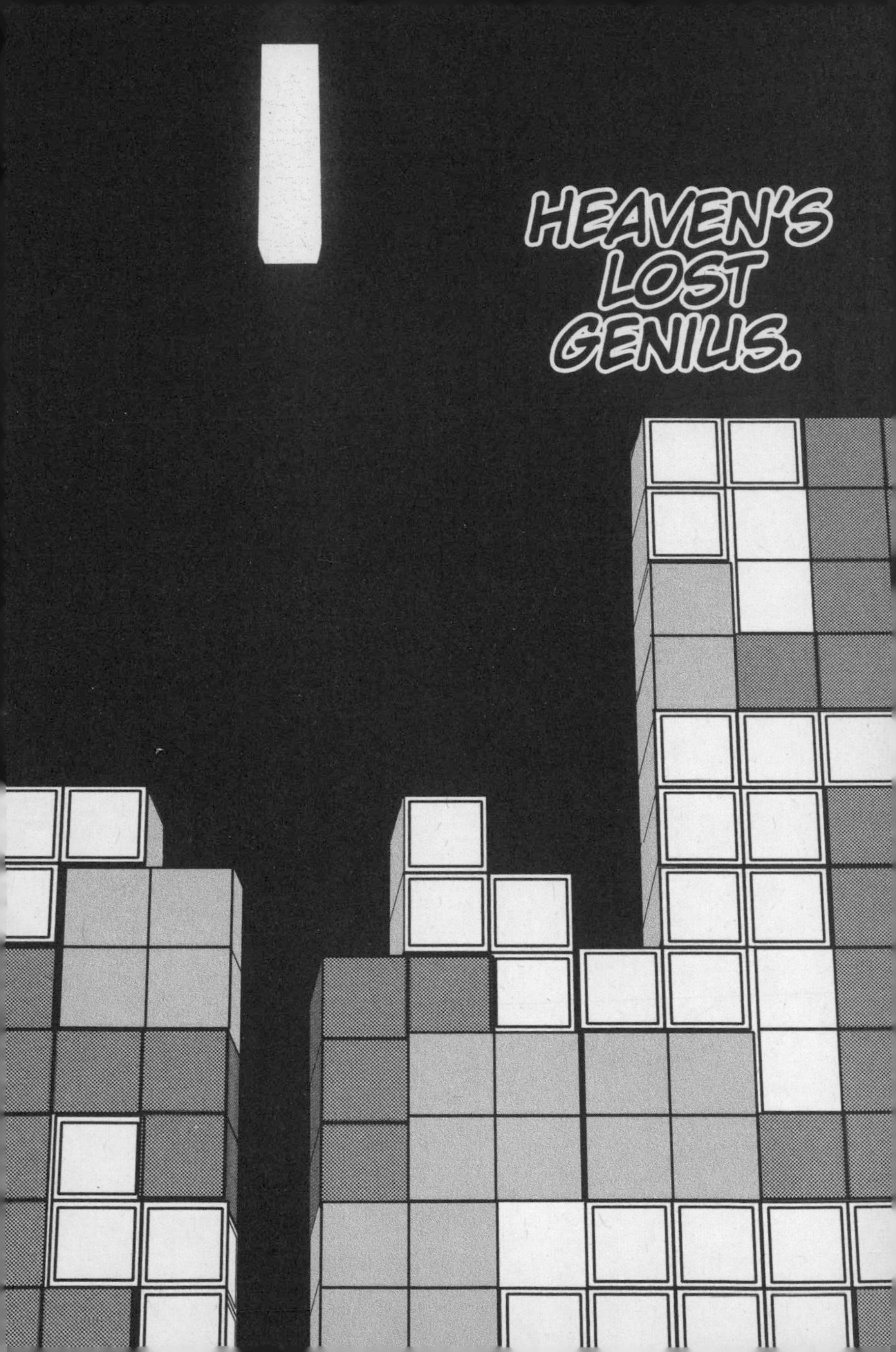
HEAVEN'S LOST GENIUS.

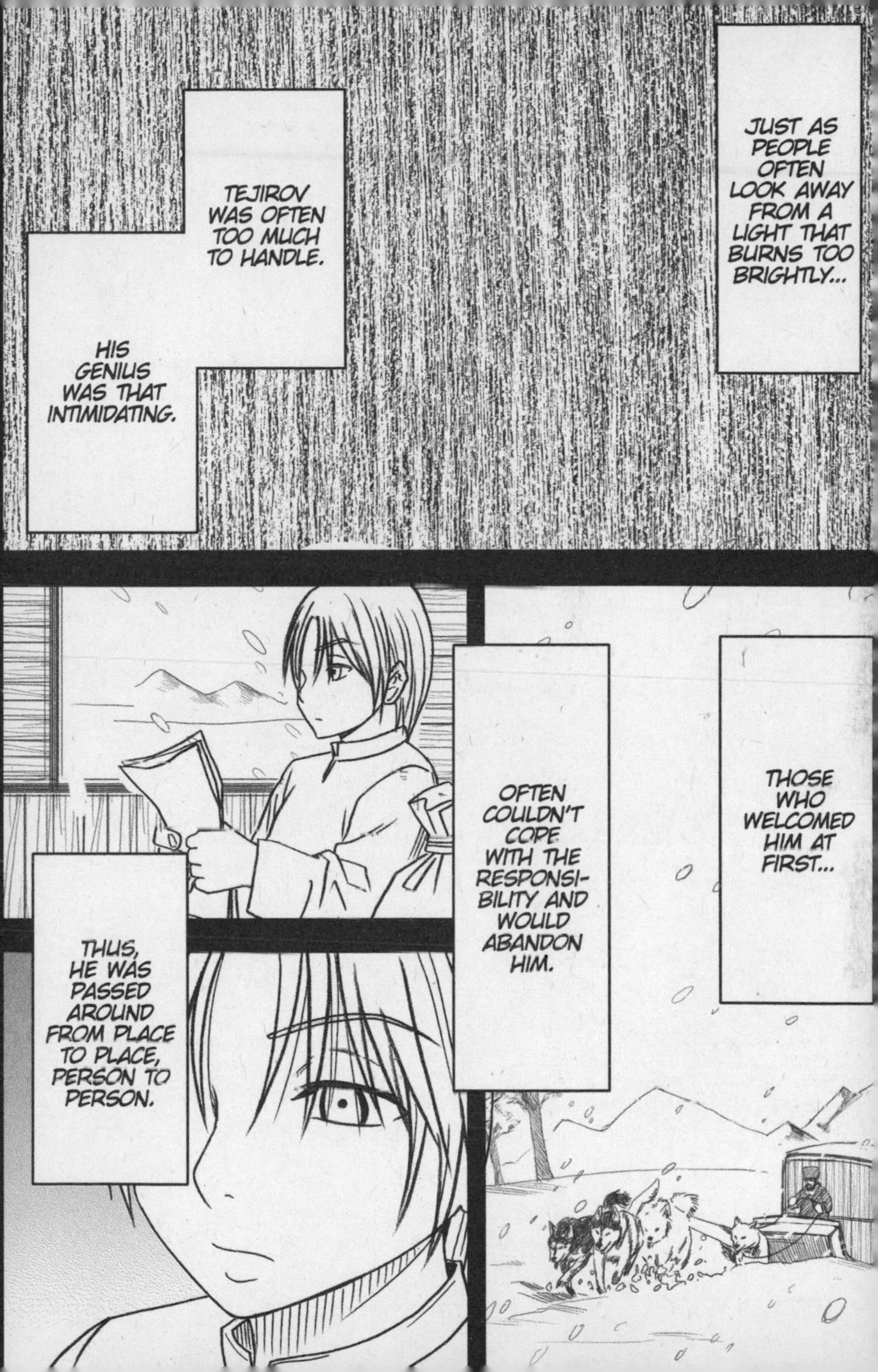
JUST AS PEOPLE OFTEN LOOK AWAY FROM A LIGHT THAT BURNS TOO BRIGHTLY...
TEJIROV WAS OFTEN TOO MUCH TO HANDLE.
HIS GENIUS WAS THAT INTIMIDATING.
THOSE WHO WELCOMED HIM AT FIRST...
OFTEN COULDN'T COPE WITH THE RESPONSI-BILITY AND WOULD ABANDON HIM.
THUS, HE WAS PASSED AROUND FROM PLACE TO PLACE, PERSON TO PERSON.

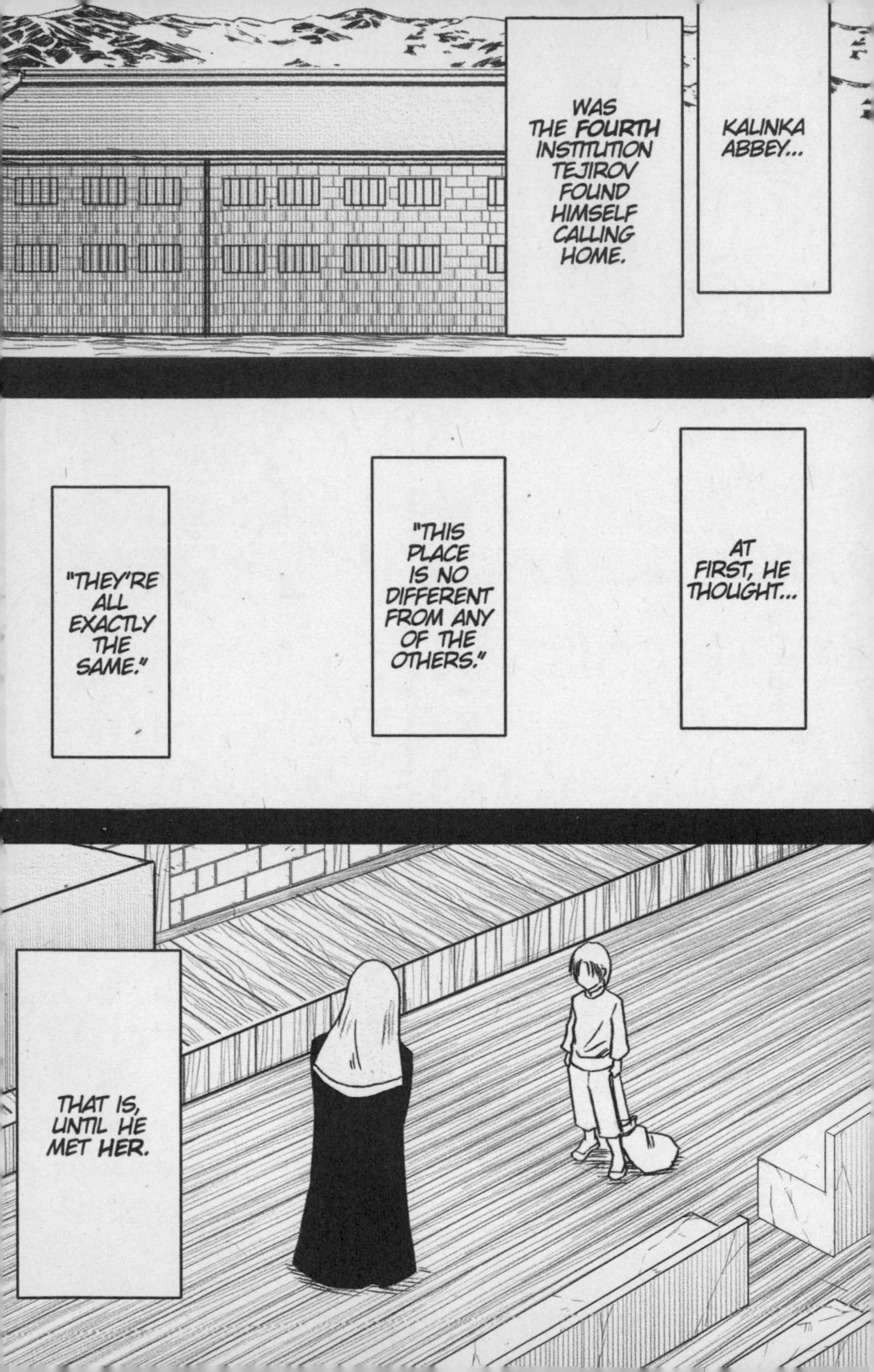
KALINKA ABBEY...
WAS THE FOURTH INSTITUTION TEJIROV FOUND HIMSELF CALLING HOME.
AT FIRST, HE THOUGHT...
"THIS PLACE IS NO DIFFERENT FROM ANY OF THE OTHERS."
"THEY'RE ALL EXACTLY THE SAME."
THAT IS, UNTIL HE MET HER.

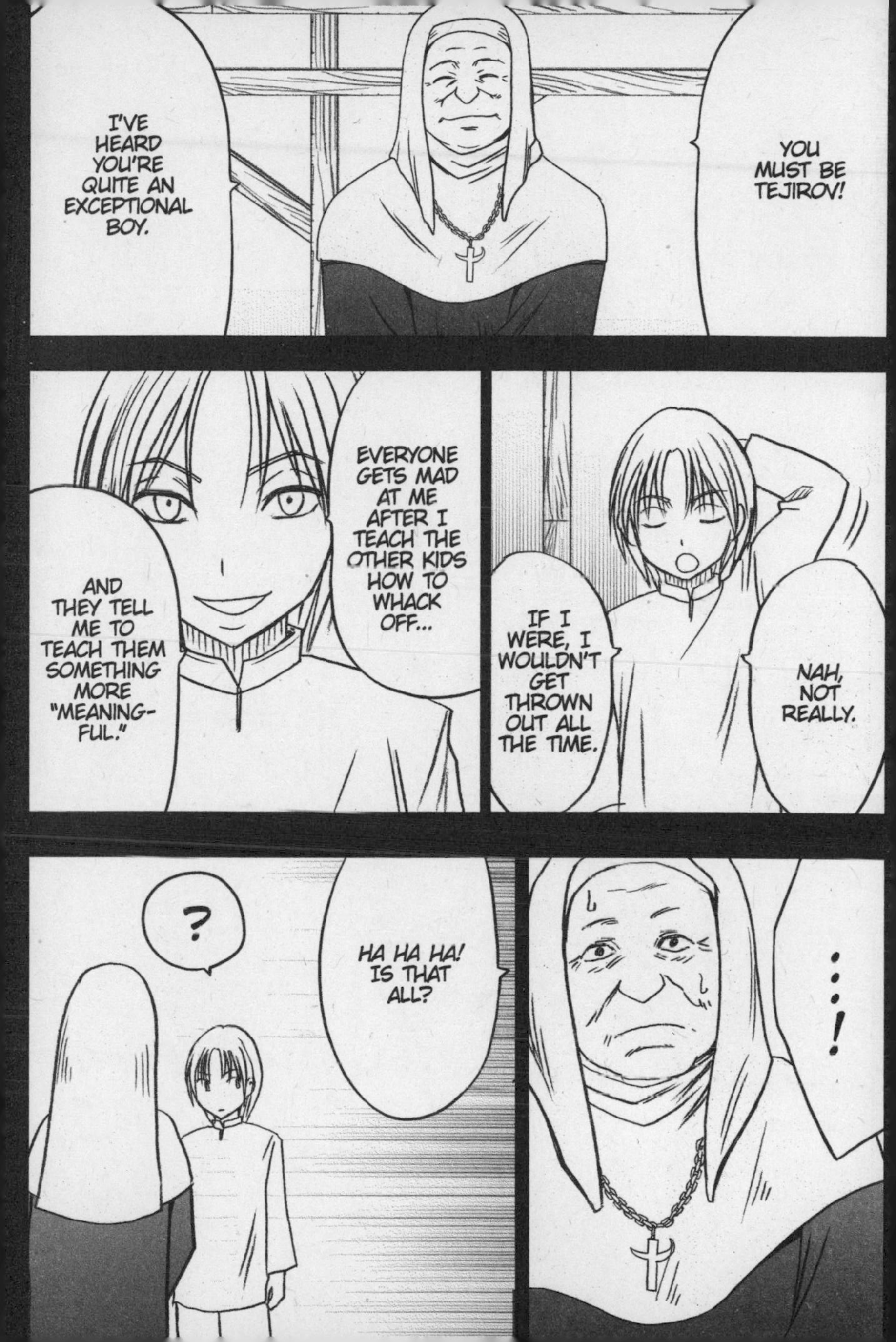
YOU MUST BE TEJIROV!
I'VE HEARD YOU'RE QUITE AN EXCEPTIONAL BOY.
NAH, NOT REALLY.
IF I WERE, I WOULDN'T GET THROWN OUT ALL THE TIME.
EVERYONE GETS MAD AT ME AFTER I TEACH THE OTHER KIDS HOW TO WHACK OFF...
AND THEY TELL ME TO TEACH THEM SOMETHING MORE "MEANING-FUL."
...!
HA HA HA! IS THAT ALL?
?

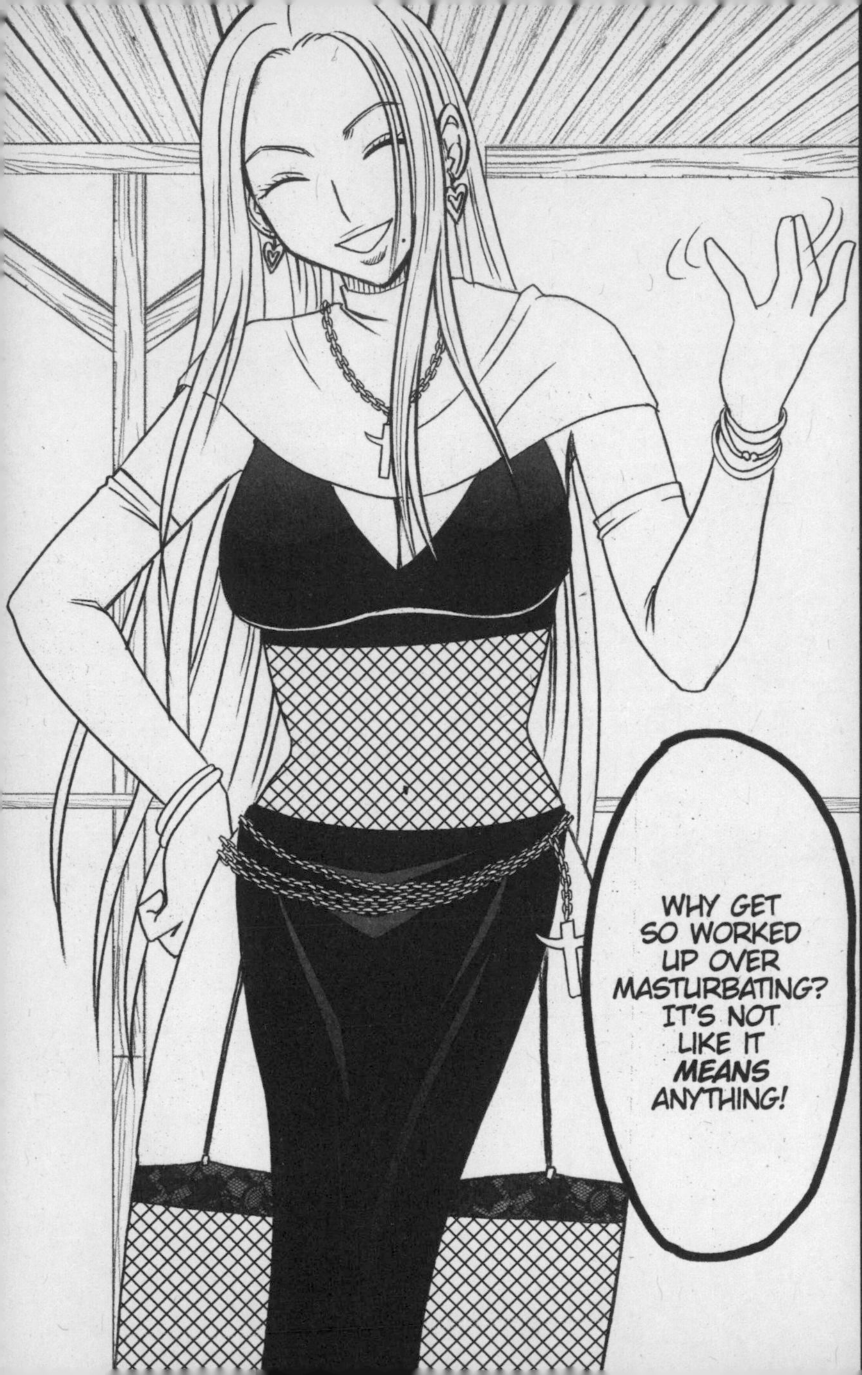
WHY GET SO WORKED UP OVER MASTURBATING? IT'S NOT LIKE IT MEANS ANYTHING!

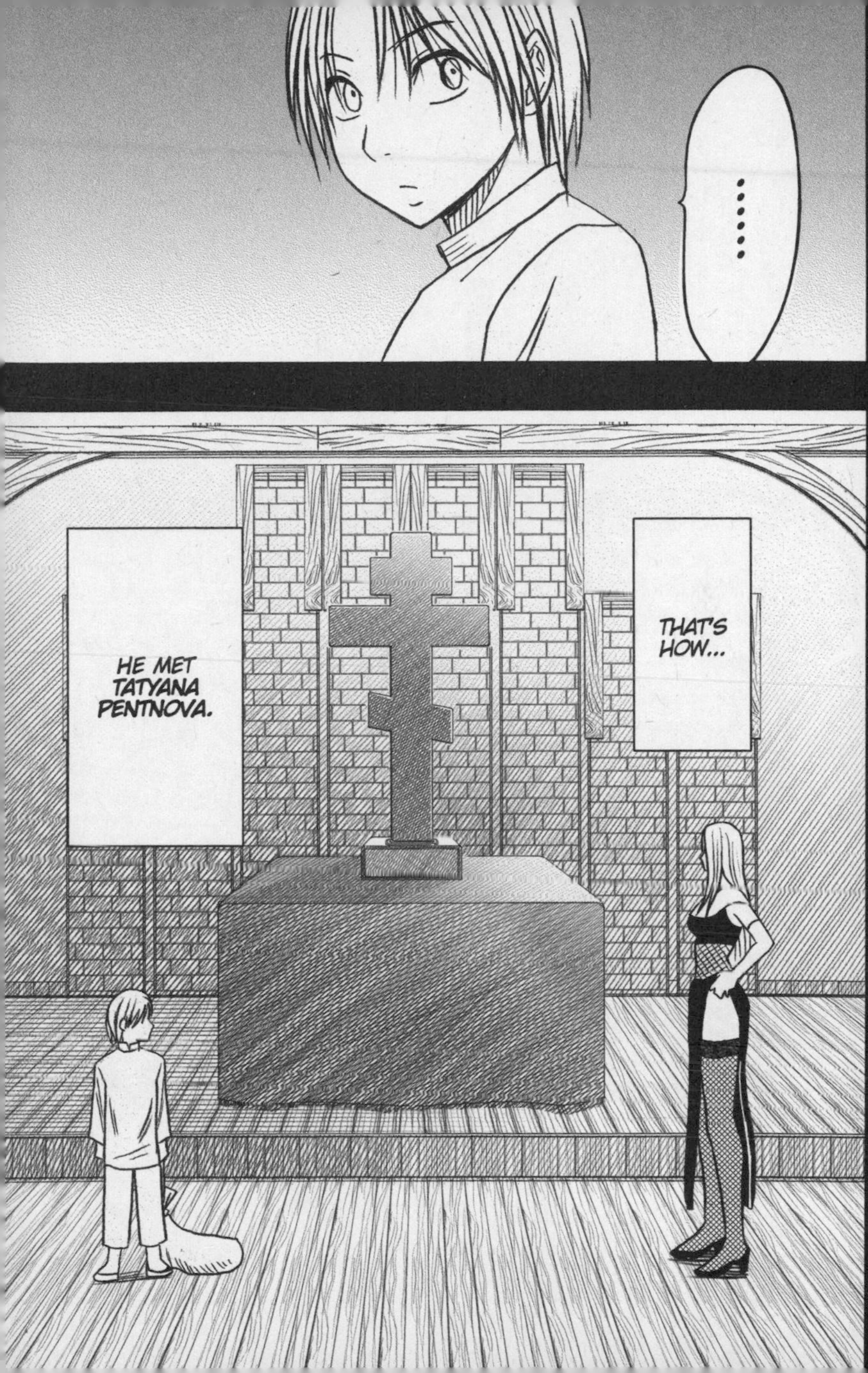
......
THAT'S HOW...
HE MET TATYANA PENTNOVA.

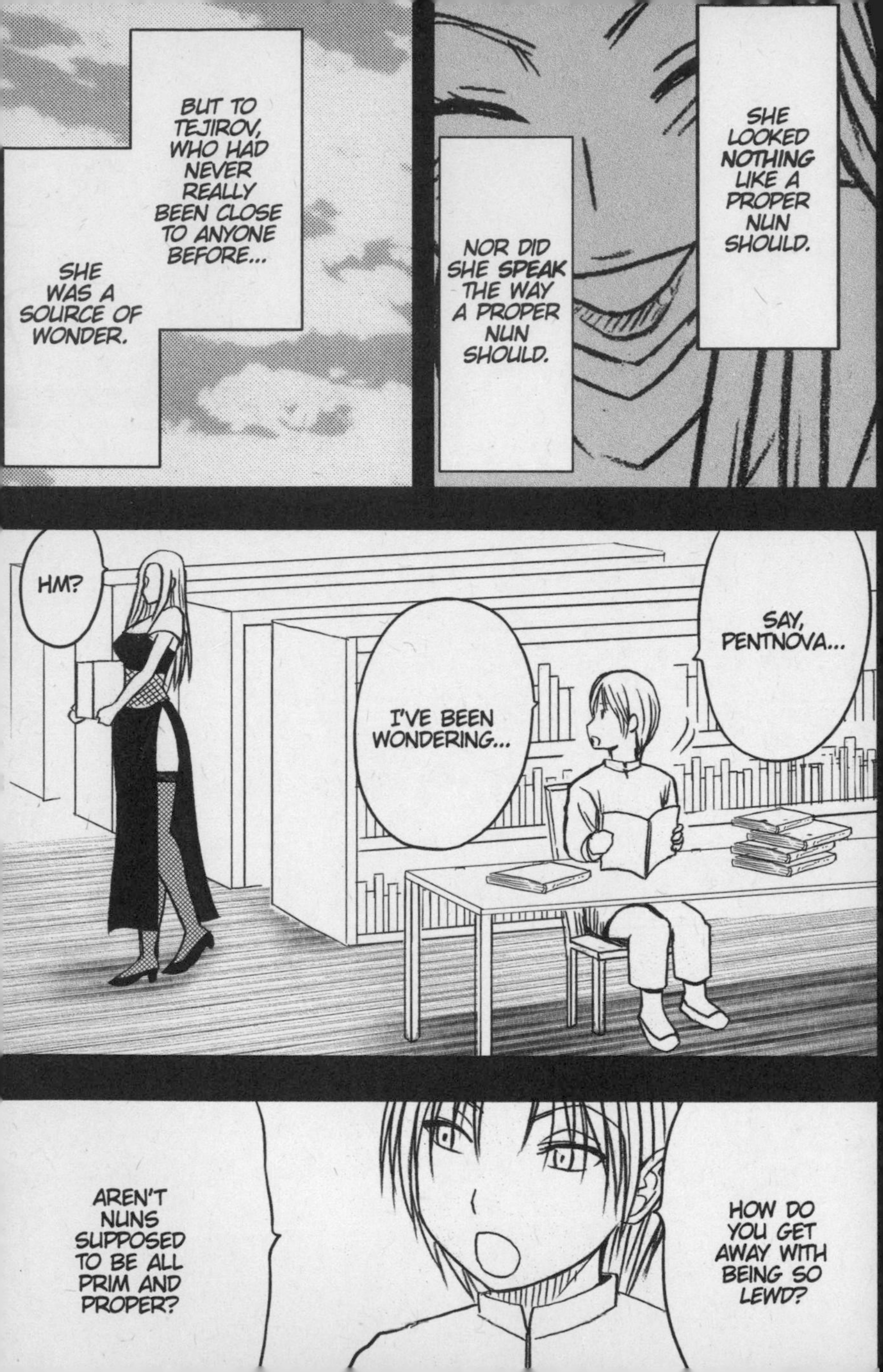
SHE LOOKED NOTHING LIKE A PROPER NUN SHOULD.
NOR DID SHE SPEAK THE WAY A PROPER NUN SHOULD.
BUT TO TEJIROV, WHO HAD NEVER REALLY BEEN CLOSE TO ANYONE BEFORE...
SHE WAS A SOURCE OF WONDER.
SAY, PENTNOVA...
I'VE BEEN WONDERING...
HM?
HOW DO YOU GET AWAY WITH BEING SO LEWD?
AREN'T NUNS SUPPOSED TO BE ALL PRIM AND PROPER?

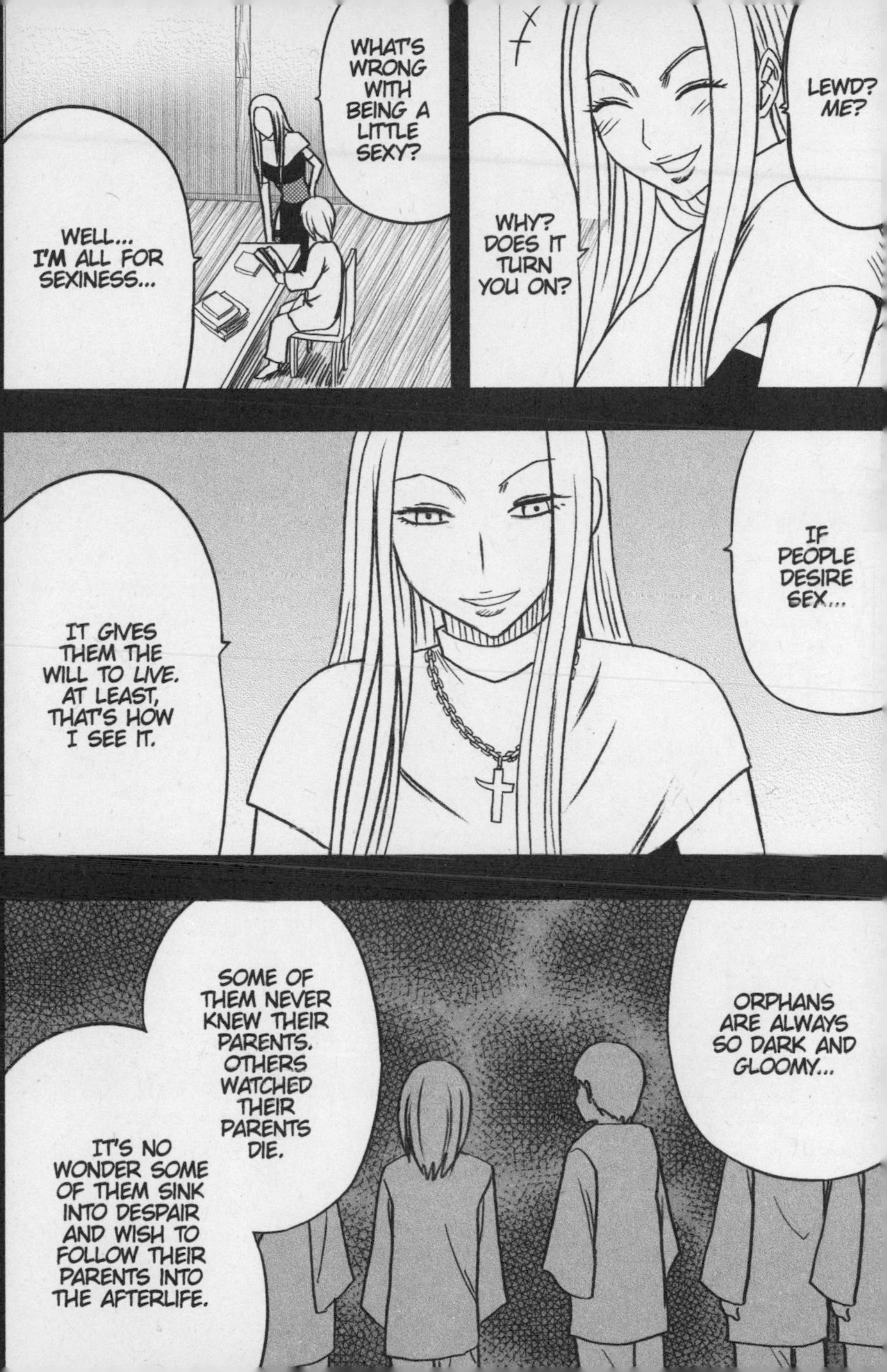
LEWD? ME?
WHY? DOES IT TURN YOU ON?
WHAT'S WRONG WITH BEING A LITTLE SEXY?
WELL... I'M ALL FOR SEXINESS...
IF PEOPLE DESIRE SEX...
IT GIVES THEM THE WILL TO LIVE. AT LEAST, THAT'S HOW I SEE IT.
ORPHANS ARE ALWAYS SO DARK AND GLOOMY...
SOME OF THEM NEVER KNEW THEIR PARENTS. OTHERS WATCHED THEIR PARENTS DIE.
IT'S NO WONDER SOME OF THEM SINK INTO DESPAIR AND WISH TO FOLLOW THEIR PARENTS INTO THE AFTERLIFE.

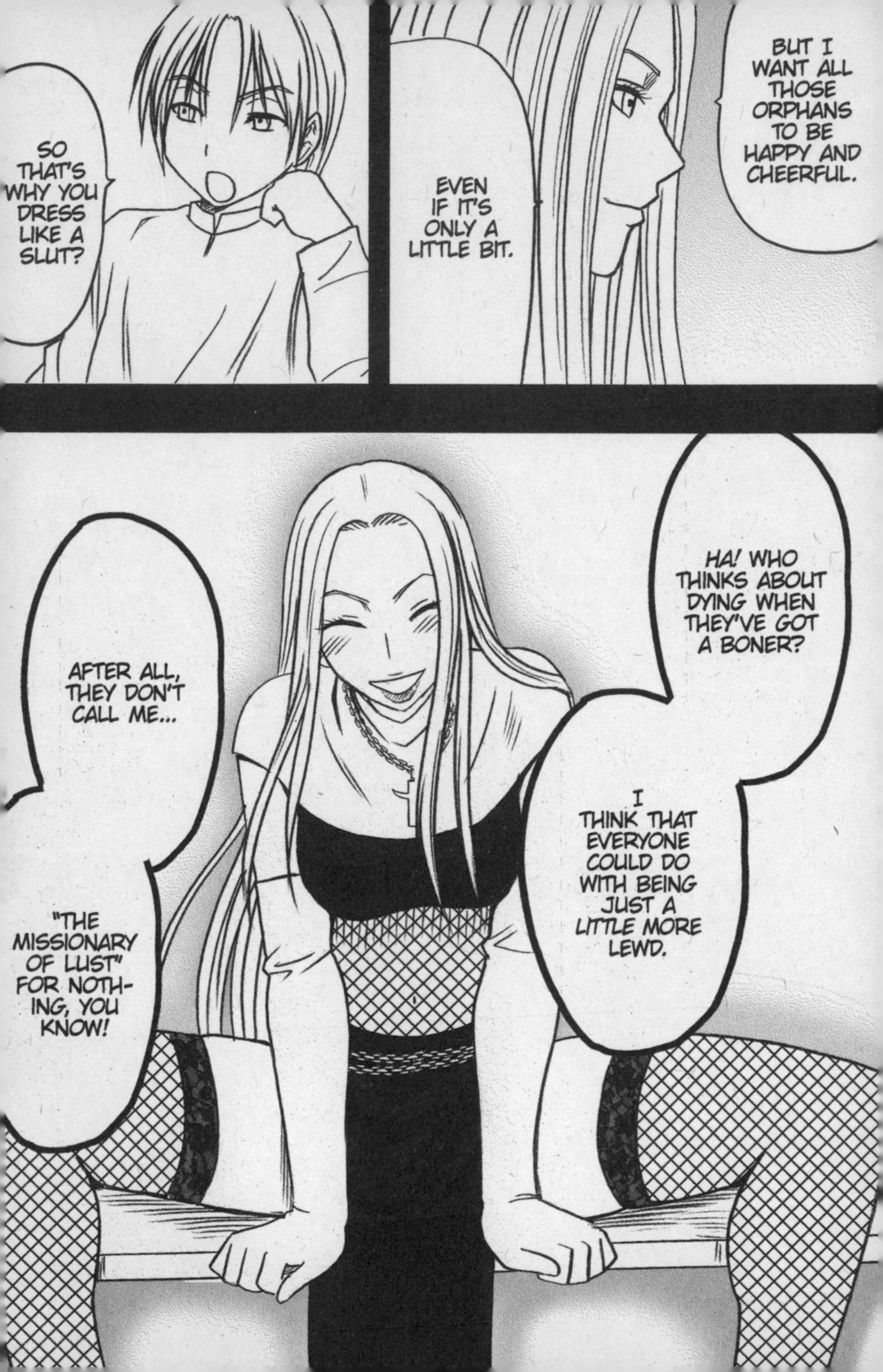
BUT I WANT ALL THOSE ORPHANS TO BE HAPPY AND CHEERFUL.
EVEN IF IT'S ONLY A LITTLE BIT.
SO THAT'S WHY YOU DRESS LIKE A SLUT?
HA! WHO THINKS ABOUT DYING WHEN THEY'VE GOT A BONER?
I THINK THAT EVERYONE COULD DO WITH BEING JUST A LITTLE MORE LEWD.
AFTER ALL, THEY DON'T CALL ME...
"THE MISSIONARY OF LUST" FOR NOTH-ING, YOU KNOW!

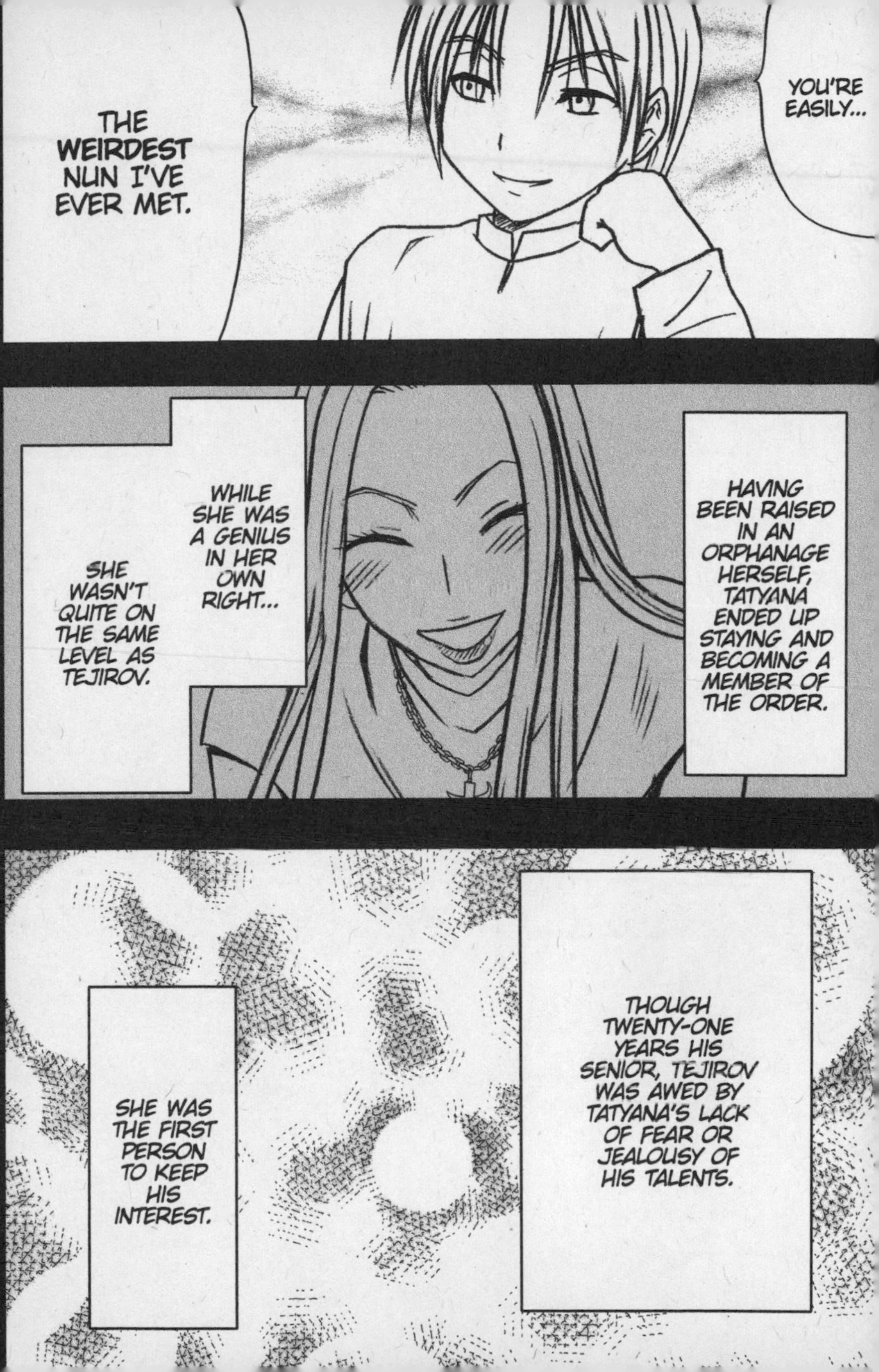
YOU'RE EASILY...
THE WEIRDEST NUN I'VE EVER MET.
HAVING BEEN RAISED IN AN ORPHANAGE HERSELF, TATYANA ENDED UP STAYING AND BECOMING A MEMBER OF THE ORDER.
WHILE SHE WAS A GENIUS IN HER OWN RIGHT...
SHE WASN'T QUITE ON THE SAME LEVEL AS TEJIROV.
THOUGH TWENTY-ONE YEARS HIS SENIOR, TEJIROV WAS AWED BY TATYANA'S LACK OF FEAR OR JEALOUSY OF HIS TALENTS.
SHE WAS THE FIRST PERSON TO KEEP HIS INTEREST.

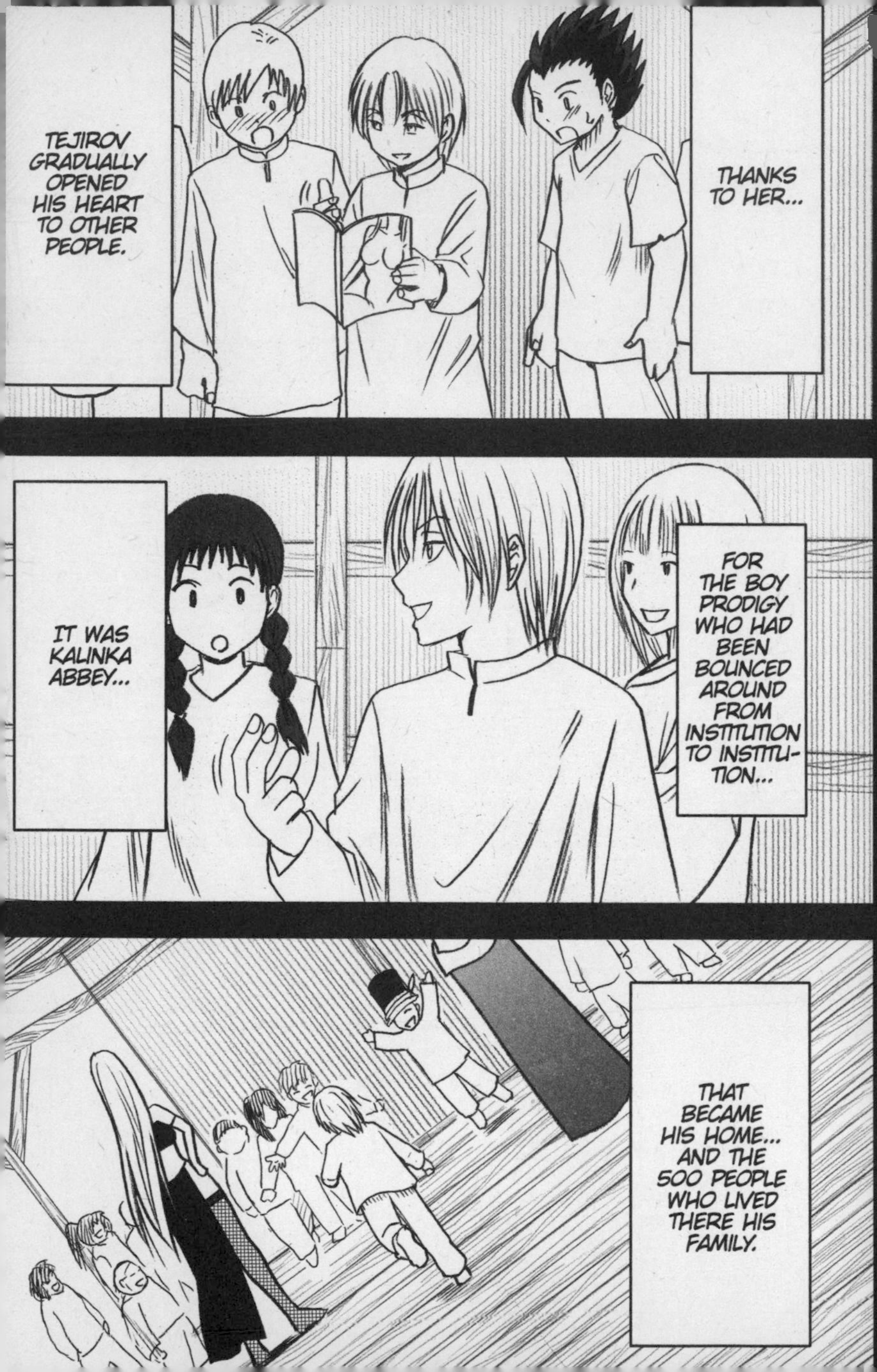
THANKS TO HER...
TEJIROV GRADUALLY OPENED HIS HEART TO OTHER PEOPLE.
FOR THE BOY PRODIGY WHO HAD BEEN BOUNCED AROUND FROM INSTITUTION TO INSTITU-TION...
IT WAS KALINKA ABBEY...
THAT BECAME HIS HOME... AND THE 500 PEOPLE WHO LIVED THERE HIS FAMILY.

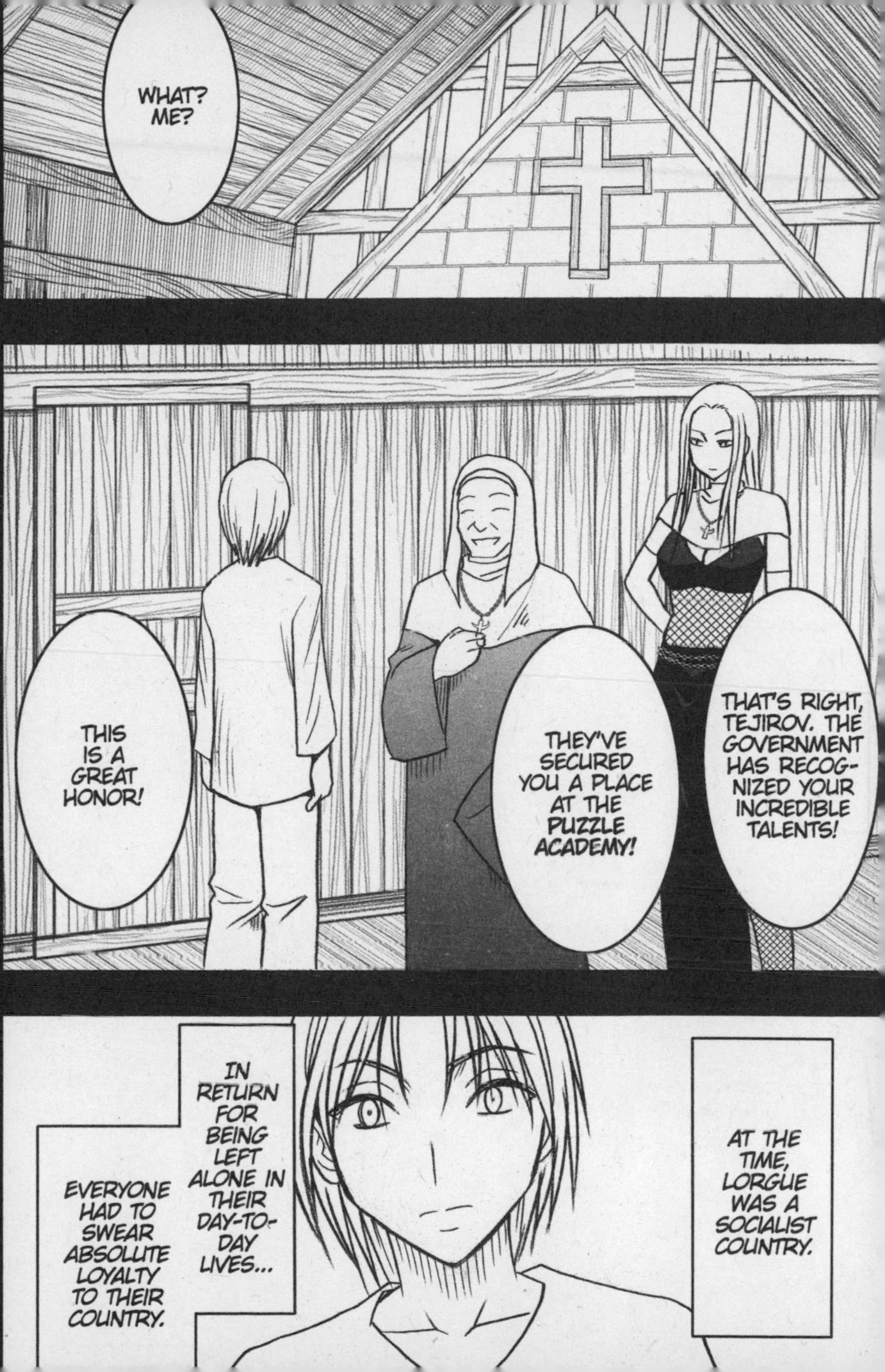
WHAT? ME?
THAT'S RIGHT, TEJIROV. THE GOVERNMENT HAS RECOGNIZED YOUR INCREDIBLE TALENTS!
THEY'VE SECURED YOU A PLACE AT THE PUZZLE ACADEMY!
THIS IS A GREAT HONOR!
AT THE TIME, LORGUE WAS A SOCIALIST COUNTRY.
IN RETURN FOR BEING LEFT ALONE IN THEIR DAY-TO-DAY LIVES...
EVERYONE HAD TO SWEAR ABSOLUTE LOYALTY TO THEIR COUNTRY.

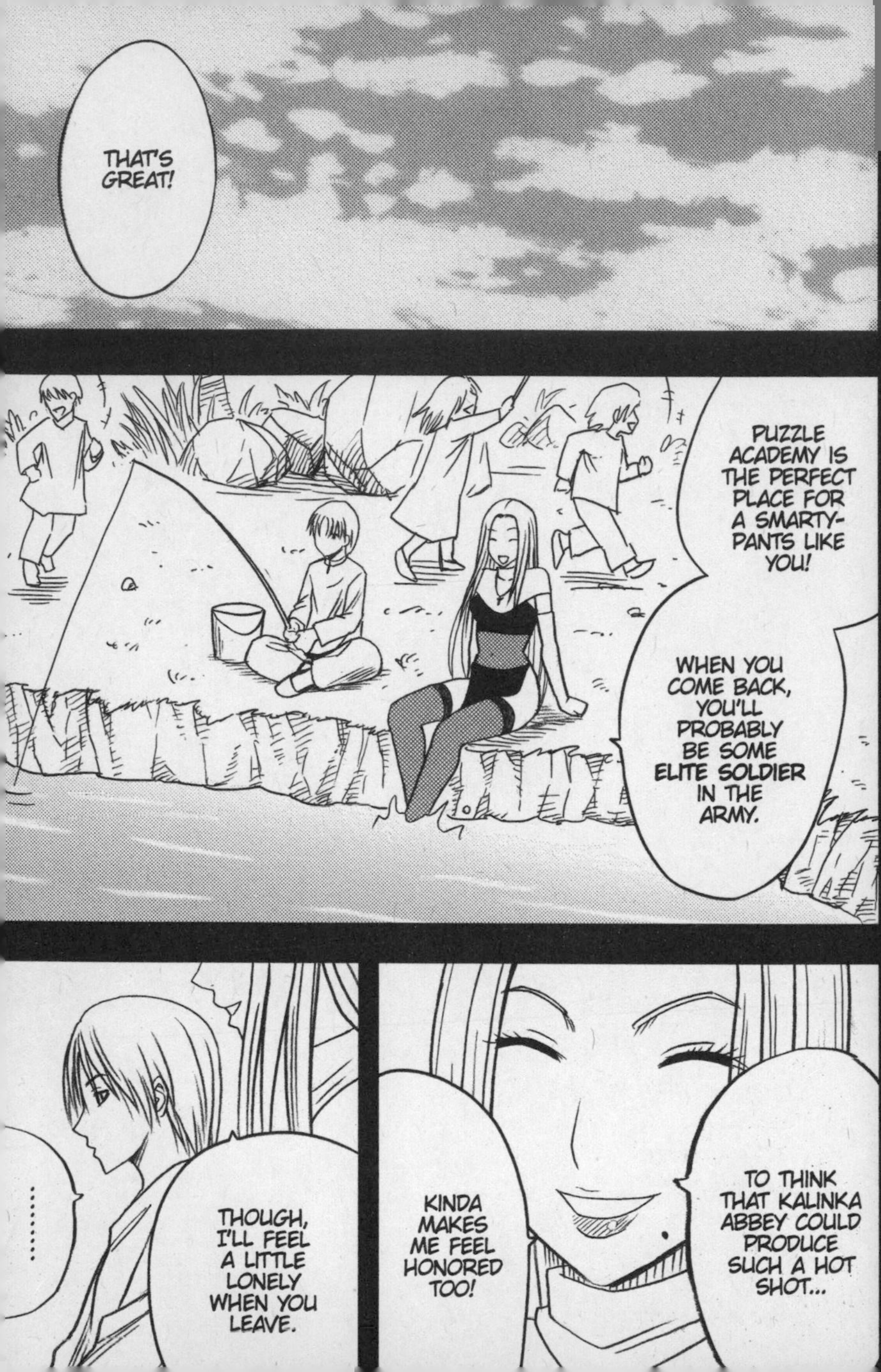
THAT'S GREAT!
PUZZLE ACADEMY IS THE PERFECT PLACE FOR A SMARTY-PANTS LIKE YOU!
WHEN YOU COME BACK, YOU'LL PROBABLY BE SOME ELITE SOLDIER IN THE ARMY.
TO THINK THAT KALINKA ABBEY COULD PRODUCE SUCH A HOT SHOT...
KINDA MAKES ME FEEL HONORED TOO!
THOUGH, I'LL FEEL A LITTLE LONELY WHEN YOU LEAVE.
........

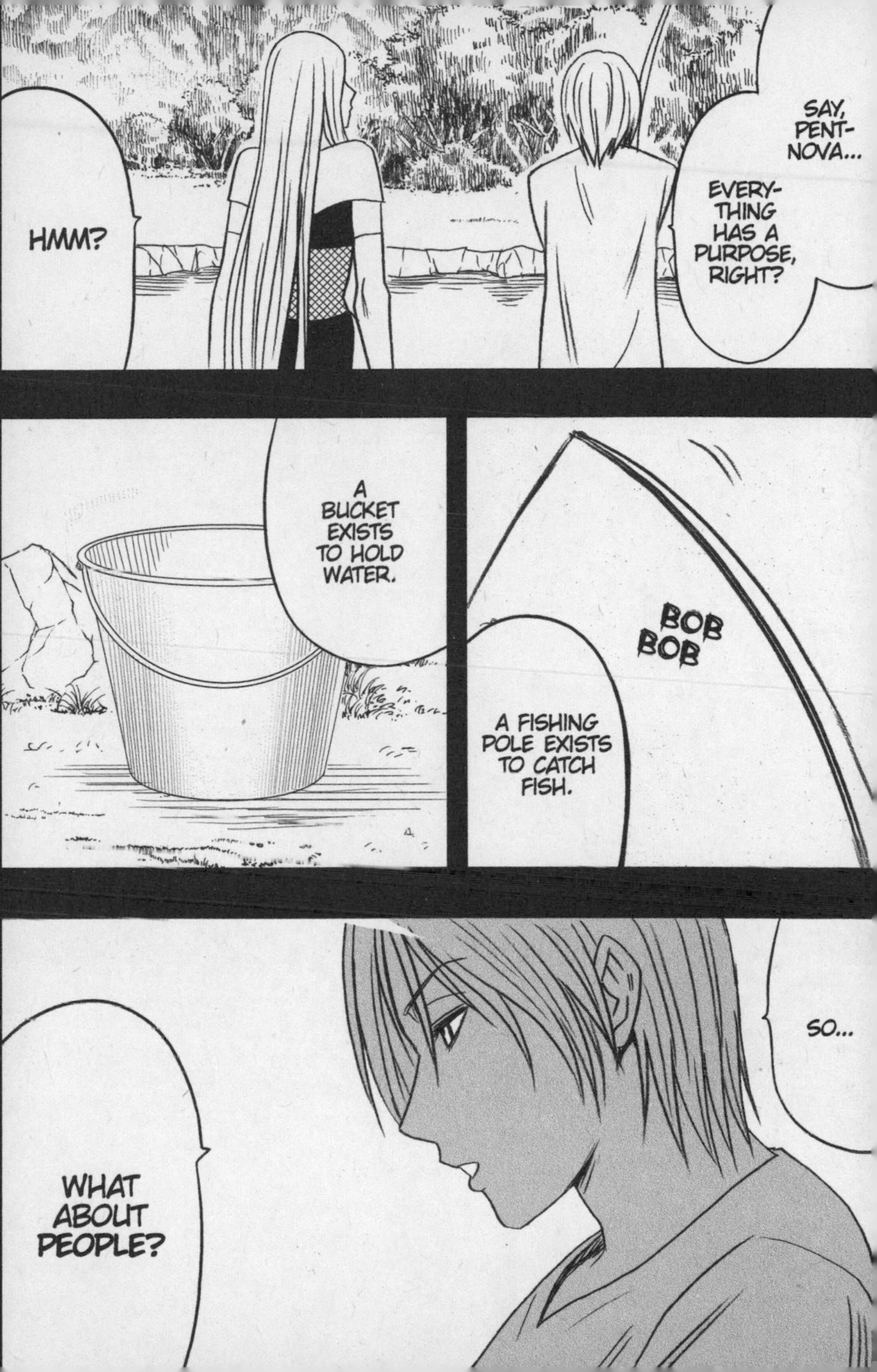
SAY, PENT-NOVA...
EVERY-THING HAS A PURPOSE, RIGHT?
HMM?
BOB BOB
A FISHING POLE EXISTS TO CATCH FISH.
A BUCKET EXISTS TO HOLD WATER.
SO...
WHAT ABOUT PEOPLE?

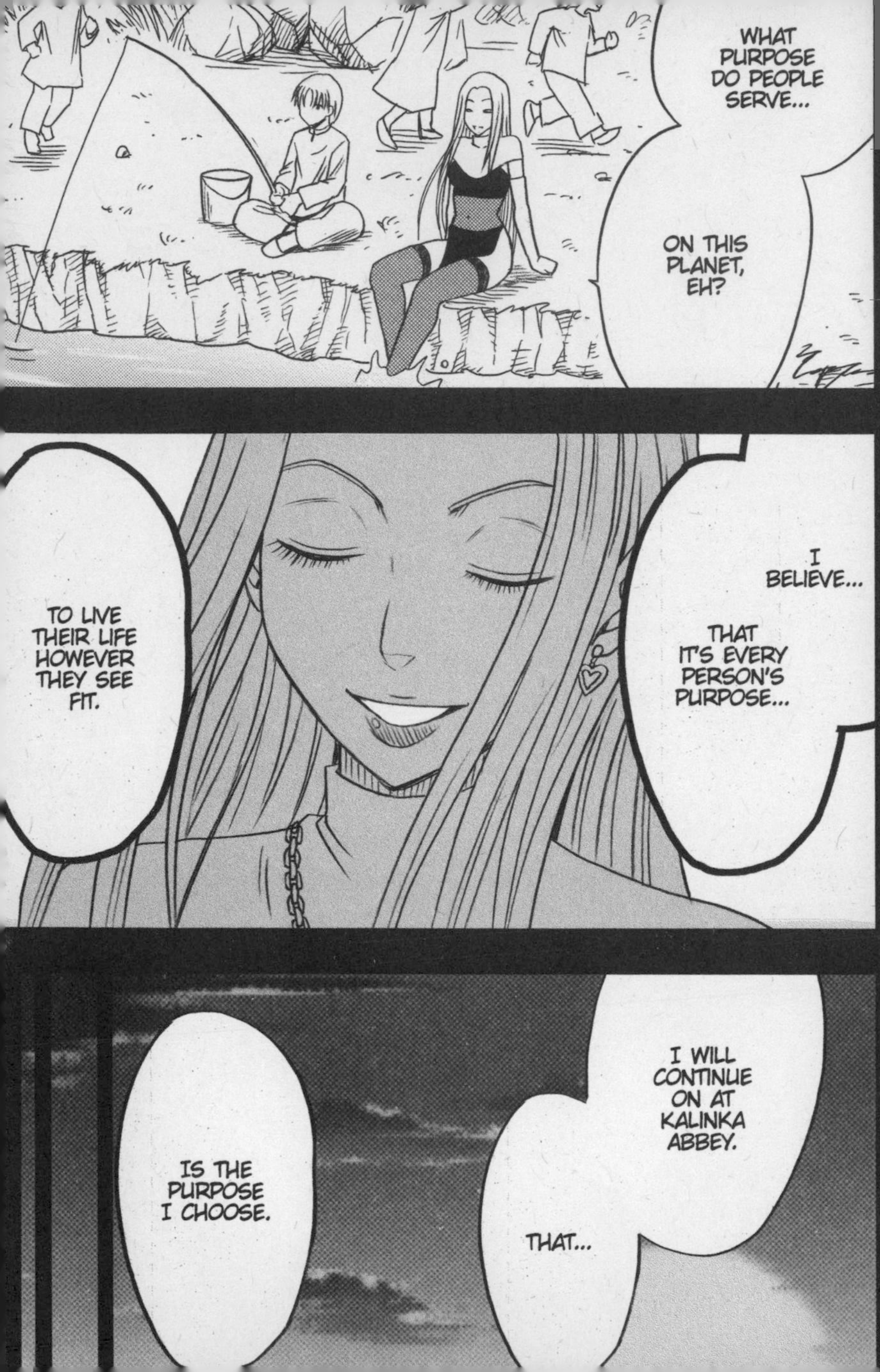
WHAT PURPOSE DO PEOPLE SERVE...
ON THIS PLANET, EH?
I BELIEVE...
THAT IT'S EVERY PERSON'S PURPOSE...
TO LIVE THEIR LIFE HOWEVER THEY SEE FIT.
I WILL CONTINUE ON AT KALINKA ABBEY.
THAT...
IS THE PURPOSE I CHOOSE.

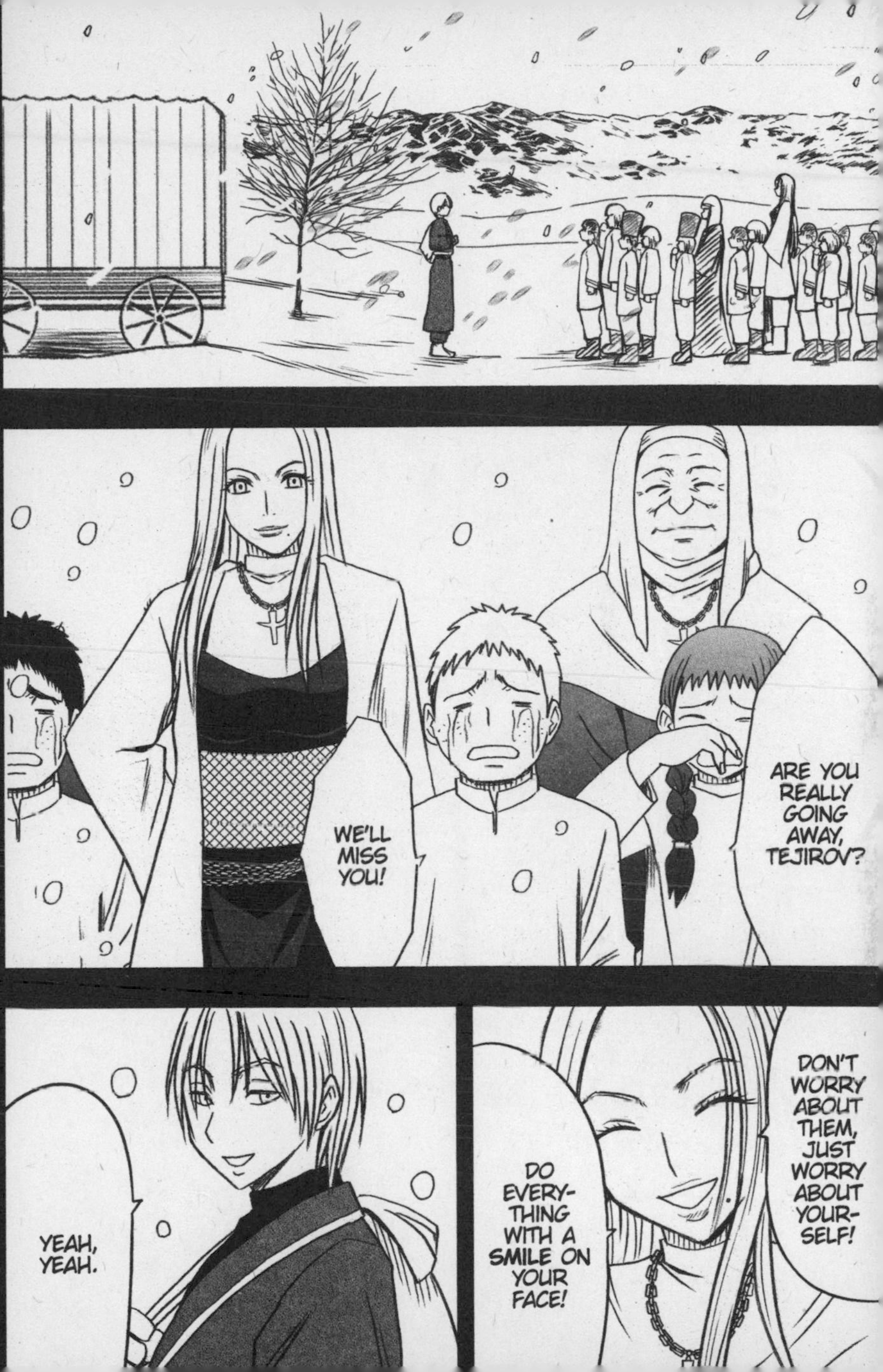
ARE YOU REALLY GOING AWAY, TEJIROV?
WE'LL MISS YOU!
DON'T WORRY ABOUT THEM, JUST WORRY ABOUT YOUR-SELF!
DO EVERY-THING WITH A SMILE ON YOUR FACE!
YEAH, YEAH.

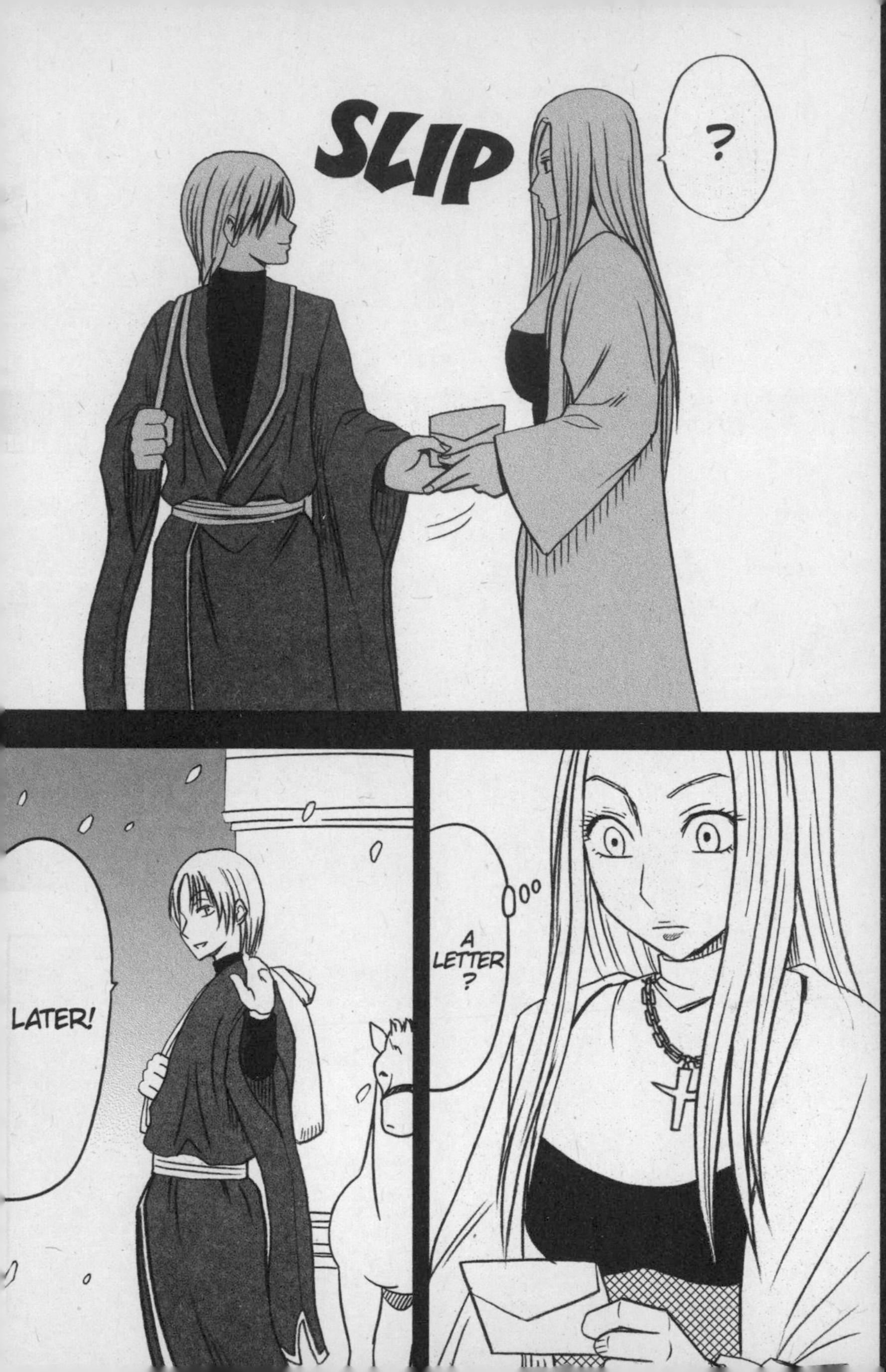
SLIP
?
A LETTER?
LATER!

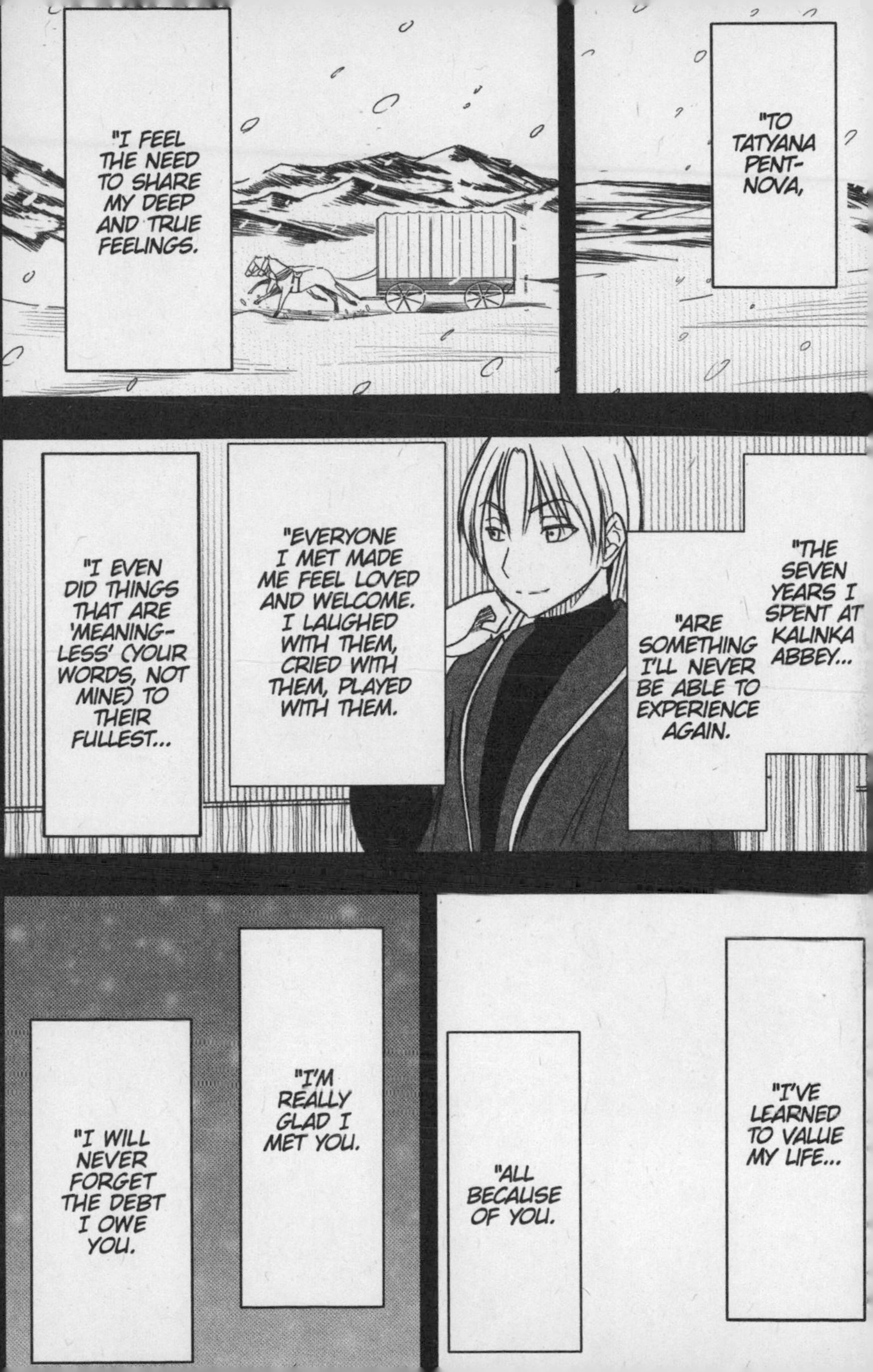
"TO TATYANA PENT-NOVA,
"I FEEL THE NEED TO SHARE MY DEEP AND TRUE FEELINGS.
"THE SEVEN YEARS I SPENT AT KALINKA ABBEY...
"ARE SOMETHING I'LL NEVER BE ABLE TO EXPERIENCE AGAIN.
"EVERYONE I MET MADE ME FEEL LOVED AND WELCOME. I LAUGHED WITH THEM, CRIED WITH THEM, PLAYED WITH THEM.
"I EVEN DID THINGS THAT ARE 'MEANING-LESS' (YOUR WORDS, NOT MINE) TO THEIR FULLEST...
"I'VE LEARNED TO VALUE MY LIFE...
"ALL BECAUSE OF YOU.
"I'M REALLY GLAD I MET YOU.
"I WILL NEVER FORGET THE DEBT I OWE YOU.

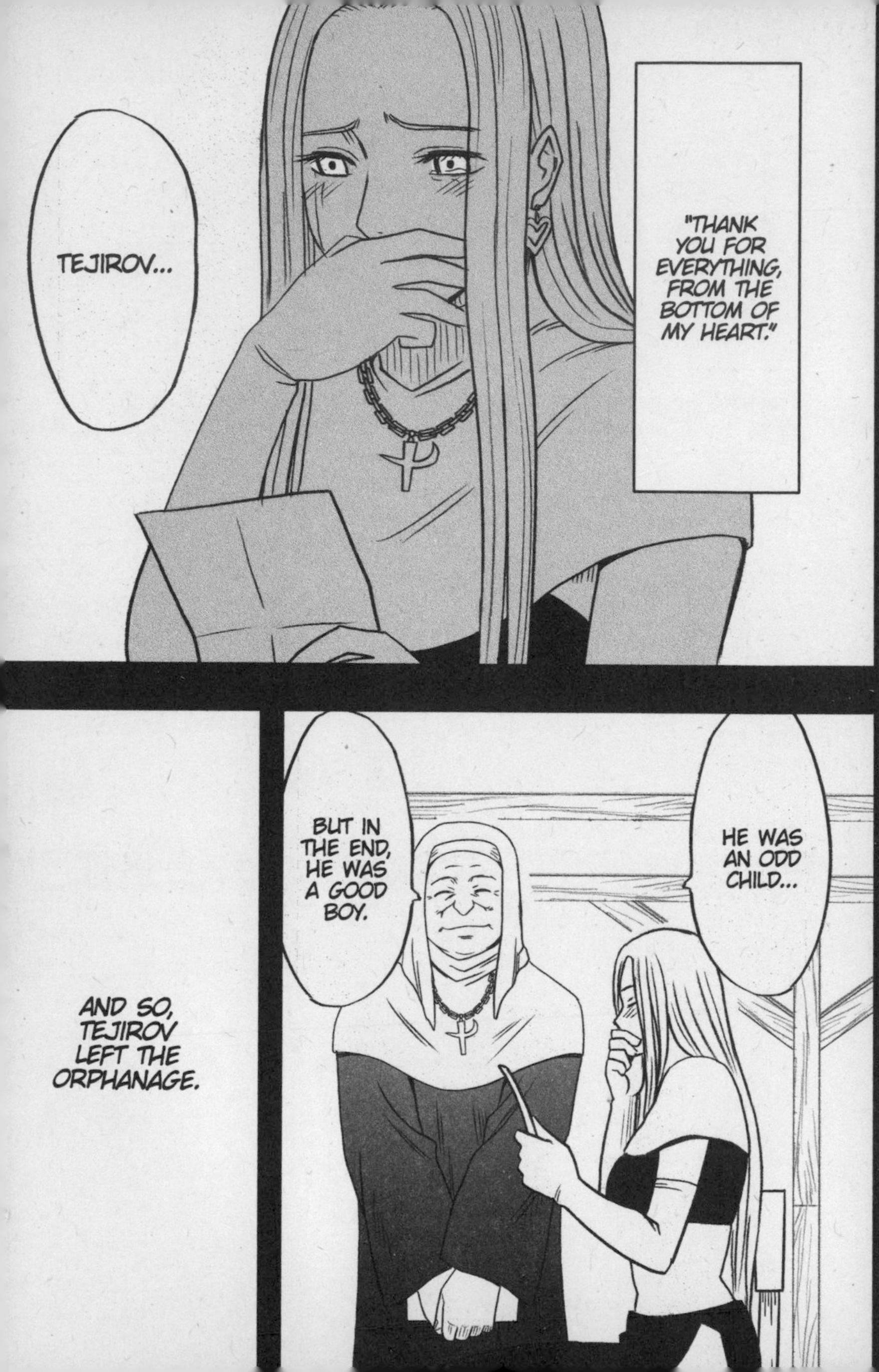
"THANK YOU FOR EVERYTHING, FROM THE BOTTOM OF MY HEART."
TEJIROV...
HE WAS AN ODD CHILD...
BUT IN THE END, HE WAS A GOOD BOY.
AND SO, TEJIROV LEFT THE ORPHANAGE.

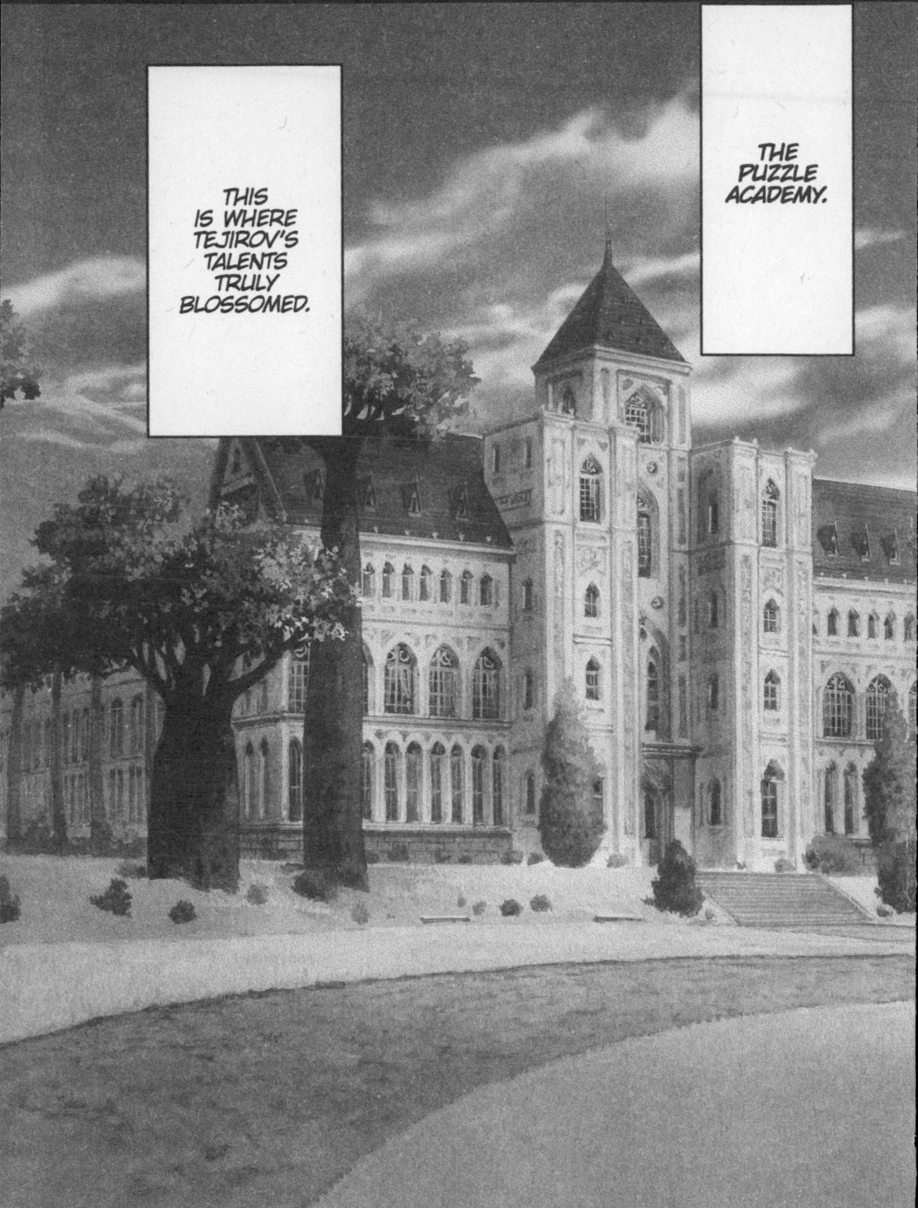
THE PUZZLE ACADEMY.
THIS IS WHERE TEJIROV'S TALENTS TRULY BLOSSOMED.

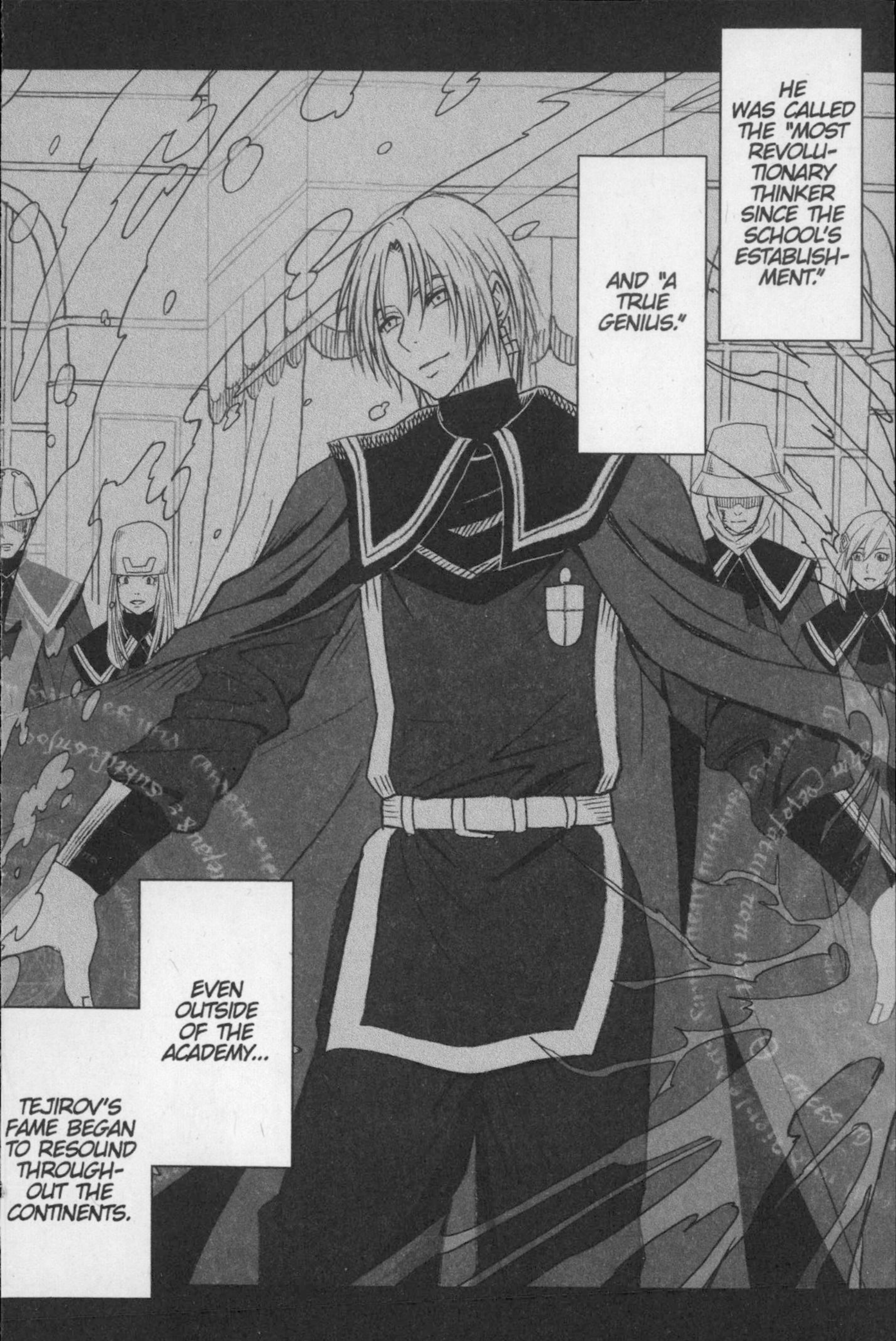
HE WAS CALLED THE "MOST REVOLUTIONARY THINKER SINCE THE SCHOOL'S ESTABLISHMENT."
AND "A TRUE GENIUS."
EVEN OUTSIDE OF THE ACADEMY...
TEJIROV'S FAME BEGAN TO RESOUND THROUGHOUT THE CONTINENTS.

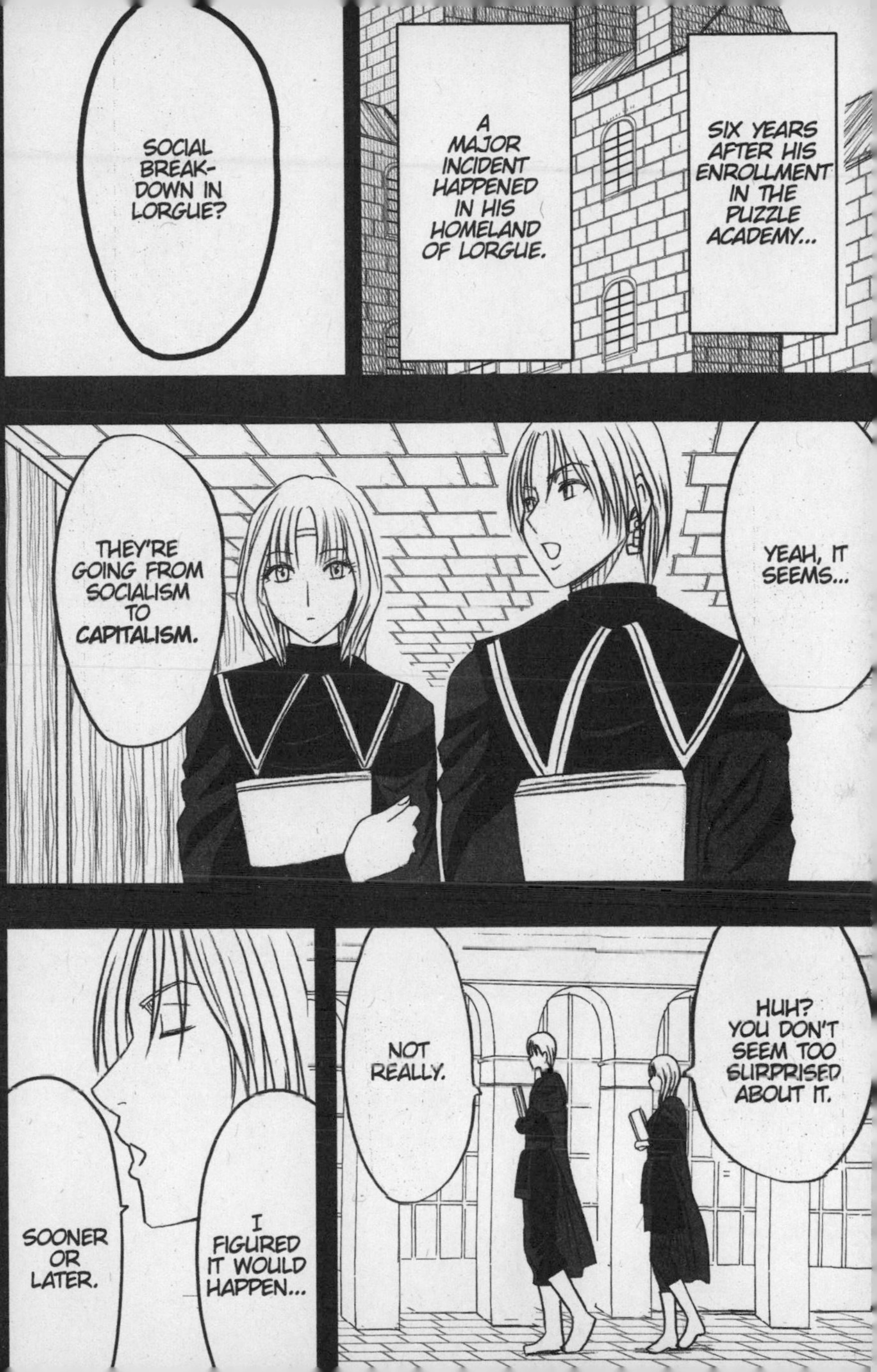
SIX YEARS AFTER HIS ENROLLMENT IN THE PUZZLE ACADEMY...
A MAJOR INCIDENT HAPPENED IN HIS HOMELAND OF LORGUE.
SOCIAL BREAK-DOWN IN LORGUE?
YEAH, IT SEEMS...
THEY'RE GOING FROM SOCIALISM TO CAPITALISM.
HUH? YOU DON'T SEEM TOO SURPRISED ABOUT IT.
NOT REALLY.
I FIGURED IT WOULD HAPPEN...
SOONER OR LATER.

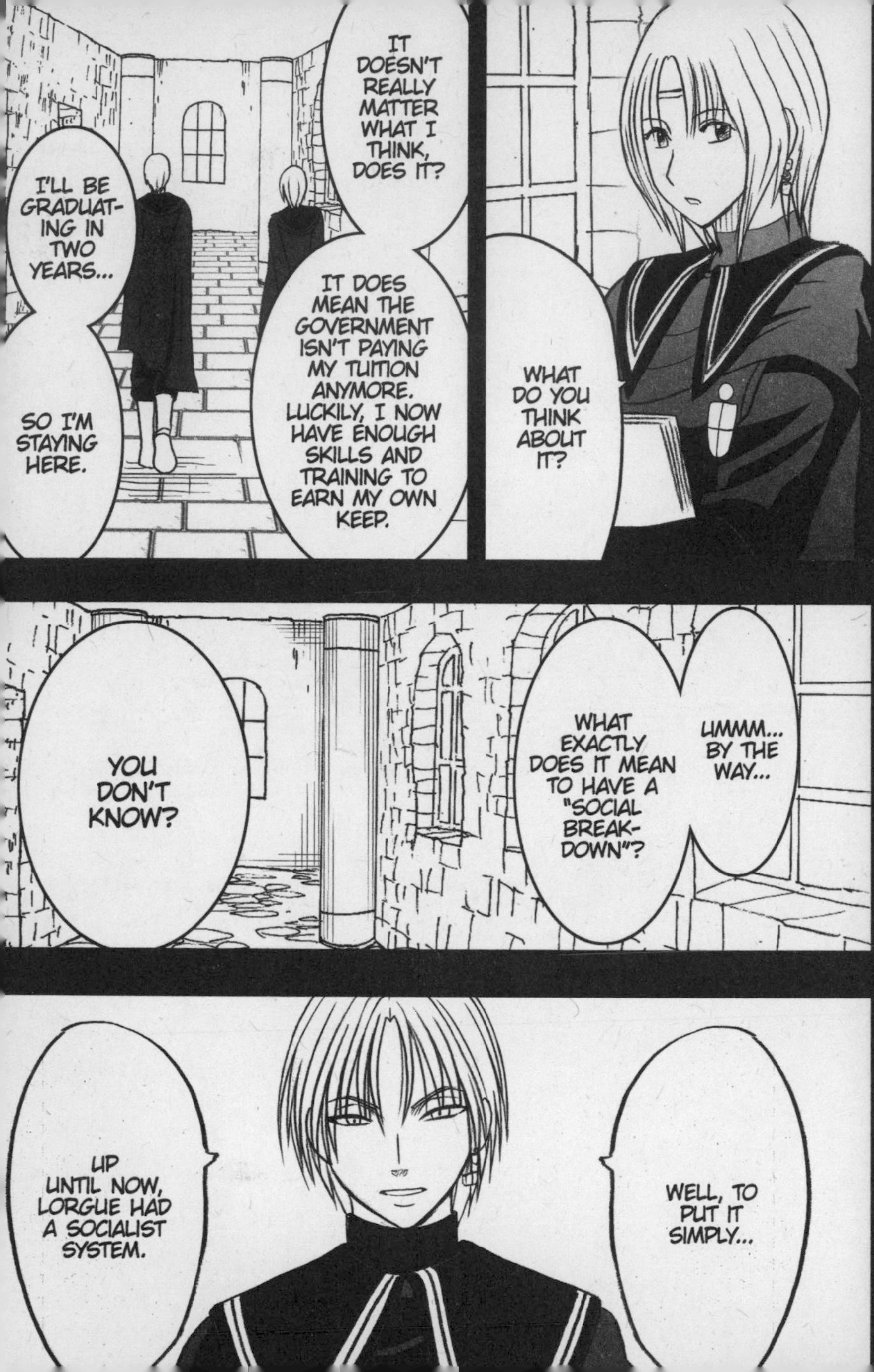
WHAT DO YOU THINK ABOUT IT?
IT DOESN'T REALLY MATTER WHAT I THINK, DOES IT?
IT DOES MEAN THE GOVERNMENT ISN'T PAYING MY TUITION ANYMORE. LUCKILY, I NOW HAVE ENOUGH SKILLS AND TRAINING TO EARN MY OWN KEEP.
I'LL BE GRADUATING IN TWO YEARS...
SO I'M STAYING HERE.
UMMM... BY THE WAY...
WHAT EXACTLY DOES IT MEAN TO HAVE A "SOCIAL BREAKDOWN"?
YOU DON'T KNOW?
WELL, TO PUT IT SIMPLY...
UP UNTIL NOW, LORGUE HAD A SOCIALIST SYSTEM.

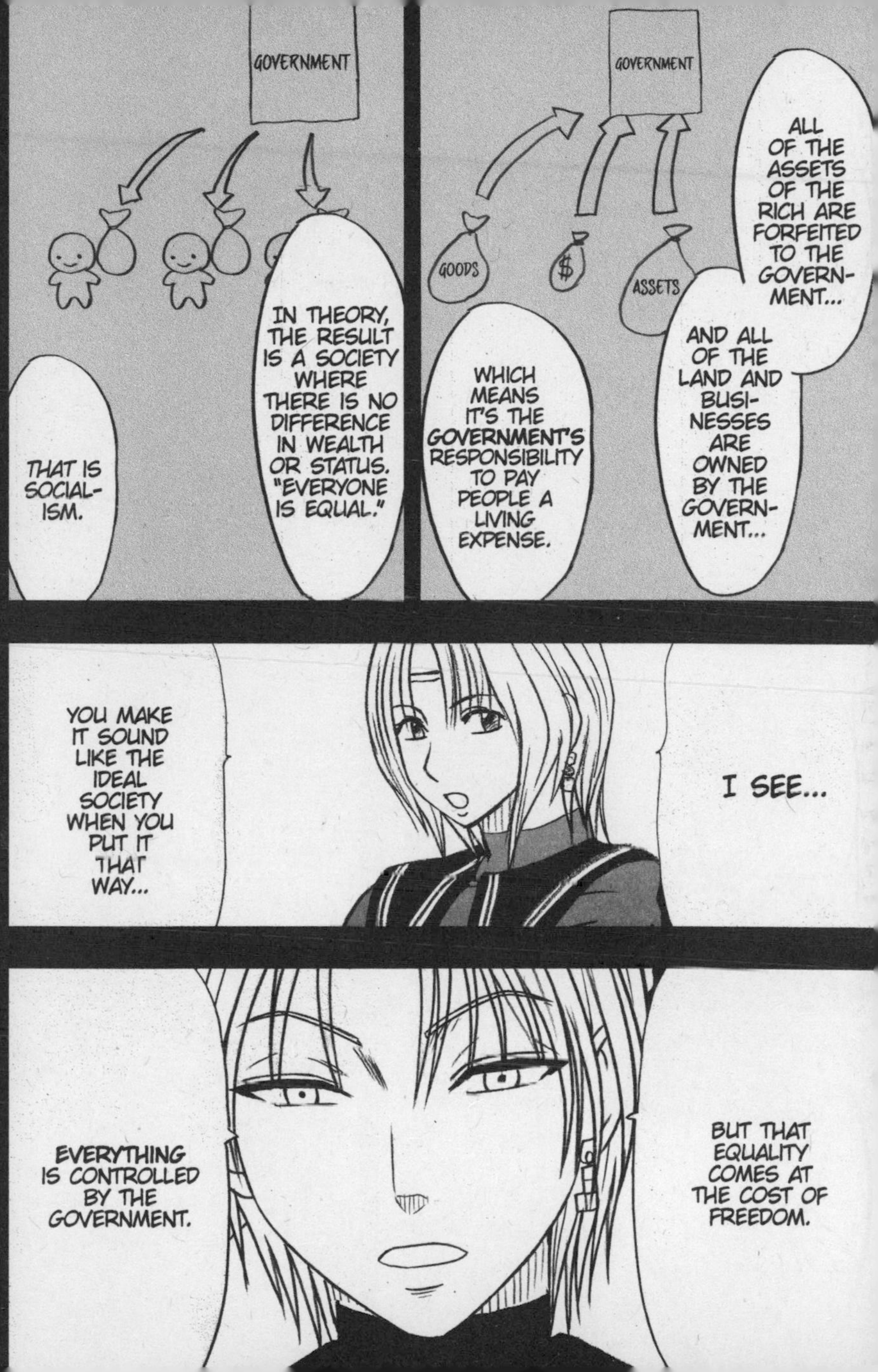
GOVERNMENT
GOODS
$
ASSETS
ALL OF THE ASSETS OF THE RICH ARE FORFEITED TO THE GOVERNMENT...
AND ALL OF THE LAND AND BUSINESSES ARE OWNED BY THE GOVERNMENT...
WHICH MEANS IT'S THE GOVERNMENT'S RESPONSIBILITY TO PAY PEOPLE A LIVING EXPENSE.
GOVERNMENT
IN THEORY, THE RESULT IS A SOCIETY WHERE THERE IS NO DIFFERENCE IN WEALTH OR STATUS. "EVERYONE IS EQUAL."
THAT IS SOCIALISM.
I SEE...
YOU MAKE IT SOUND LIKE THE IDEAL SOCIETY WHEN YOU PUT IT THAT WAY...
BUT THAT EQUALITY COMES AT THE COST OF FREEDOM.
EVERYTHING IS CONTROLLED BY THE GOVERNMENT.

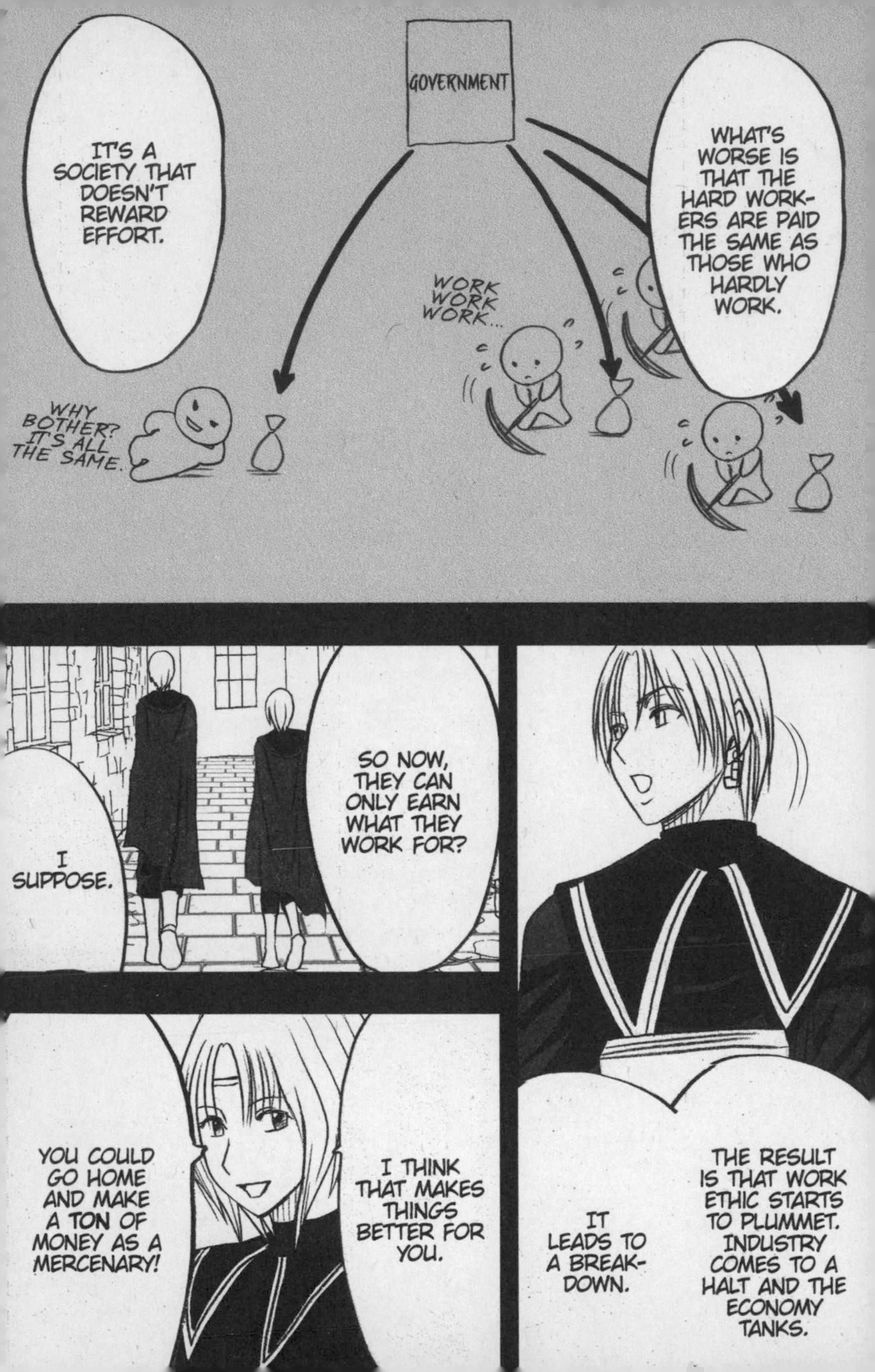
GOVERNMENT
IT'S A SOCIETY THAT DOESN'T REWARD EFFORT.
WHAT'S WORSE IS THAT THE HARD WORKERS ARE PAID THE SAME AS THOSE WHO HARDLY WORK.
WORK WORK WORK...
WHY BOTHER? IT'S ALL THE SAME.
THE RESULT IS THAT WORK ETHIC STARTS TO PLUMMET. INDUSTRY COMES TO A HALT AND THE ECONOMY TANKS.
IT LEADS TO A BREAKDOWN.
SO NOW, THEY CAN ONLY EARN WHAT THEY WORK FOR?
I SUPPOSE.
I THINK THAT MAKES THINGS BETTER FOR YOU.
YOU COULD GO HOME AND MAKE A TON OF MONEY AS A MERCENARY!

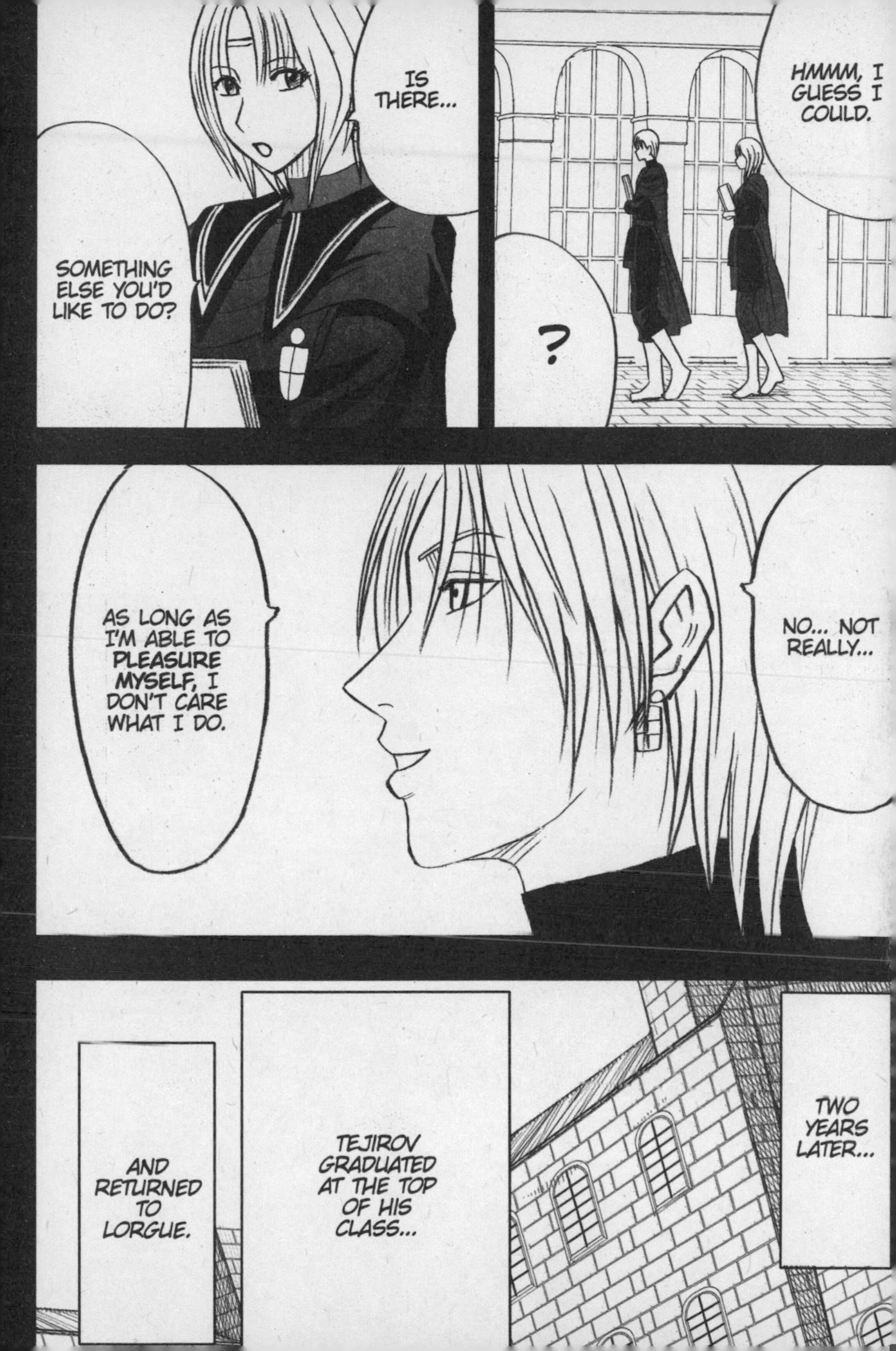
HMMM, I GUESS I COULD.
?
IS THERE...
SOMETHING ELSE YOU'D LIKE TO DO?
NO... NOT REALLY...
AS LONG AS I'M ABLE TO PLEASURE MYSELF, I DON'T CARE WHAT I DO.
TWO YEARS LATER...
TEJIROV GRADUATED AT THE TOP OF HIS CLASS...
AND RETURNED TO LORGUE.

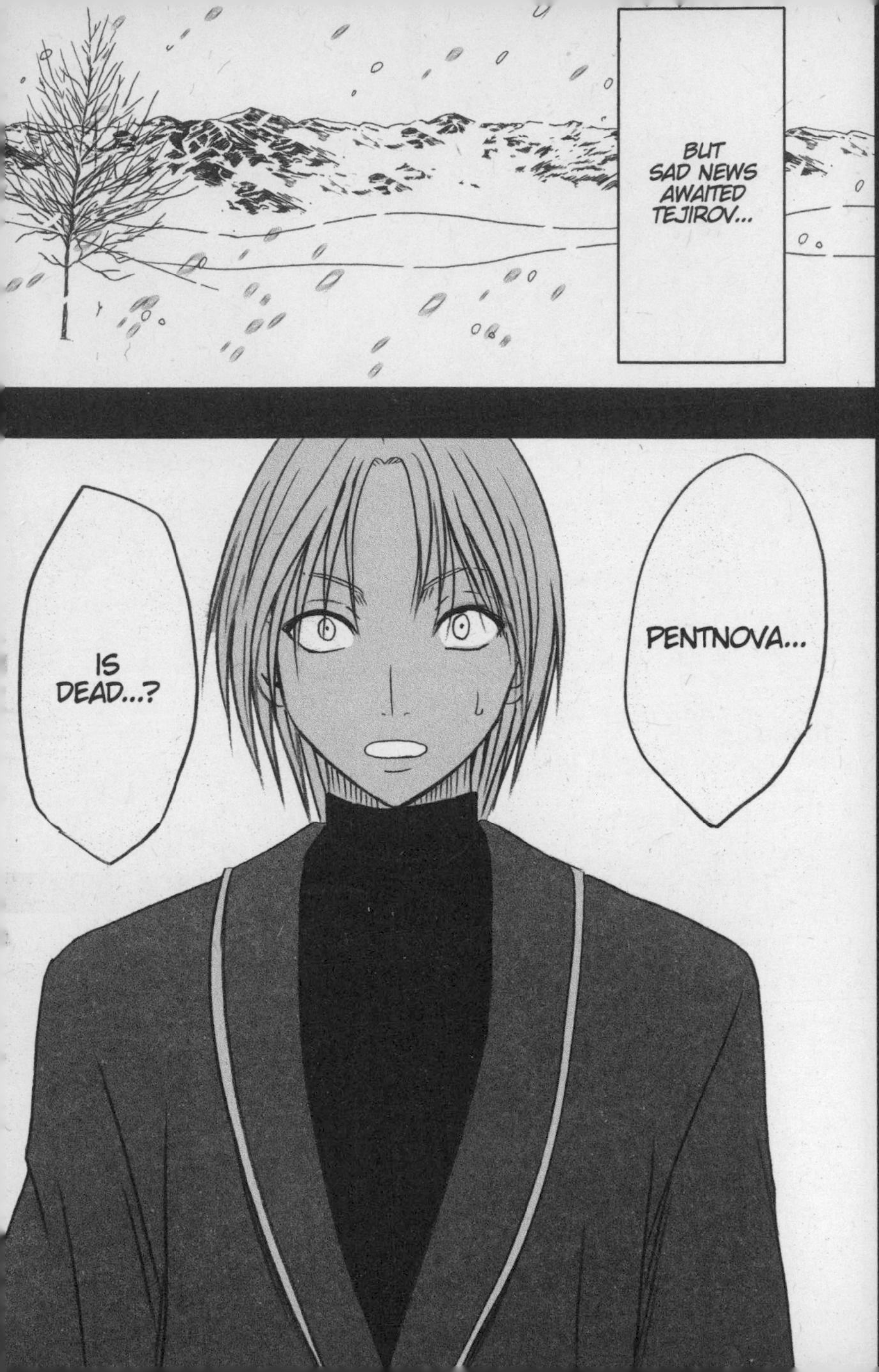
BUT SAD NEWS AWAITED TEJIROV...
PENTNOVA...
IS DEAD...?

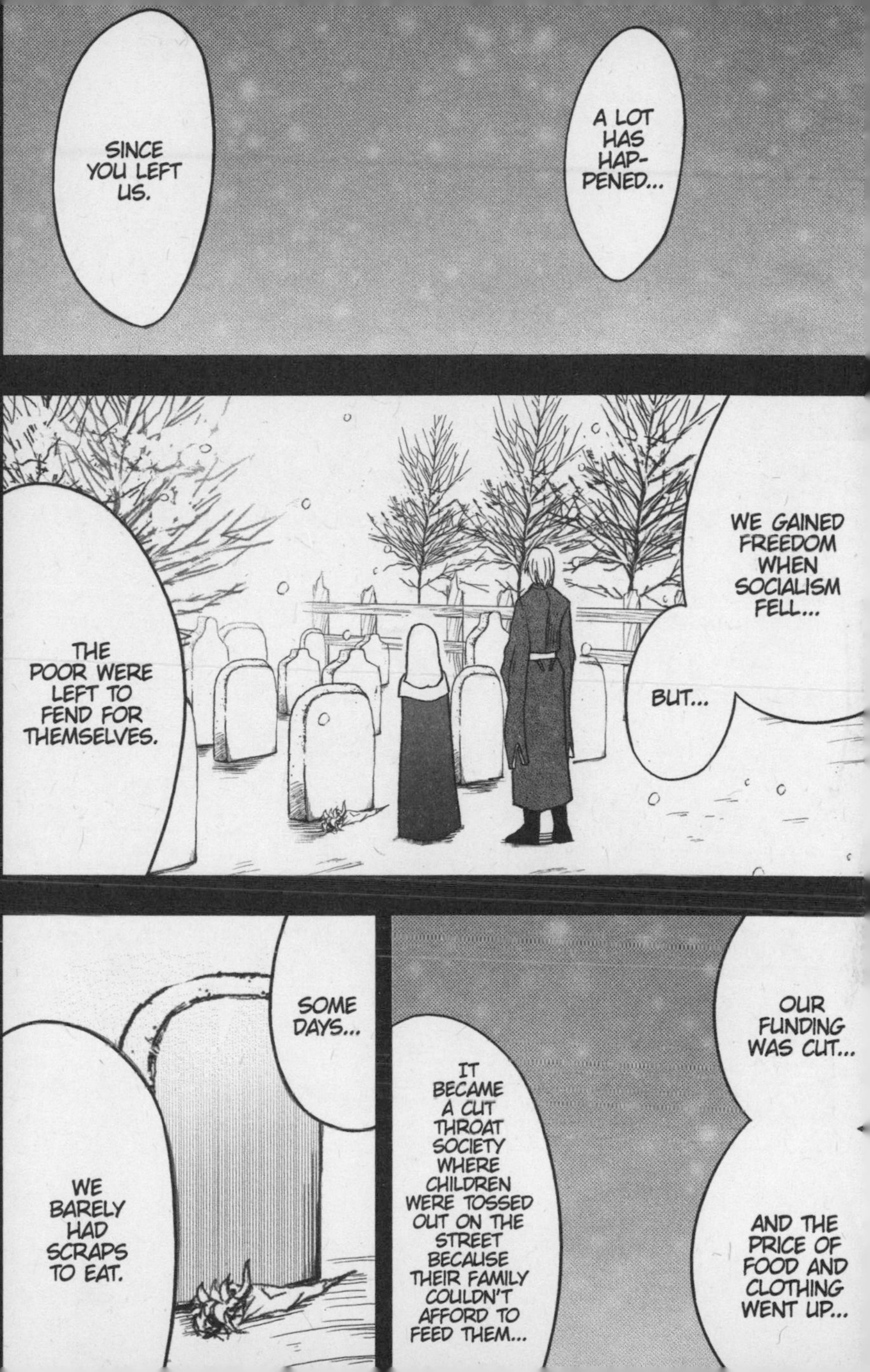
A LOT HAS HAP-PENED...
SINCE YOU LEFT US.
WE GAINED FREEDOM WHEN SOCIALISM FELL...
BUT...
THE POOR WERE LEFT TO FEND FOR THEMSELVES.
OUR FUNDING WAS CUT...
AND THE PRICE OF FOOD AND CLOTHING WENT UP...
IT BECAME A CUT THROAT SOCIETY WHERE CHILDREN WERE TOSSED OUT ON THE STREET BECAUSE THEIR FAMILY COULDN'T AFFORD TO FEED THEM...
SOME DAYS...
WE BARELY HAD SCRAPS TO EAT.

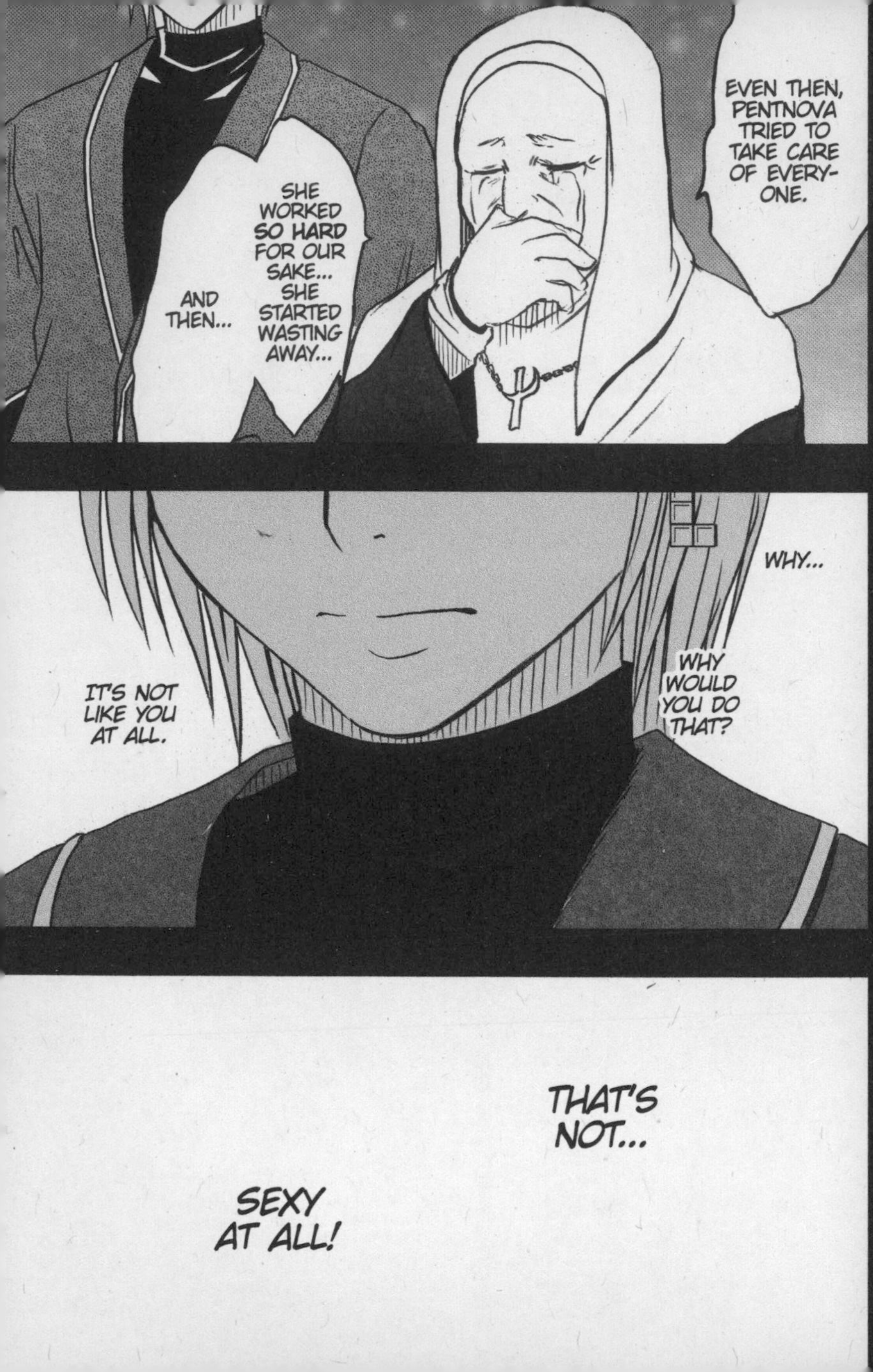
EVEN THEN, PENTNOVA TRIED TO TAKE CARE OF EVERY-ONE.
SHE WORKED SO HARD FOR OUR SAKE... SHE STARTED WASTING AWAY...
AND THEN...
WHY...
WHY WOULD YOU DO THAT?
IT'S NOT LIKE YOU AT ALL.
THAT'S NOT...
SEXY AT ALL!

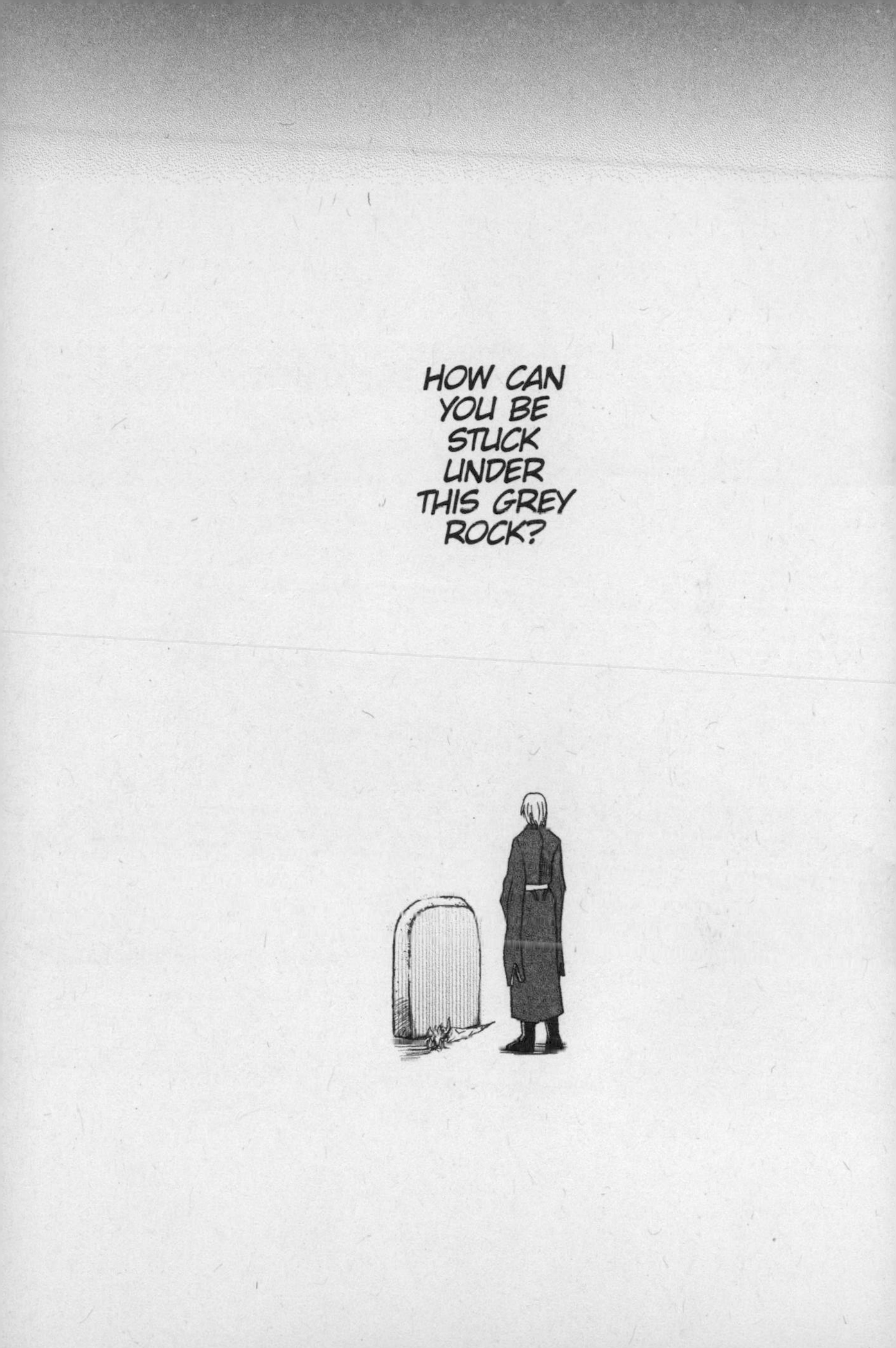
HOW CAN YOU BE STUCK UNDER THIS GREY ROCK?

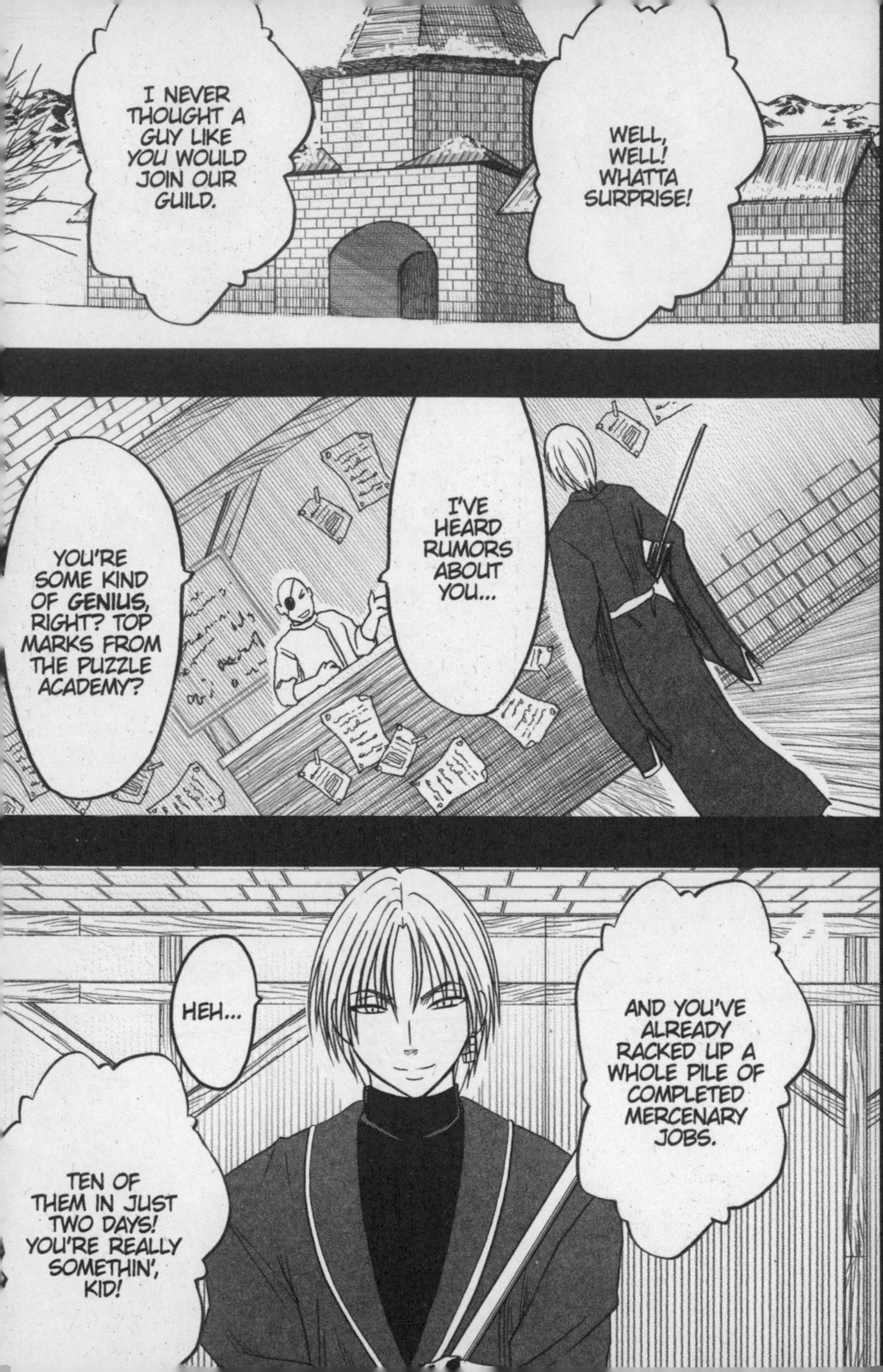
WELL, WELL! WHATTA SURPRISE!
I NEVER THOUGHT A GUY LIKE YOU WOULD JOIN OUR GUILD.
I'VE HEARD RUMORS ABOUT YOU...
YOU'RE SOME KIND OF GENIUS, RIGHT? TOP MARKS FROM THE PUZZLE ACADEMY?
AND YOU'VE ALREADY RACKED UP A WHOLE PILE OF COMPLETED MERCENARY JOBS.
HEH...
TEN OF THEM IN JUST TWO DAYS! YOU'RE REALLY SOMETHIN', KID!

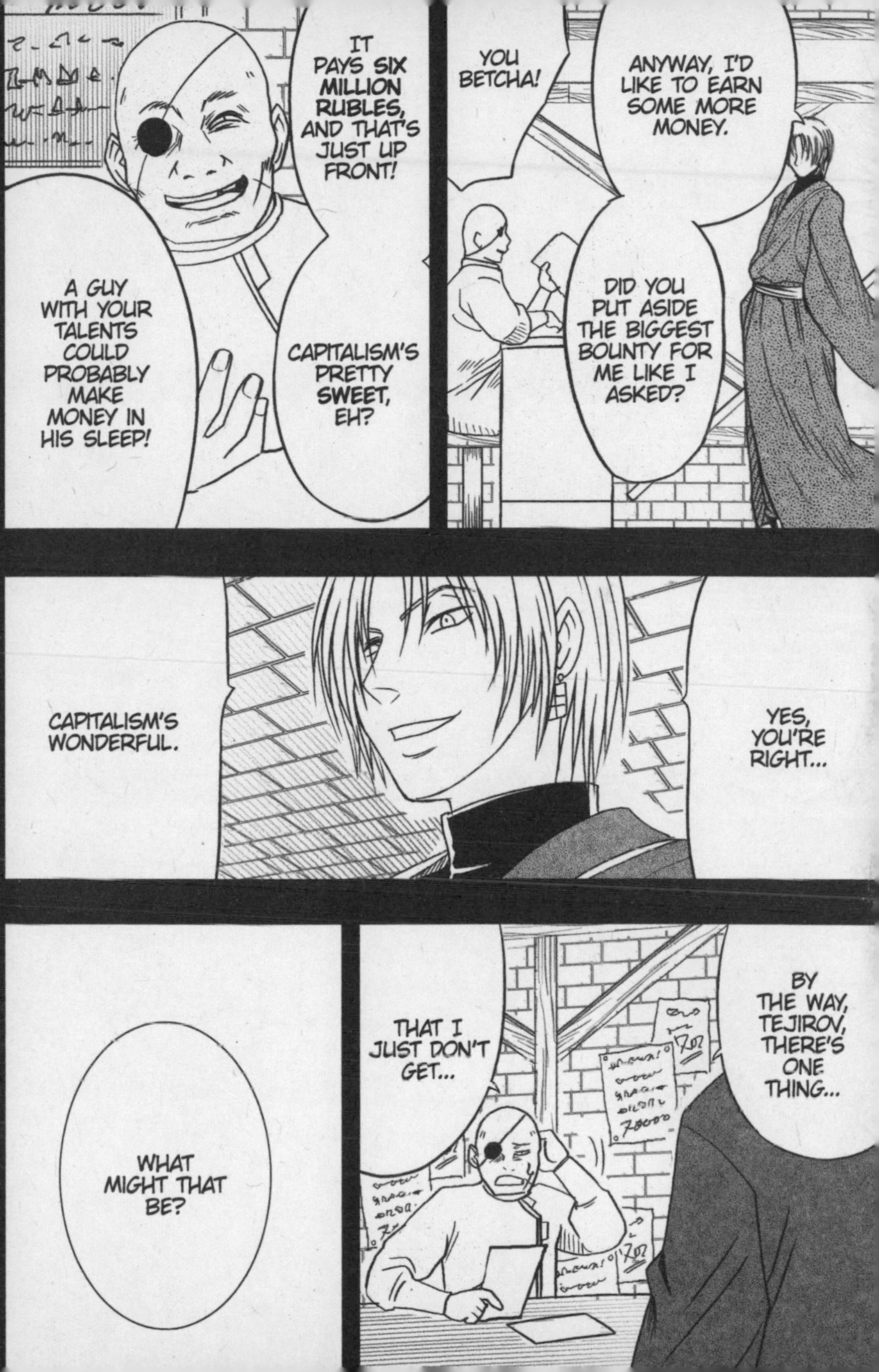
ANYWAY, I'D LIKE TO EARN SOME MORE MONEY.
DID YOU PUT ASIDE THE BIGGEST BOUNTY FOR ME LIKE I ASKED?
YOU BETCHA!
IT PAYS SIX MILLION RUBLES, AND THAT'S JUST UP FRONT!
CAPITALISM'S PRETTY SWEET, EH?
A GUY WITH YOUR TALENTS COULD PROBABLY MAKE MONEY IN HIS SLEEP!
YES, YOU'RE RIGHT...
CAPITALISM'S WONDERFUL.
BY THE WAY, TEJIROV, THERE'S ONE THING...
THAT I JUST DON'T GET...
WHAT MIGHT THAT BE?

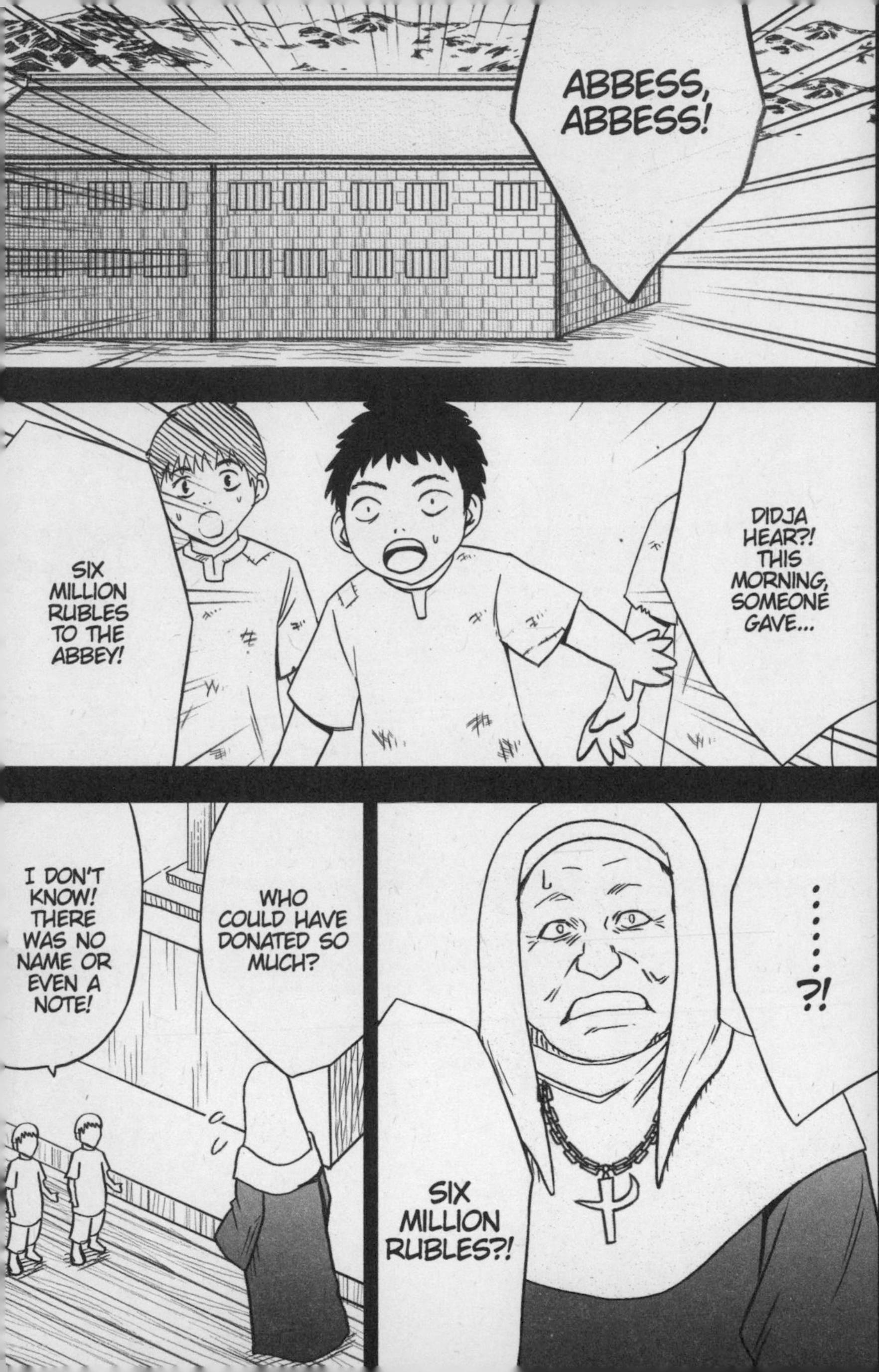
ABBESS, ABBESS!
DIDJA HEAR?! THIS MORNING, SOMEONE GAVE...
SIX MILLION RUBLES TO THE ABBEY!
......?!
SIX MILLION RUBLES?!
WHO COULD HAVE DONATED SO MUCH?
I DON'T KNOW! THERE WAS NO NAME OR EVEN A NOTE!

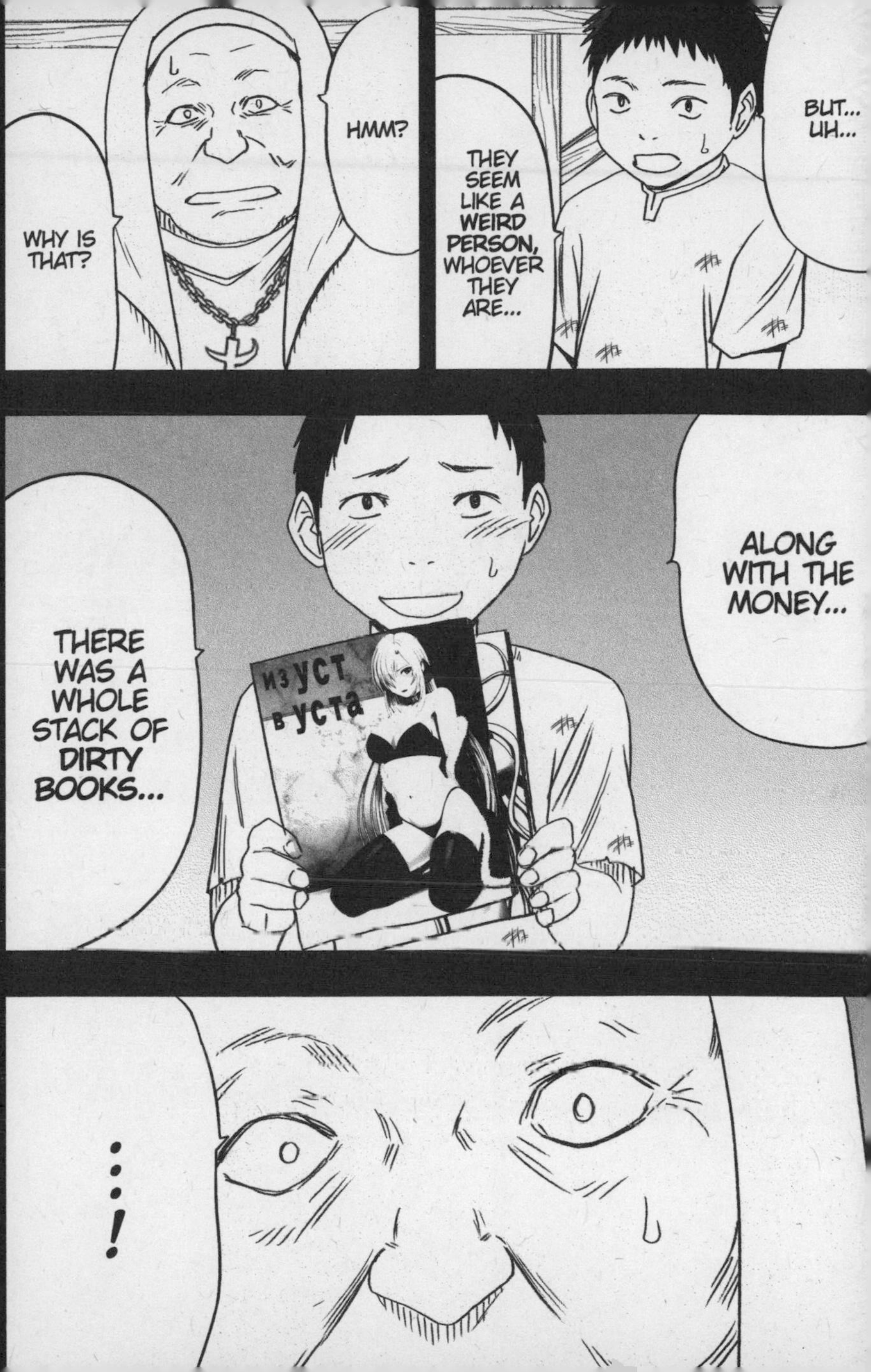
BUT... UH...
THEY SEEM LIKE A WEIRD PERSON, WHOEVER THEY ARE...
HMM?
WHY IS THAT?
ALONG WITH THE MONEY...
THERE WAS A WHOLE STACK OF DIRTY BOOKS...
из уст в уста
...!

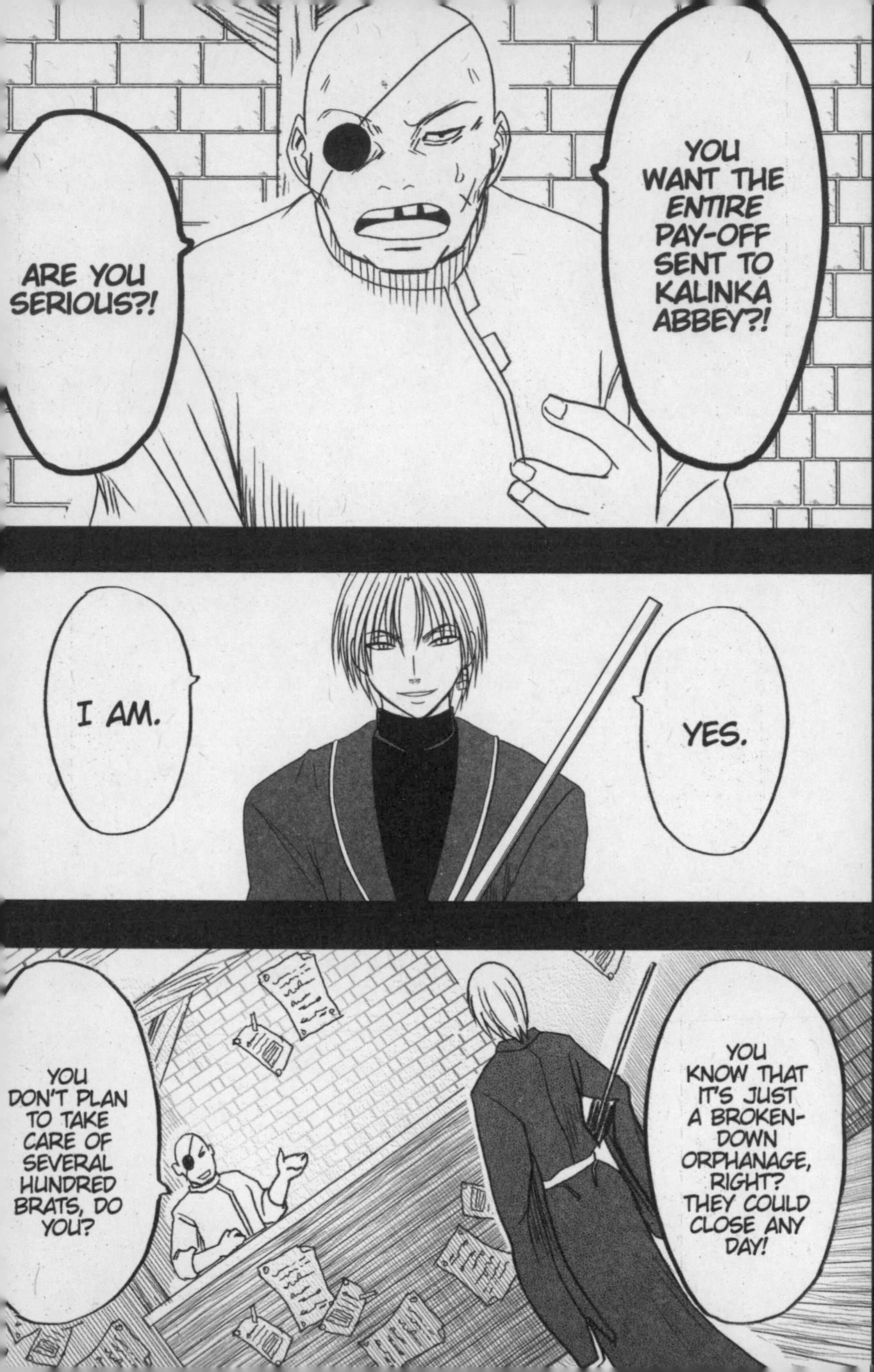
YOU WANT THE ENTIRE PAY-OFF SENT TO KALINKA ABBEY?!
ARE YOU SERIOUS?!
YES.
I AM.
YOU KNOW THAT IT'S JUST A BROKEN-DOWN ORPHANAGE, RIGHT? THEY COULD CLOSE ANY DAY!
YOU DON'T PLAN TO TAKE CARE OF SEVERAL HUNDRED BRATS, DO YOU?

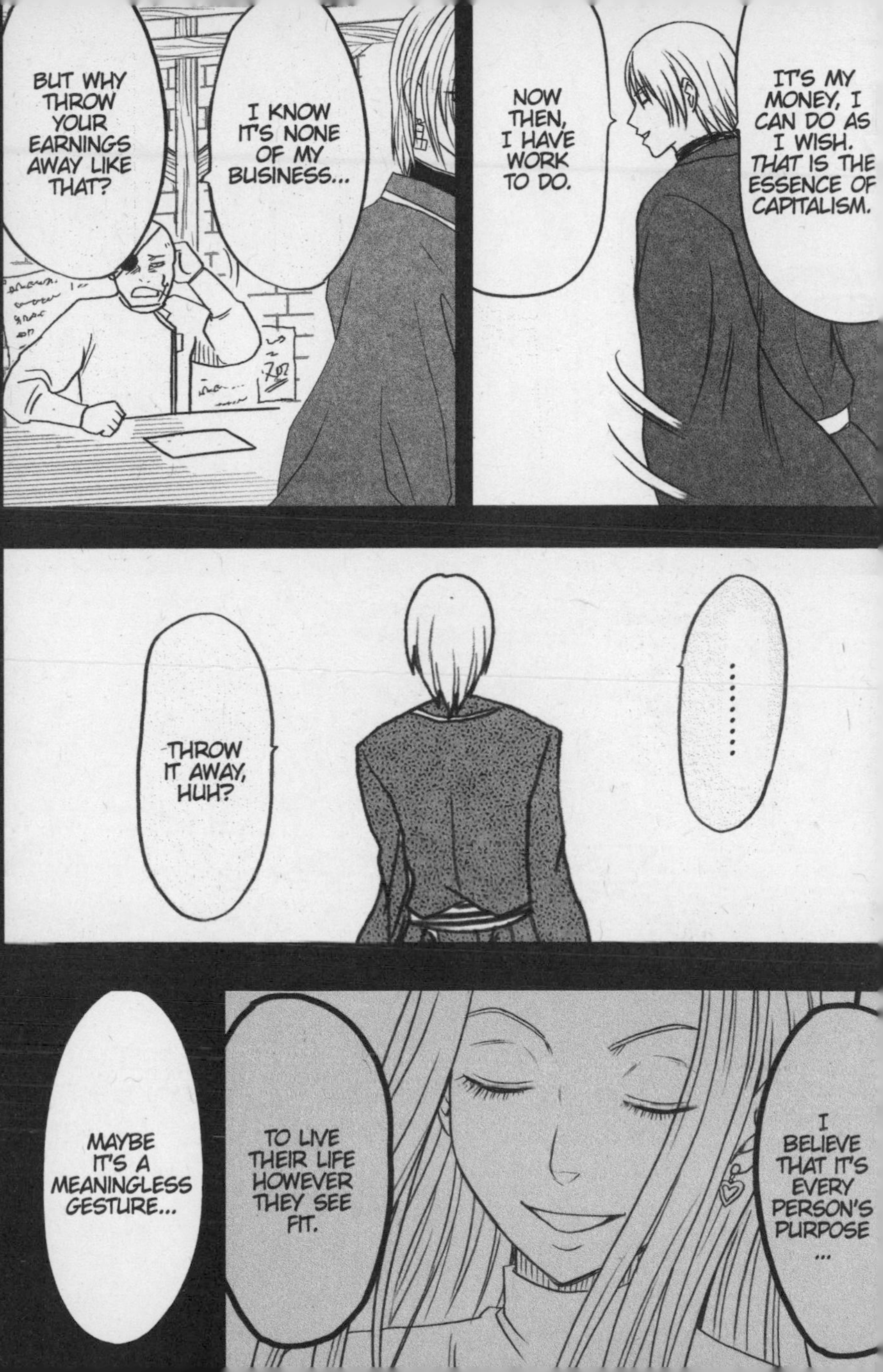
I KNOW IT'S NONE OF MY BUSINESS...
BUT WHY THROW YOUR EARNINGS AWAY LIKE THAT?
IT'S MY MONEY, I CAN DO AS I WISH. *THAT* IS THE ESSENCE OF CAPITALISM.
NOW THEN, I HAVE WORK TO DO.
......
THROW IT AWAY, HUH?
I BELIEVE THAT IT'S EVERY PERSON'S PURPOSE...
TO LIVE THEIR LIFE HOWEVER THEY SEE FIT.
MAYBE IT'S A MEANINGLESS GESTURE...

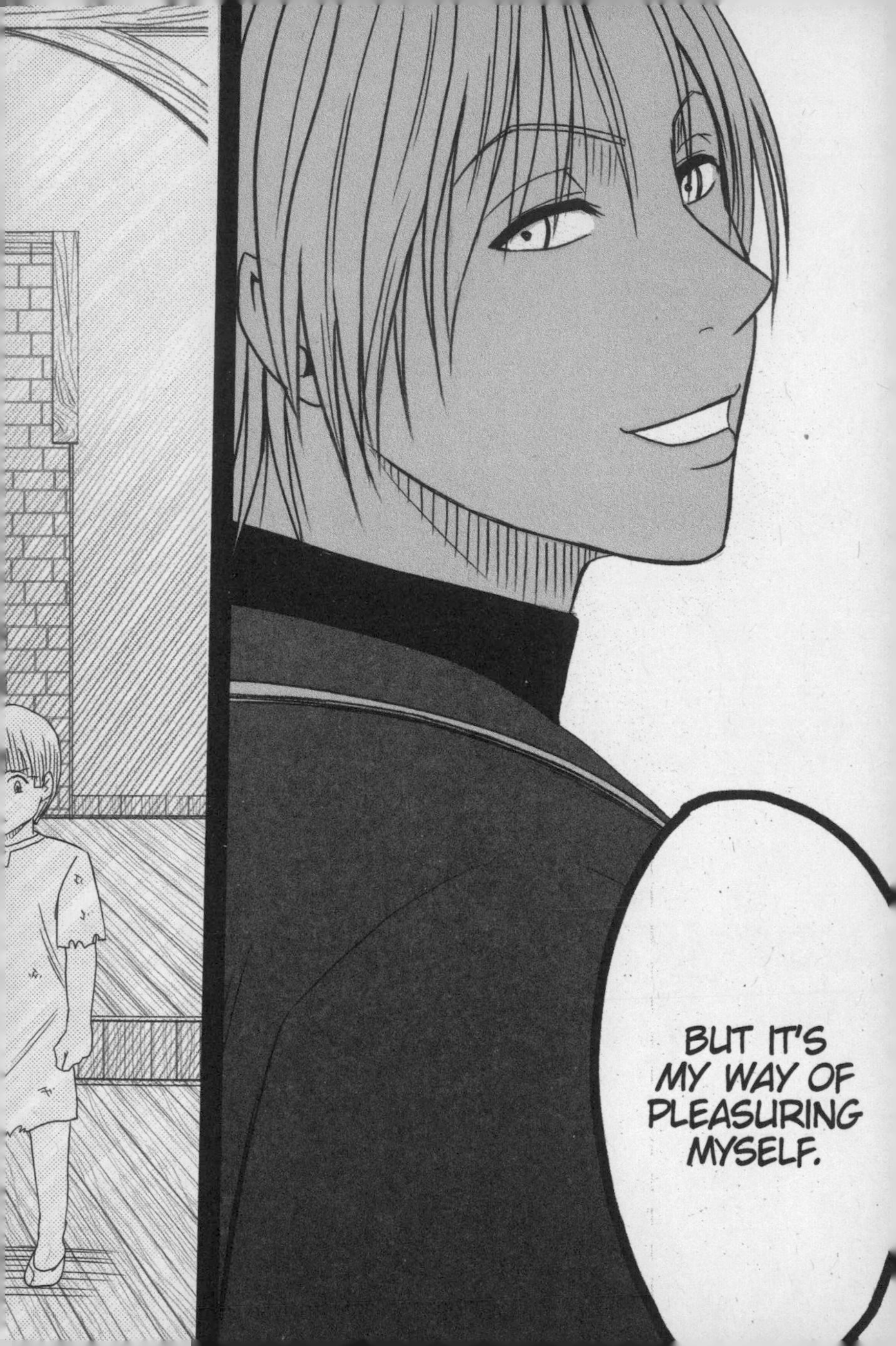
BUT IT'S MY WAY OF PLEASURING MYSELF.

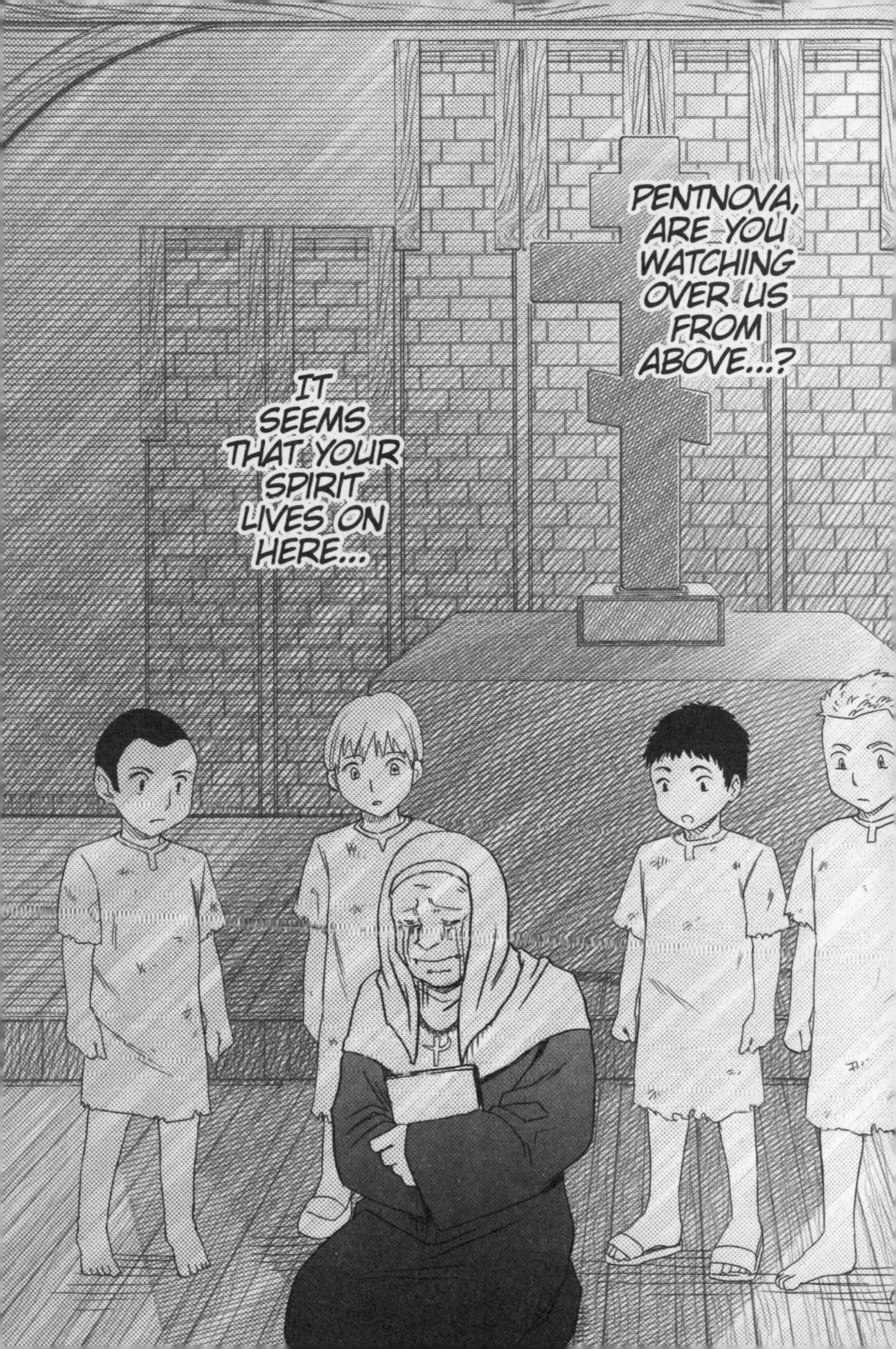
PENTNOVA, ARE YOU WATCHING OVER US FROM ABOVE...?
IT SEEMS THAT YOUR SPIRIT LIVES ON HERE...

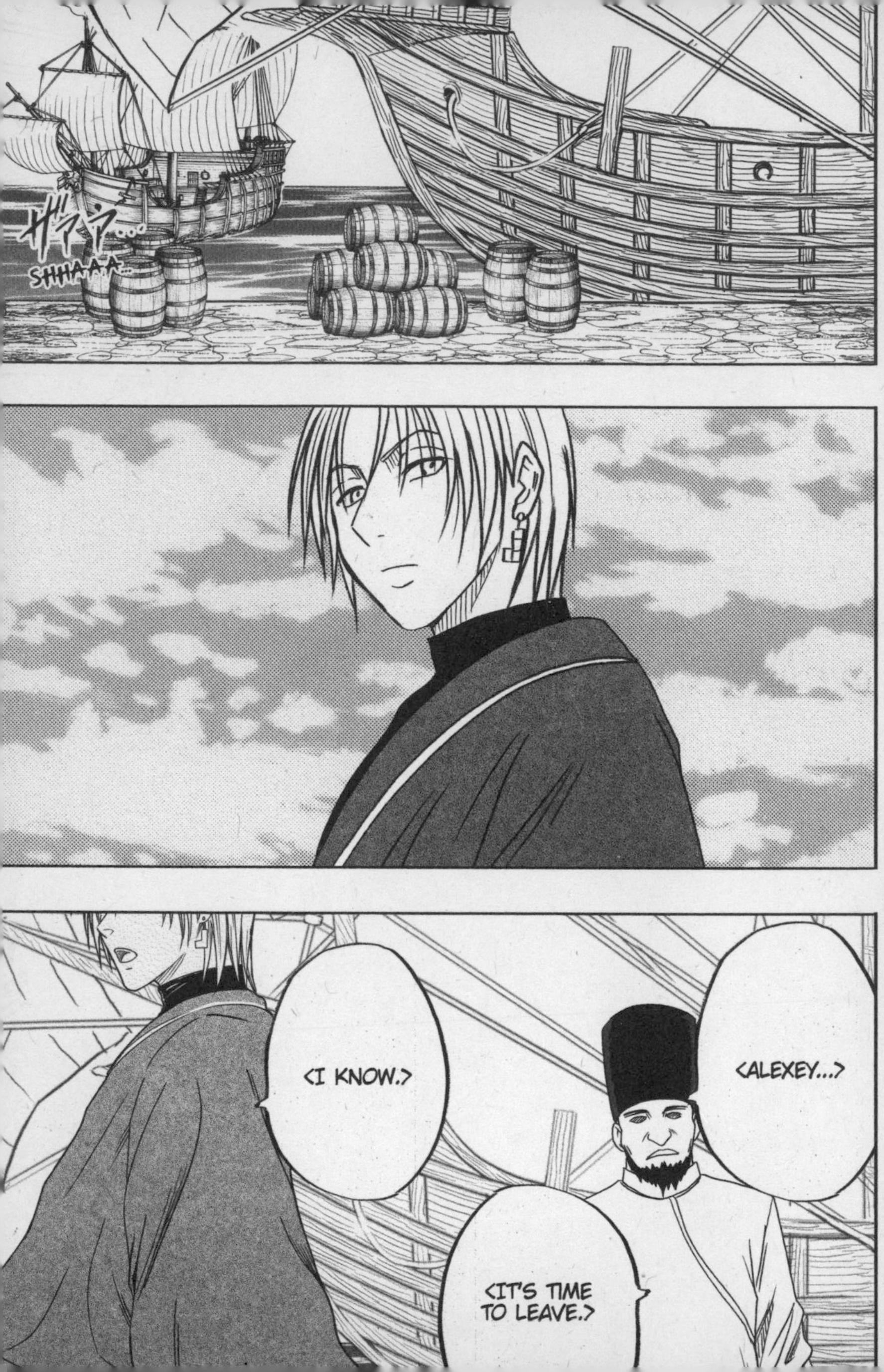
ザァァ…
SHHAAA...
<ALEXEY...>
<IT'S TIME TO LEAVE.>
<I KNOW.>

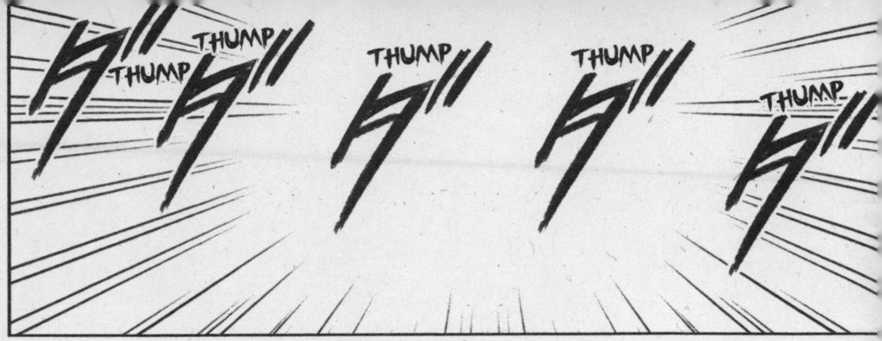
ダ
THUMP
ダ
THUMP
ダ
THUMP
ダ
THUMP
ダ
THUMP

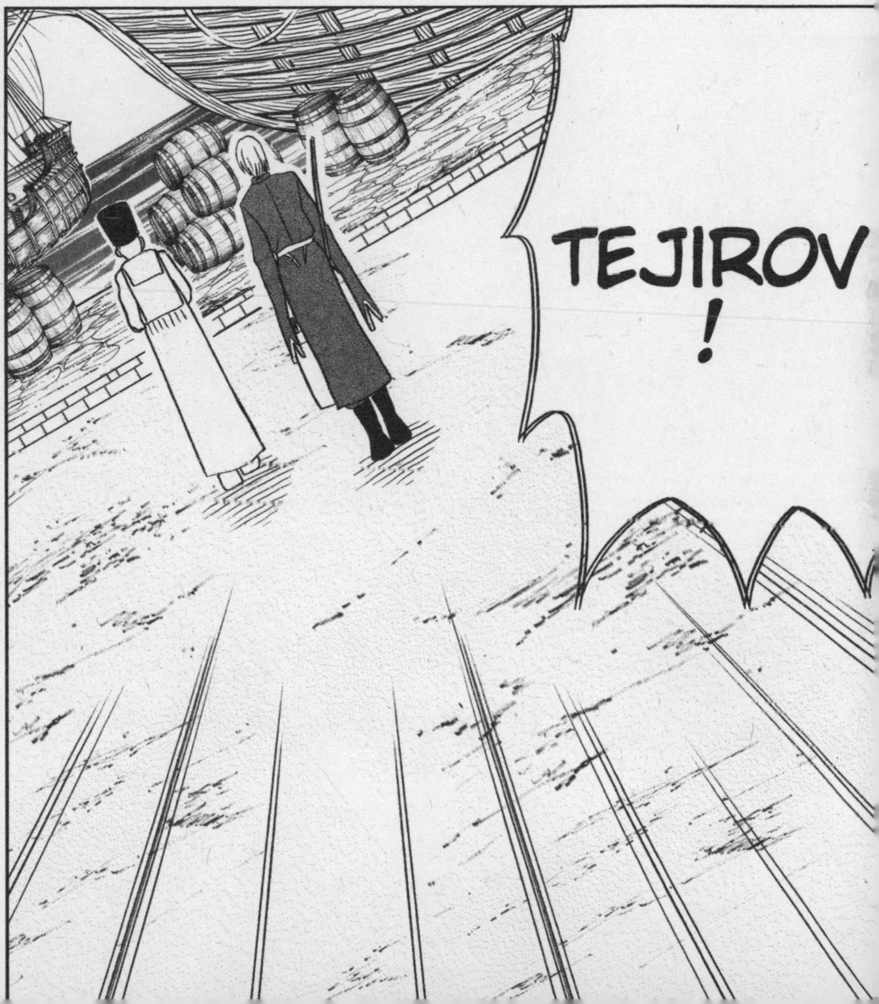
TEJIROV!

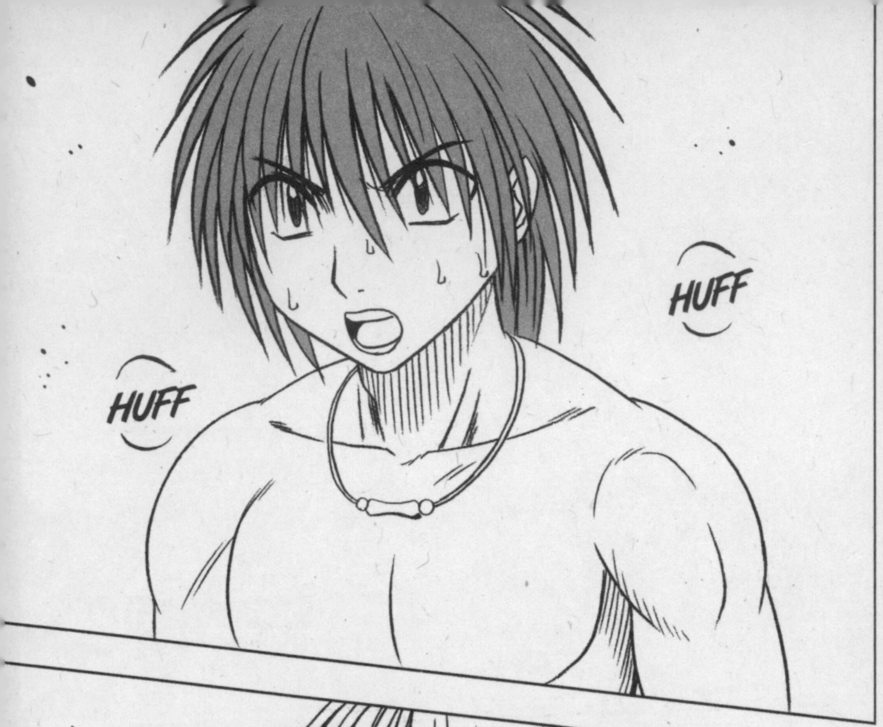
HUFF
HUFF
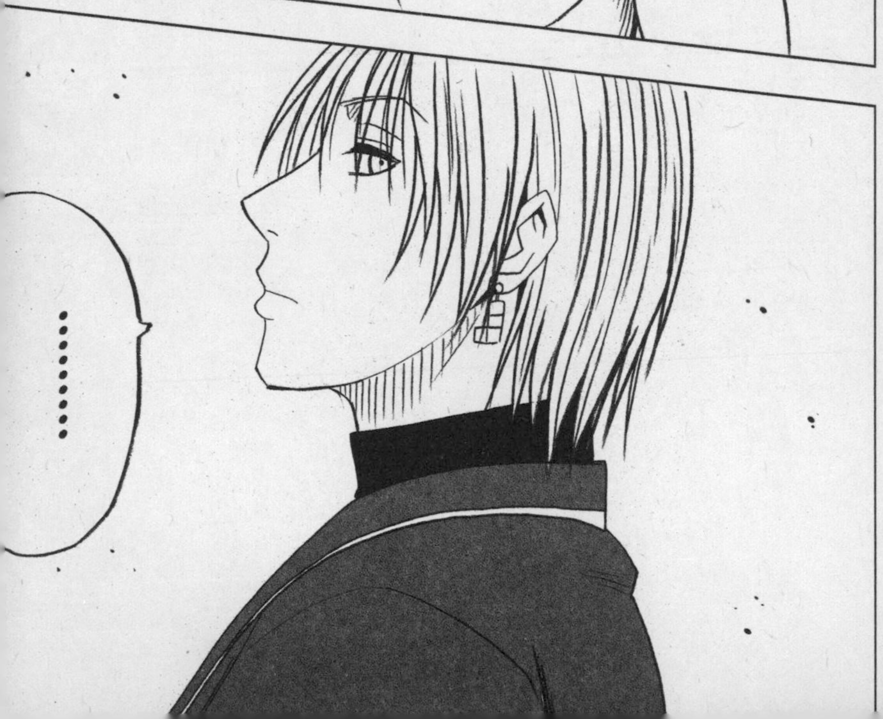
......

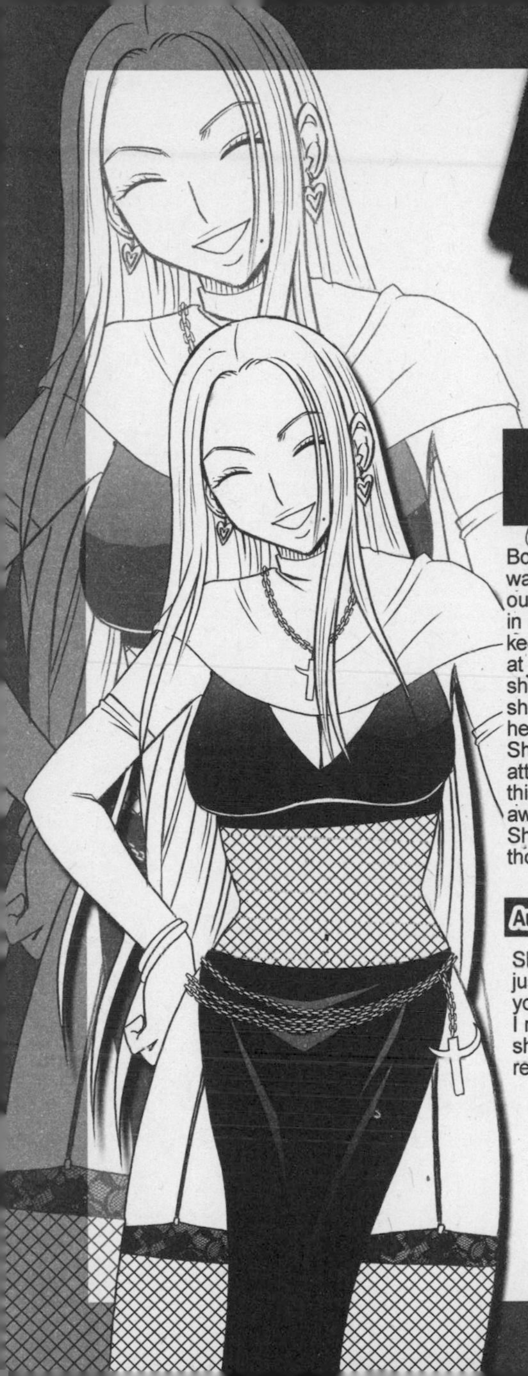

# WORLD WAR BLUE
## CHARACTER INTRODUCTION

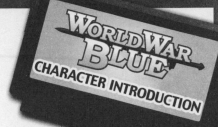

## TATYANA PENTNOVA

Born in Lorgue. When she was young, she was tossed out by her parents and raised in an orphanage. With her keen intelligence, she excelled at logic and philosophy. Since she loved to debate things, she often caused problems for her teachers at the orphanage. She stopped devoting all her attention to logic when something happened that made her aware of her womanly charms. She became a nun, even though she isn't very religious.

### Author Comment

She is a character that you just can't leave out when you're talking about Tejirov. I really wish I could have shown even more of their relationship.

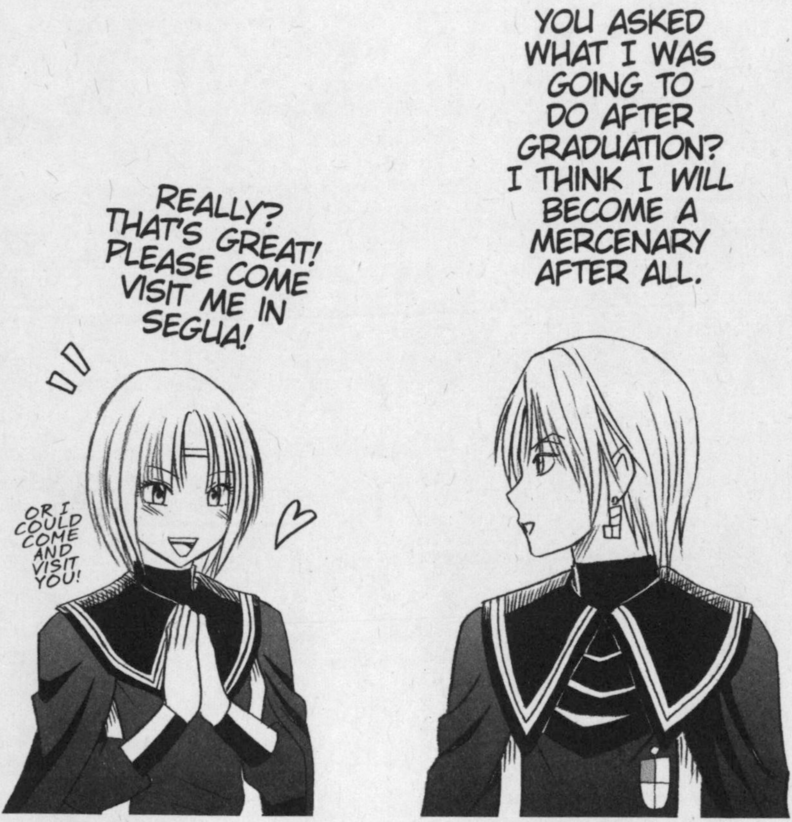
YOU ASKED WHAT I WAS GOING TO DO AFTER GRADUATION? I THINK I WILL BECOME A MERCENARY AFTER ALL.
REALLY? THAT'S GREAT! PLEASE COME VISIT ME IN SEGUA!
OR I COULD COME AND VISIT YOU!

Part 2

# CHAPTER 14

# GRAND MASTER

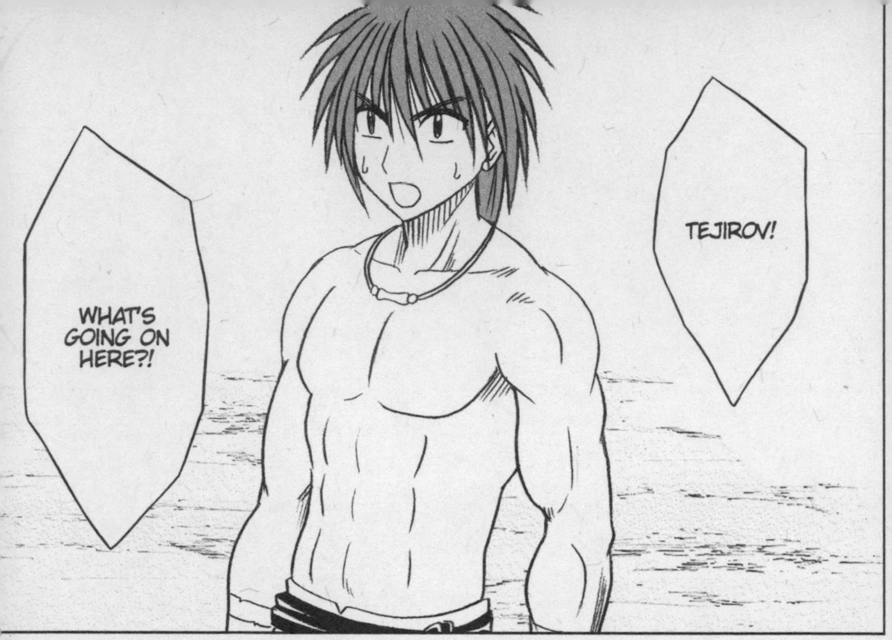
TEJIROV!
WHAT'S GOING ON HERE?!
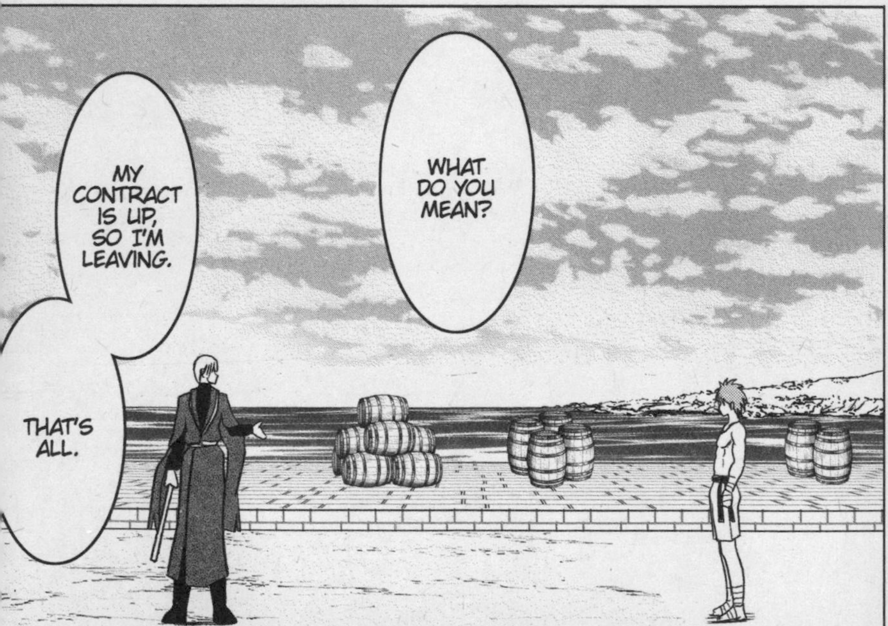
WHAT DO YOU MEAN?
MY CONTRACT IS UP, SO I'M LEAVING.
THAT'S ALL.

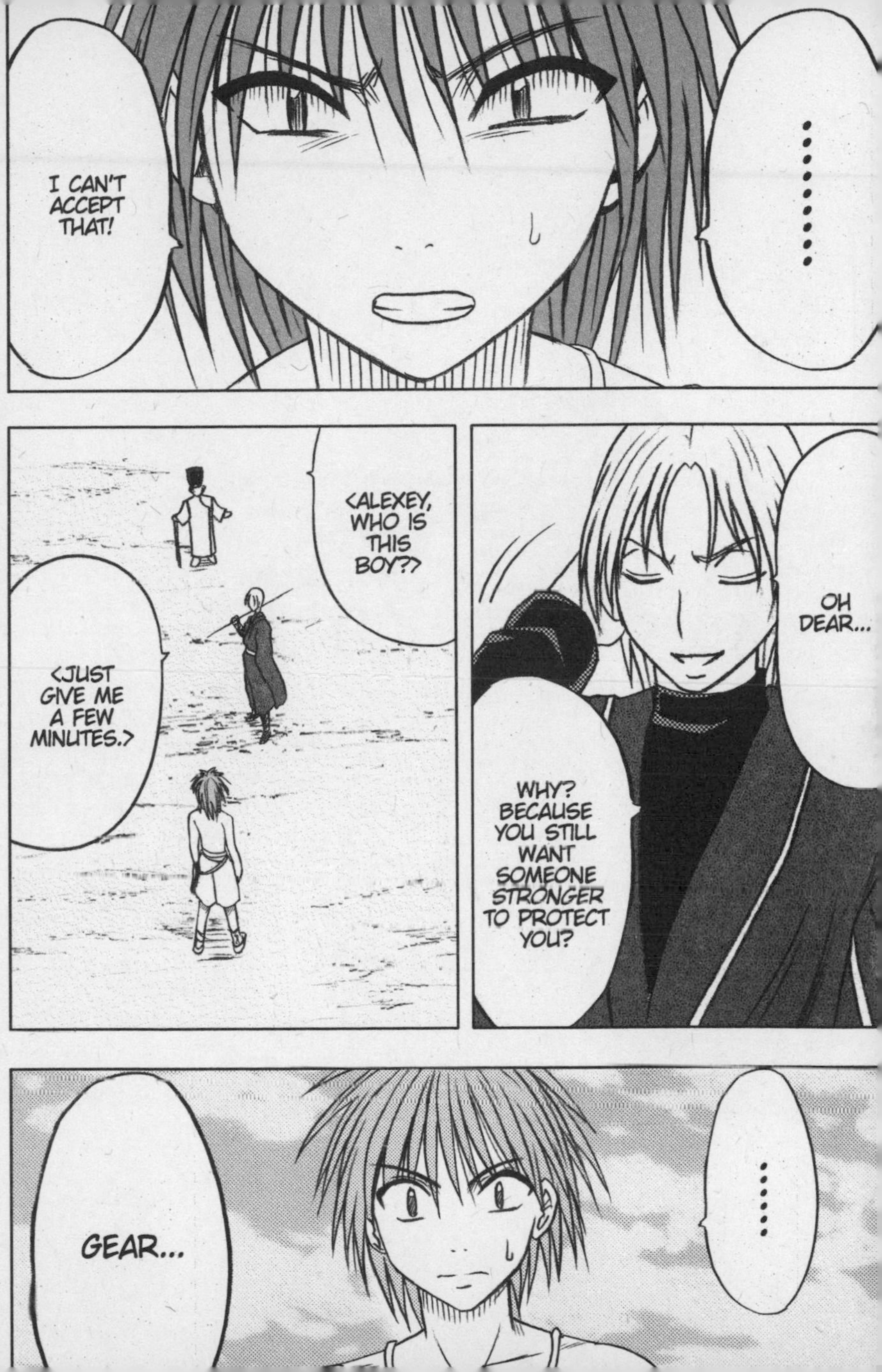

.........
I CAN'T ACCEPT THAT!
OH DEAR...
WHY? BECAUSE YOU STILL WANT SOMEONE STRONGER TO PROTECT YOU?
<ALEXEY, WHO IS THIS BOY?>
<JUST GIVE ME A FEW MINUTES.>
......
GEAR...

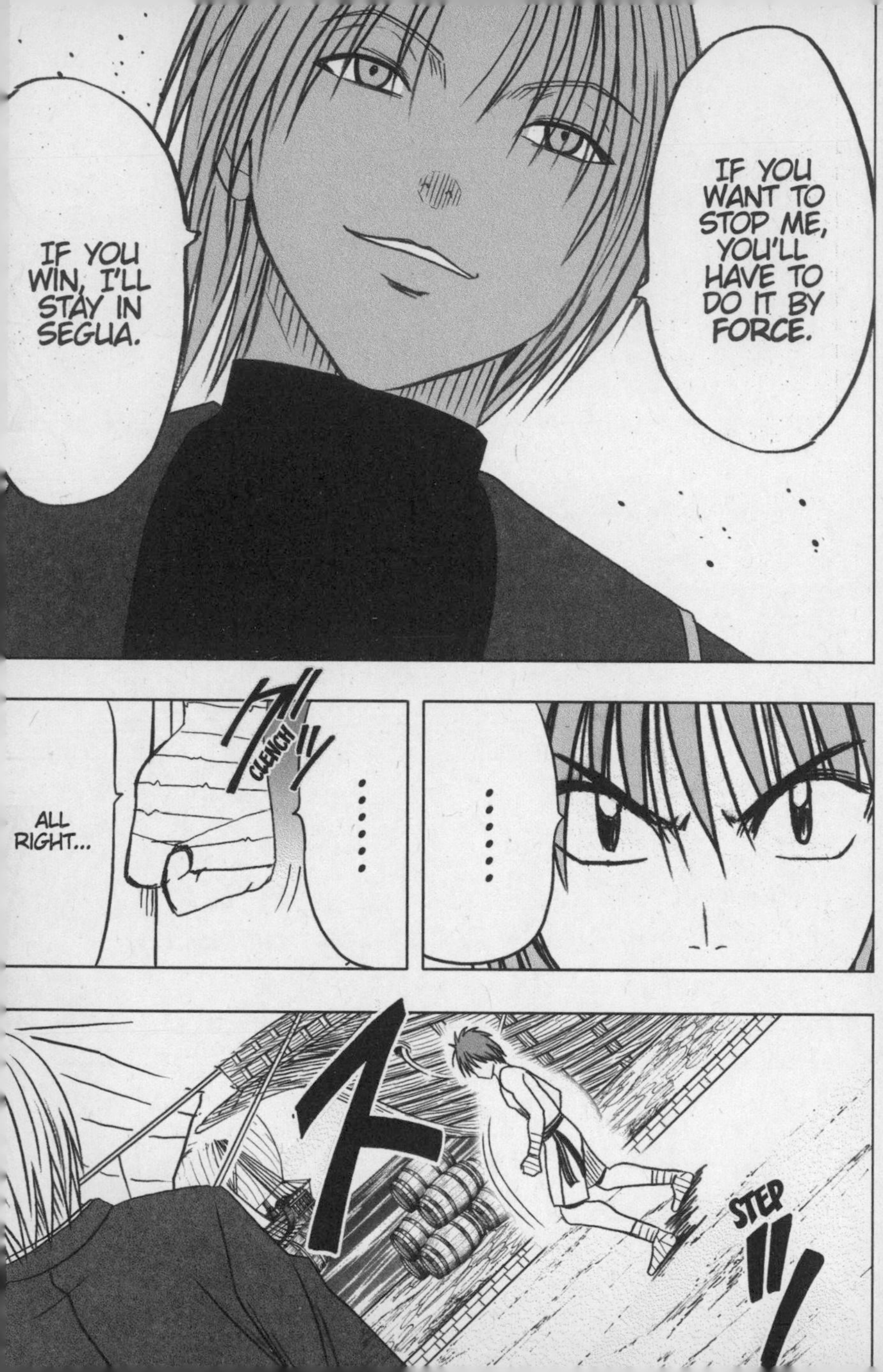
IF YOU WANT TO STOP ME, YOU'LL HAVE TO DO IT BY FORCE.
IF YOU WIN, I'LL STAY IN SEGUA.
......
......
CLENCH
ALL RIGHT...
STEP

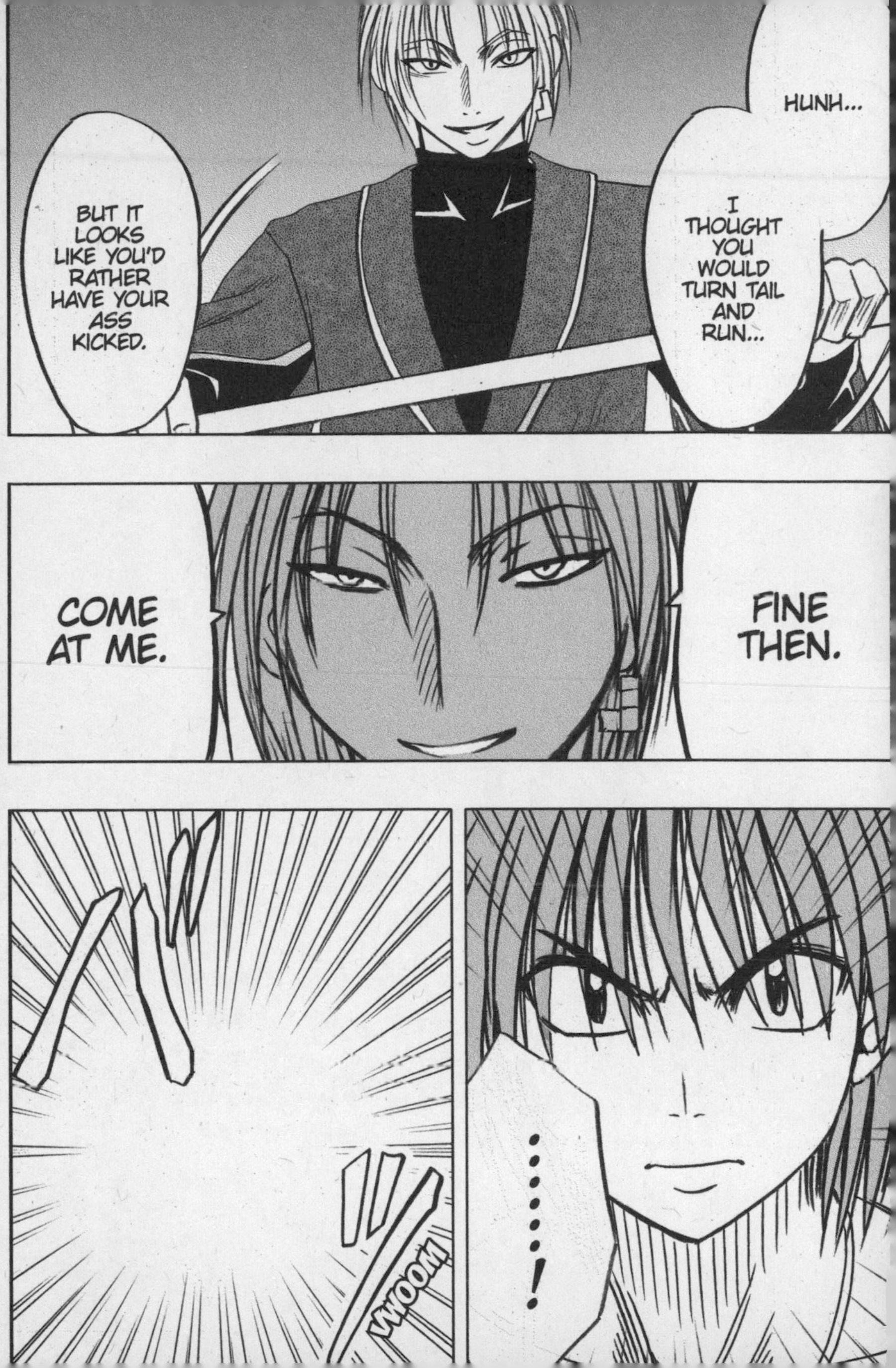
HUNH...
I THOUGHT YOU WOULD TURN TAIL AND RUN...
BUT IT LOOKS LIKE YOU'D RATHER HAVE YOUR ASS KICKED.
FINE THEN.
COME AT ME.
......!
VWOOM

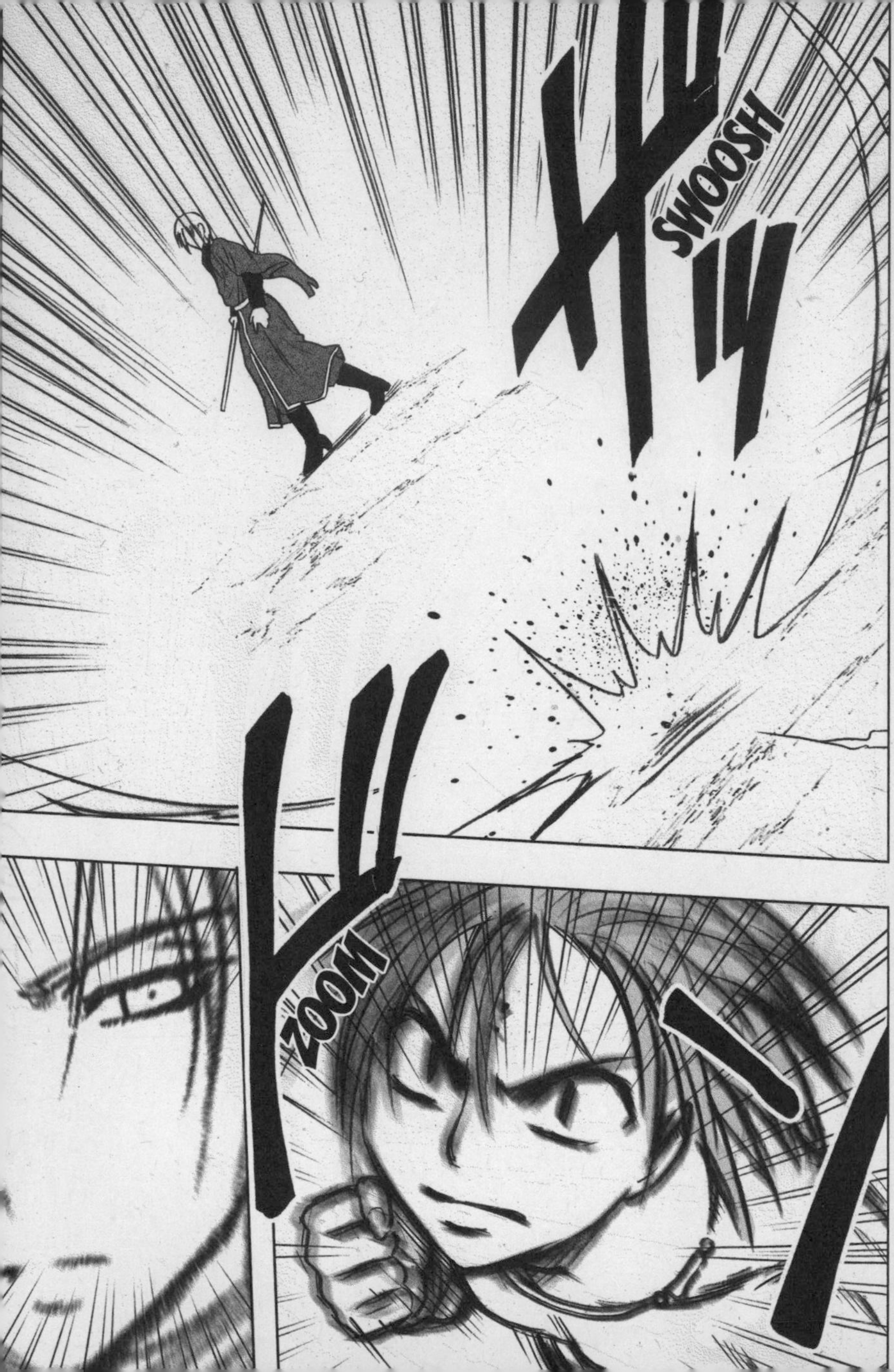
SWOOSH
ZOOM

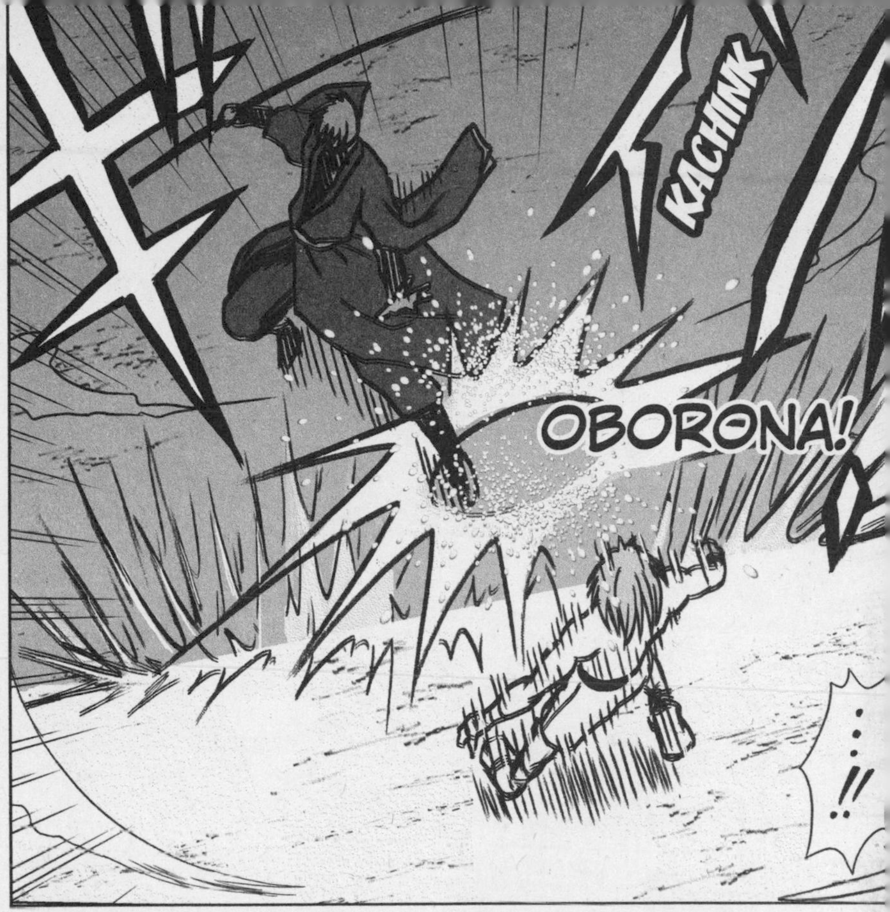
KACHINK
OBORONA!
...!!
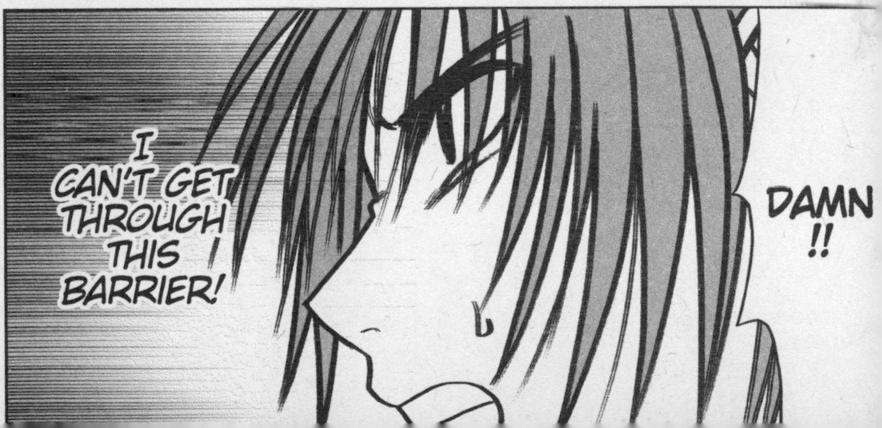
DAMN !!
I CAN'T GET THROUGH THIS BARRIER!

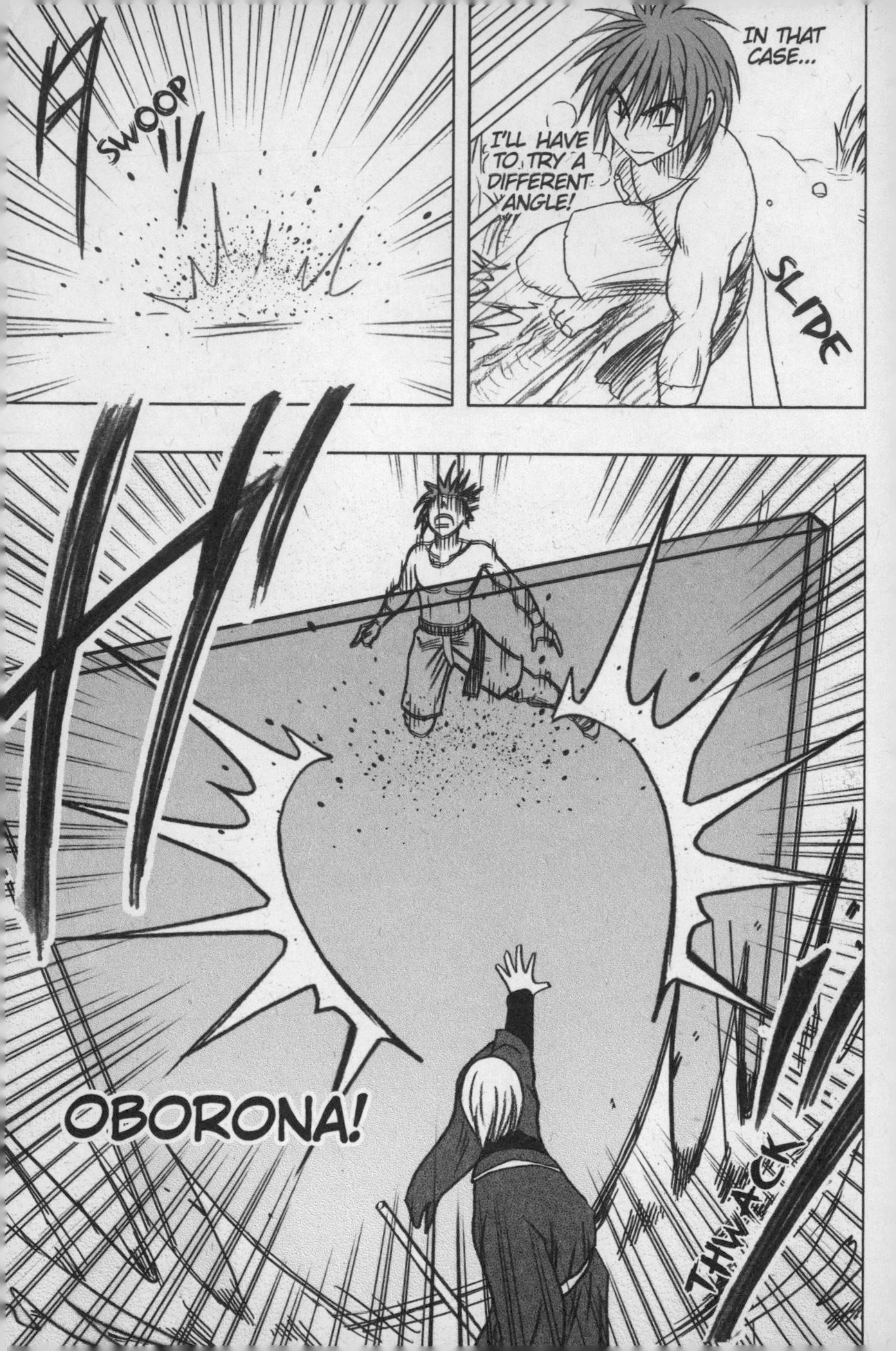
IN THAT CASE...
I'LL HAVE TO TRY A DIFFERENT ANGLE!
SLIDE
SWOOP
OBORONA!
THWACK

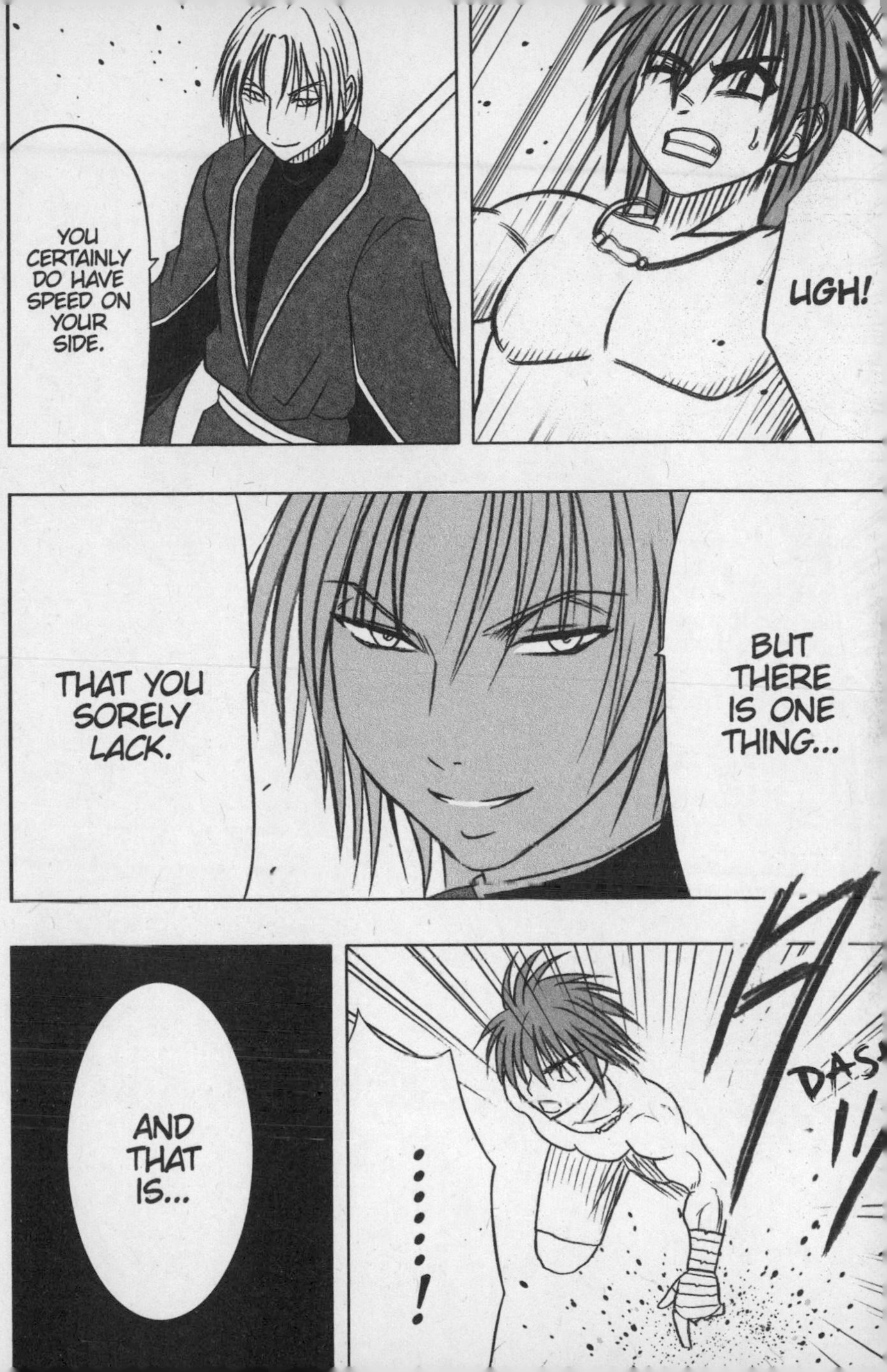
UGH!
YOU CERTAINLY DO HAVE SPEED ON YOUR SIDE.
BUT THERE IS ONE THING...
THAT YOU SORELY LACK.
DAS
......!
AND THAT IS...

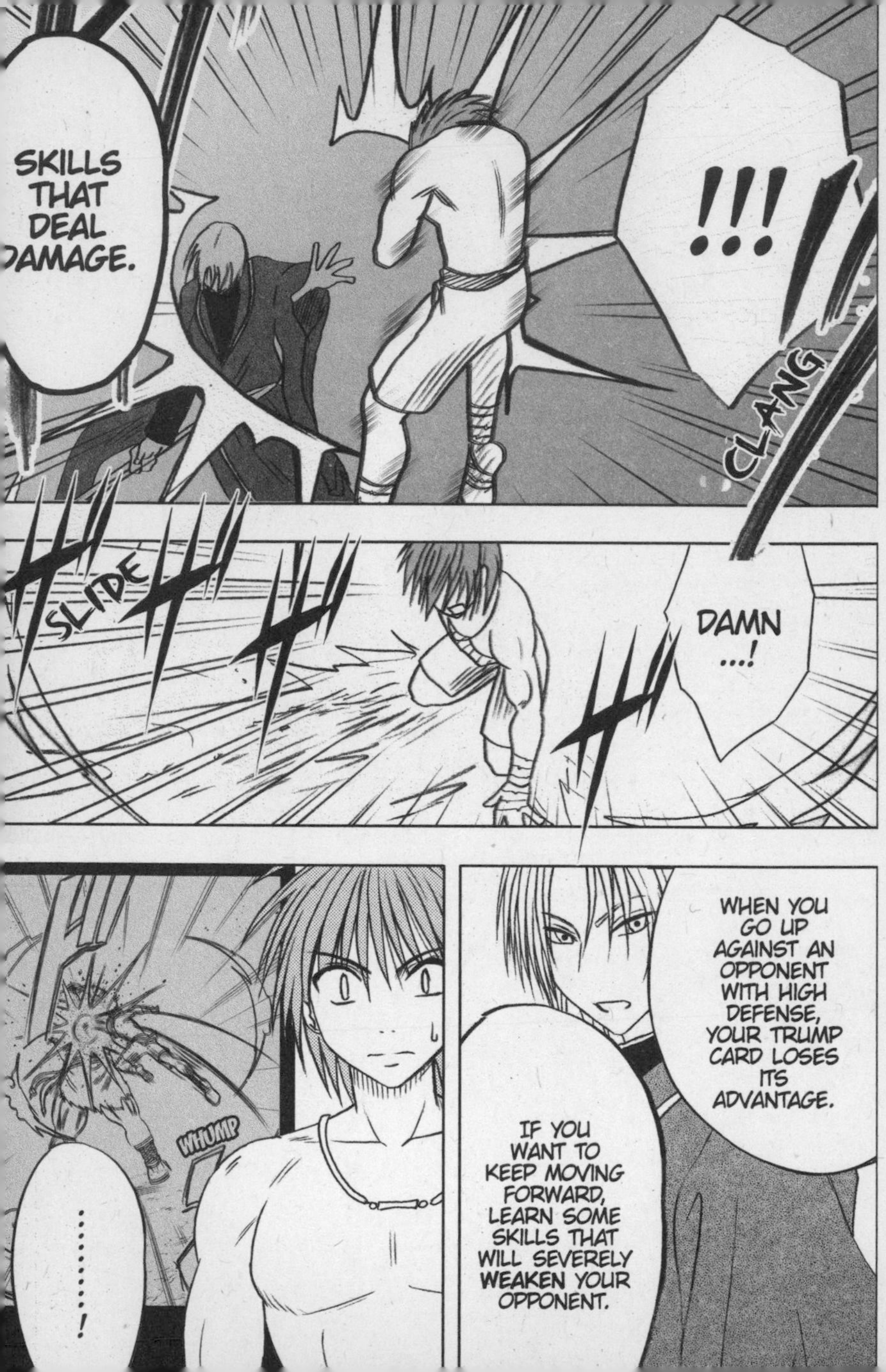
!!!
SKILLS THAT DEAL DAMAGE.
CLANG
DAMN ...!
SLIDE
WHEN YOU GO UP AGAINST AN OPPONENT WITH HIGH DEFENSE, YOUR TRUMP CARD LOSES ITS ADVANTAGE.
IF YOU WANT TO KEEP MOVING FORWARD, LEARN SOME SKILLS THAT WILL SEVERELY WEAKEN YOUR OPPONENT.
WHUMP
.........!

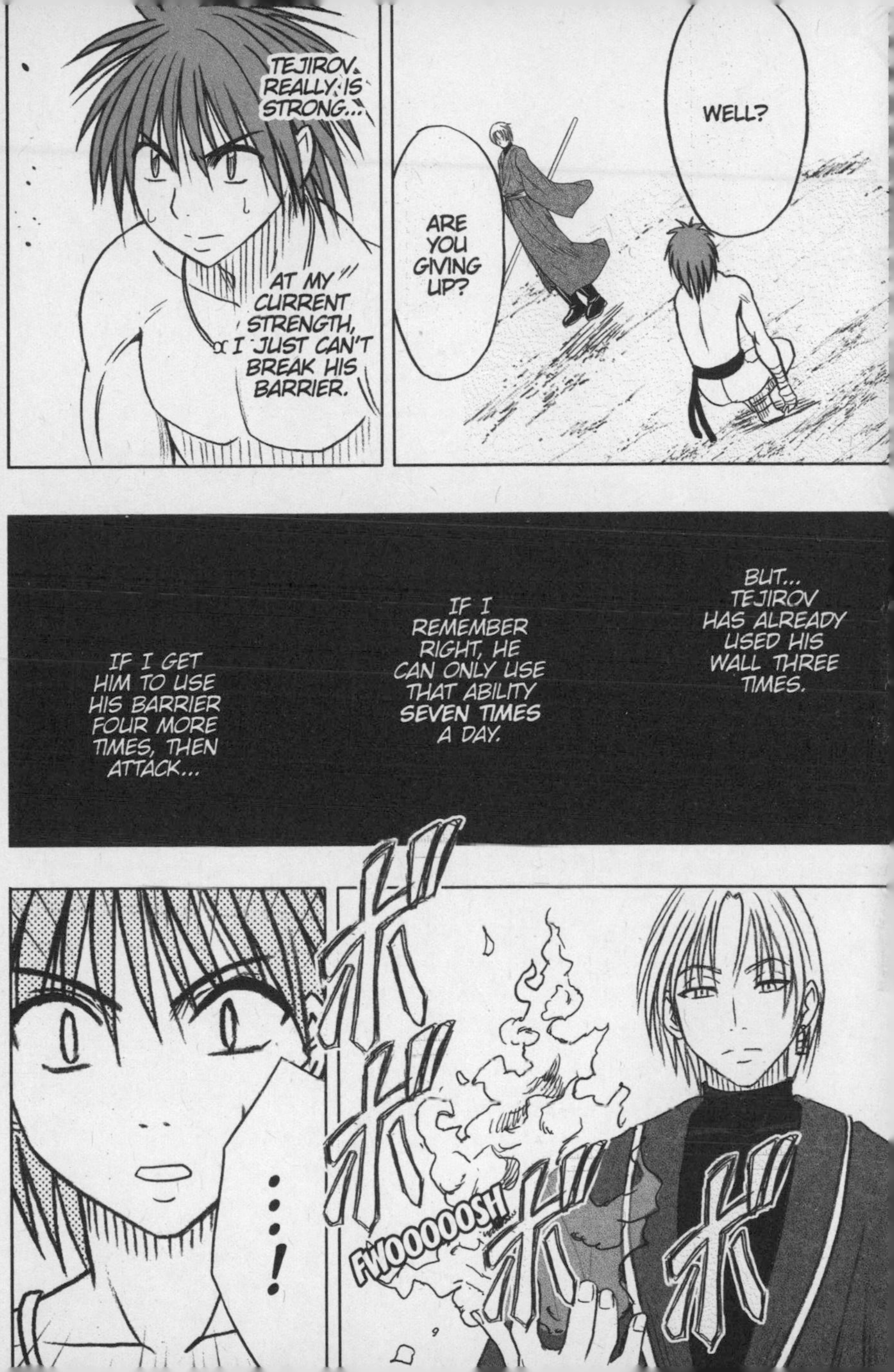
WELL?
ARE YOU GIVING UP?
TEJIROV REALLY IS STRONG...
AT MY CURRENT STRENGTH, I JUST CAN'T BREAK HIS BARRIER.
BUT... TEJIROV HAS ALREADY USED HIS WALL THREE TIMES.
IF I REMEMBER RIGHT, HE CAN ONLY USE THAT ABILITY SEVEN TIMES A DAY.
IF I GET HIM TO USE HIS BARRIER FOUR MORE TIMES, THEN ATTACK...
FWOOOOOSH
...!

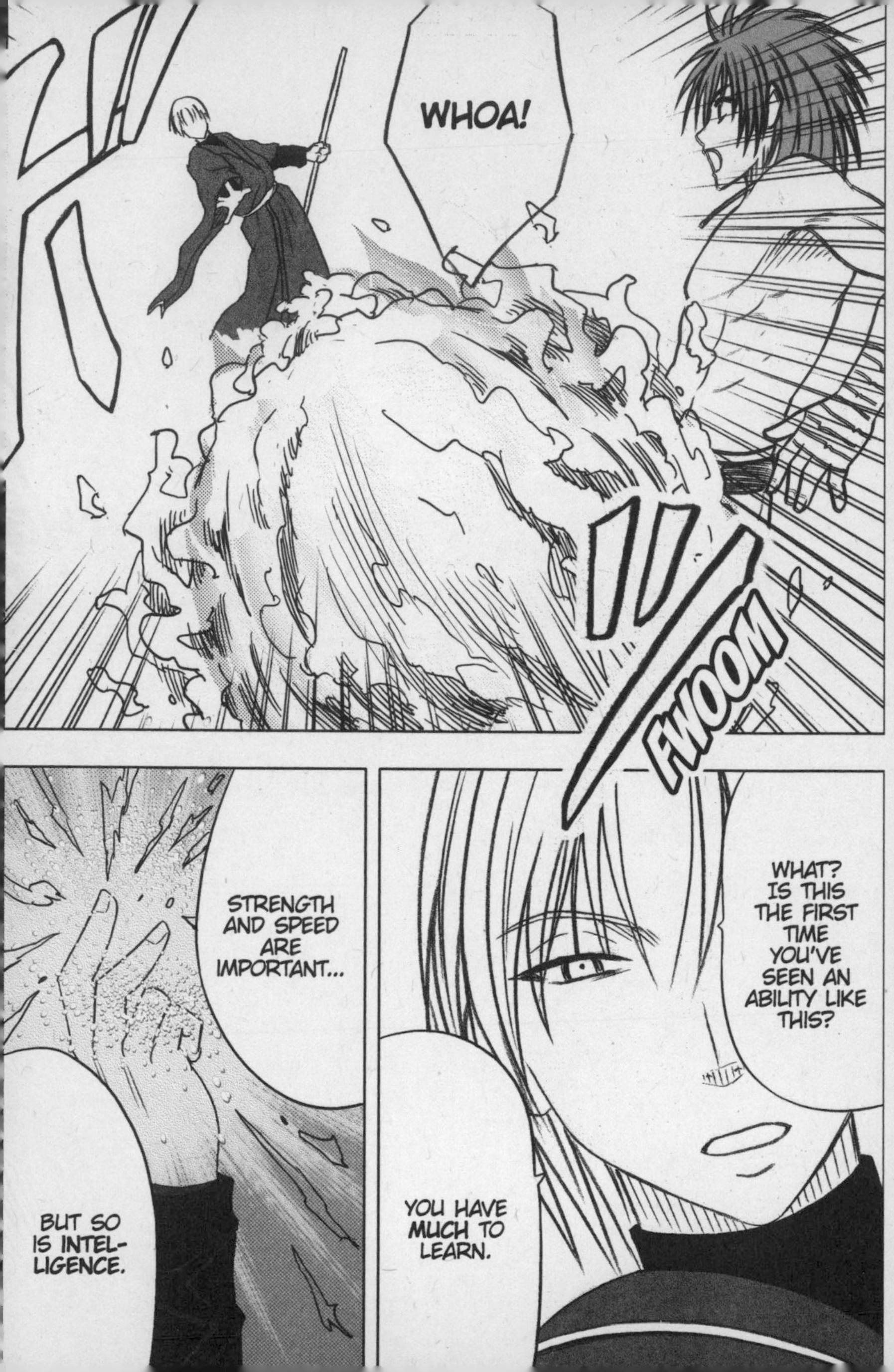
WHOA!
FWOOM
WHAT? IS THIS THE FIRST TIME YOU'VE SEEN AN ABILITY LIKE THIS?
YOU HAVE MUCH TO LEARN.
STRENGTH AND SPEED ARE IMPORTANT...
BUT SO IS INTEL-LIGENCE.

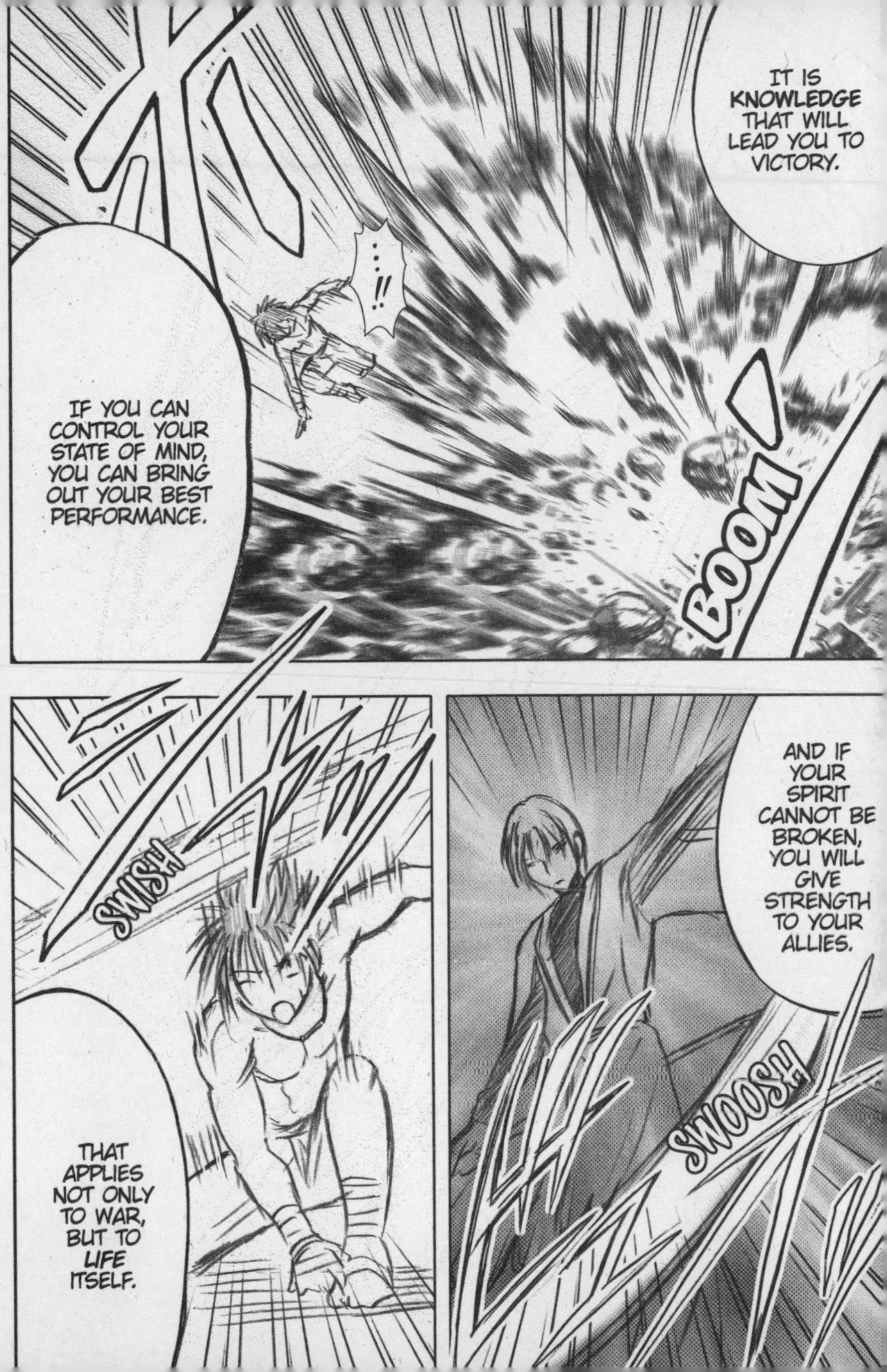
IT IS KNOWLEDGE THAT WILL LEAD YOU TO VICTORY.
...!!
BOOM
IF YOU CAN CONTROL YOUR STATE OF MIND, YOU CAN BRING OUT YOUR BEST PERFORMANCE.
AND IF YOUR SPIRIT CANNOT BE BROKEN, YOU WILL GIVE STRENGTH TO YOUR ALLIES.
SWOOSH
SWISH
THAT APPLIES NOT ONLY TO WAR, BUT TO LIFE ITSELF.

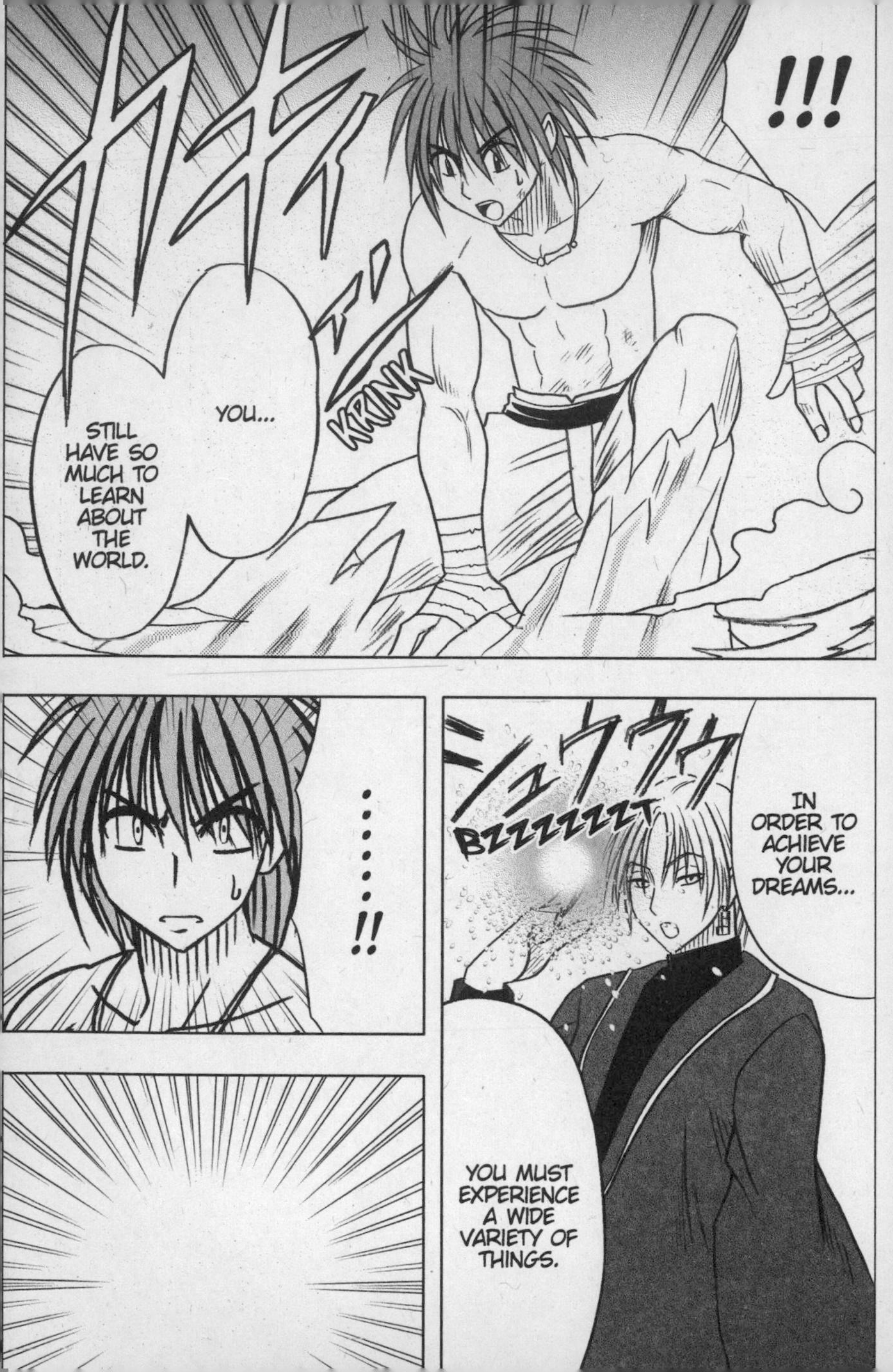
!!!
KRINK
YOU...
STILL HAVE SO MUCH TO LEARN ABOUT THE WORLD.
BZZZZZZZT
IN ORDER TO ACHIEVE YOUR DREAMS...
YOU MUST EXPERIENCE A WIDE VARIETY OF THINGS.
......!!

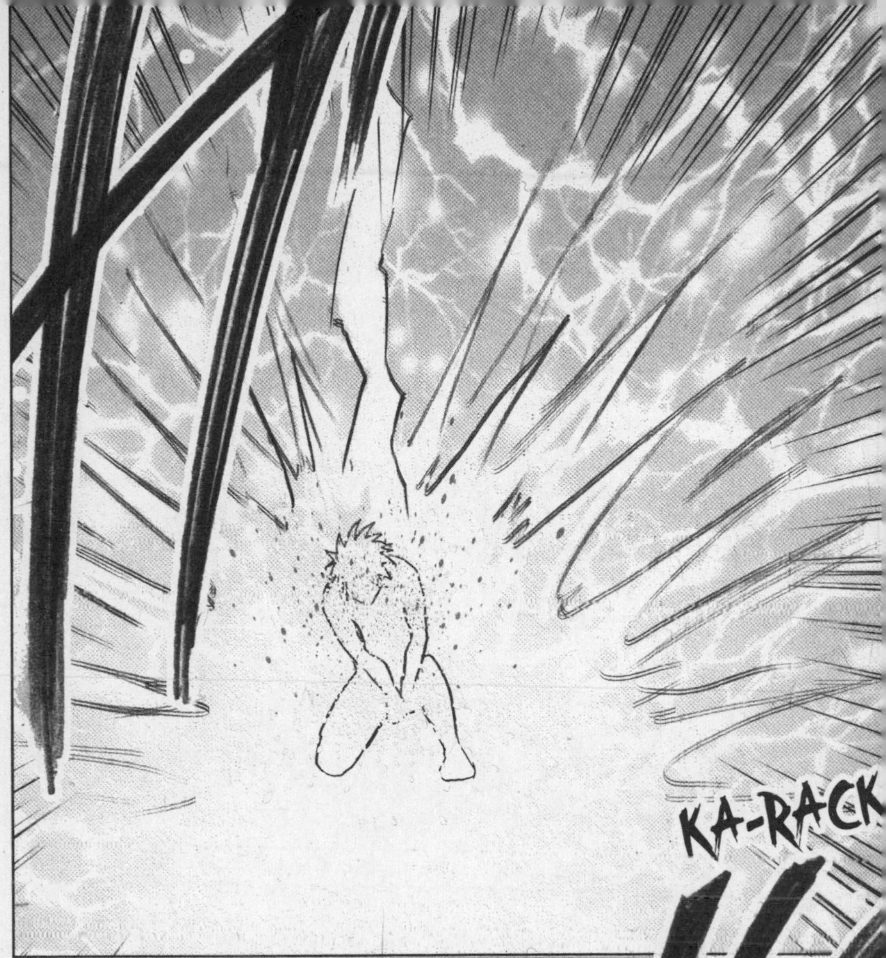
KA-RACK
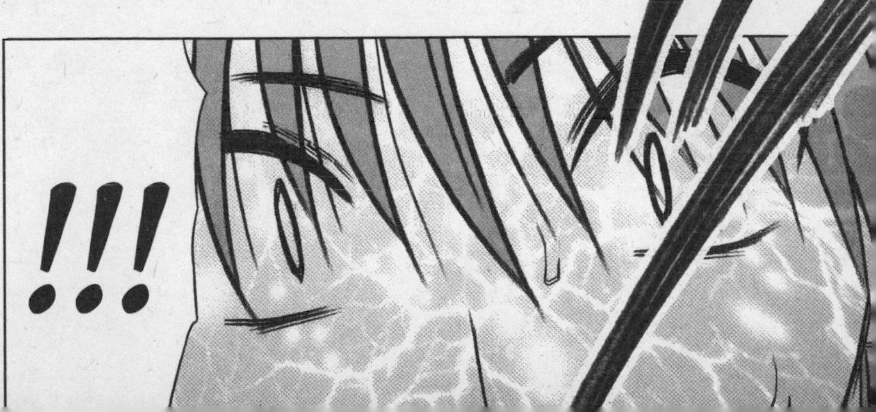
!!!

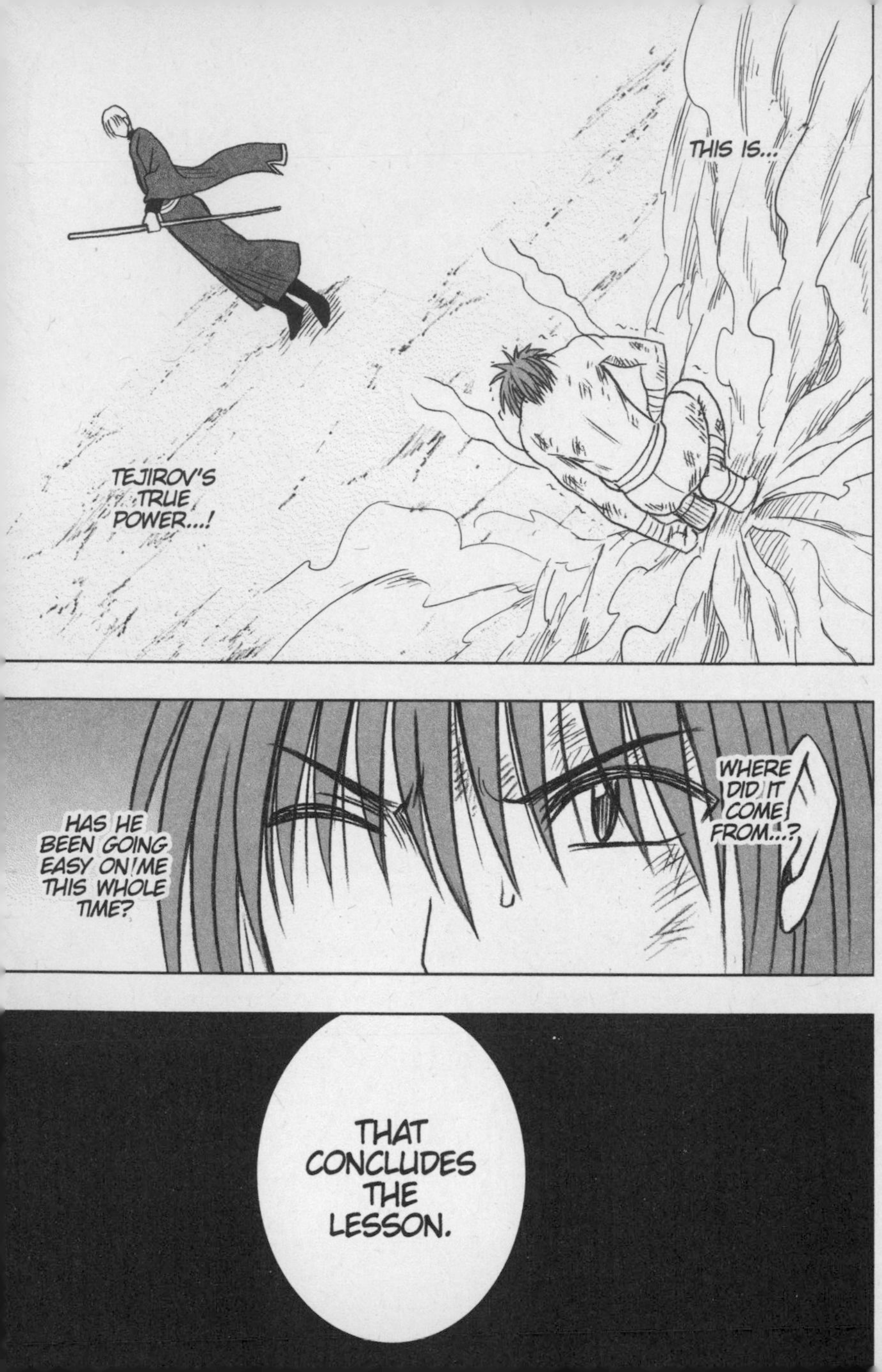
THIS IS...
TEJIROV'S TRUE POWER...!
WHERE DID IT COME FROM...?
HAS HE BEEN GOING EASY ON ME THIS WHOLE TIME?
THAT CONCLUDES THE LESSON.

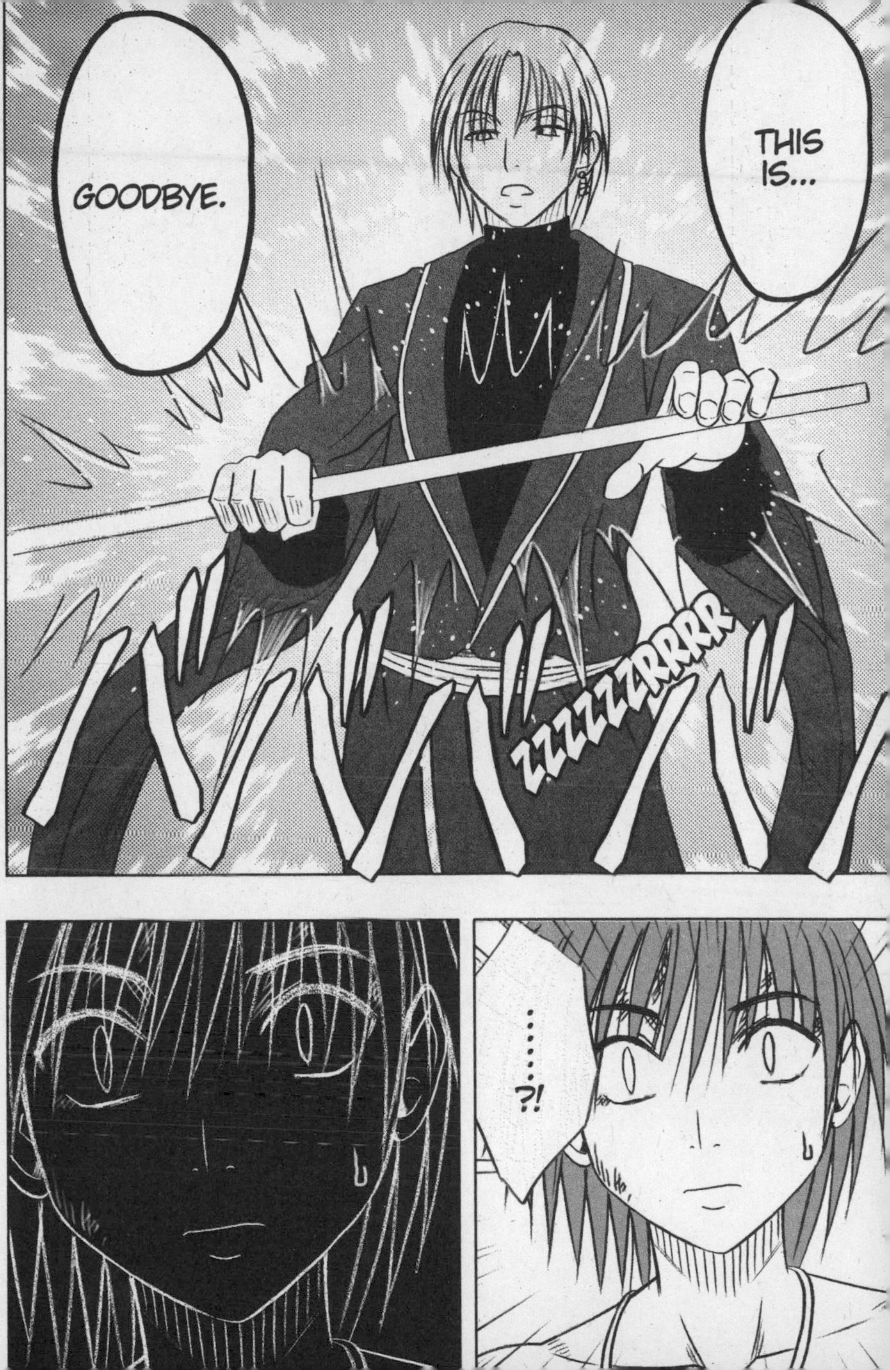
THIS IS...
GOODBYE.
ZZZZZZZRRRR
......?!

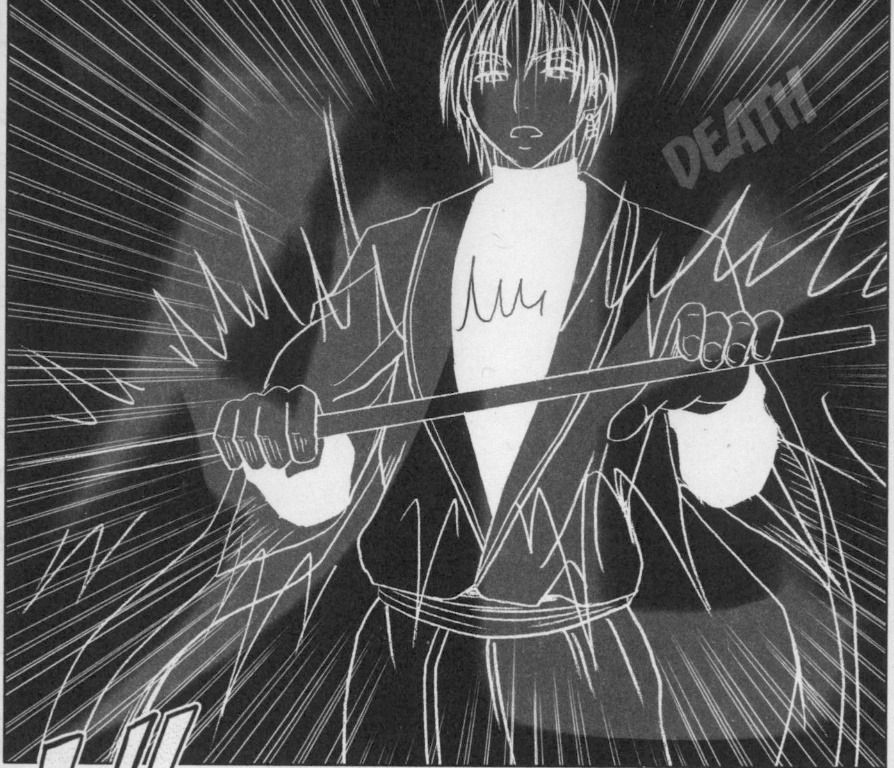
DEATH
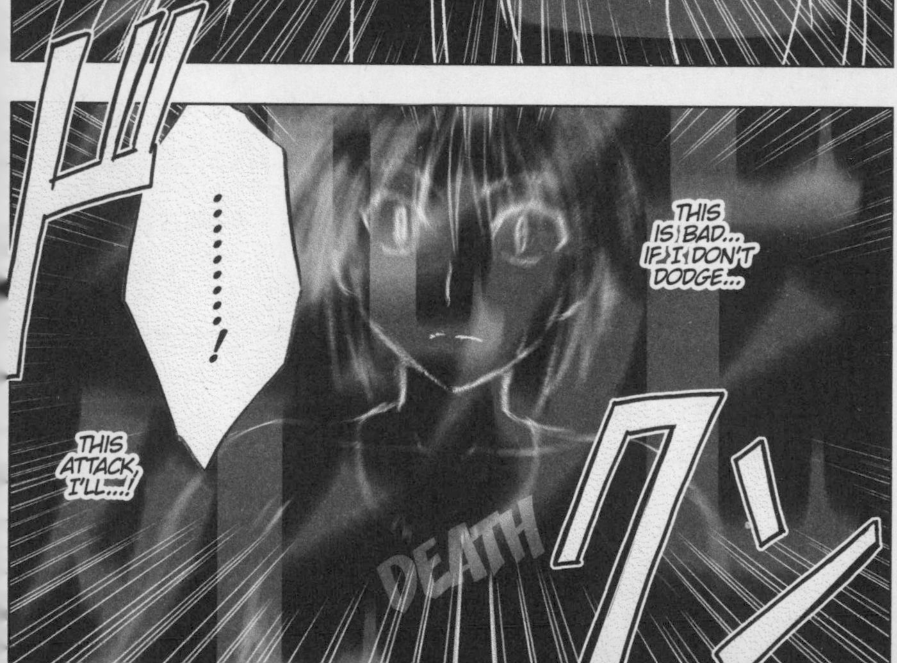
THIS IS BAD... IF I DON'T DODGE...
.........!
THIS ATTACK, I'LL...!
DEATH

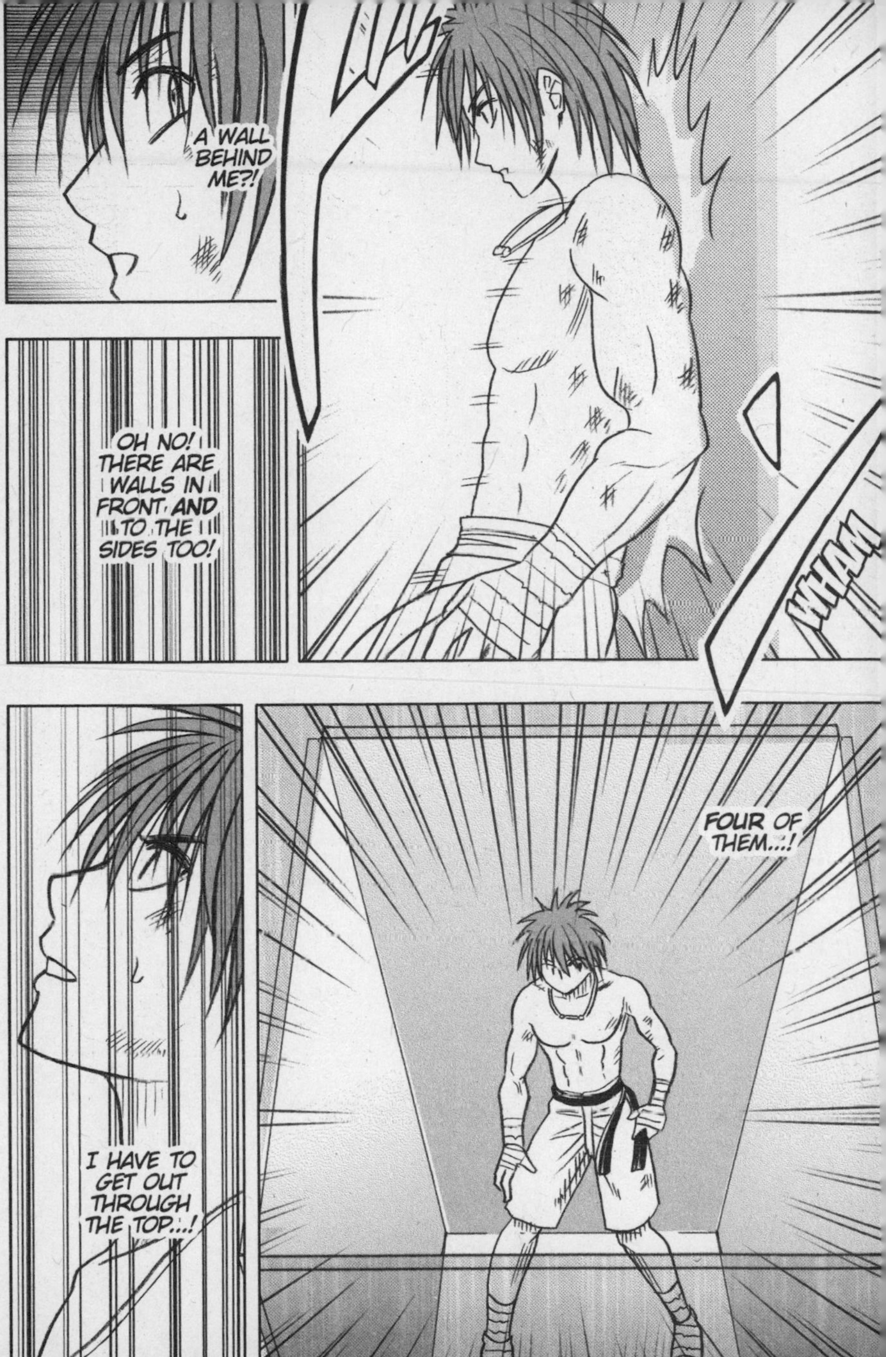
WHAM
A WALL BEHIND ME?!
OH NO! THERE ARE WALLS IN FRONT AND TO THE SIDES TOO!
FOUR OF THEM...!
I HAVE TO GET OUT THROUGH THE TOP...!

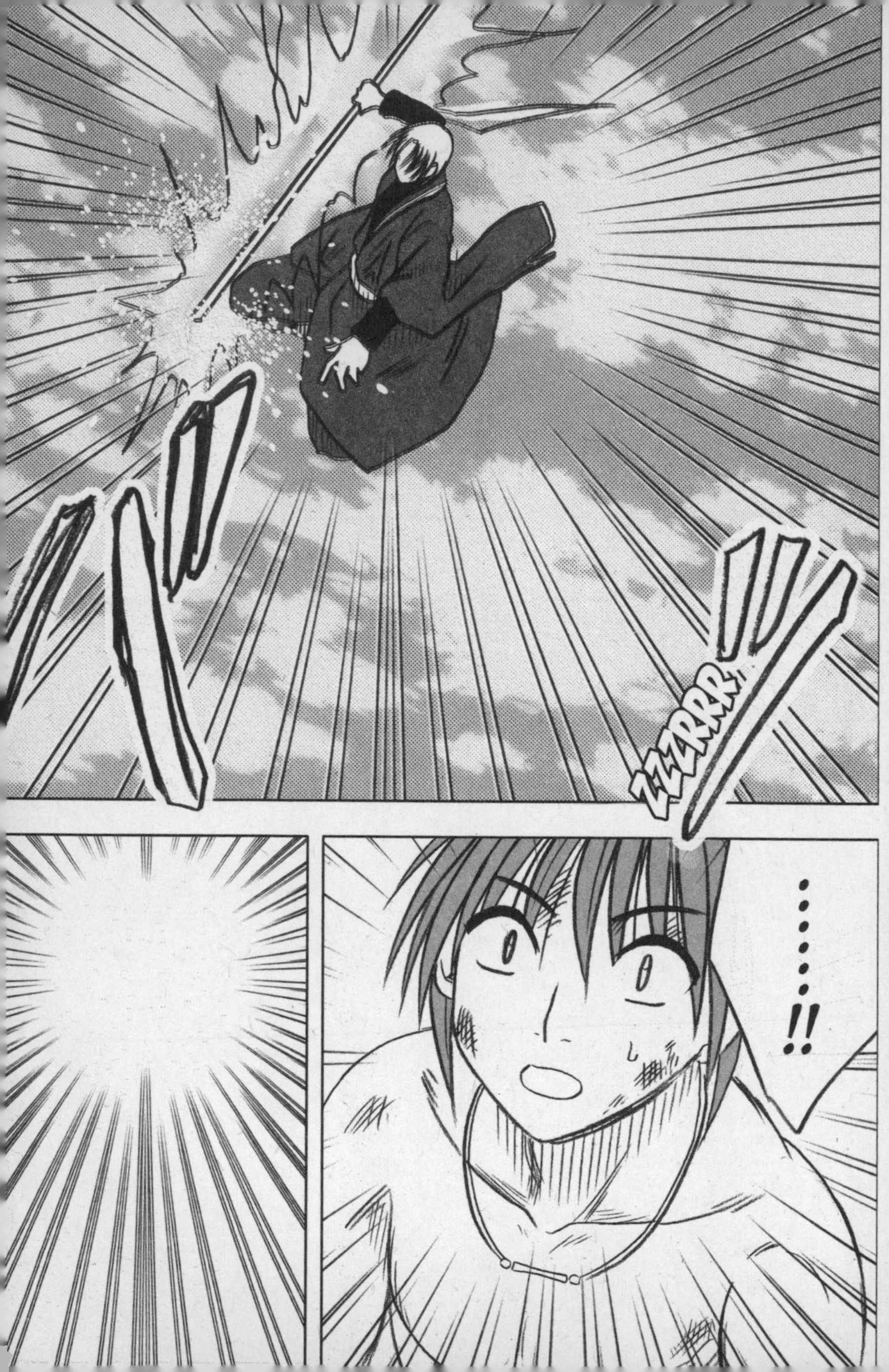
ZZZRRR
......!!

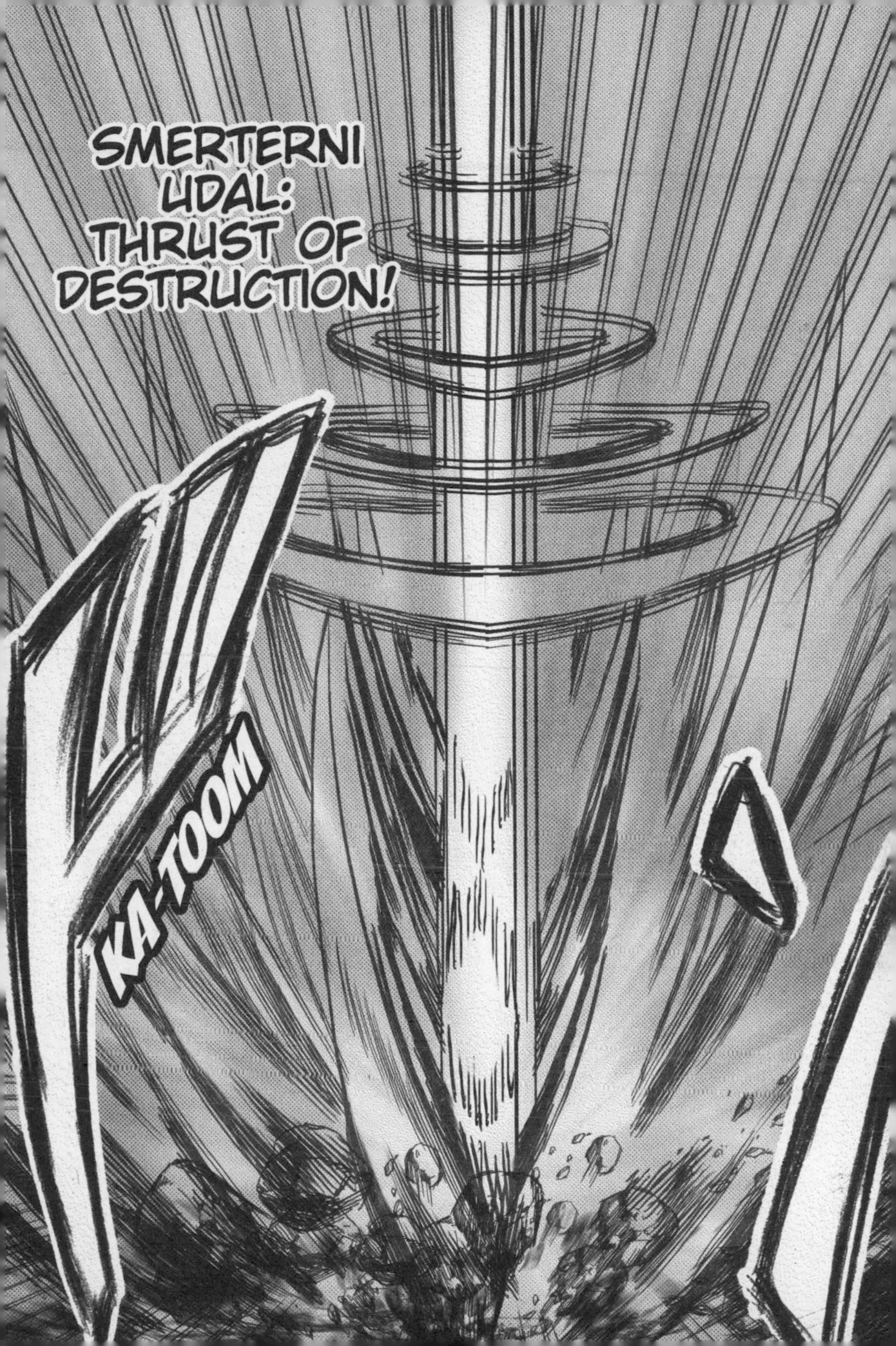
SMERTERNI UDAL: THRUST OF DESTRUCTION!
KA-TOOM

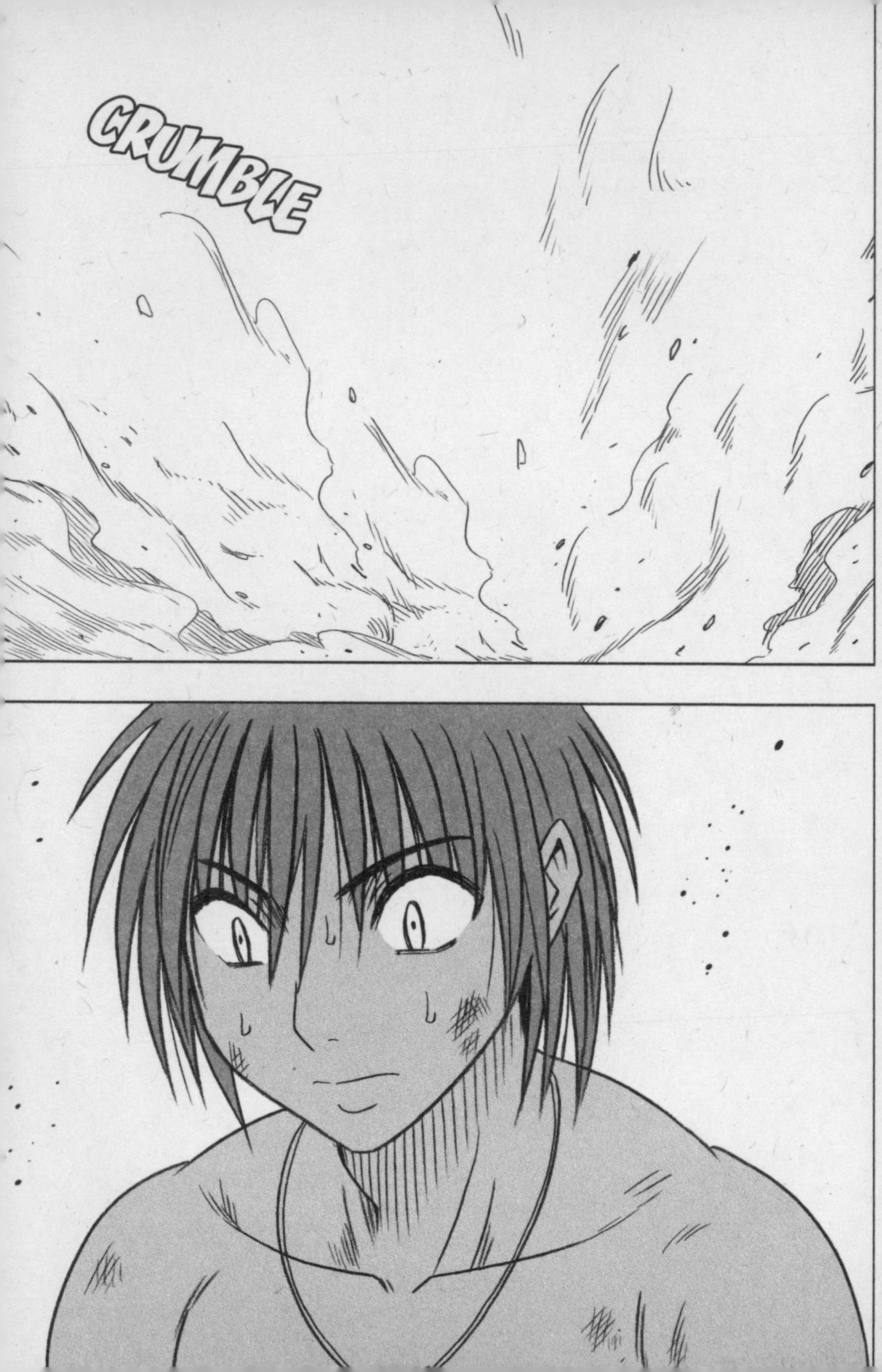
CRUMBLE

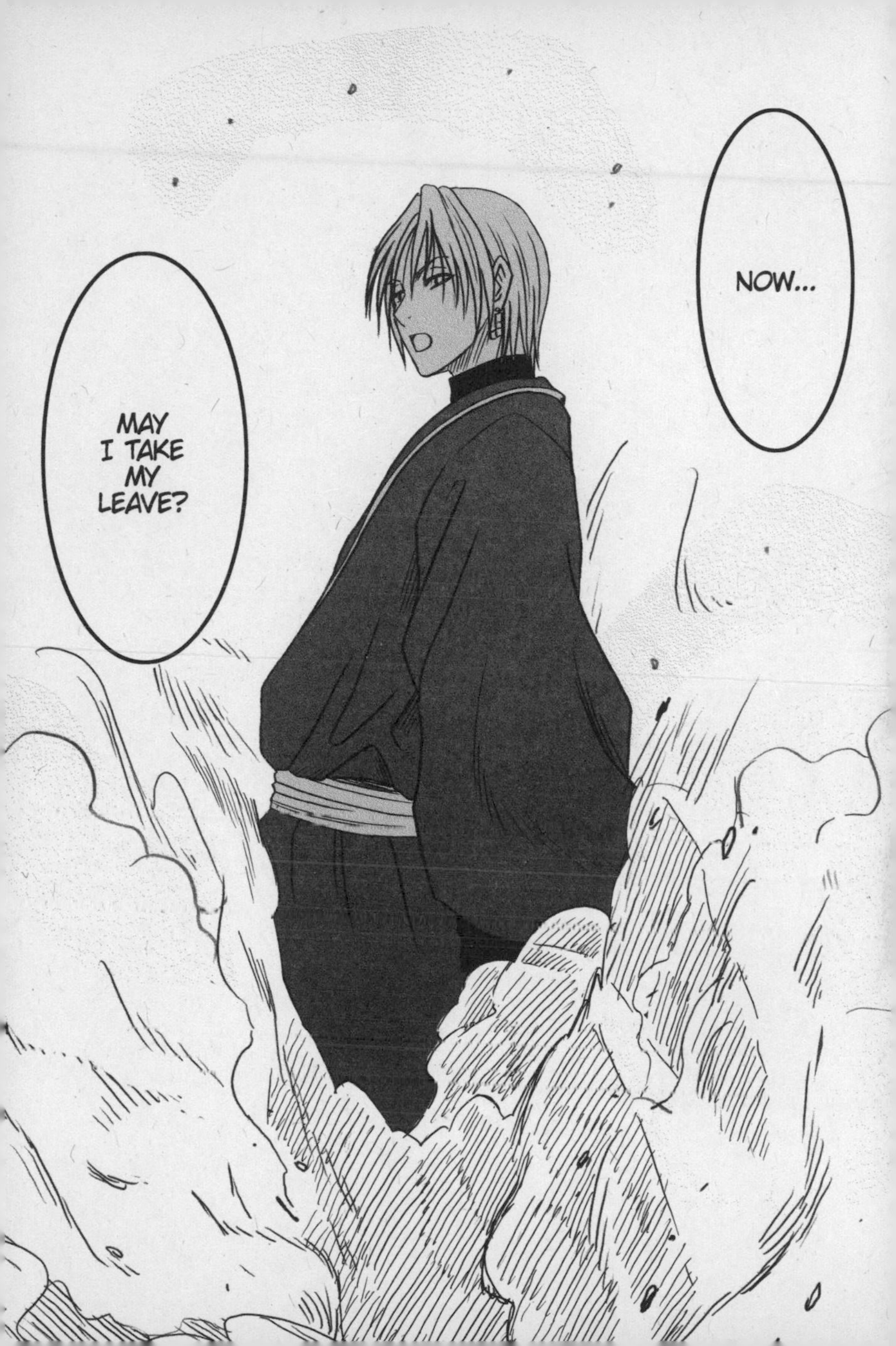
NOW...
MAY I TAKE MY LEAVE?

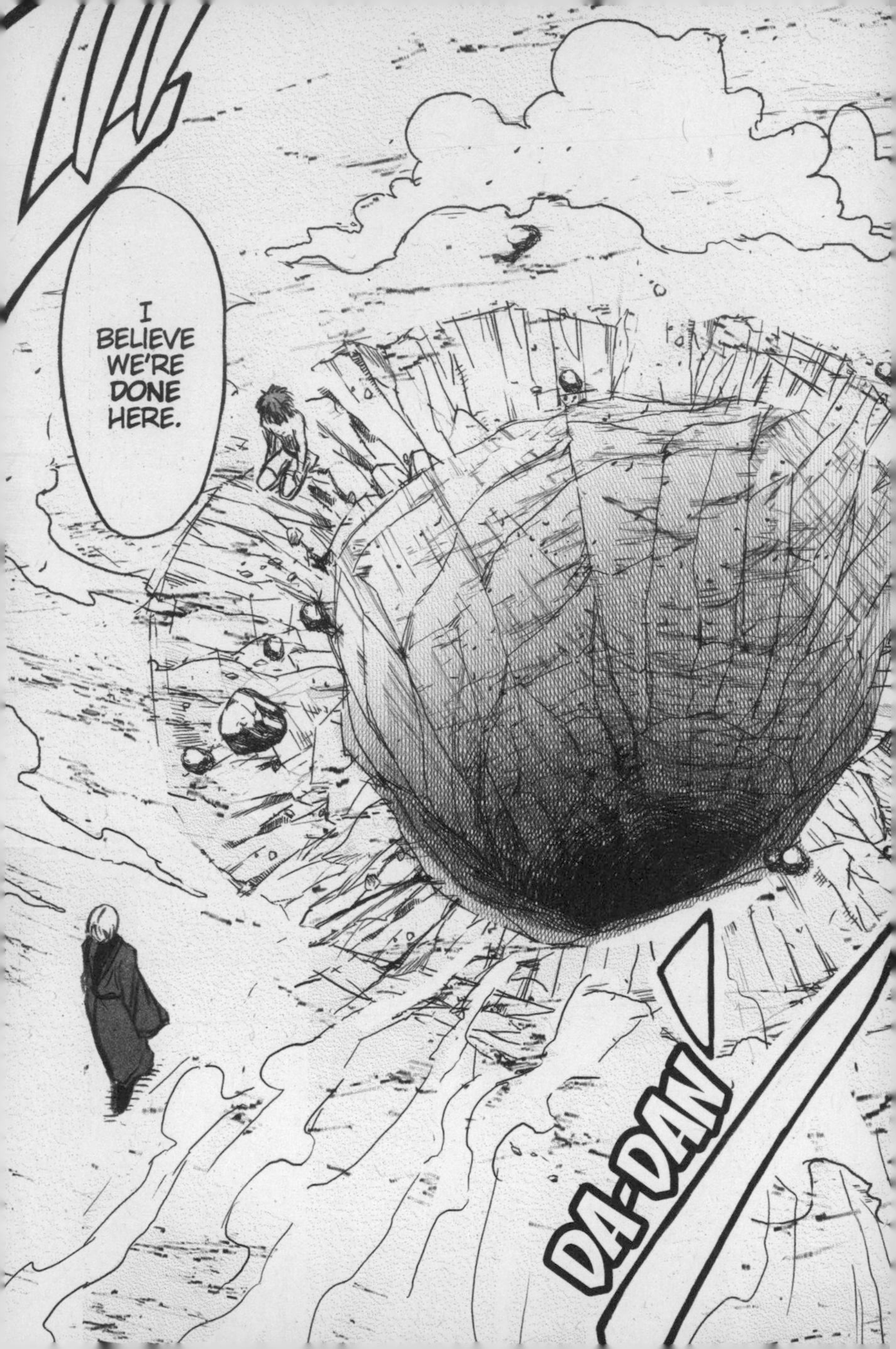
I BELIEVE WE'RE DONE HERE.
DA-DAN

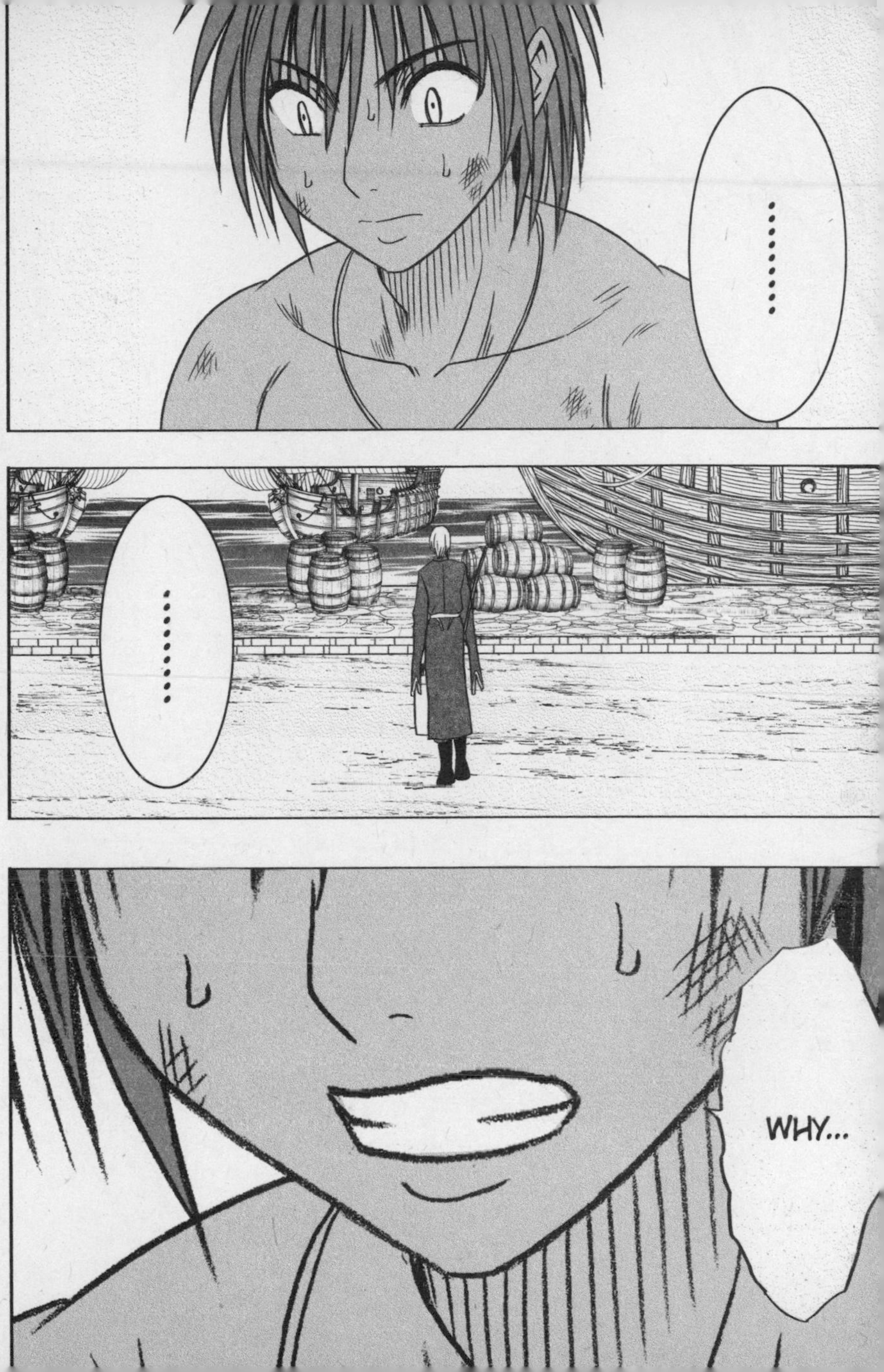
........
........
WHY...

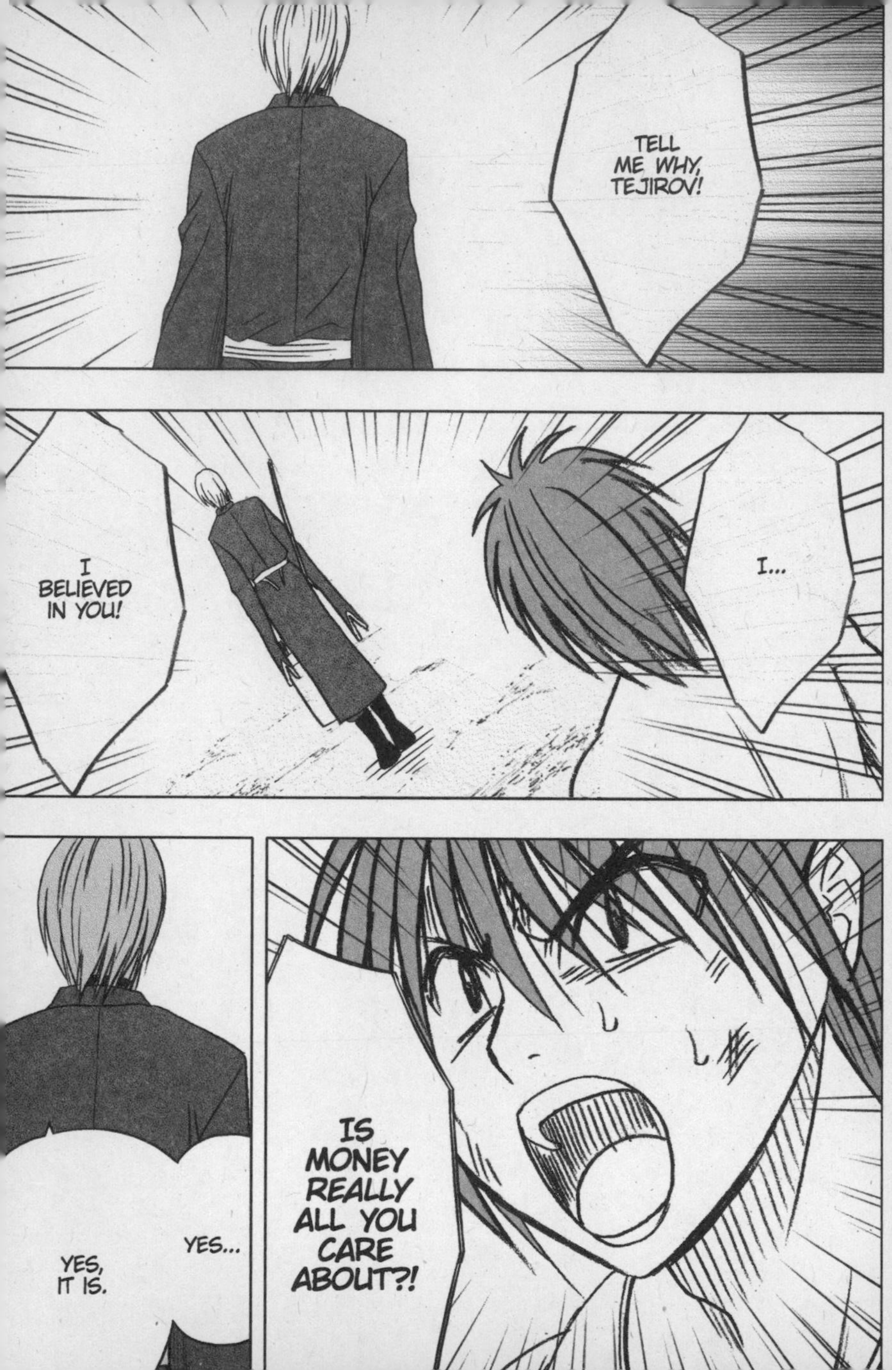
TELL ME WHY, TEJIROV!
I...
I BELIEVED IN YOU!
IS MONEY REALLY ALL YOU CARE ABOUT?!
YES...
YES, IT IS.

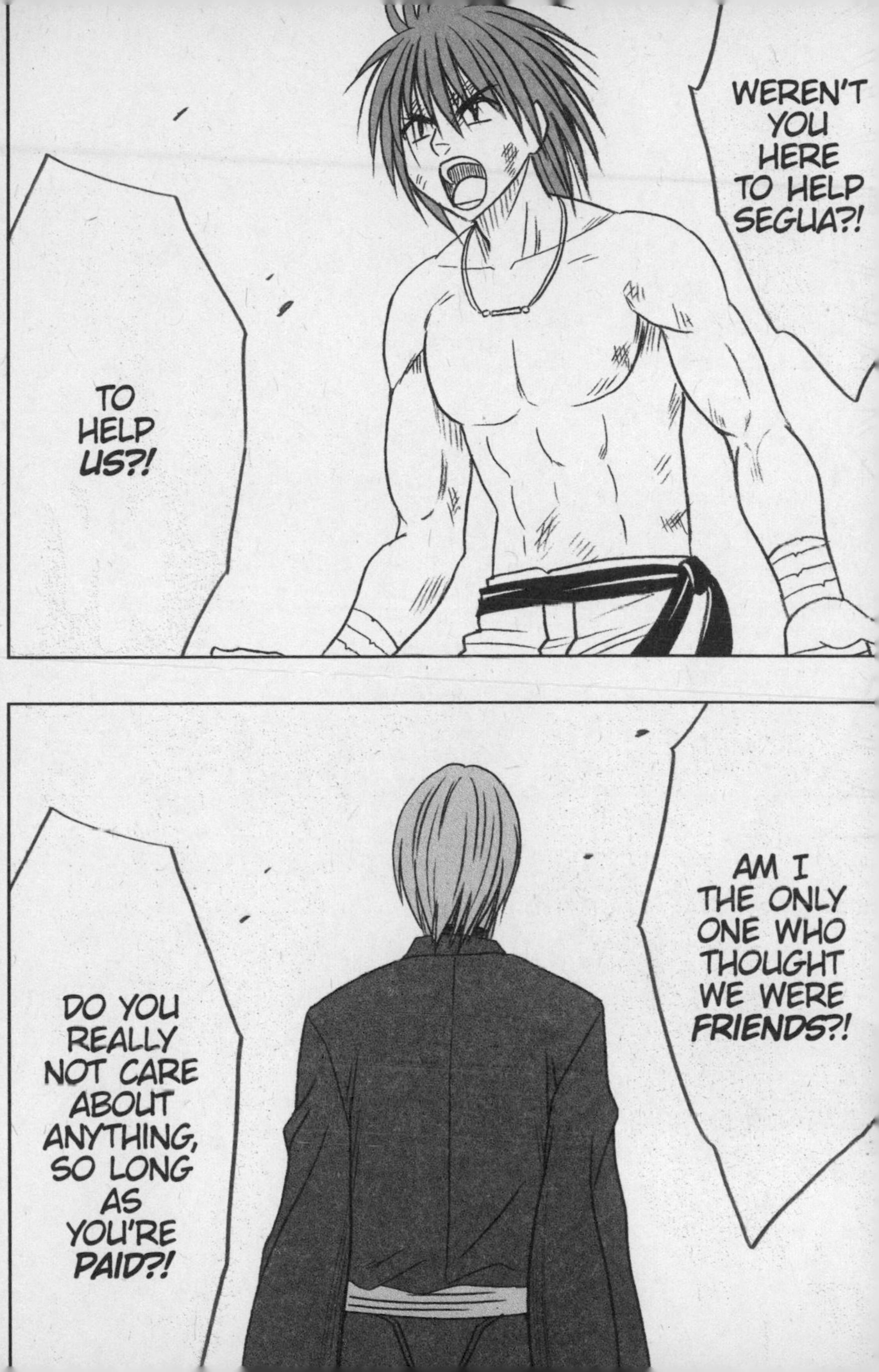
WEREN'T YOU HERE TO HELP SEGUA?!
TO HELP US?!
AM I THE ONLY ONE WHO THOUGHT WE WERE FRIENDS?!
DO YOU REALLY NOT CARE ABOUT ANYTHING, SO LONG AS YOU'RE PAID?!

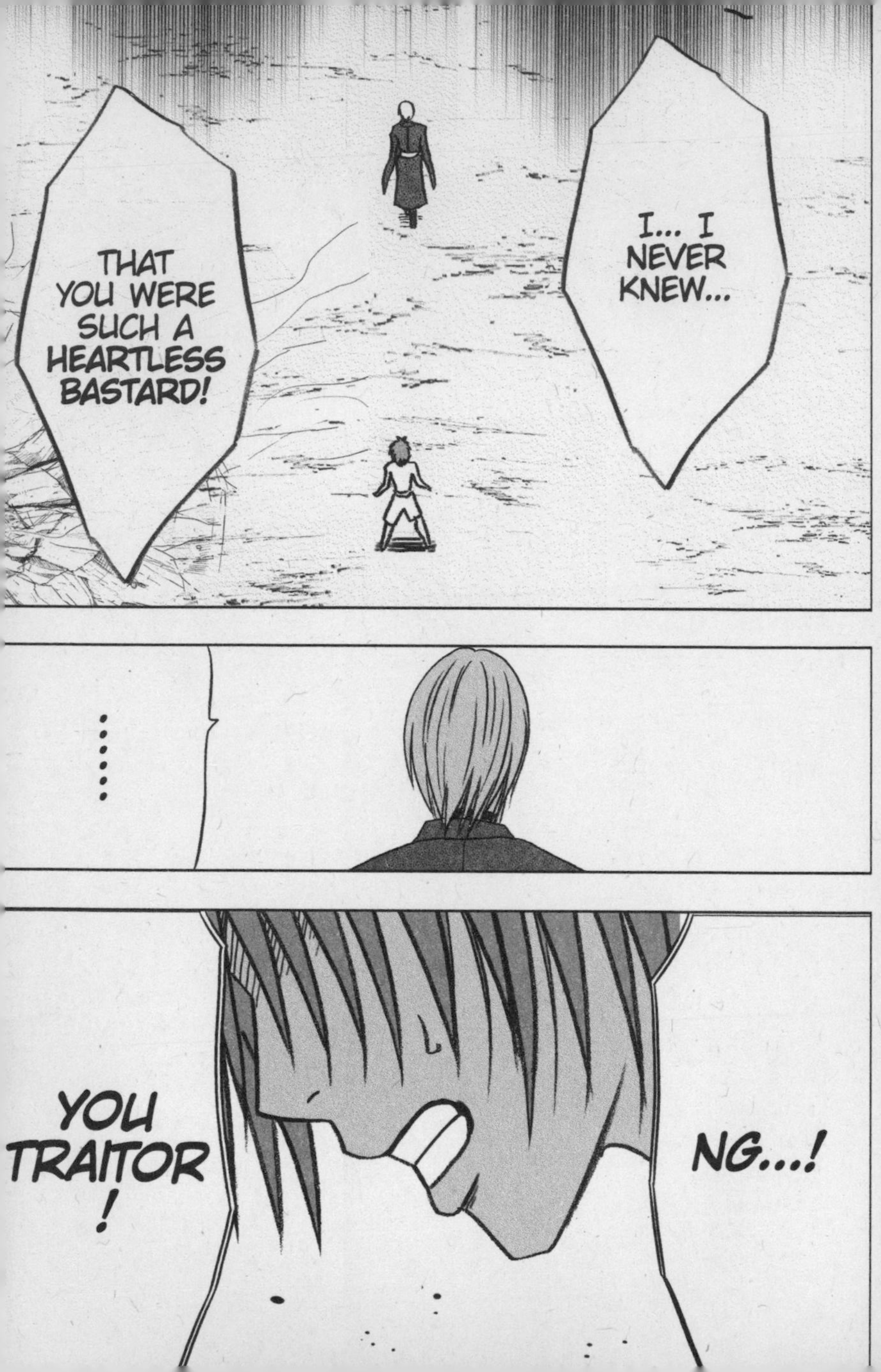
I... I NEVER KNEW...
THAT YOU WERE SUCH A HEARTLESS BASTARD!
......
NG...!
YOU TRAITOR!

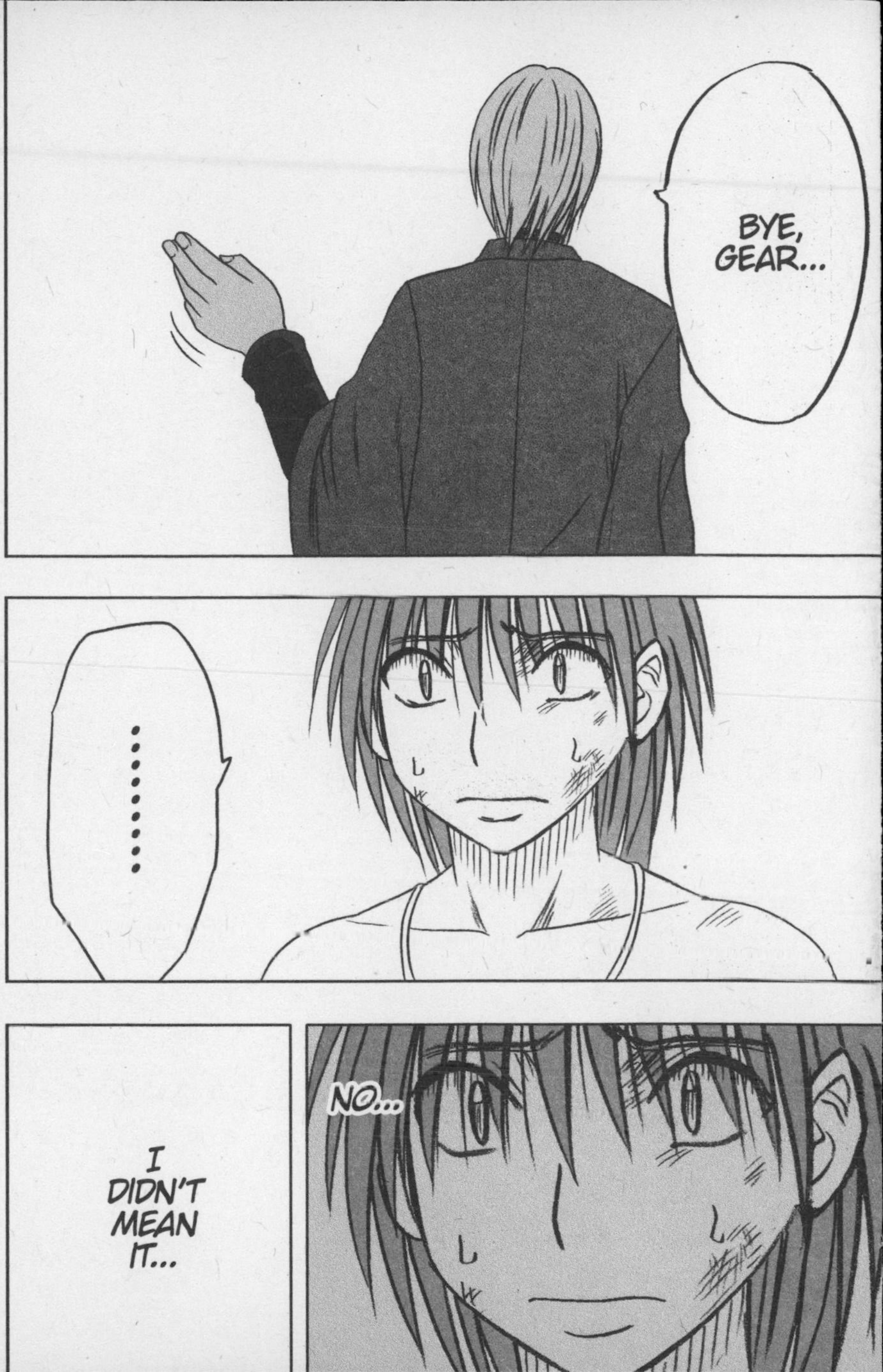
BYE, GEAR...
........
NO...
I DIDN'T MEAN IT...

THAT'S
NOT WHAT
I MEANT...

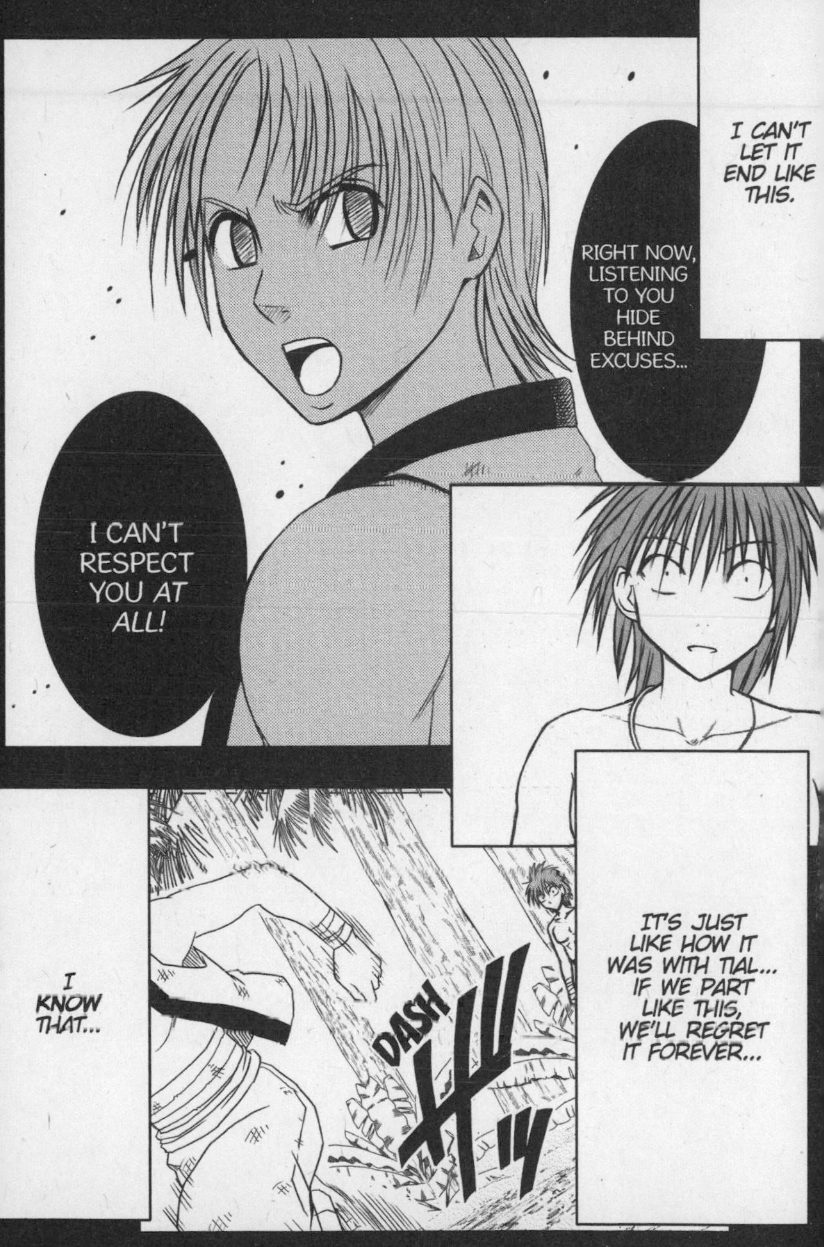
I CAN'T LET IT END LIKE THIS.
RIGHT NOW, LISTENING TO YOU HIDE BEHIND EXCUSES...
I CAN'T RESPECT YOU AT ALL!
IT'S JUST LIKE HOW IT WAS WITH TIAL... IF WE PART LIKE THIS, WE'LL REGRET IT FOREVER...
DASH
I KNOW THAT...

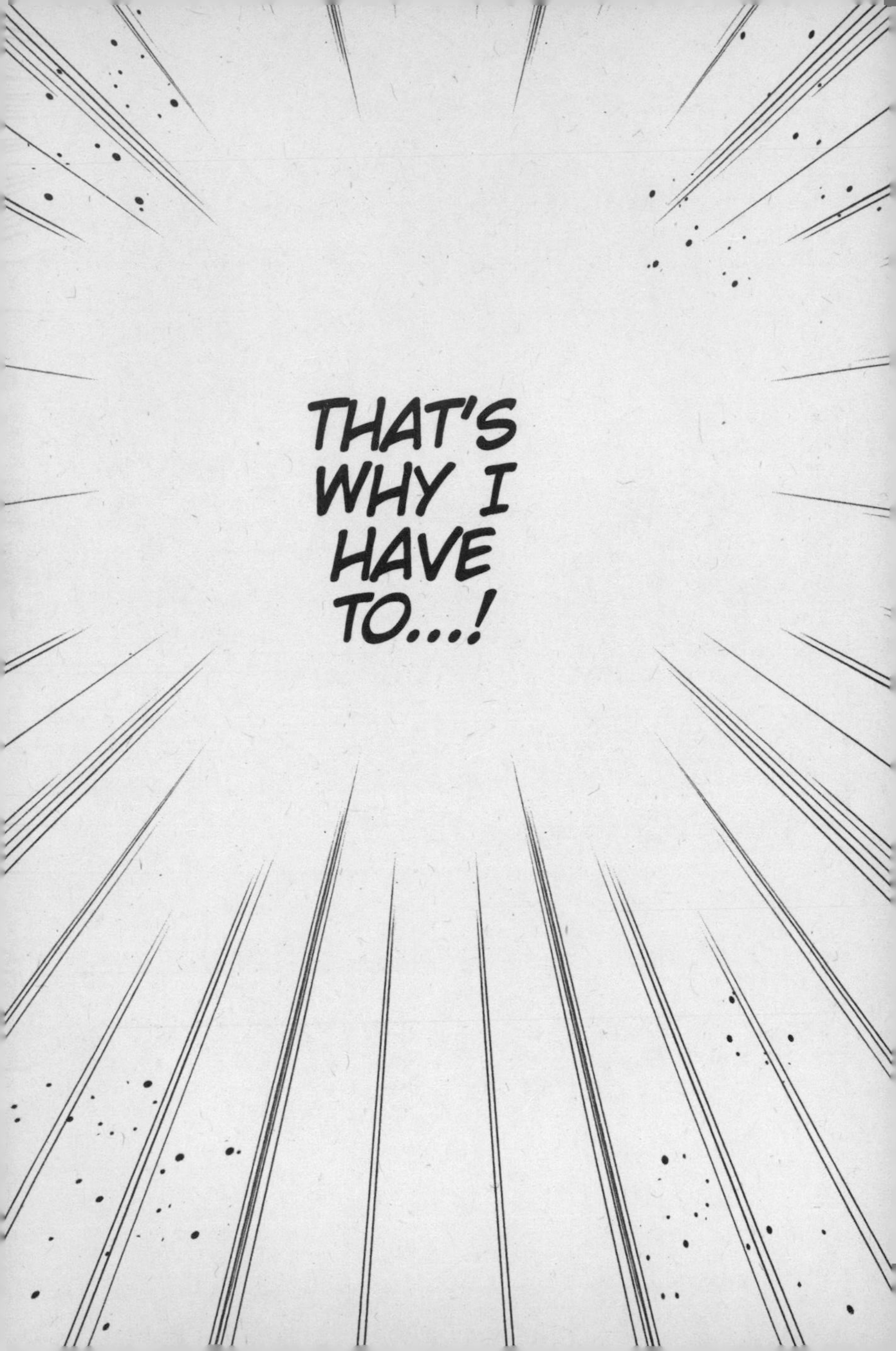
THAT'S WHY I HAVE TO...!

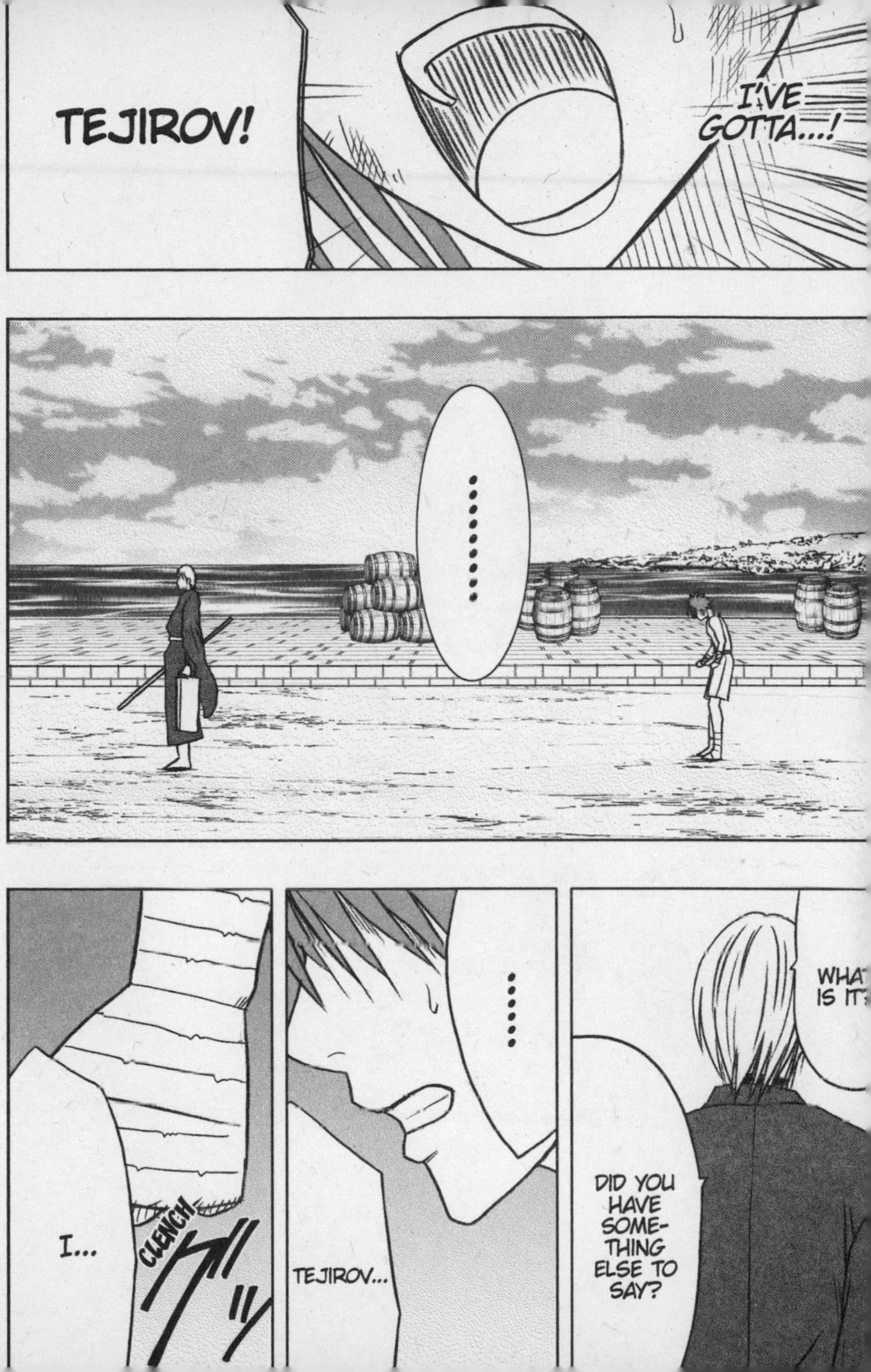
I'VE GOTTA...!
TEJIROV!
........
WHAT IS IT
DID YOU HAVE SOME-THING ELSE TO SAY?
......
TEJIROV...
CLENCH
I...

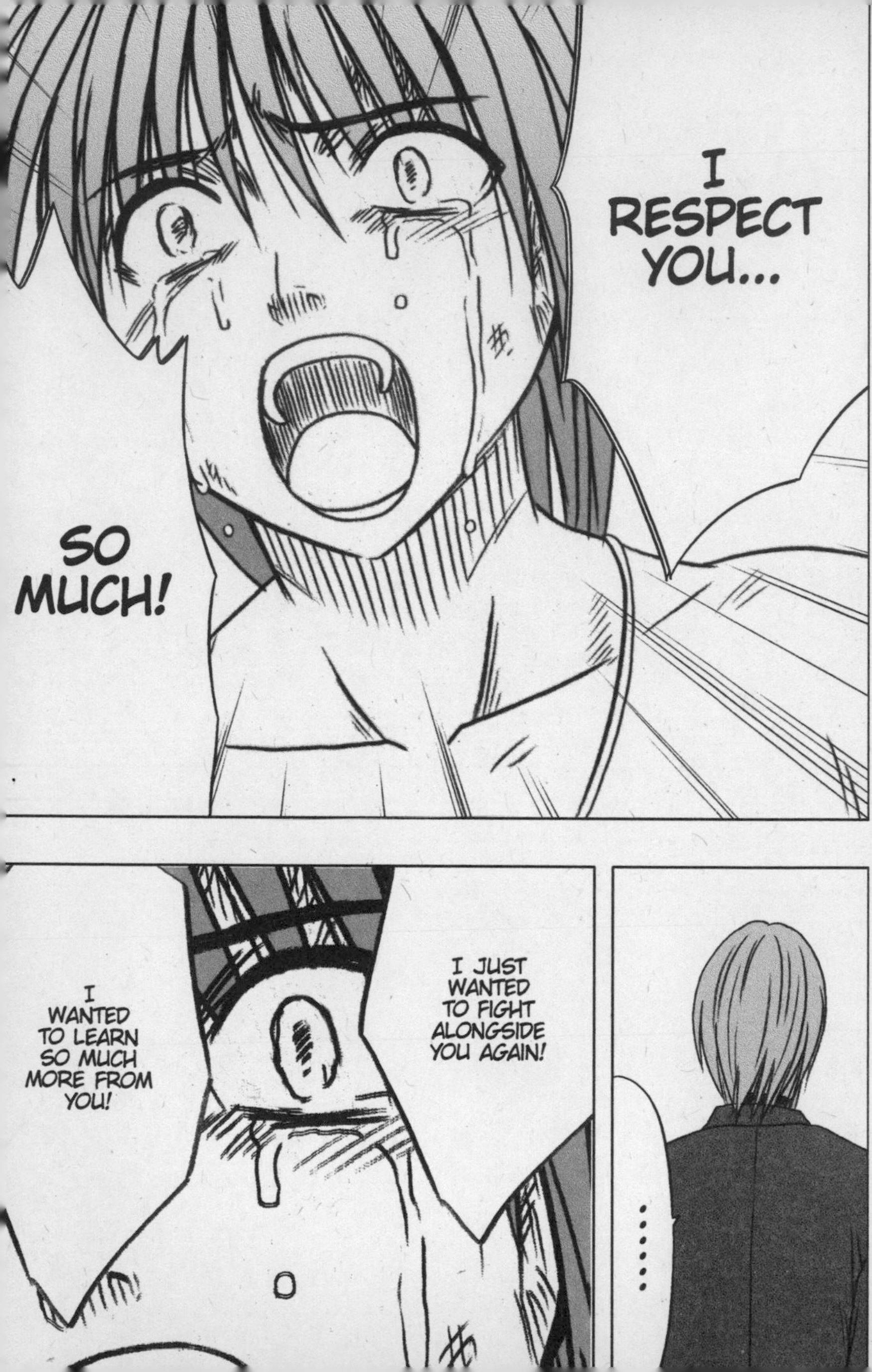
I RESPECT YOU...
SO MUCH!
......
I JUST WANTED TO FIGHT ALONGSIDE YOU AGAIN!
I WANTED TO LEARN SO MUCH MORE FROM YOU!

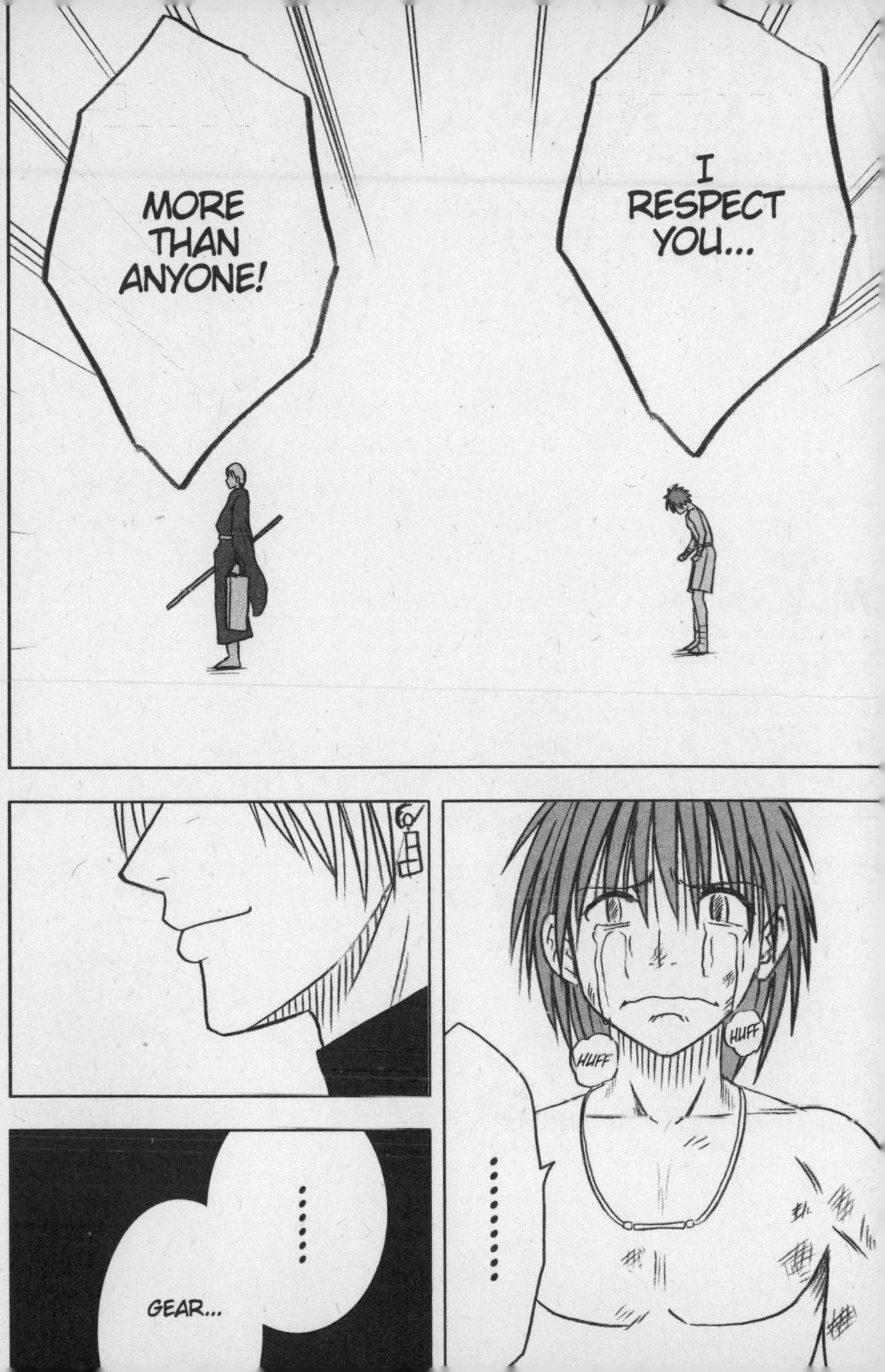
I RESPECT YOU...
MORE THAN ANYONE!
HUFF
HUFF
......
......
GEAR...

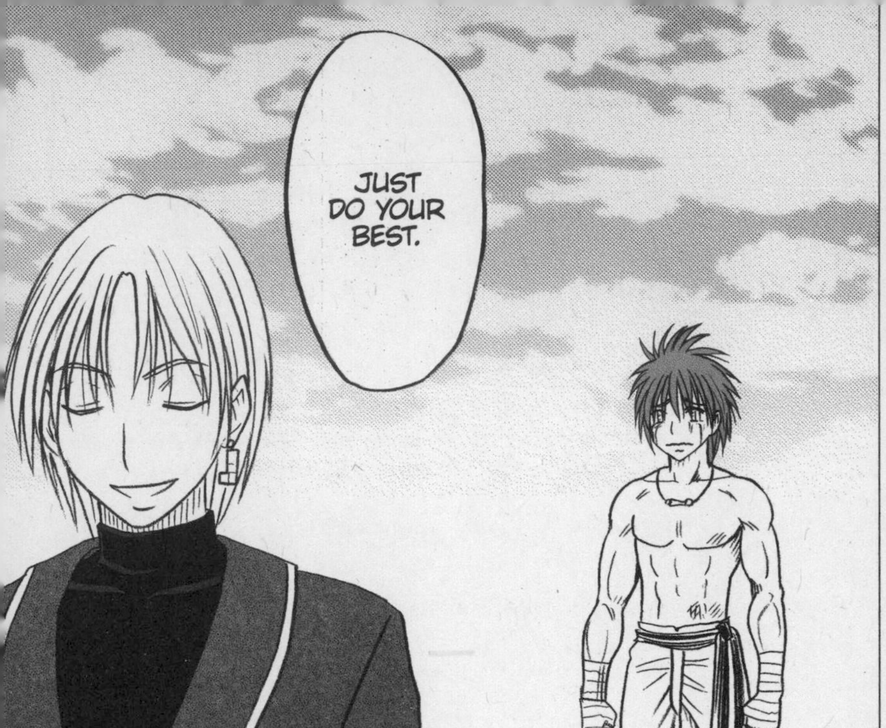
JUST DO YOUR BEST.

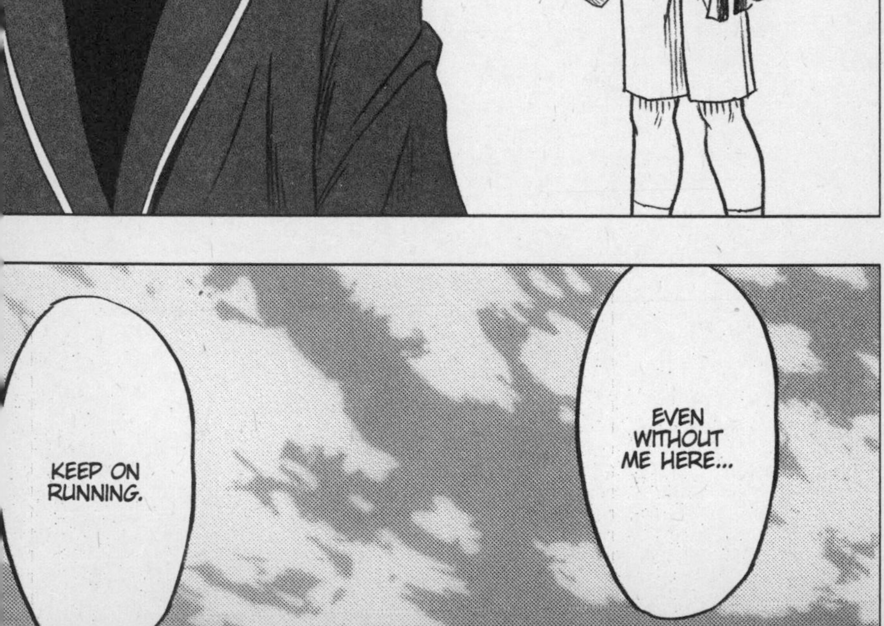
EVEN WITHOUT ME HERE...
KEEP ON RUNNING.

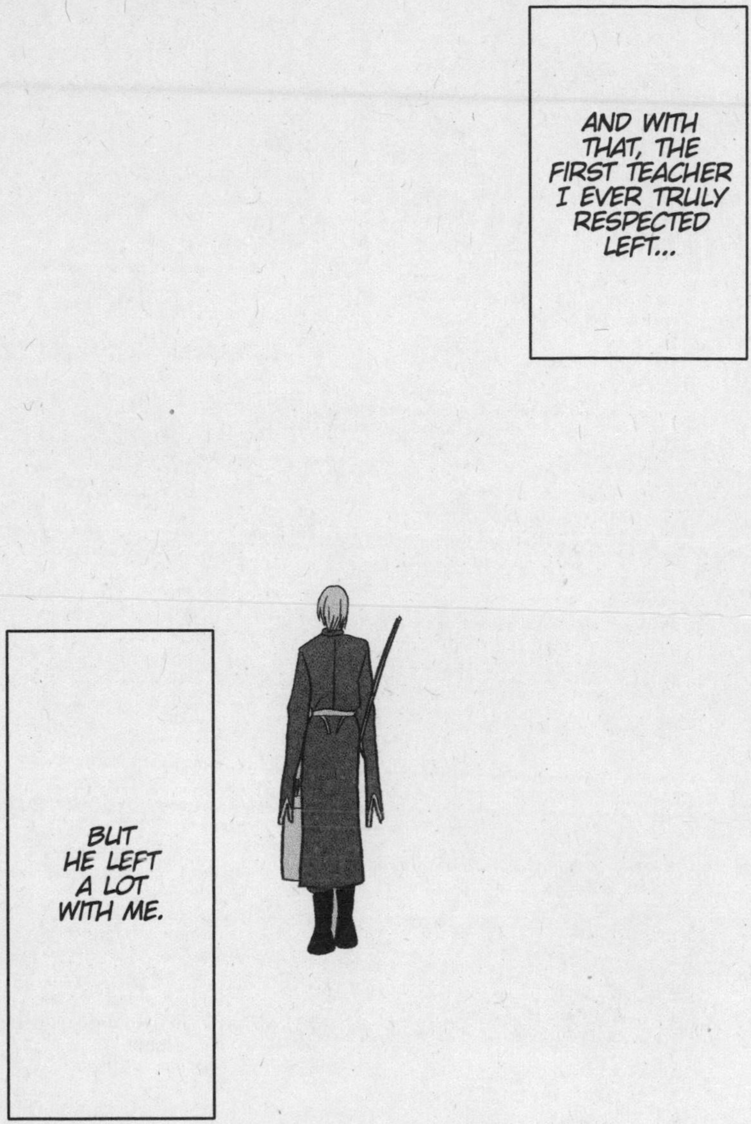
AND WITH THAT, THE FIRST TEACHER I EVER TRULY RESPECTED LEFT...
BUT HE LEFT A LOT WITH ME.

Perusing Video Game History

# ON THE EDGE OF THE BLUE WORLD

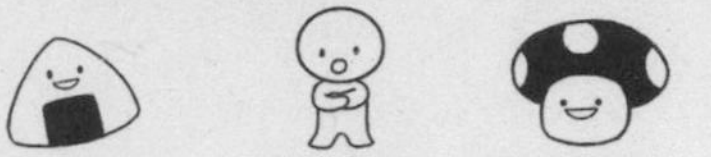

Dr. Onigiri   Mr. Why   Prof. Mushroom

Today's Topic

## TETRIS

**Mr. Why:** It's finally here, our introduction to *Tetris*! It's been a long time coming!

**Prof. Mushroom:** Well, it's a national puzzle game, after all. It started off as a dropping block puzzle game, but, to this day, it's been said that no other game has ever surpassed it.

**Dr. Onigiri:** But, you know, this game wasn't actually made in Japan.

**Mr. Why:** What? Really?

**Prof. Mushroom:** Really. It started off in a cold country far north of Japan, the Soviet Union (which is now Russia).

**Dr. Onigiri:** The creator was a computer engineer by the name of Alexey Pajitnov. He took the idea from pentaminoes (geometric shapes made up of five equal squares joined edge to edge) and designed the program as a learning tool. Foreign game makers saw the software, licensed it and sold it as a game.

**Mr. Why:** Oh! He must have made a killing off it!

**Prof. Mushroom:** Actually, he didn't make much at all.

**Dr. Onigiri:** At the time, the Soviet Union had a socialist economic system.

**Mr. Why:** Oh. I think I may have learned something like that in Social Studies. People who hardly worked at all got paid the same as those who did work hard. Communism or something like that. It was the reason the Soviet Union broke up, wasn't it?

**Prof. Mushroom:** Well, the reasons are far more complex and detailed than that and would lead us off the topic of games, so for our purposes, that's okay. Right now, Russia is capitalist, but we can't really say that the change came around due to *Tetris*.

To be continued...

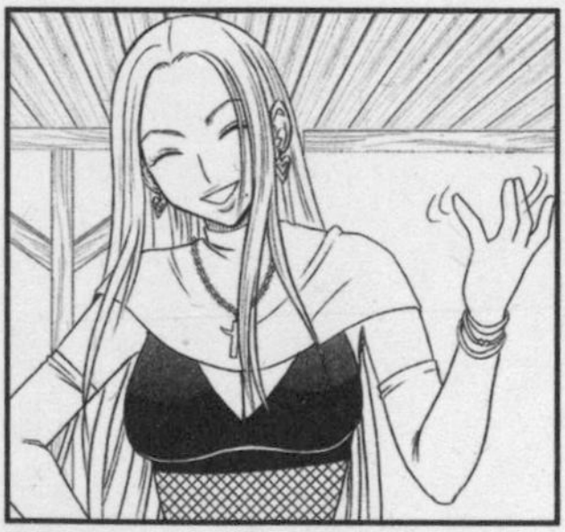

**The person who understood Tejirov and became his teacher, Pentnova. Upon her death, the ultimate mercenary, Tejirov, was born.**

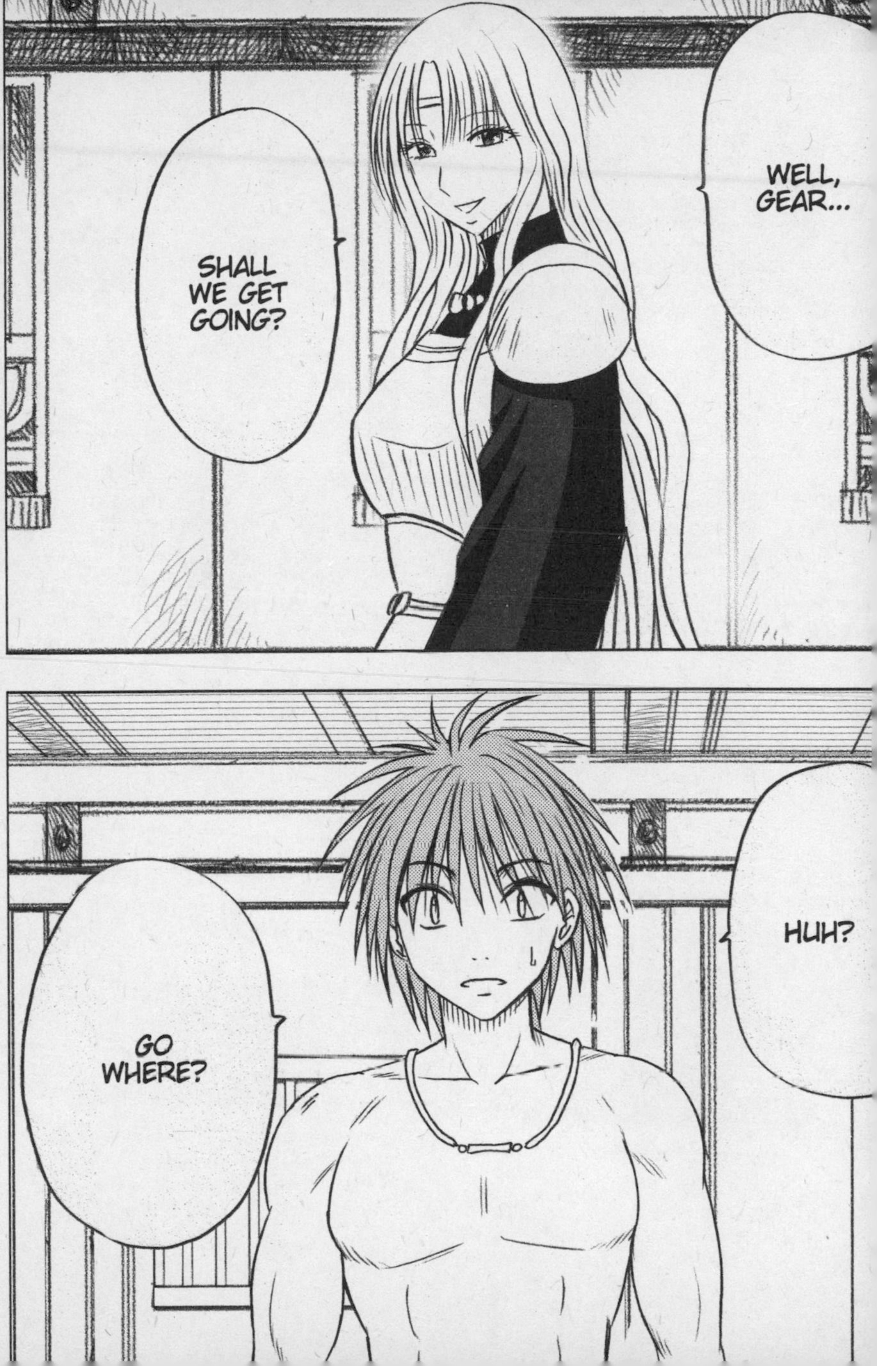
WELL, GEAR...
SHALL WE GET GOING?
HUH?
GO WHERE?

Part 2

CHAPTER 15

# ACTION

DISC 1

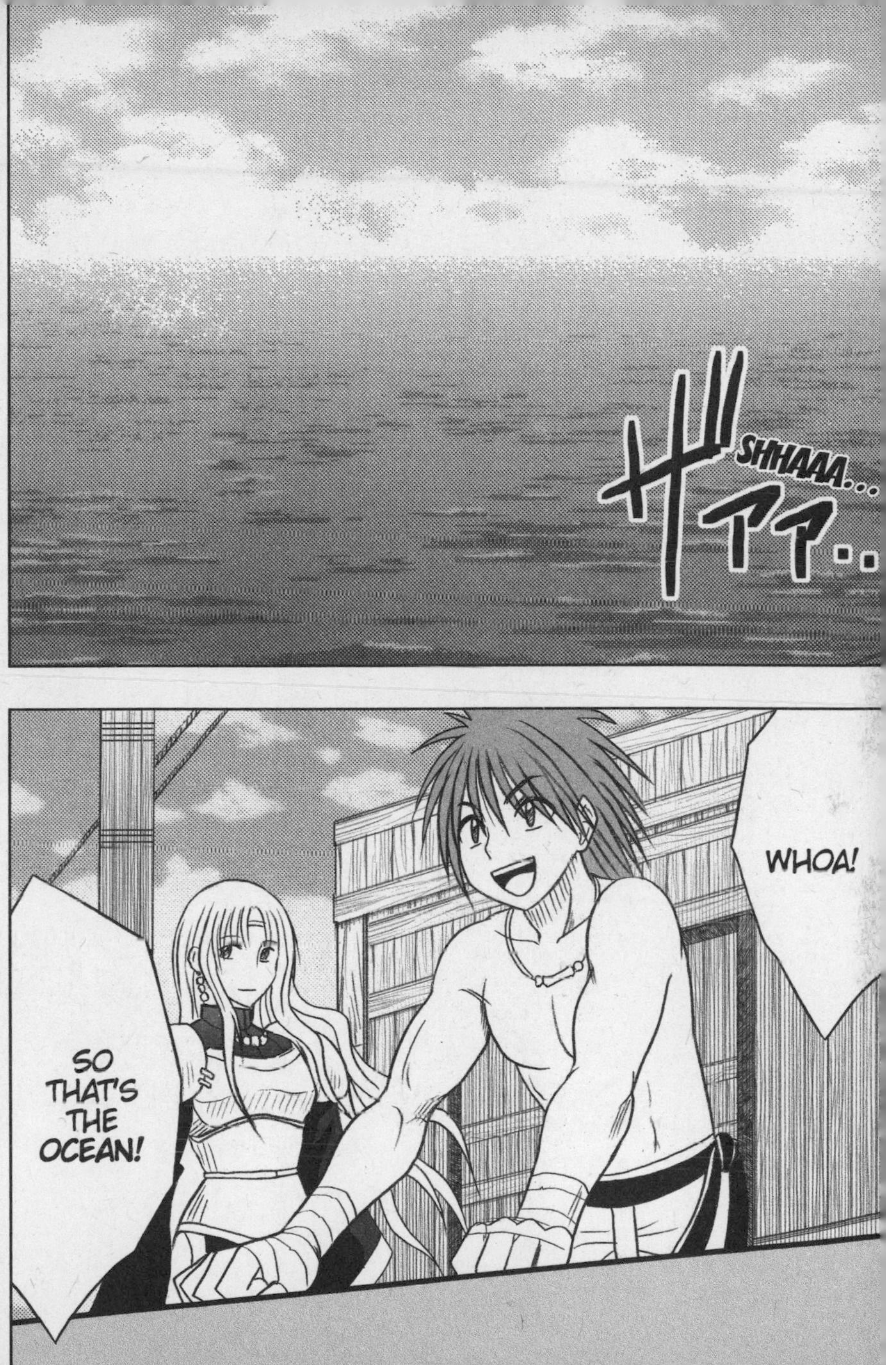
ザァァ..
SHHAAA...
WHOA!
SO THAT'S THE OCEAN!

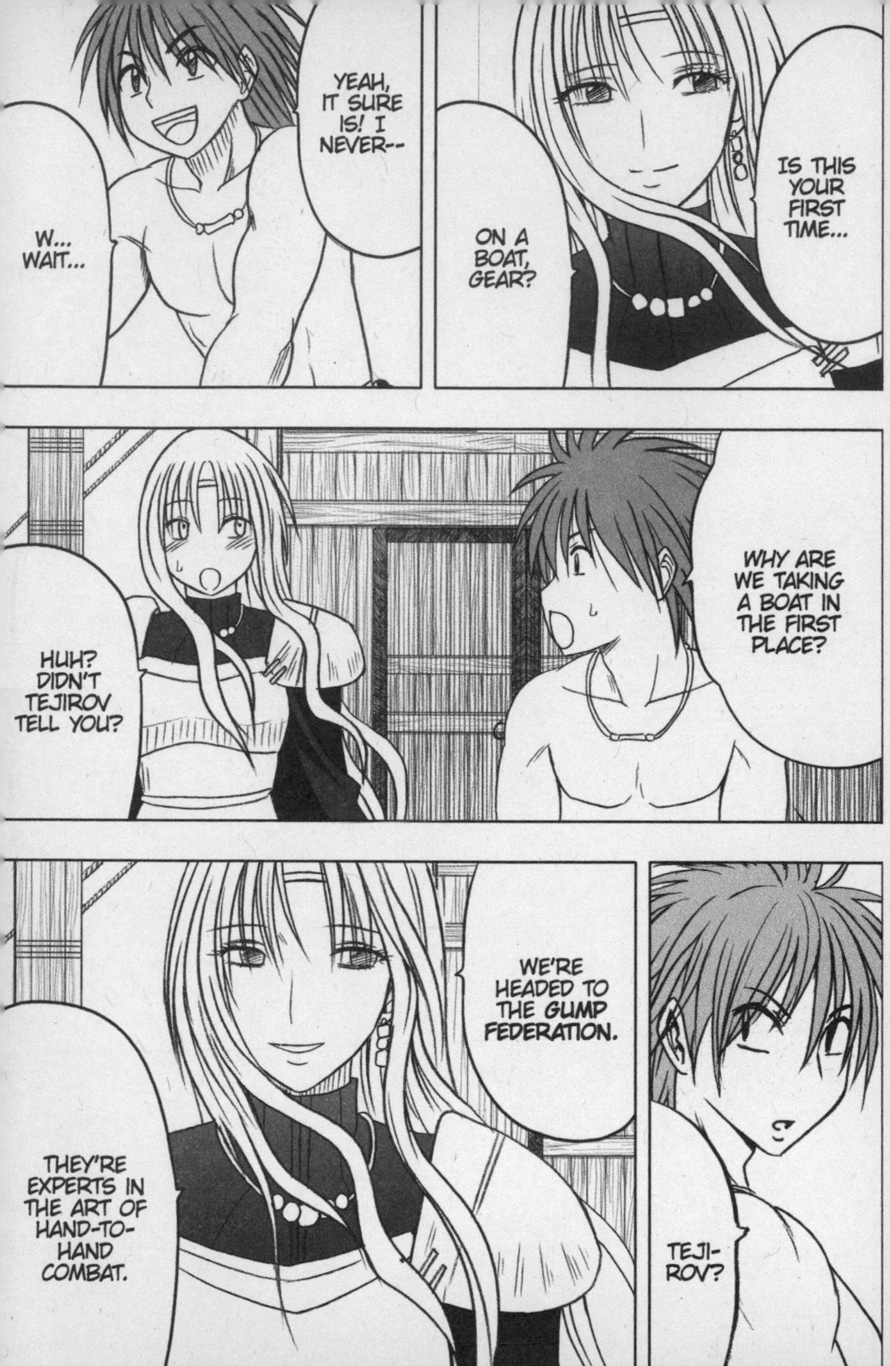
IS THIS YOUR FIRST TIME...
ON A BOAT, GEAR?
YEAH, IT SURE IS! I NEVER--
W... WAIT...
WHY ARE WE TAKING A BOAT IN THE FIRST PLACE?
HUH? DIDN'T TEJIROV TELL YOU?
TEJI-ROV?
WE'RE HEADED TO THE GUMP FEDERATION.
THEY'RE EXPERTS IN THE ART OF HAND-TO-HAND COMBAT.

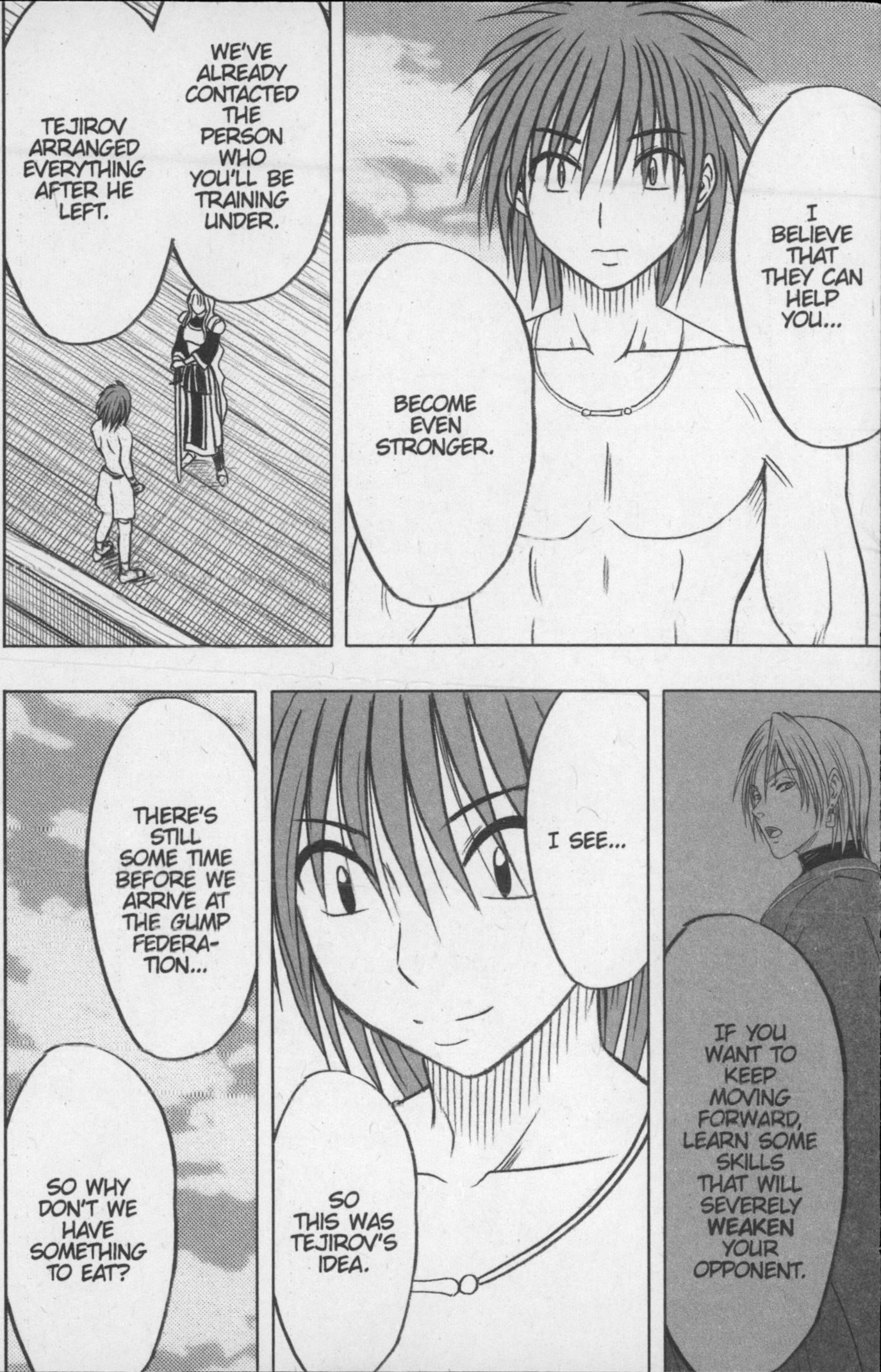
I BELIEVE THAT THEY CAN HELP YOU...
BECOME EVEN STRONGER.
WE'VE ALREADY CONTACTED THE PERSON WHO YOU'LL BE TRAINING UNDER.
TEJIROV ARRANGED EVERYTHING AFTER HE LEFT.
IF YOU WANT TO KEEP MOVING FORWARD, LEARN SOME SKILLS THAT WILL SEVERELY WEAKEN YOUR OPPONENT.
I SEE...
SO THIS WAS TEJIROV'S IDEA.
THERE'S STILL SOME TIME BEFORE WE ARRIVE AT THE GUMP FEDERA-TION...
SO WHY DON'T WE HAVE SOMETHING TO EAT?

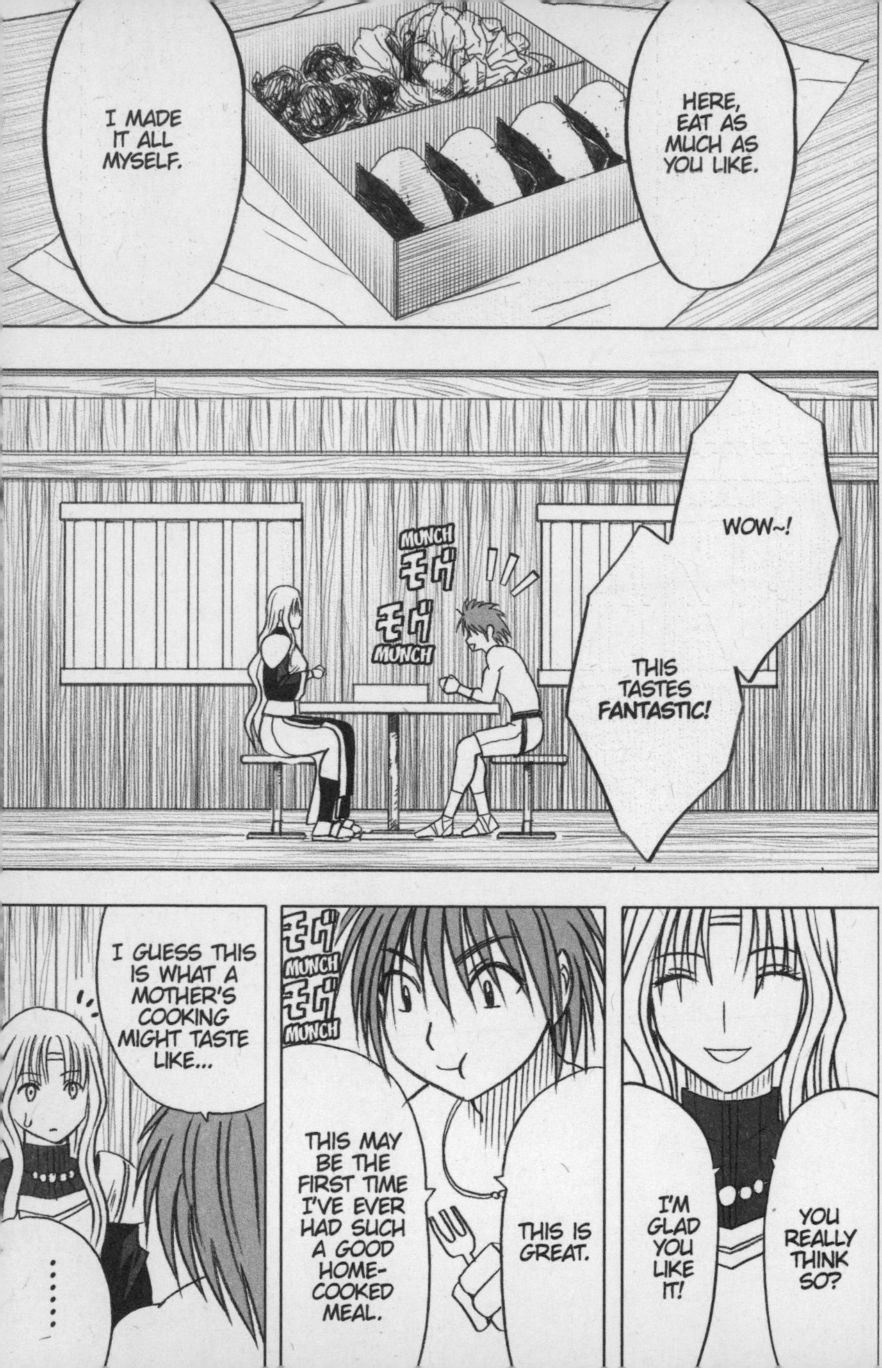
HERE, EAT AS MUCH AS YOU LIKE.
I MADE IT ALL MYSELF.
WOW~!
THIS TASTES FANTASTIC!
MUNCH
モグ
モグ
MUNCH
YOU REALLY THINK SO?
I'M GLAD YOU LIKE IT!
THIS IS GREAT.
THIS MAY BE THE FIRST TIME I'VE EVER HAD SUCH A GOOD HOME-COOKED MEAL.
モグ
MUNCH
モグ
MUNCH
I GUESS THIS IS WHAT A MOTHER'S COOKING MIGHT TASTE LIKE...
......

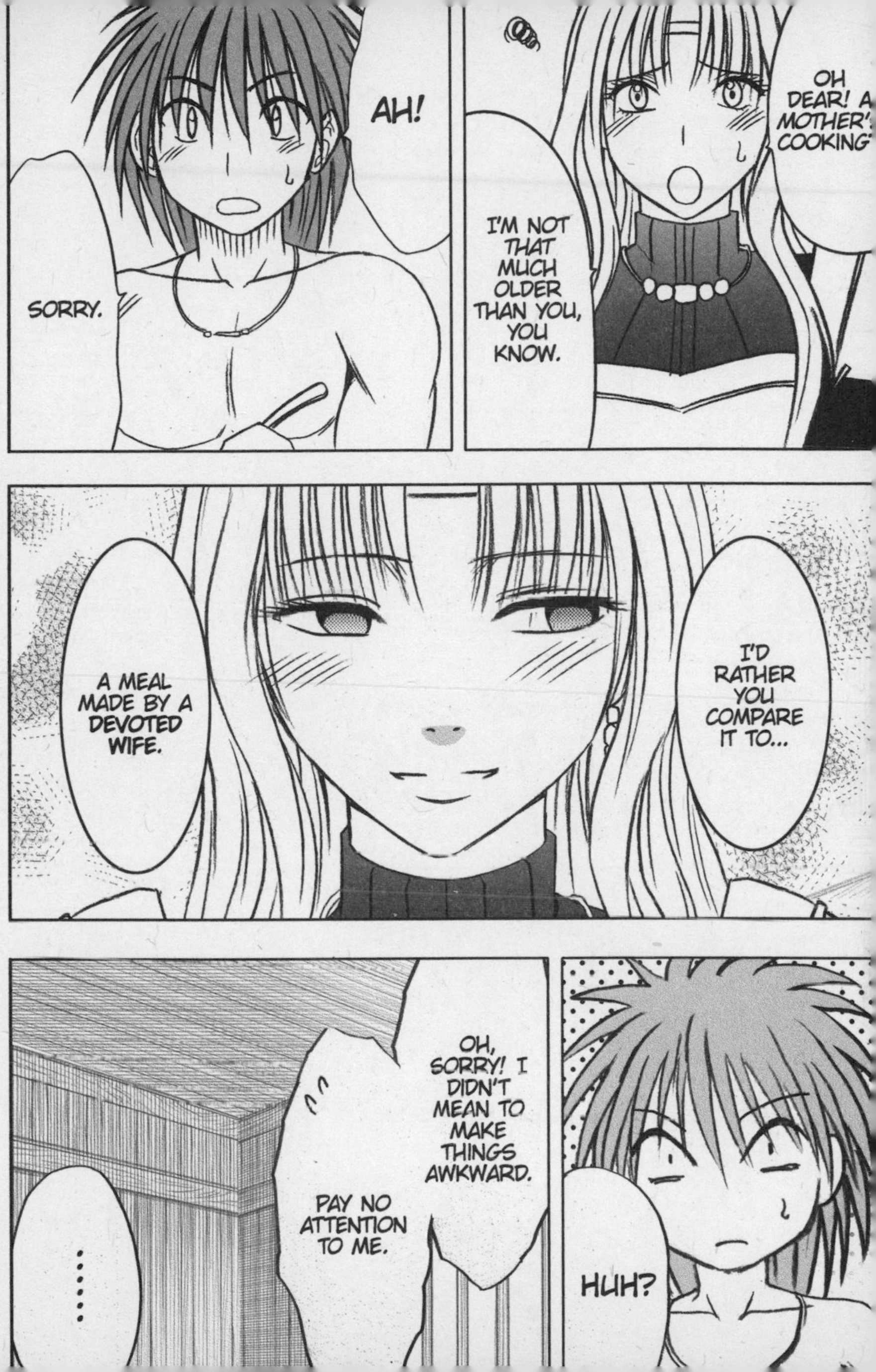

OH DEAR! A MOTHER'S COOKING?
I'M NOT THAT MUCH OLDER THAN YOU, YOU KNOW.
AH!
SORRY.
I'D RATHER YOU COMPARE IT TO...
A MEAL MADE BY A DEVOTED WIFE.
HUH?
OH, SORRY! I DIDN'T MEAN TO MAKE THINGS AWKWARD.
PAY NO ATTENTION TO ME.
......

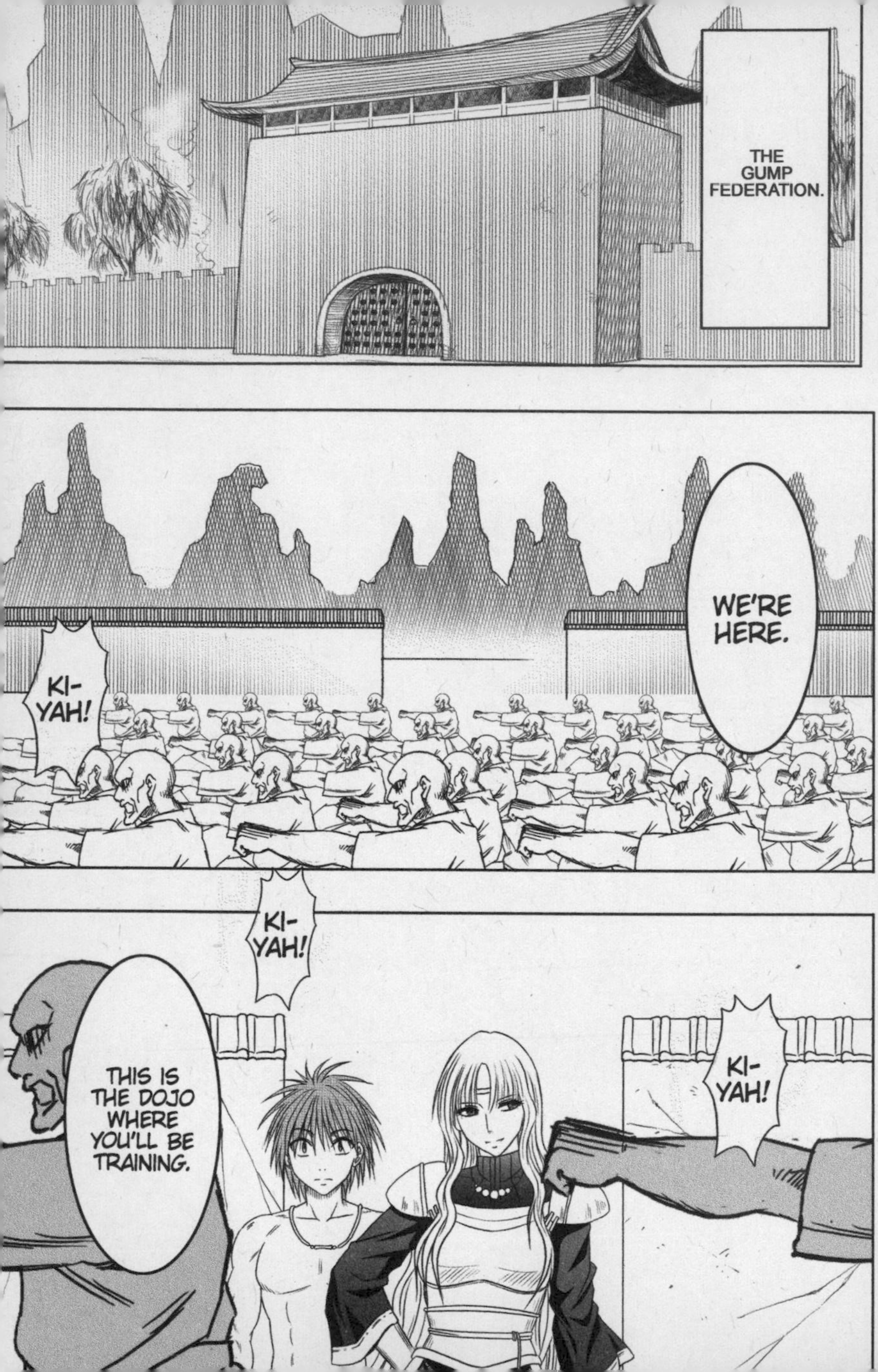
THE GUMP FEDERATION.
WE'RE HERE.
KI-YAH!
KI-YAH!
KI-YAH!
THIS IS THE DOJO WHERE YOU'LL BE TRAINING.

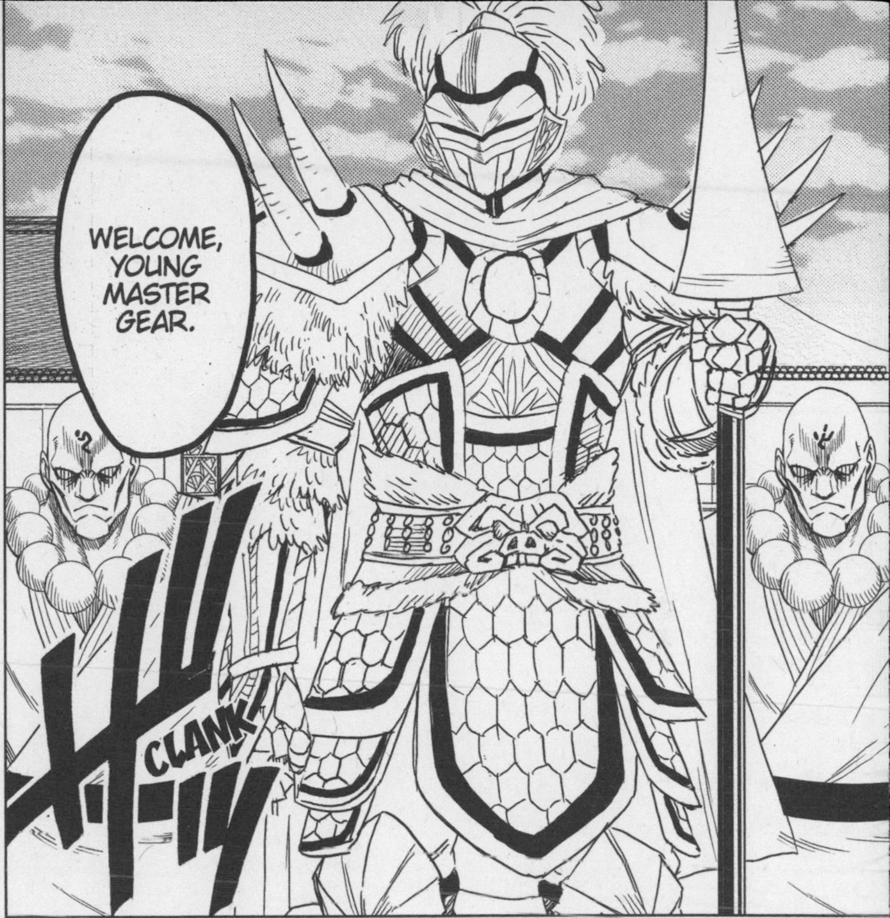
WELCOME, YOUNG MASTER GEAR.
CLANK
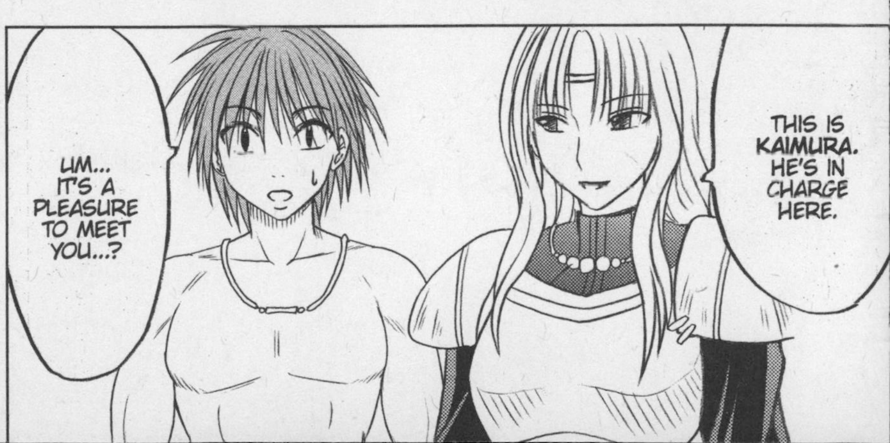
THIS IS KAIMURA. HE'S IN CHARGE HERE.
UM... IT'S A PLEASURE TO MEET YOU...?

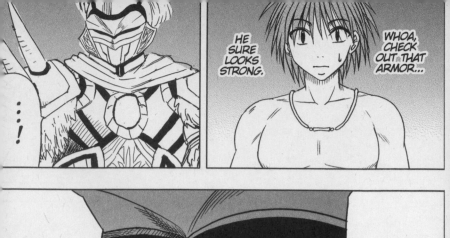

WHOA, CHECK OUT THAT ARMOR...
HE SURE LOOKS STRONG.
...!
HMM...
GEAR...
...?
YOUR CLOTHING...
HUH?
IS THERE SOMETHING WRONG WITH THEM?

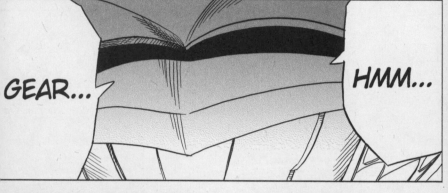

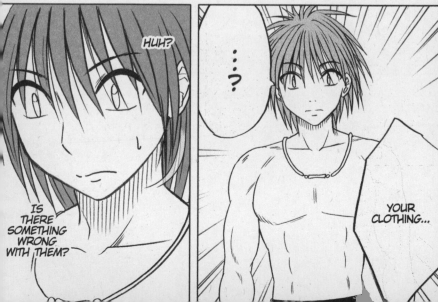

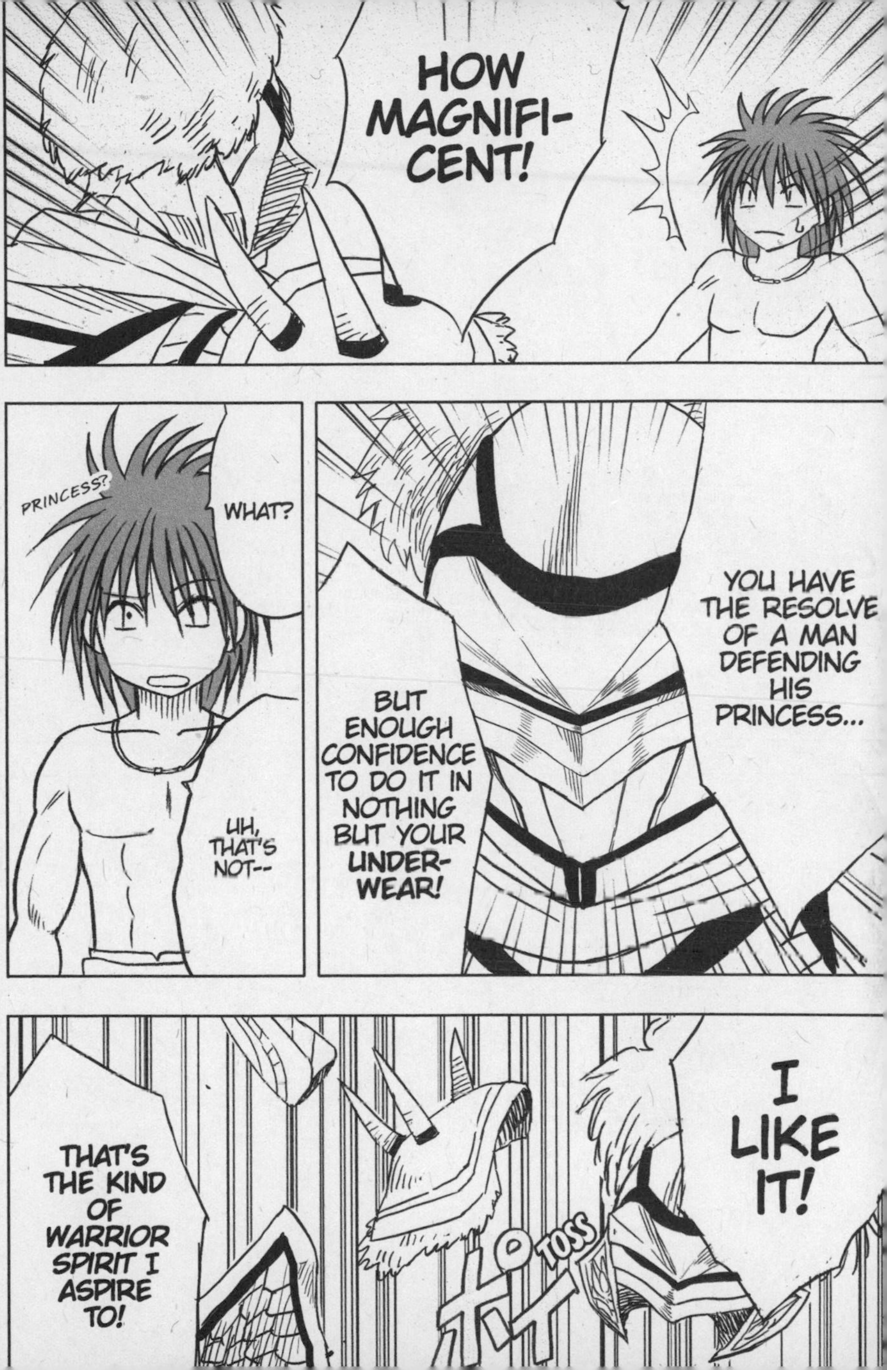
HOW MAGNIFI-CENT!
YOU HAVE THE RESOLVE OF A MAN DEFENDING HIS PRINCESS...
BUT ENOUGH CONFIDENCE TO DO IT IN NOTHING BUT YOUR UNDER-WEAR!
WHAT?
PRINCESS?
UH, THAT'S NOT--
I LIKE IT!
THAT'S THE KIND OF WARRIOR SPIRIT I ASPIRE TO!
TOSS

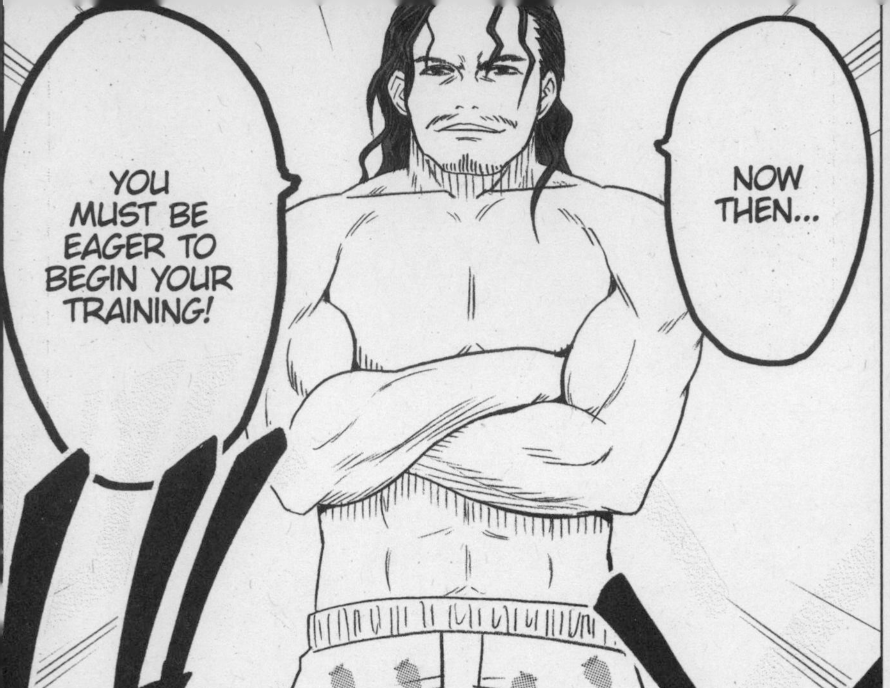
NOW THEN...
YOU MUST BE EAGER TO BEGIN YOUR TRAINING!
DA-DAH

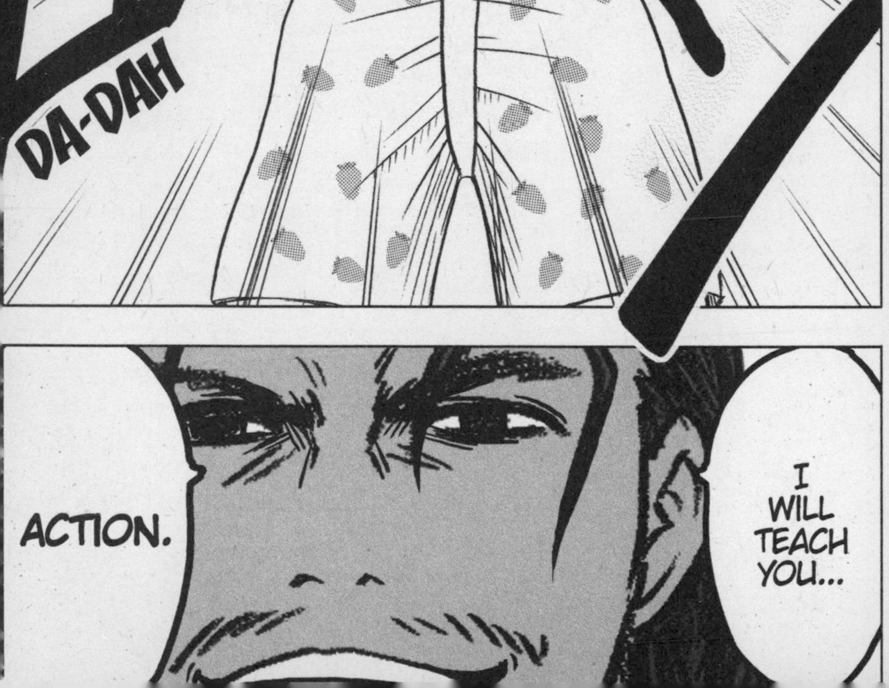
I WILL TEACH YOU...
ACTION.

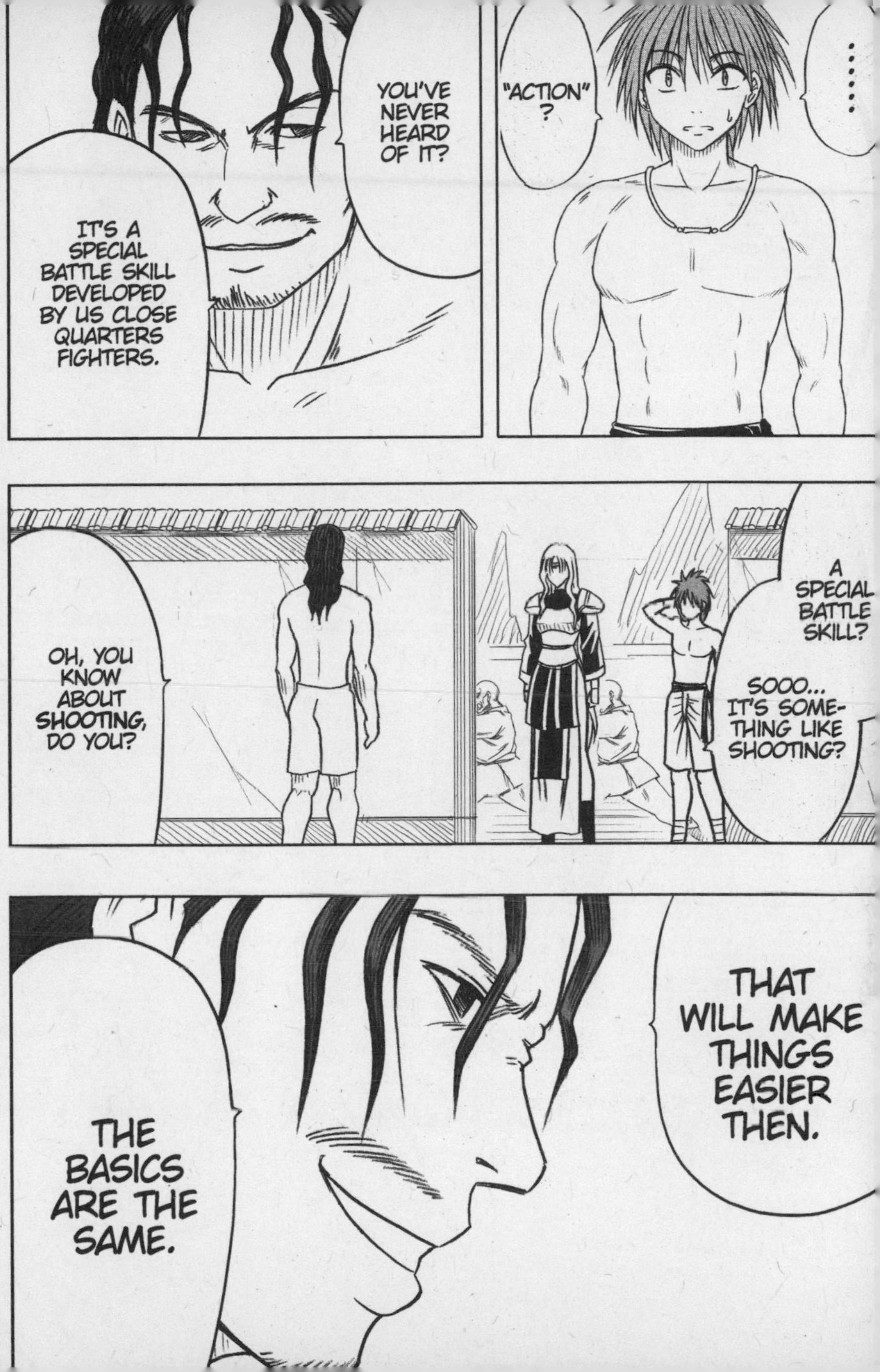
......
"ACTION"?
YOU'VE NEVER HEARD OF IT?
IT'S A SPECIAL BATTLE SKILL DEVELOPED BY US CLOSE QUARTERS FIGHTERS.
A SPECIAL BATTLE SKILL?
SOOO... IT'S SOME-THING LIKE SHOOTING?
OH, YOU KNOW ABOUT SHOOTING, DO YOU?
THAT WILL MAKE THINGS EASIER THEN.
THE BASICS ARE THE SAME.

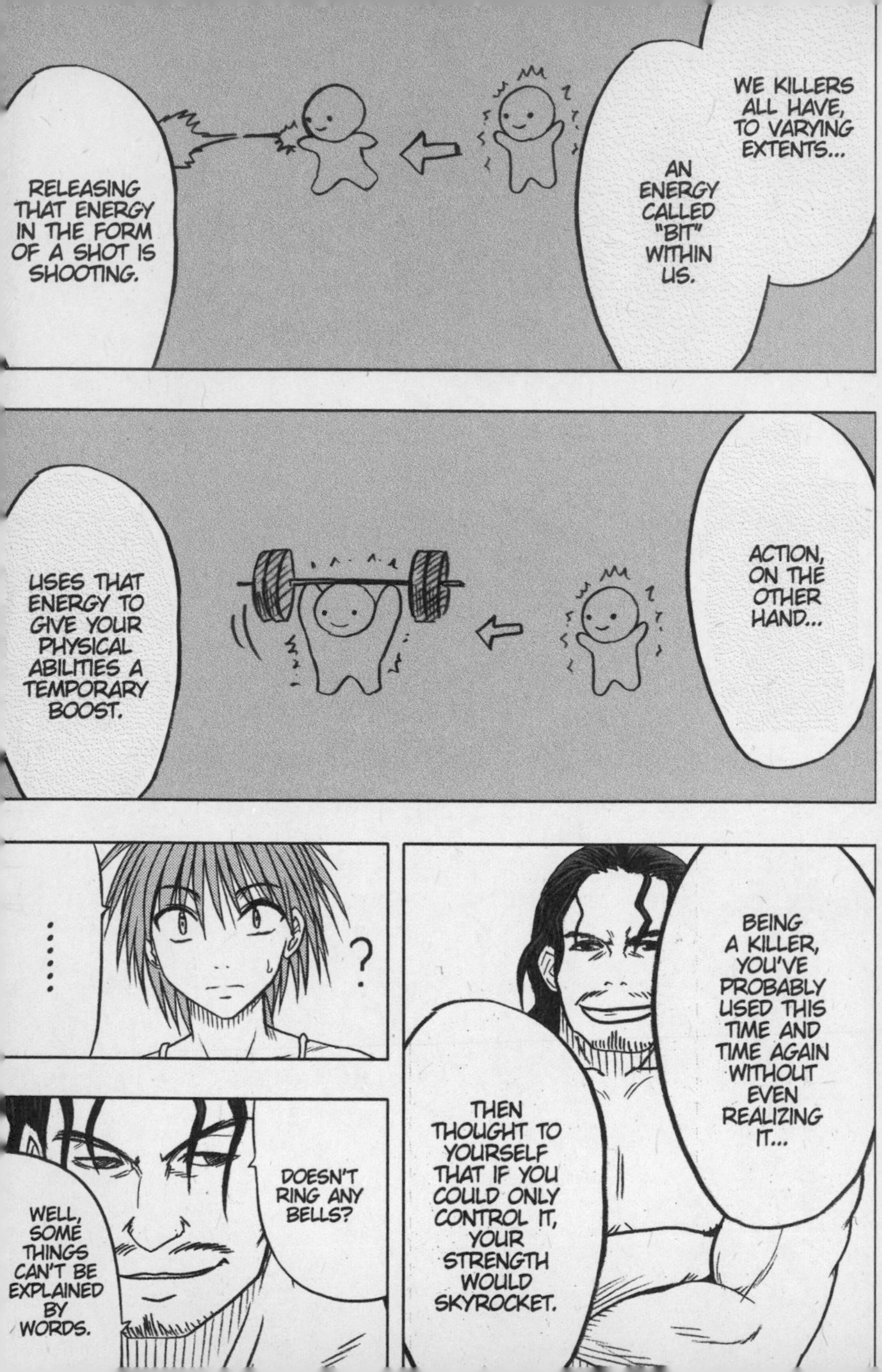
WE KILLERS ALL HAVE, TO VARYING EXTENTS...
AN ENERGY CALLED "BIT" WITHIN US.
RELEASING THAT ENERGY IN THE FORM OF A SHOT IS SHOOTING.
ACTION, ON THE OTHER HAND...
USES THAT ENERGY TO GIVE YOUR PHYSICAL ABILITIES A TEMPORARY BOOST.
BEING A KILLER, YOU'VE PROBABLY USED THIS TIME AND TIME AGAIN WITHOUT EVEN REALIZING IT...
THEN THOUGHT TO YOURSELF THAT IF YOU COULD ONLY CONTROL IT, YOUR STRENGTH WOULD SKYROCKET.
......
?
DOESN'T RING ANY BELLS?
WELL, SOME THINGS CAN'T BE EXPLAINED BY WORDS.

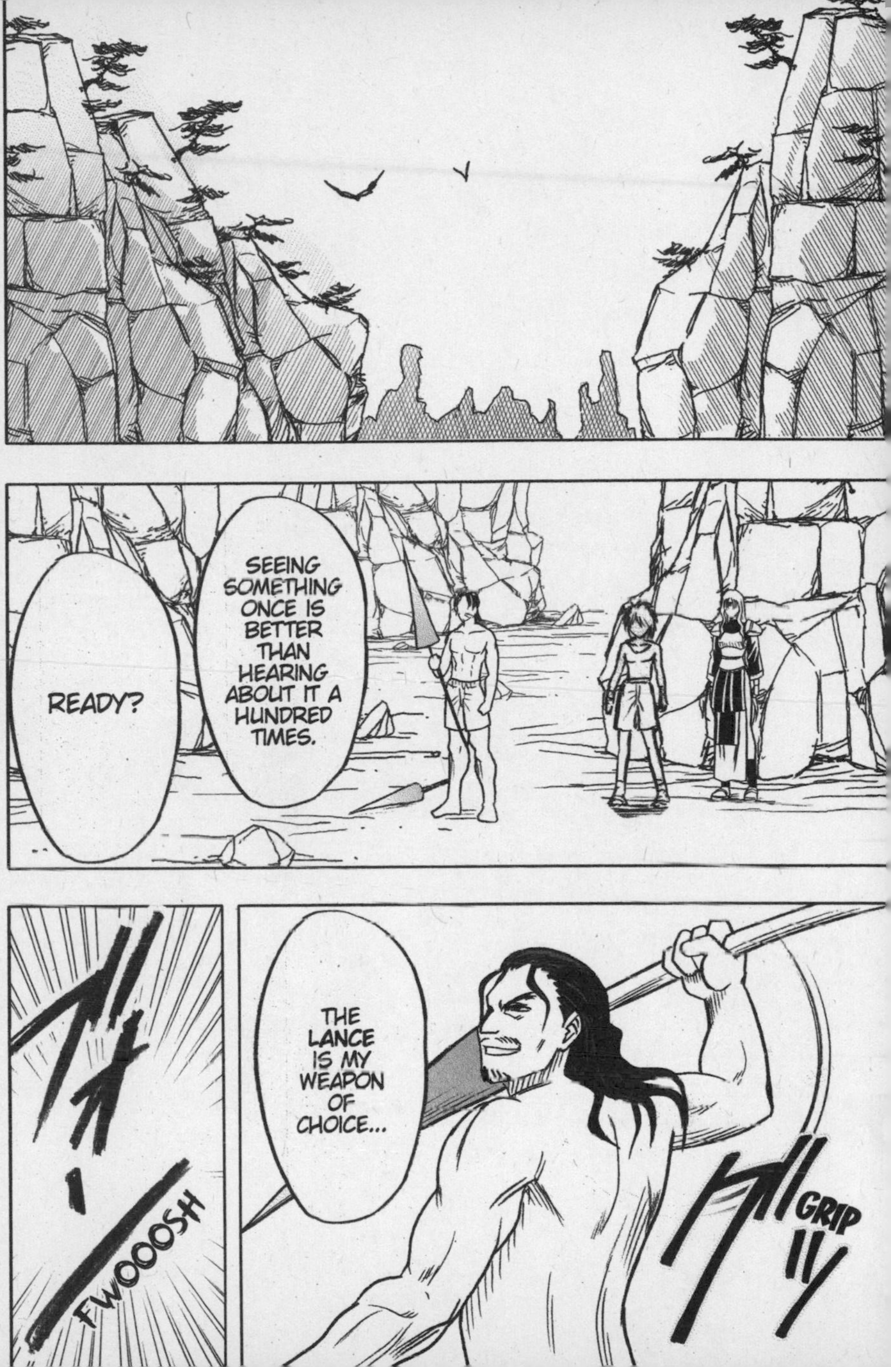
SEEING SOMETHING ONCE IS BETTER THAN HEARING ABOUT IT A HUNDRED TIMES.
READY?
THE LANCE IS MY WEAPON OF CHOICE...
GRIP
FWOOOSH

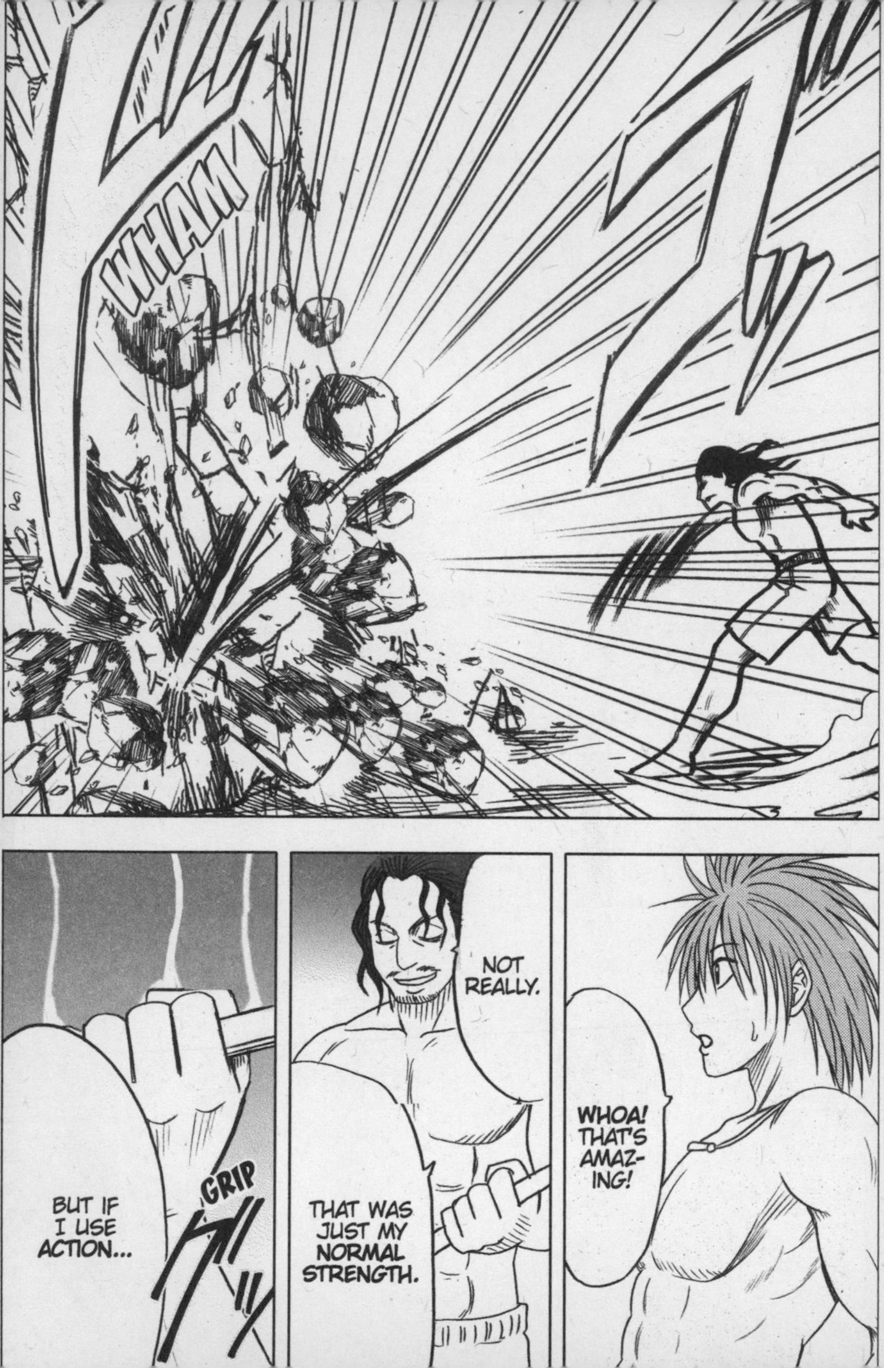
WHAM
WHOA! THAT'S AMAZ-ING!
NOT REALLY.
THAT WAS JUST MY NORMAL STRENGTH.
GRIP
BUT IF I USE ACTION...

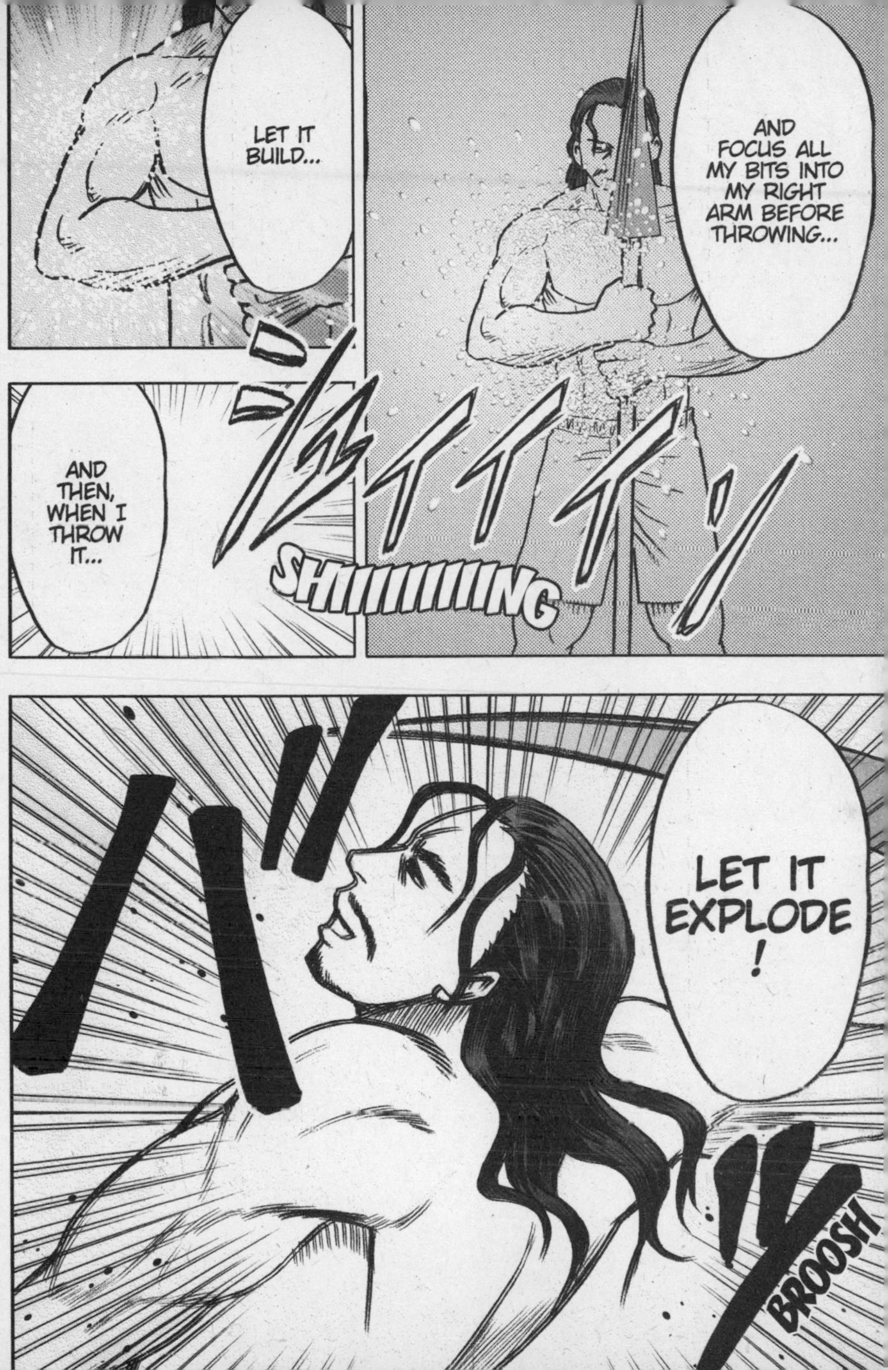
LET IT BUILD...
AND FOCUS ALL MY BITS INTO MY RIGHT ARM BEFORE THROWING...
SHIIIIIIIIING
AND THEN, WHEN I THROW IT...
LET IT EXPLODE!
BROOSH

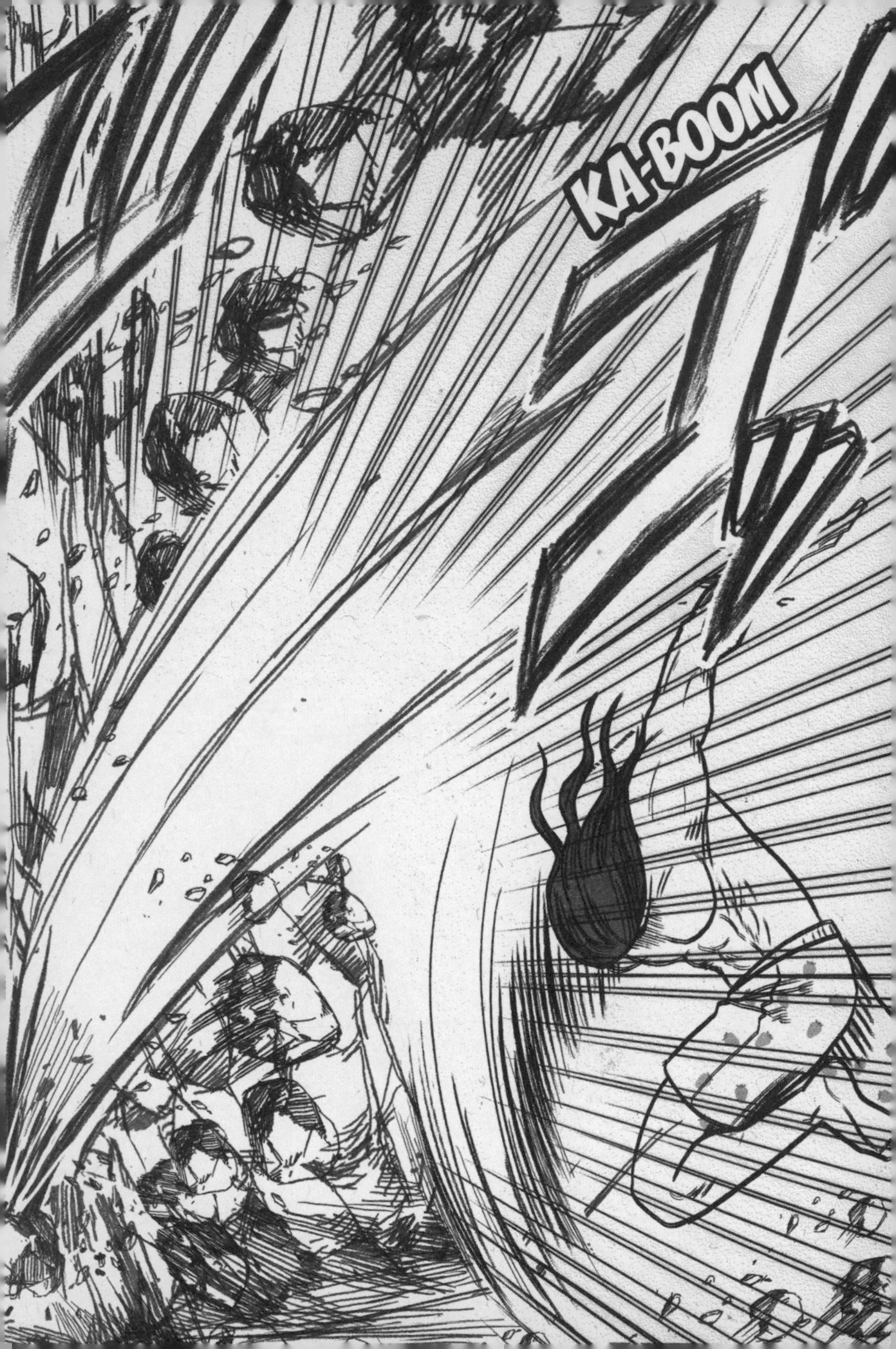
KA-BOOM

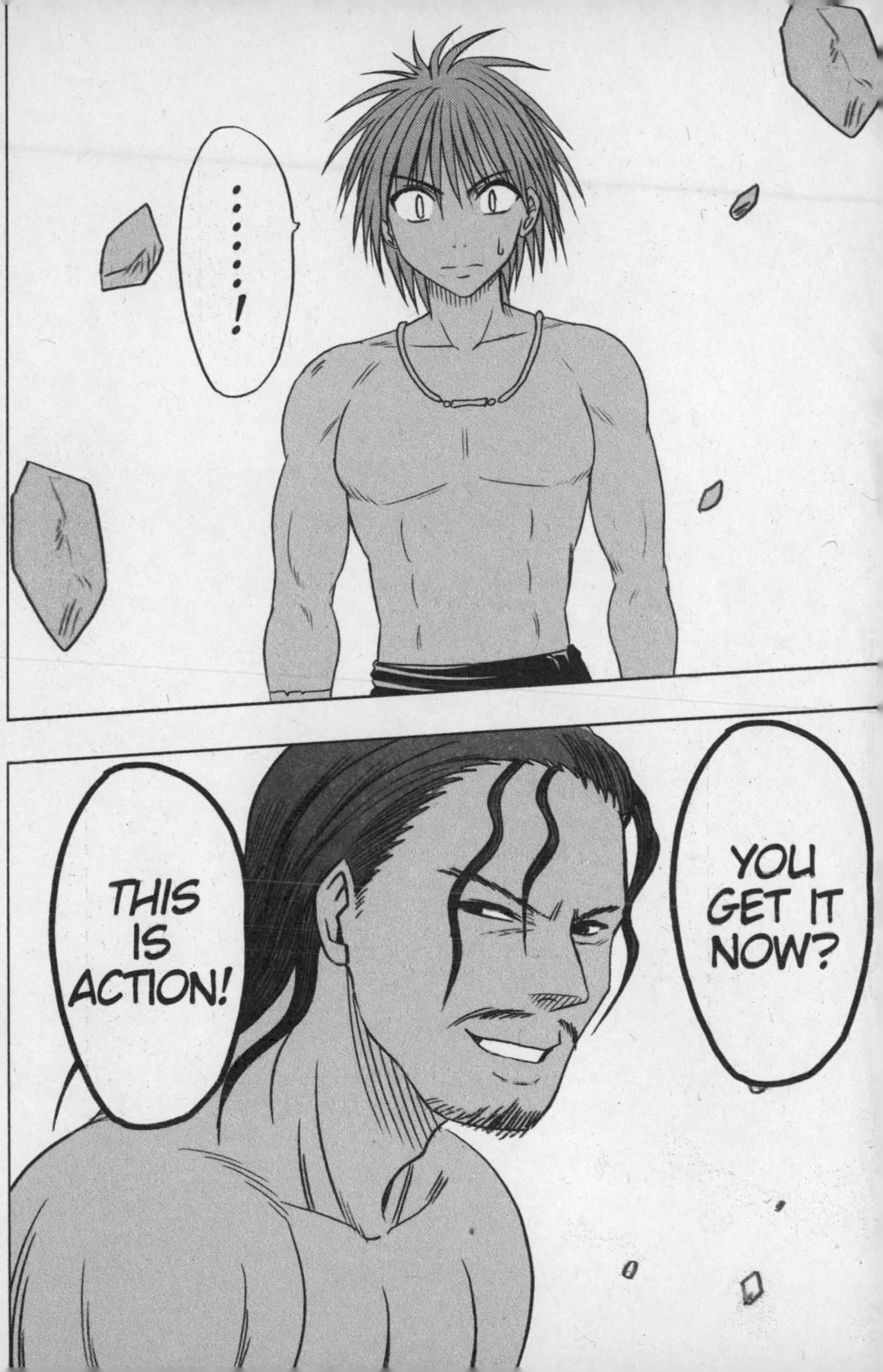
......!
YOU GET IT NOW?
THIS IS ACTION!

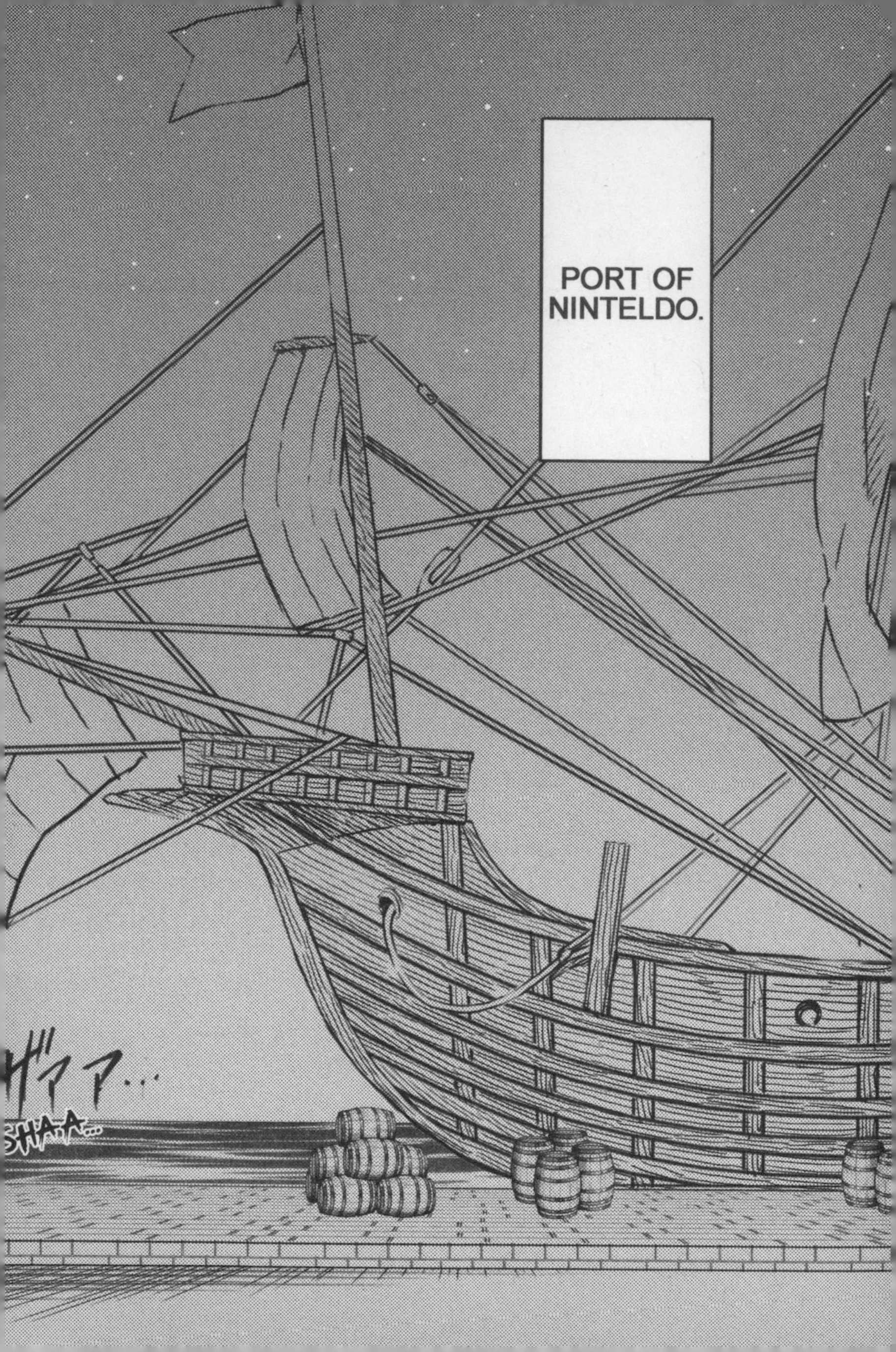
PORT OF NINTELDO.
ザァア…
SHAA...

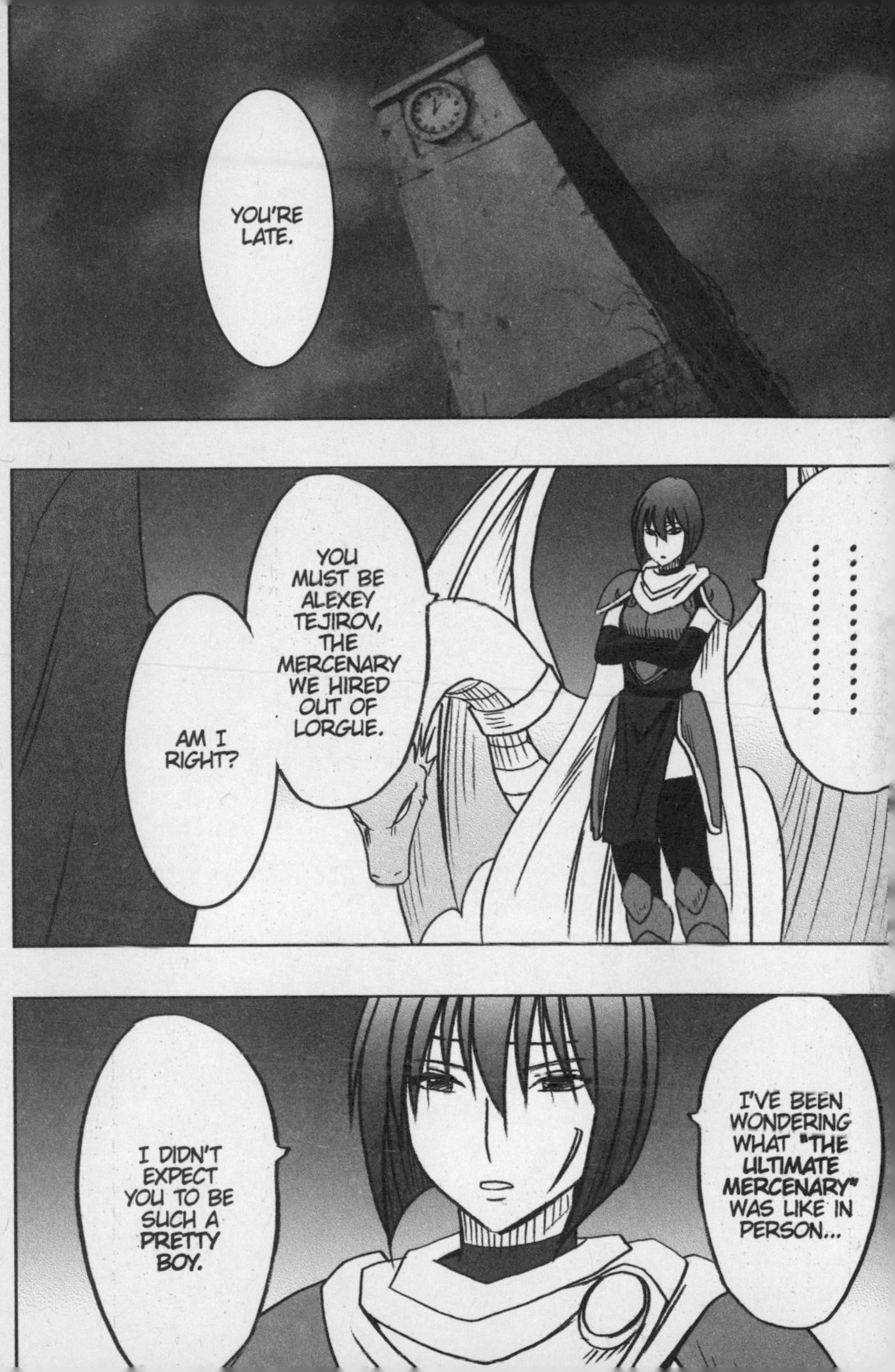
YOU'RE LATE.
..........
YOU MUST BE ALEXEY TEJIROV, THE MERCENARY WE HIRED OUT OF LORGUE.
AM I RIGHT?
I'VE BEEN WONDERING WHAT "THE ULTIMATE MERCENARY" WAS LIKE IN PERSON...
I DIDN'T EXPECT YOU TO BE SUCH A PRETTY BOY.

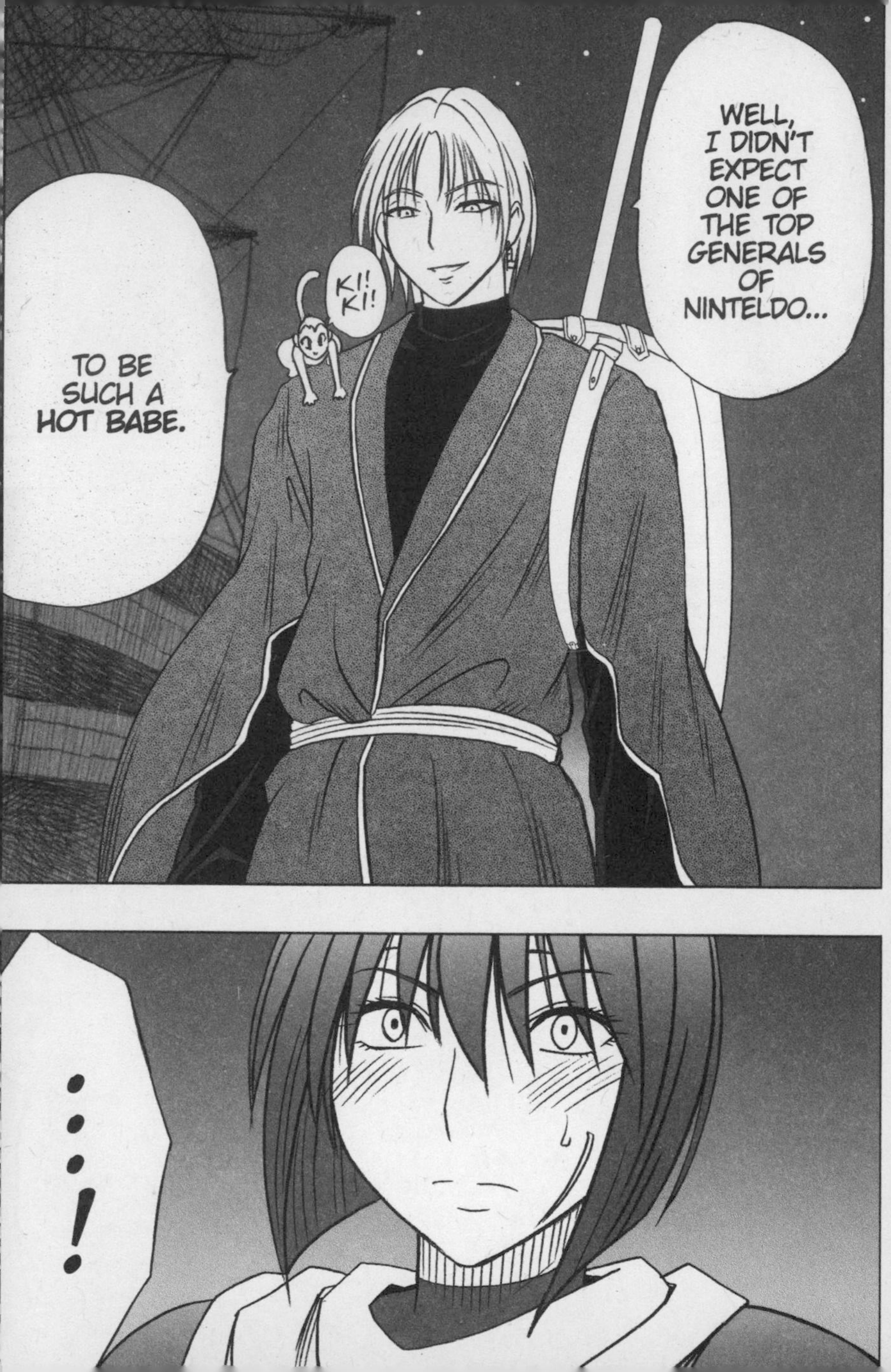
WELL, I DIDN'T EXPECT ONE OF THE TOP GENERALS OF NINTELDO...
KI! KI!
TO BE SUCH A HOT BABE.
...!

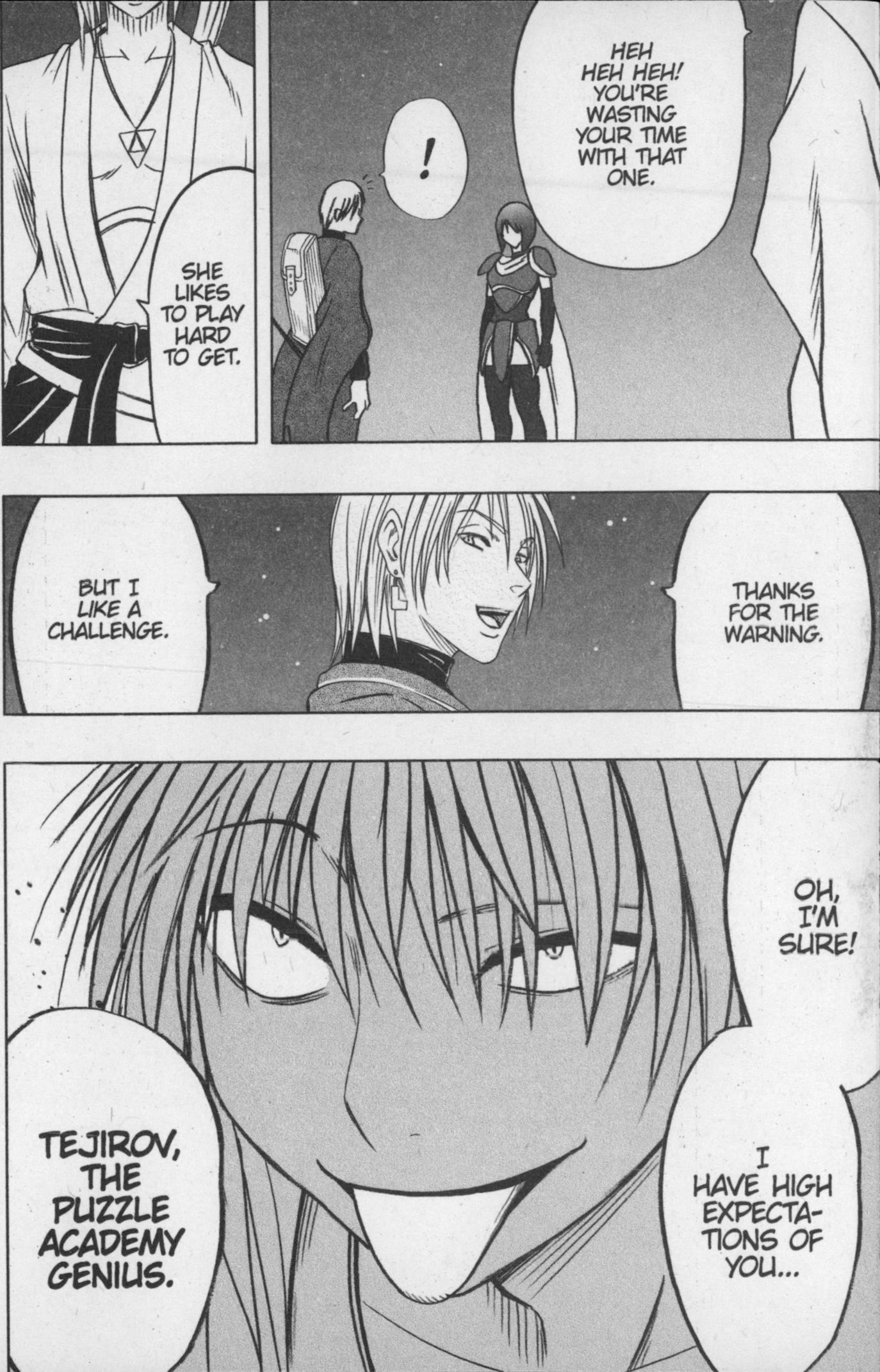
HEH HEH HEH! YOU'RE WASTING YOUR TIME WITH THAT ONE.
!
SHE LIKES TO PLAY HARD TO GET.
THANKS FOR THE WARNING.
BUT I LIKE A CHALLENGE.
OH, I'M SURE!
I HAVE HIGH EXPECTA-TIONS OF YOU...
TEJIROV, THE PUZZLE ACADEMY GENIUS.

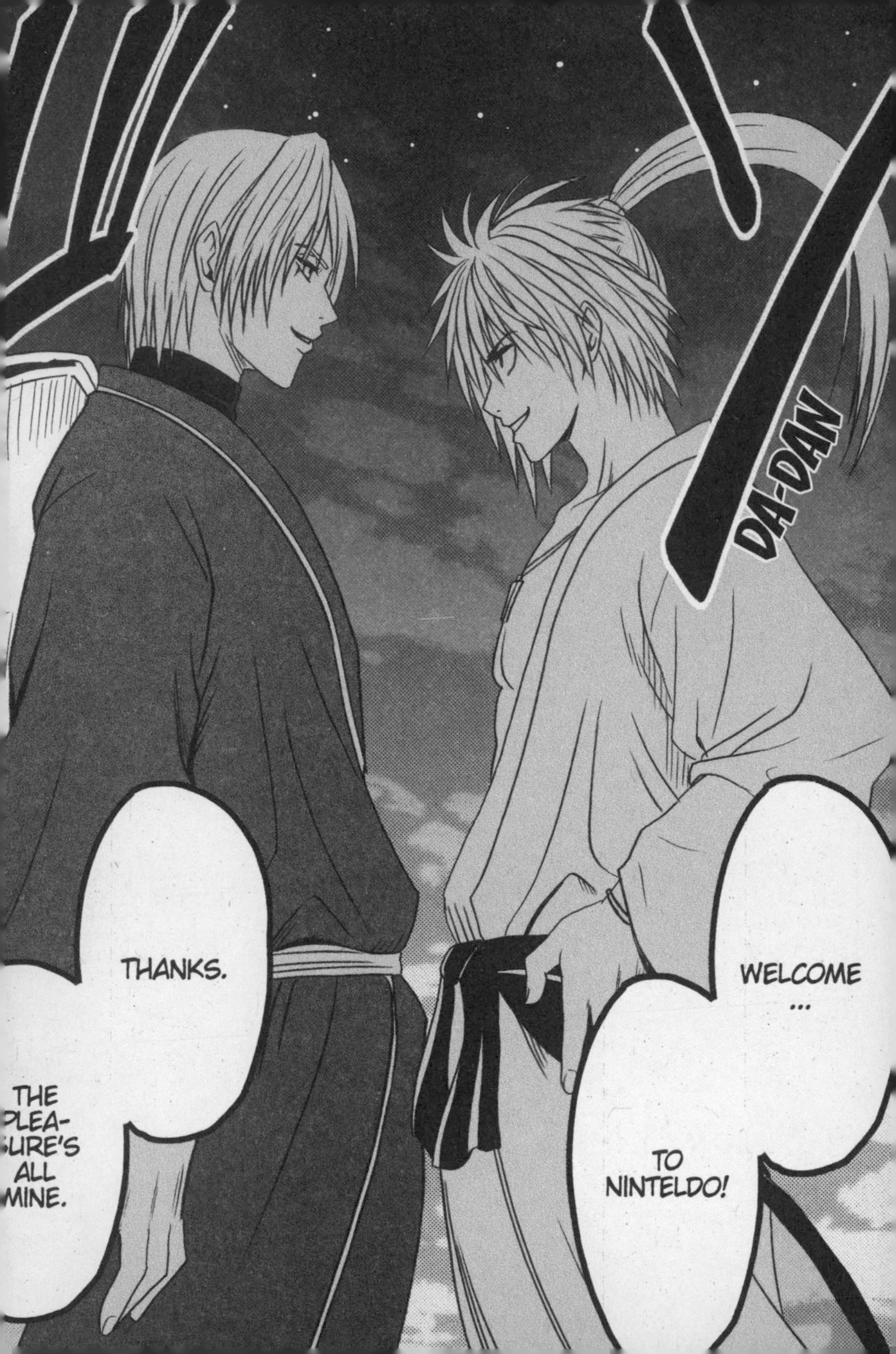
DA-DAN
WELCOME ... TO NINTELDO!
THANKS.
THE PLEA-SURE'S ALL MINE.

WORLD WAR BLUE

CHARACTER INTRODUCTION

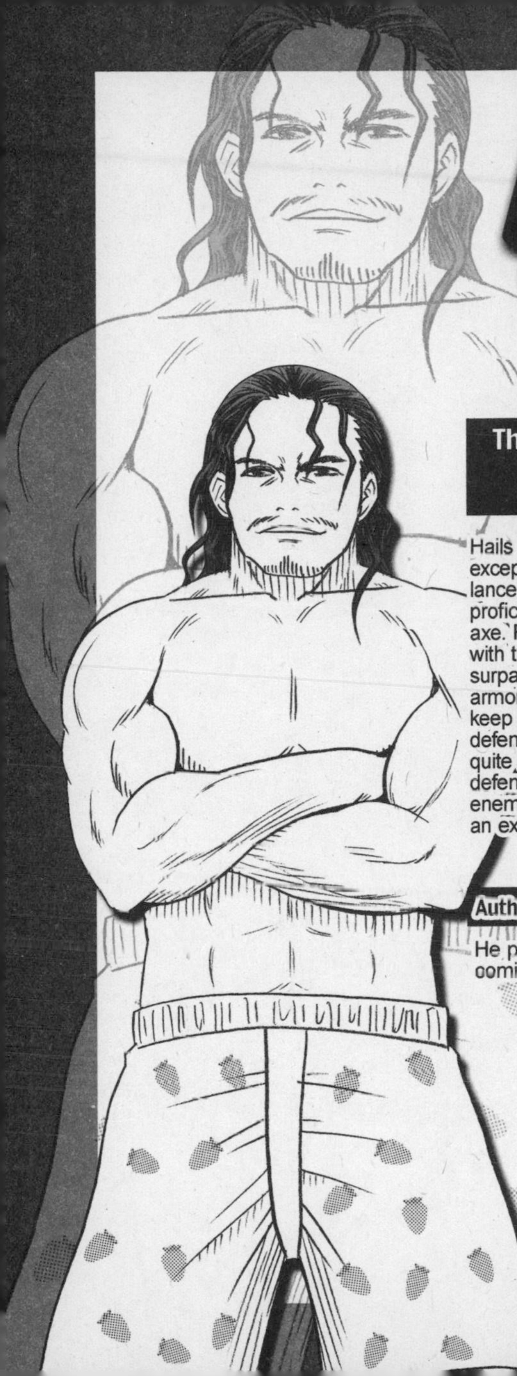

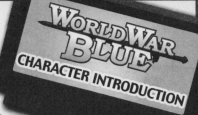

## The Naked Knight
## KAIMURA

Hails from Gump. While exceptionally skilled with the lance, he is also quite proficient with a sword and axe. Rumors are that his skill with throwing knives surpasses them all. While his armor looks sturdy, in order to keep it lightweight, its defensive value is actually quite low. In fact, it can only defend against a single enemy attack. He's a bit of an exhibitionist.

**Author Comment**

He pretty much just exists for comic relief...

Kaimura

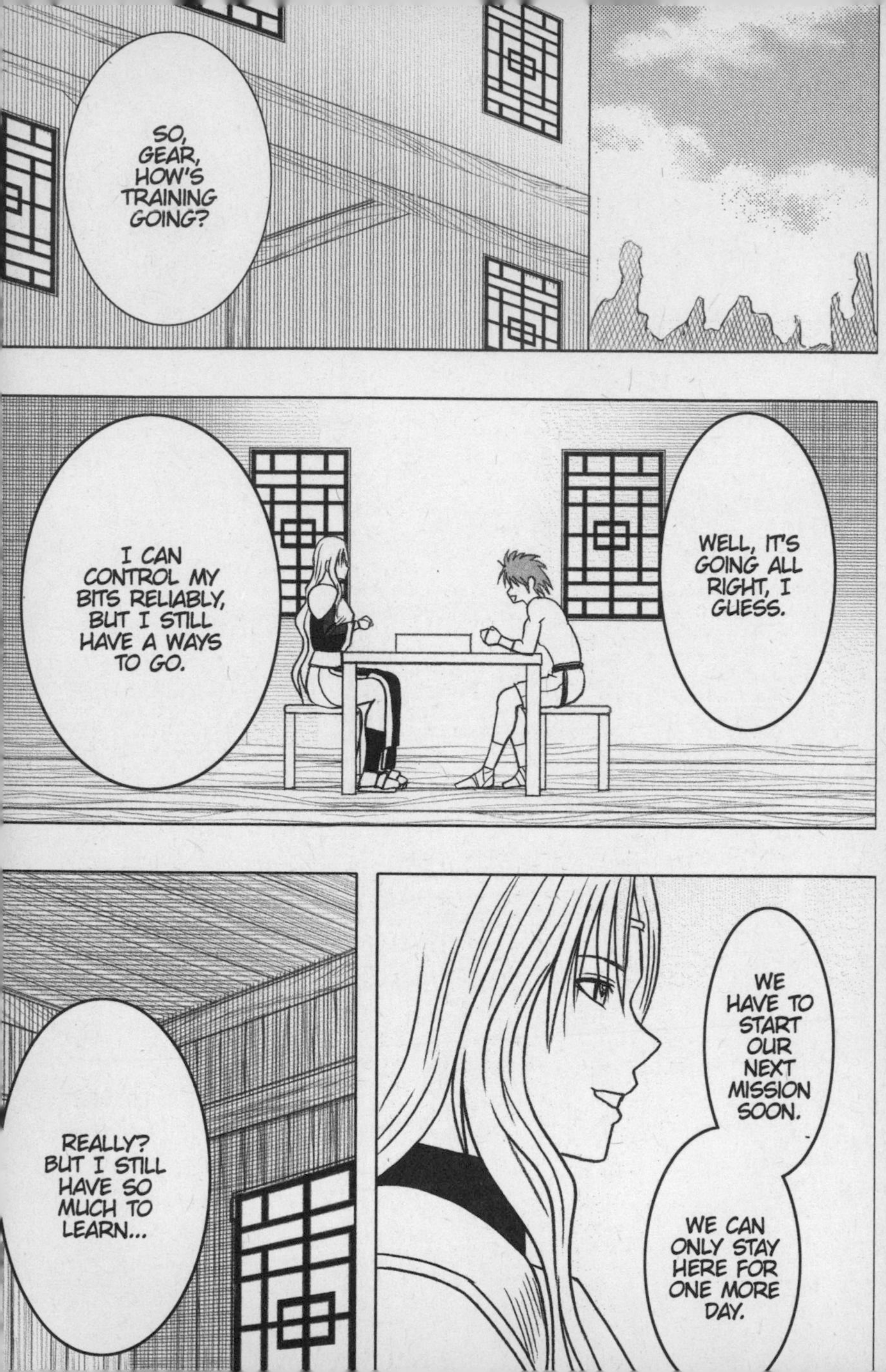
SO, GEAR, HOW'S TRAINING GOING?
WELL, IT'S GOING ALL RIGHT, I GUESS.
I CAN CONTROL MY BITS RELIABLY, BUT I STILL HAVE A WAYS TO GO.
WE HAVE TO START OUR NEXT MISSION SOON.
WE CAN ONLY STAY HERE FOR ONE MORE DAY.
REALLY? BUT I STILL HAVE SO MUCH TO LEARN...

Part 2

# CHAPTER 15

# ACTION

DISC 2

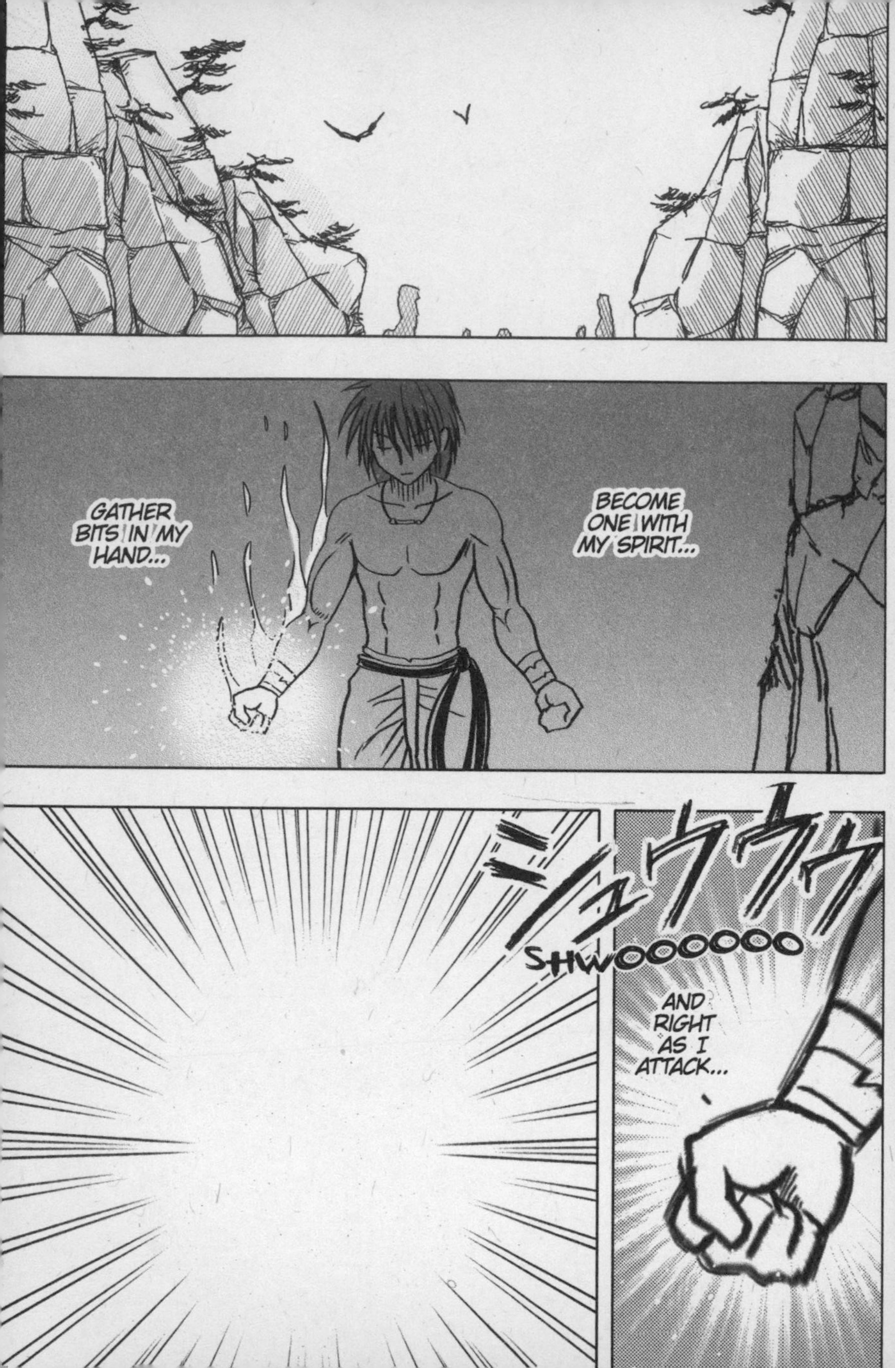
BECOME ONE WITH MY SPIRIT...
GATHER BITS IN MY HAND...
ジュウウウ
SHWOOOOOOO
AND RIGHT AS I ATTACK...

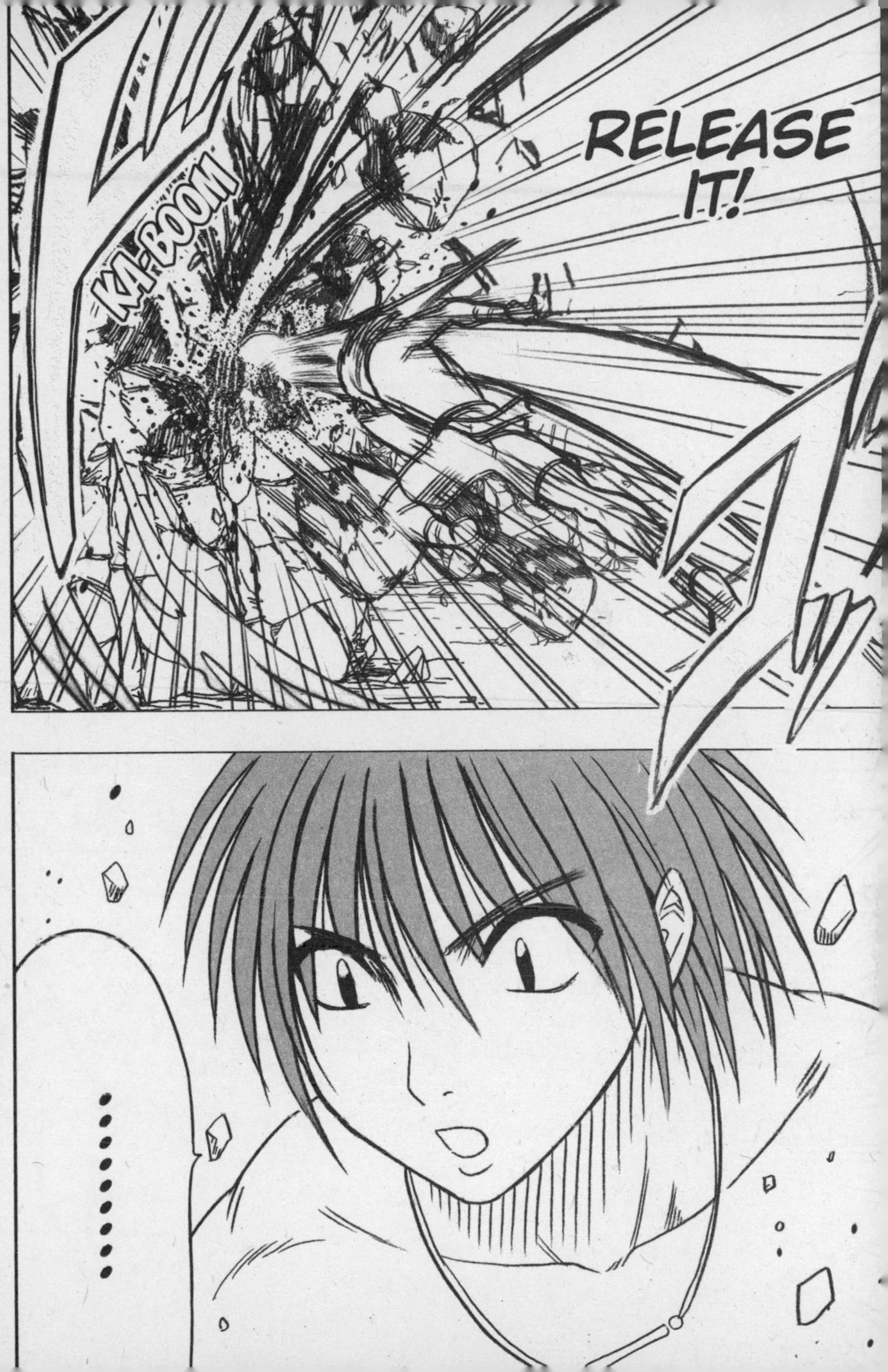
RELEASE IT!
KA-BOOM
........

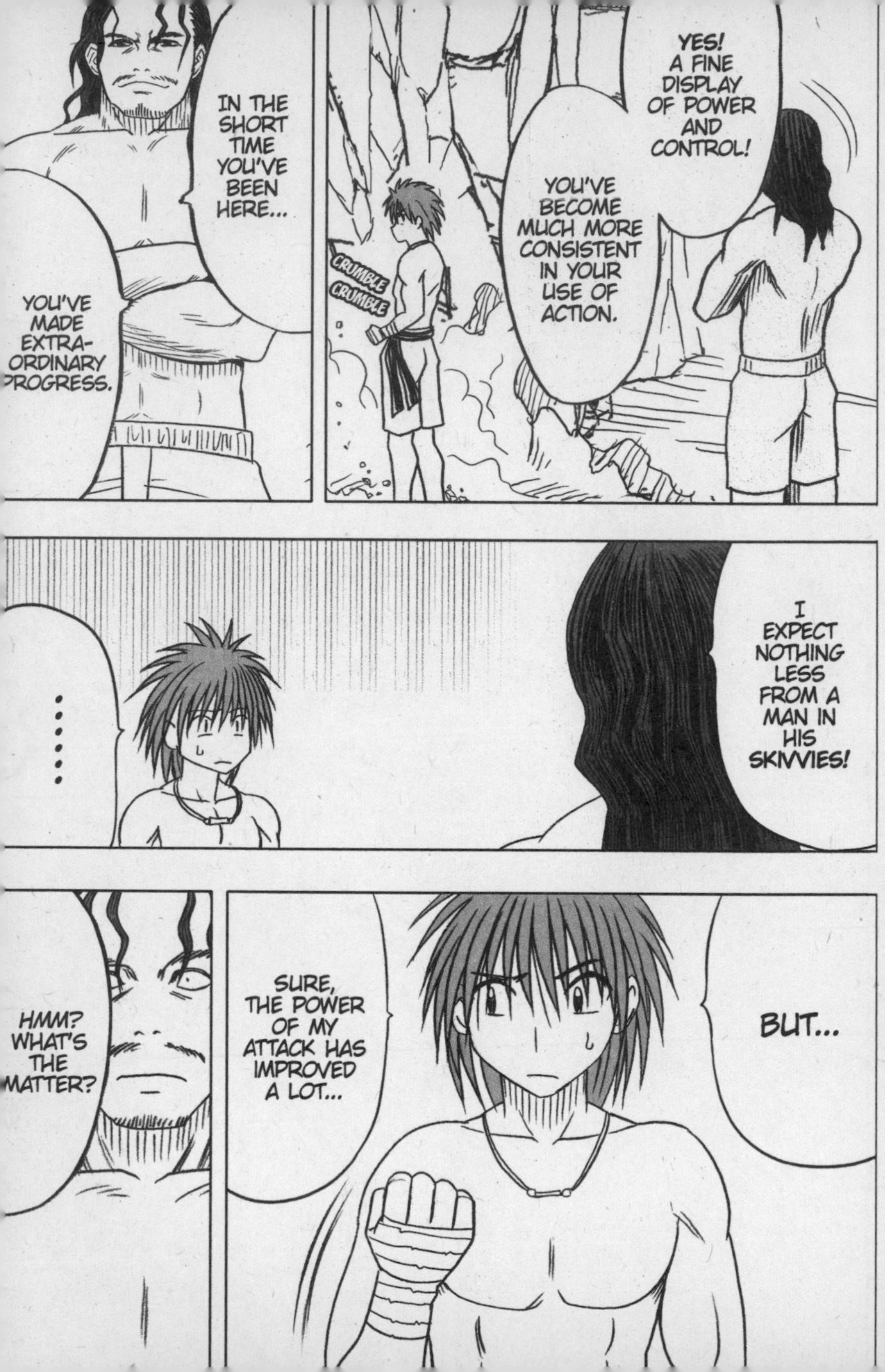
YES! A FINE DISPLAY OF POWER AND CONTROL!
YOU'VE BECOME MUCH MORE CONSISTENT IN YOUR USE OF ACTION.
CRUMBLE CRUMBLE
IN THE SHORT TIME YOU'VE BEEN HERE...
YOU'VE MADE EXTRA-ORDINARY PROGRESS.
I EXPECT NOTHING LESS FROM A MAN IN HIS SKIVVIES!
......
SURE, THE POWER OF MY ATTACK HAS IMPROVED A LOT...
BUT...
HMM? WHAT'S THE MATTER?

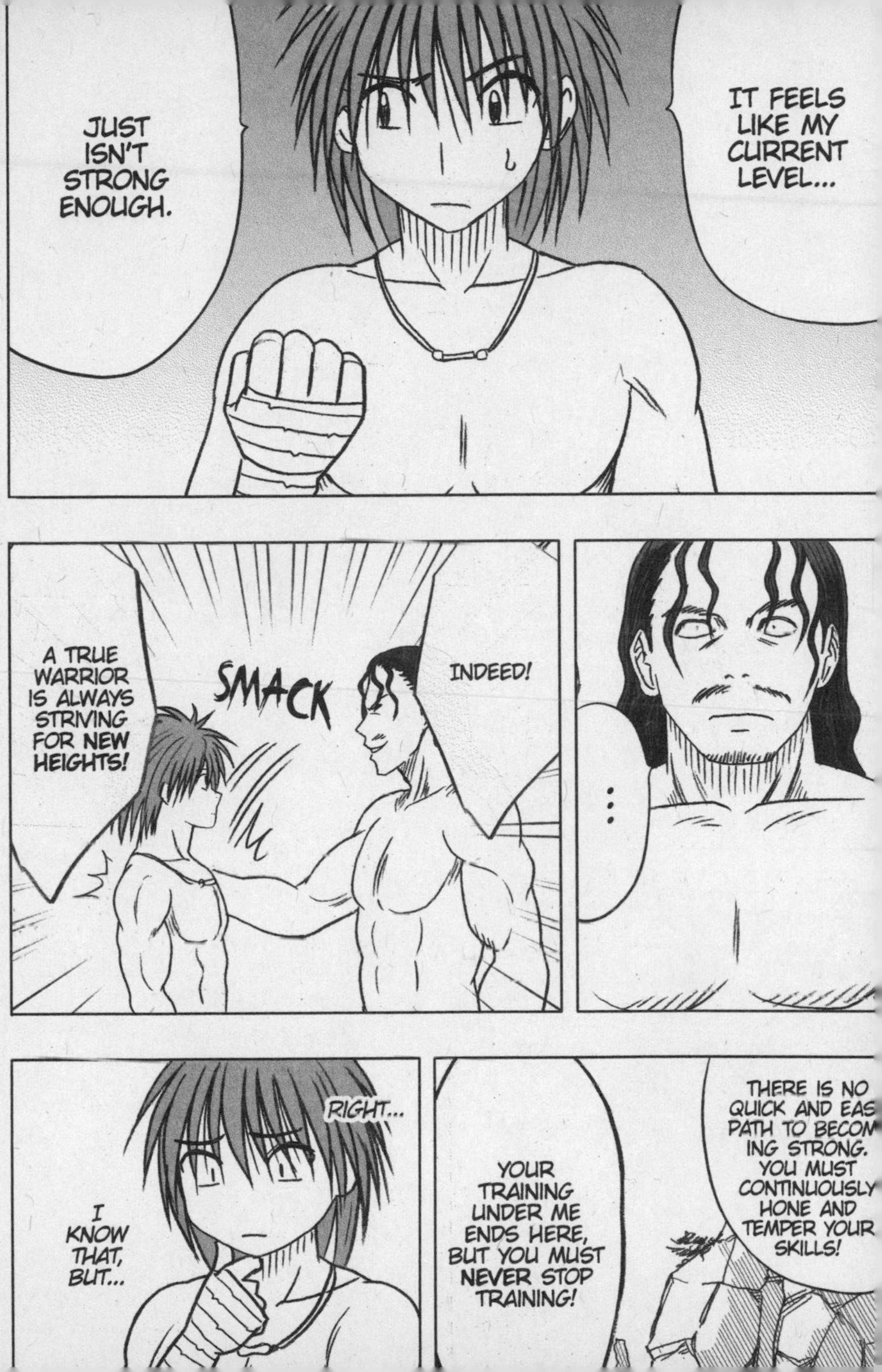
IT FEELS LIKE MY CURRENT LEVEL...
JUST ISN'T STRONG ENOUGH.
...
INDEED!
SMACK
A TRUE WARRIOR IS ALWAYS STRIVING FOR NEW HEIGHTS!
THERE IS NO QUICK AND EAS PATH TO BECOM ING STRONG. YOU MUST CONTINUOUSLY HONE AND TEMPER YOUR SKILLS!
YOUR TRAINING UNDER ME ENDS HERE, BUT YOU MUST NEVER STOP TRAINING!
RIGHT...
I KNOW THAT, BUT...

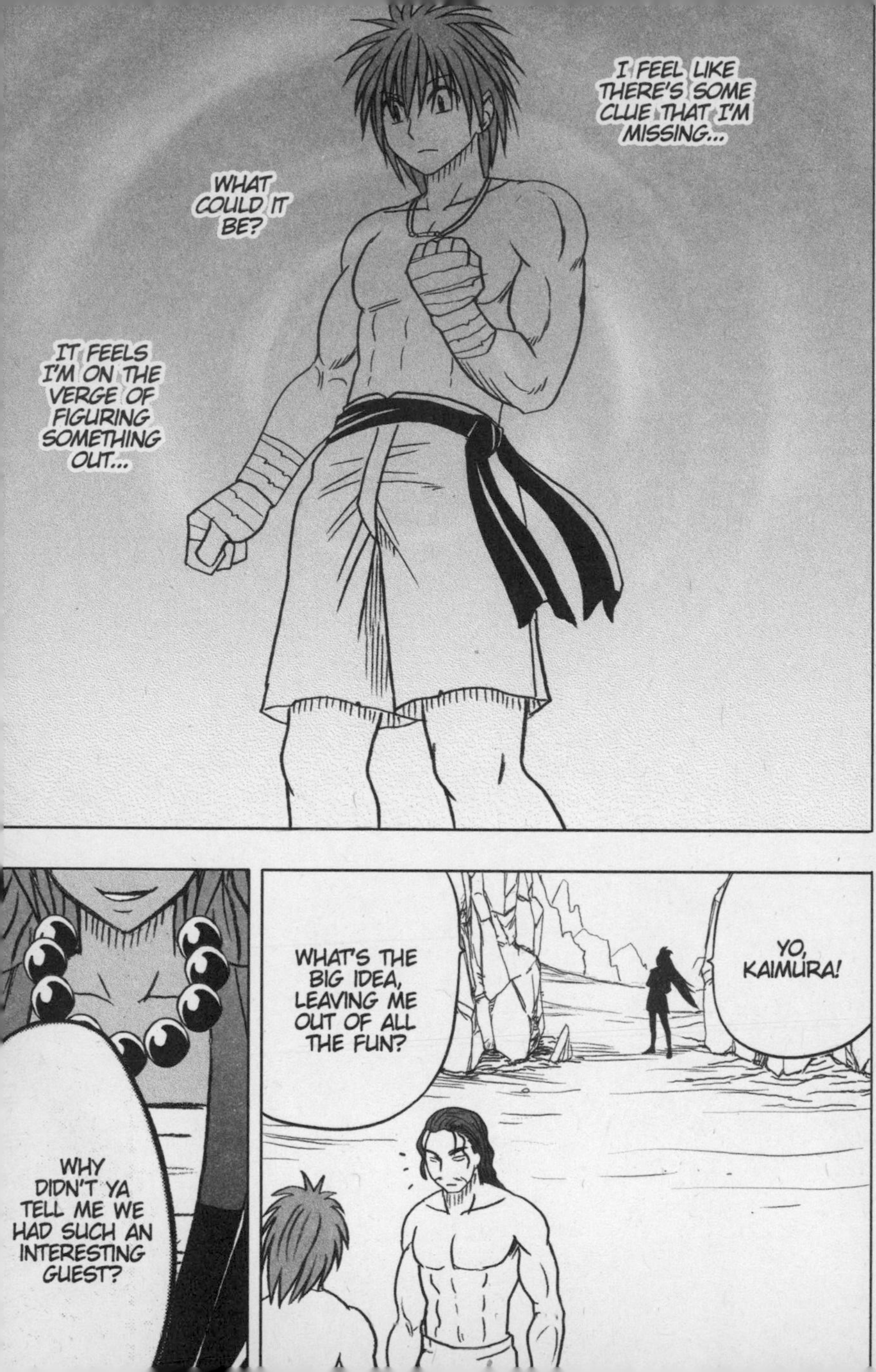
I FEEL LIKE THERE'S SOME CLUE THAT I'M MISSING...
WHAT COULD IT BE?
IT FEELS I'M ON THE VERGE OF FIGURING SOMETHING OUT...
YO, KAIMURA!
WHAT'S THE BIG IDEA, LEAVING ME OUT OF ALL THE FUN?
WHY DIDN'T YA TELL ME WE HAD SUCH AN INTERESTING GUEST?

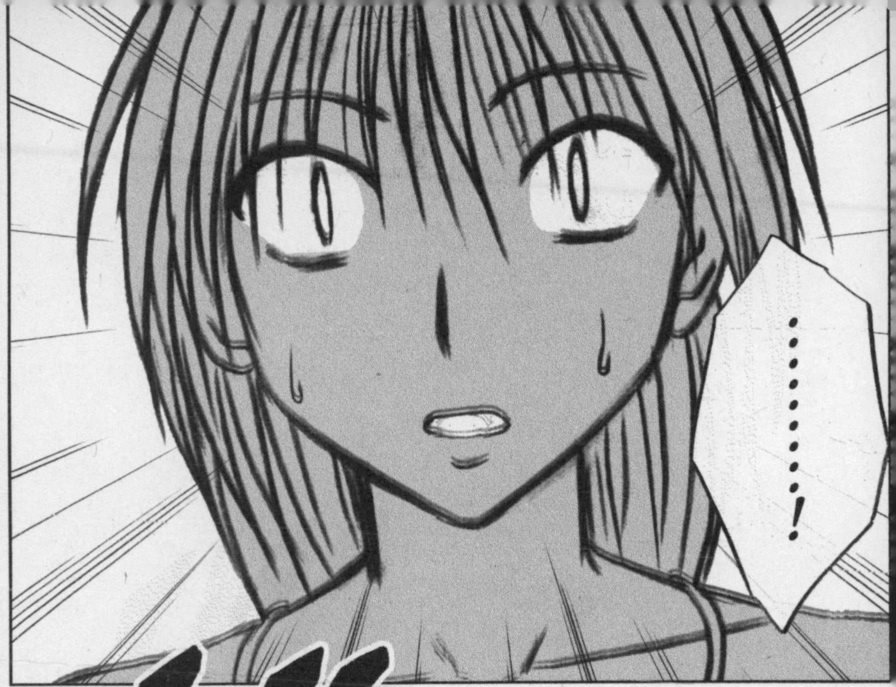
.........!
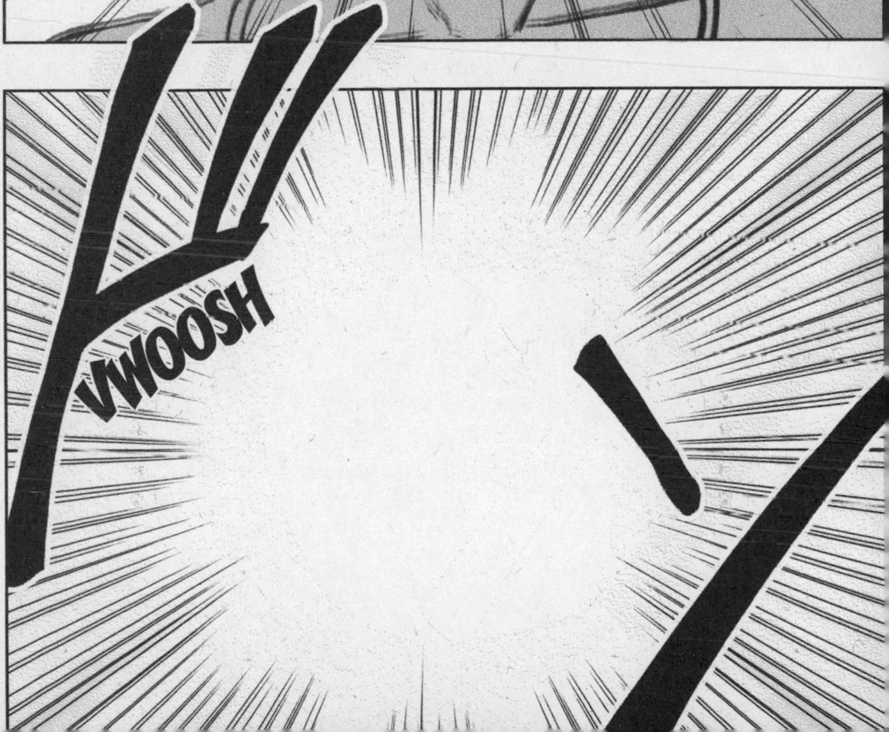
VWOOSH

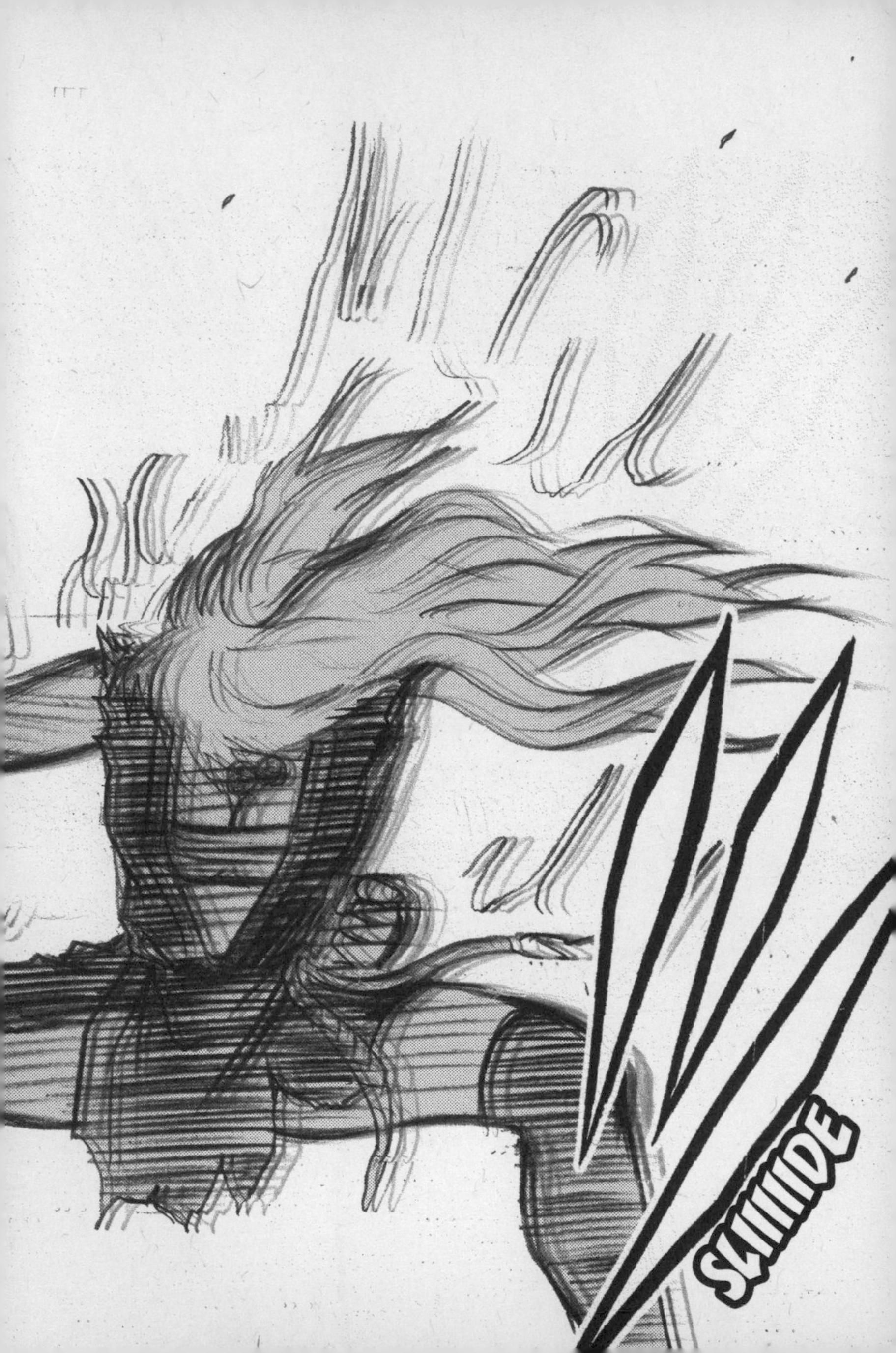
SLIIIIDE

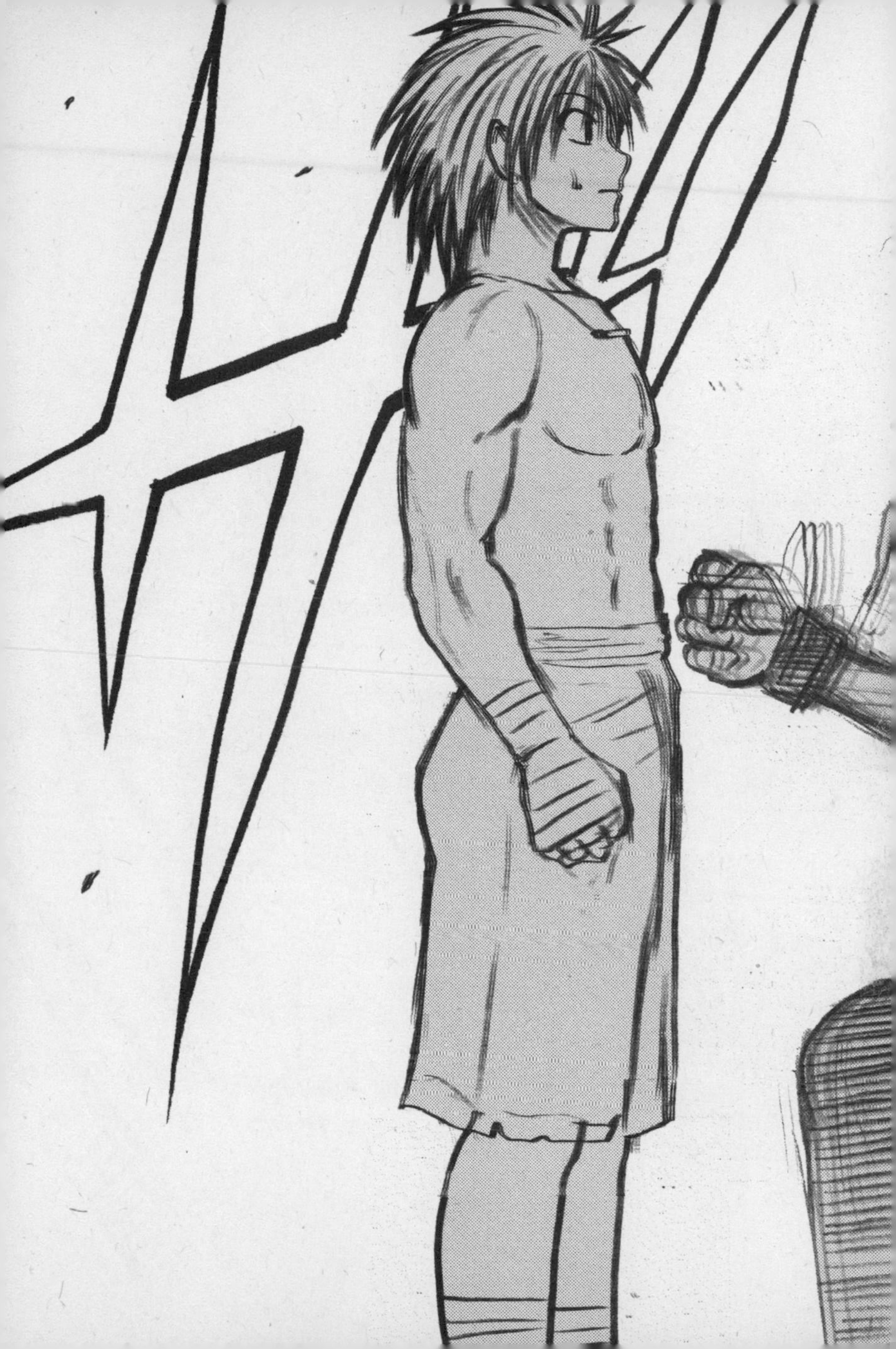

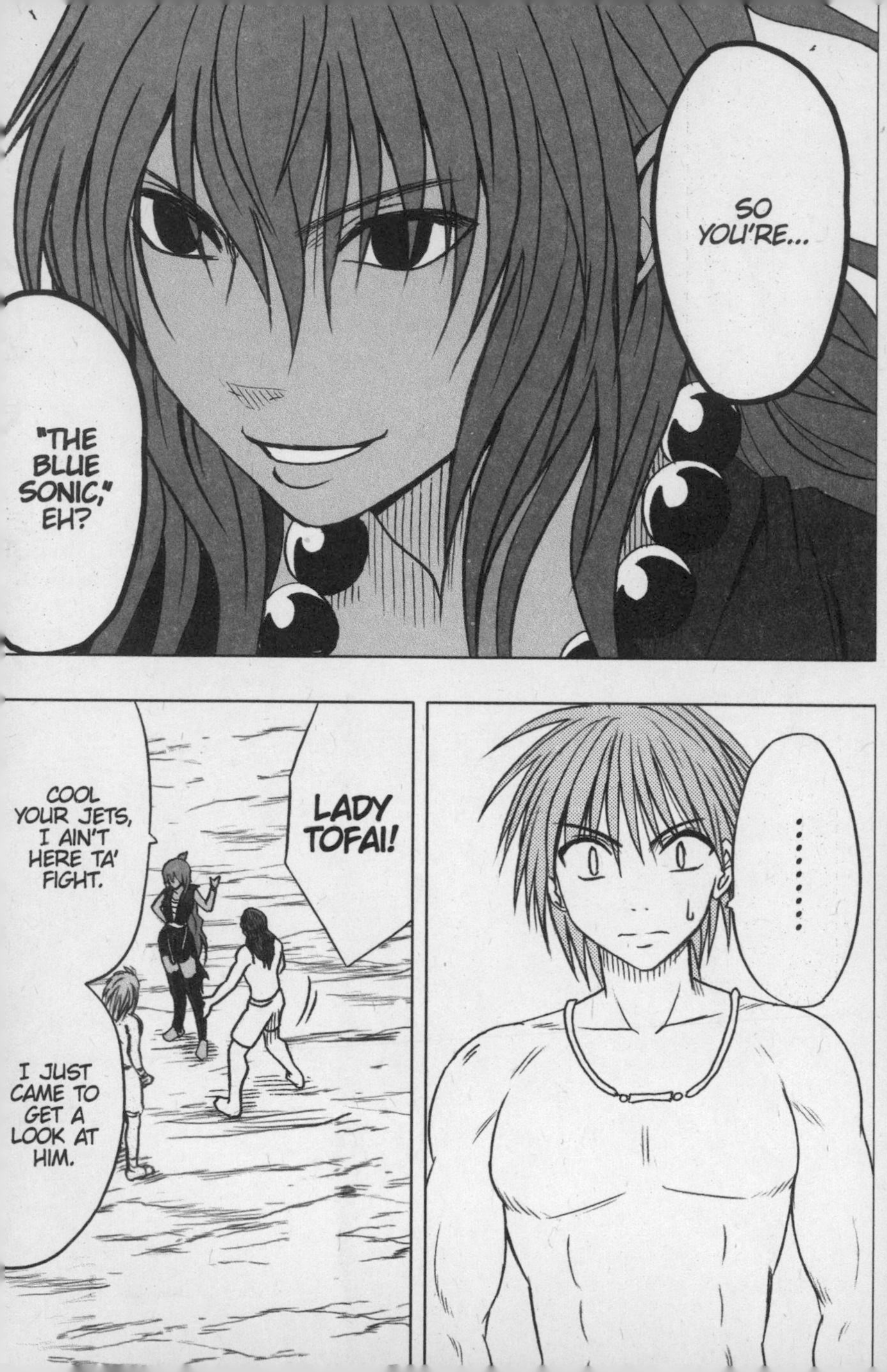
SO YOU'RE...
"THE BLUE SONIC," EH?
......
LADY TOFAI!
COOL YOUR JETS, I AIN'T HERE TA' FIGHT.
I JUST CAME TO GET A LOOK AT HIM.

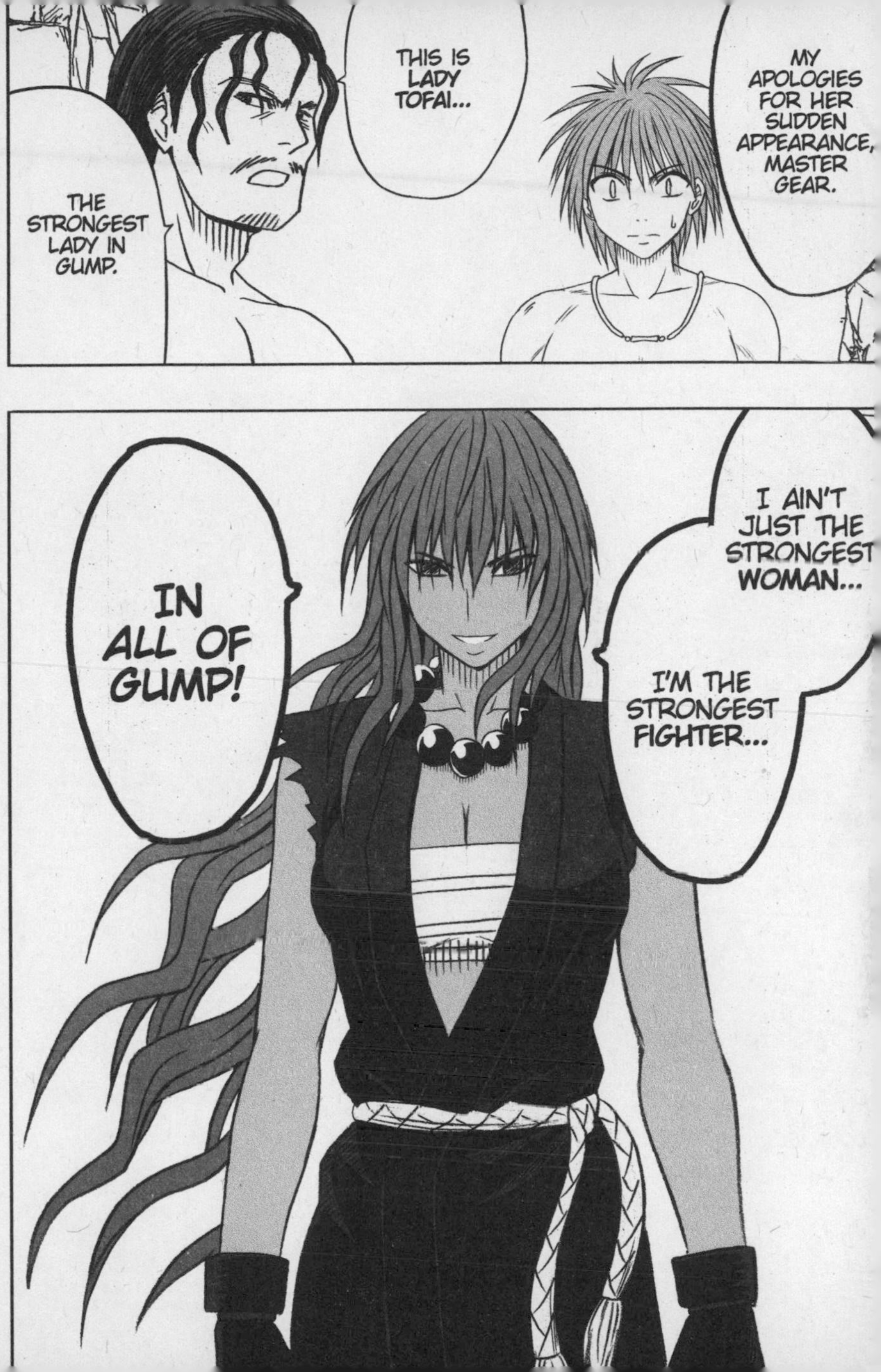
MY APOLOGIES FOR HER SUDDEN APPEARANCE, MASTER GEAR.
THIS IS LADY TOFAI...
THE STRONGEST LADY IN GUMP.
I AIN'T JUST THE STRONGEST WOMAN...
I'M THE STRONGEST FIGHTER...
IN ALL OF GUMP!

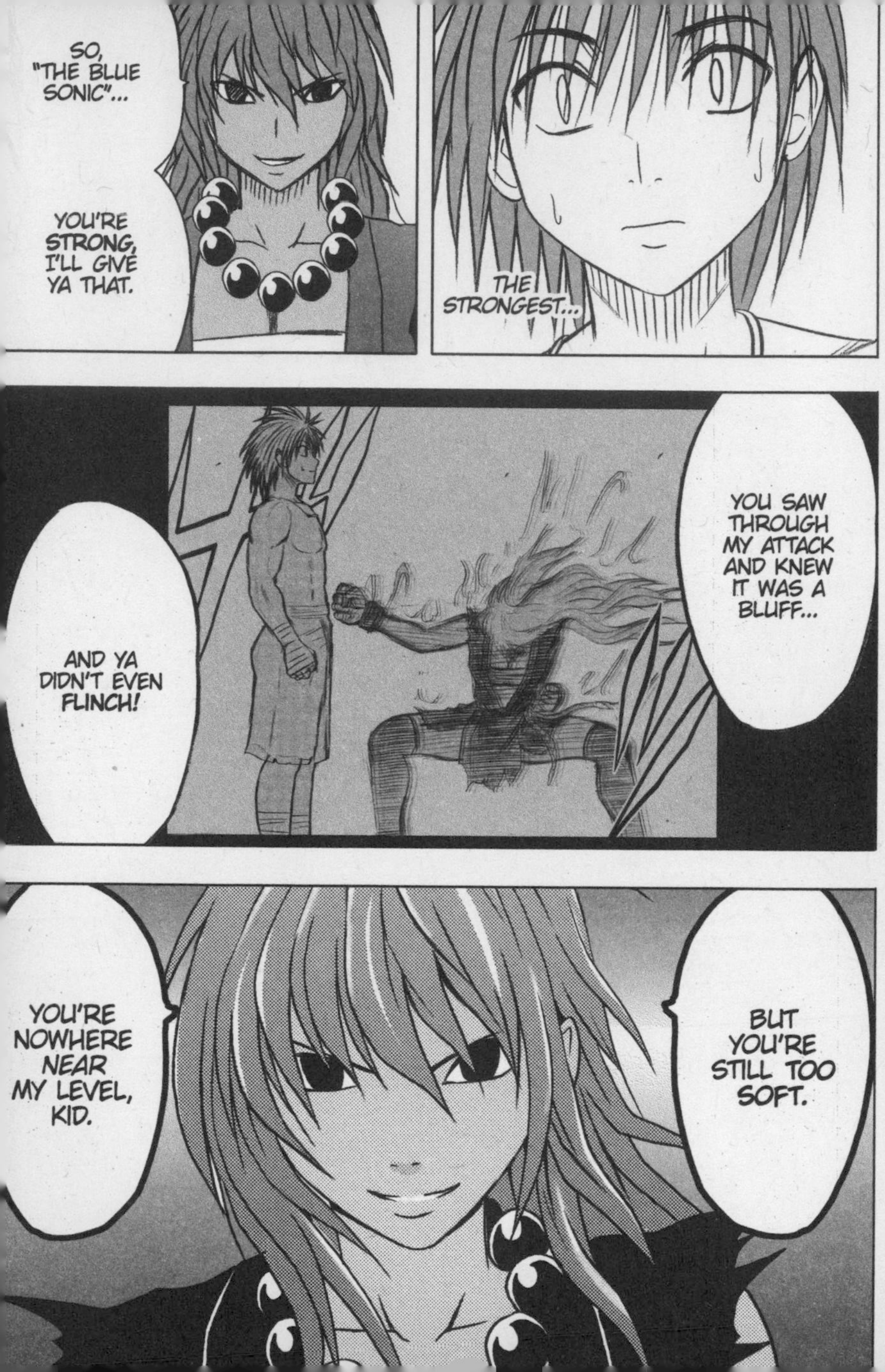
THE STRONGEST...
SO, "THE BLUE SONIC"...
YOU'RE STRONG, I'LL GIVE YA THAT.
YOU SAW THROUGH MY ATTACK AND KNEW IT WAS A BLUFF...
AND YA DIDN'T EVEN FLINCH!
BUT YOU'RE STILL TOO SOFT.
YOU'RE NOWHERE NEAR MY LEVEL, KID.

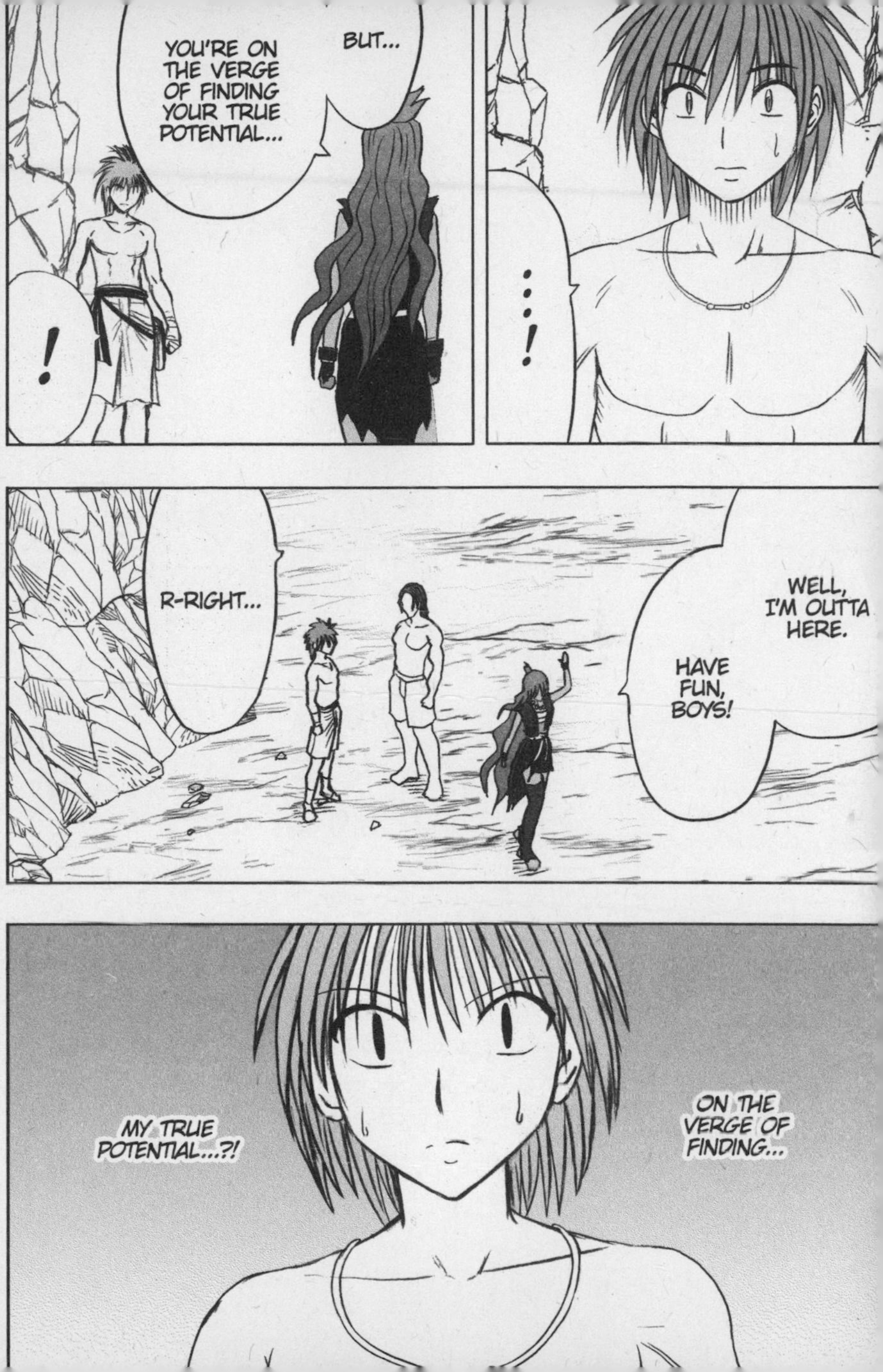
...!
BUT...
YOU'RE ON THE VERGE OF FINDING YOUR TRUE POTENTIAL...
!
WELL, I'M OUTTA HERE.
HAVE FUN, BOYS!
R-RIGHT...
ON THE VERGE OF FINDING...
MY TRUE POTENTIAL...?!

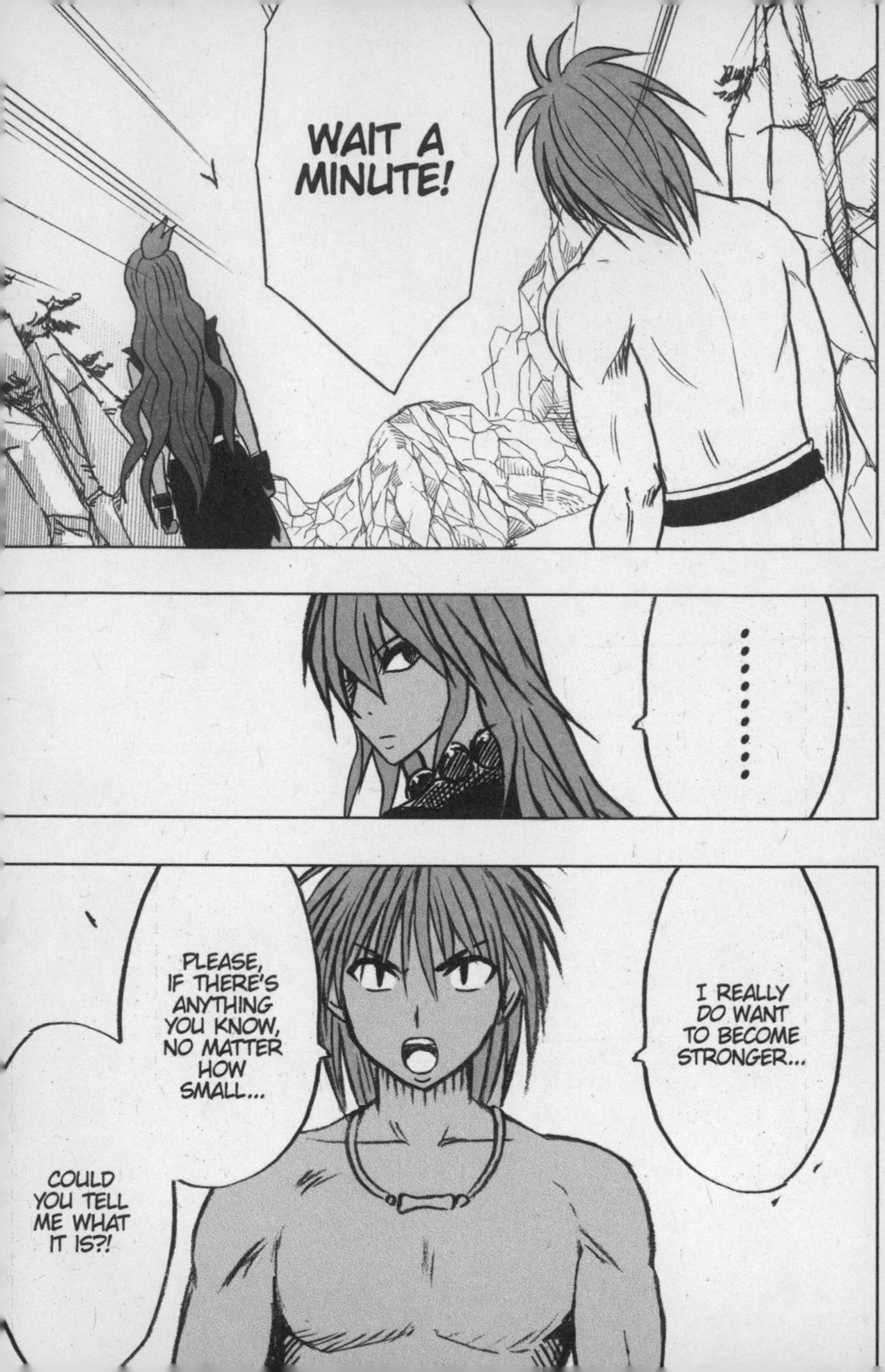
WAIT A MINUTE!
........
I REALLY DO WANT TO BECOME STRONGER...
PLEASE, IF THERE'S ANYTHING YOU KNOW, NO MATTER HOW SMALL...
COULD YOU TELL ME WHAT IT IS?!

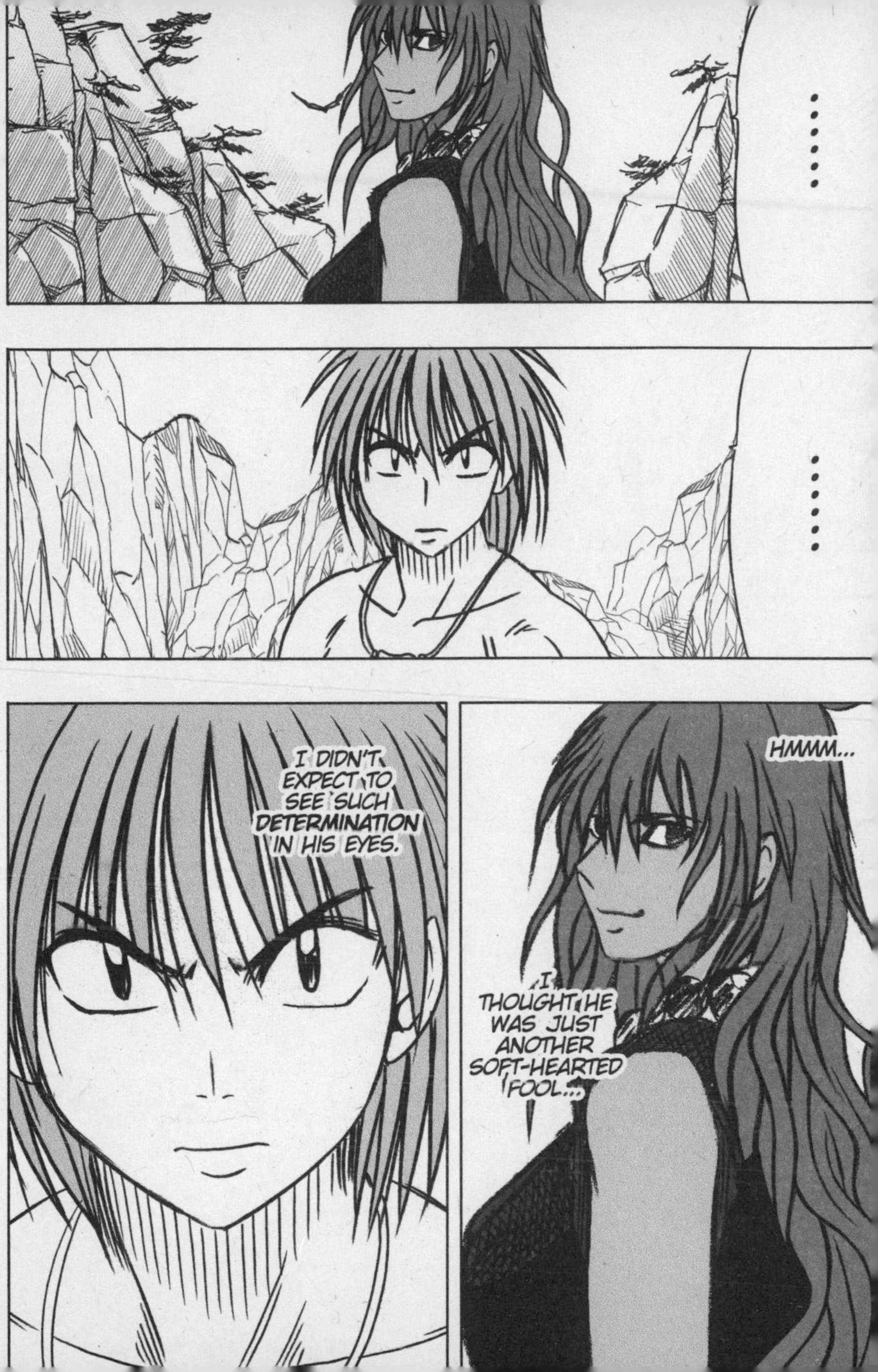
.....
......
HMMM...
I THOUGHT HE WAS JUST ANOTHER SOFT-HEARTED FOOL...
I DIDN'T EXPECT TO SEE SUCH DETERMINATION IN HIS EYES.

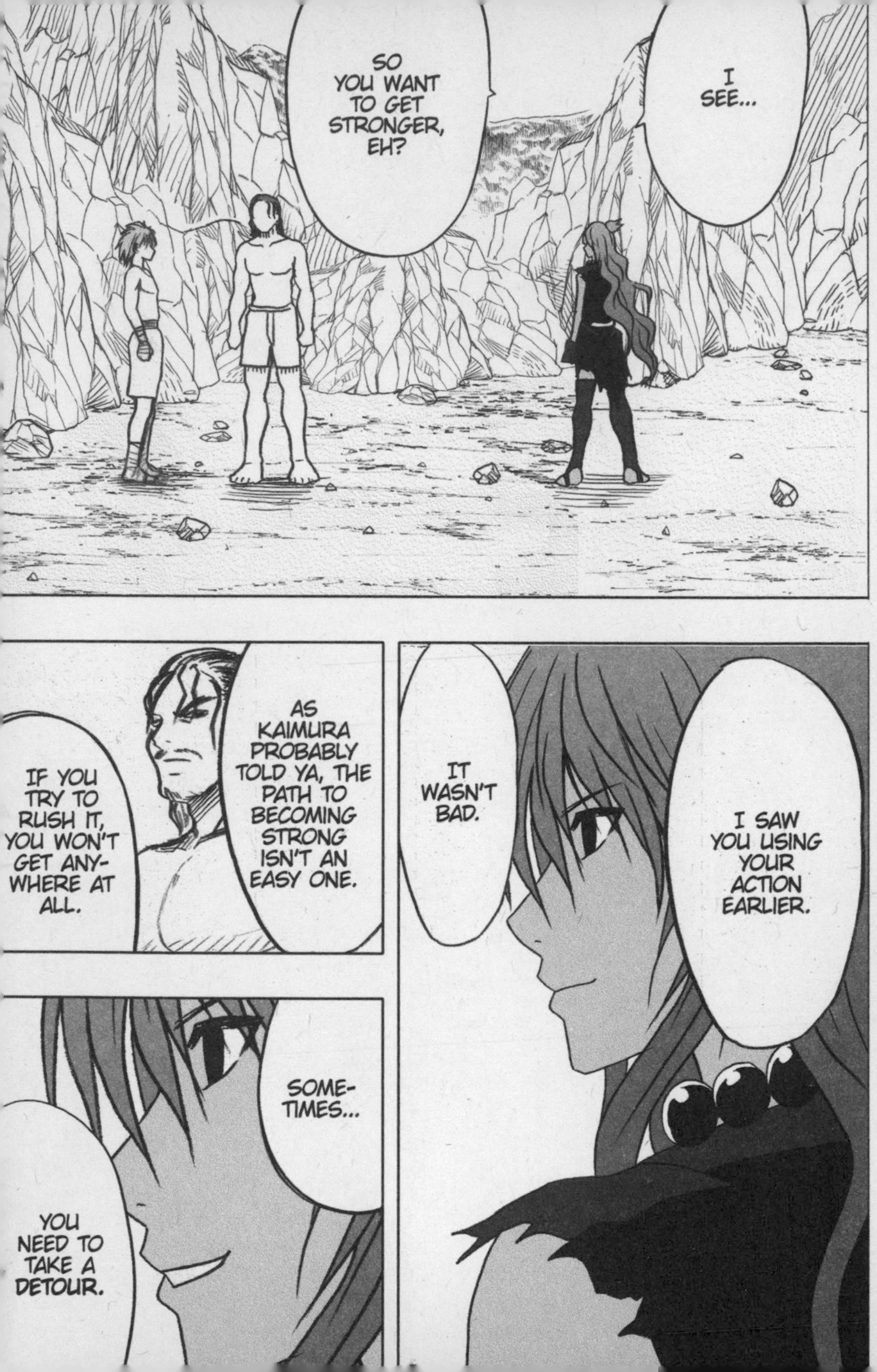
I SEE...
SO YOU WANT TO GET STRONGER, EH?
I SAW YOU USING YOUR ACTION EARLIER.
IT WASN'T BAD.
AS KAIMURA PROBABLY TOLD YA, THE PATH TO BECOMING STRONG ISN'T AN EASY ONE.
IF YOU TRY TO RUSH IT, YOU WON'T GET ANY-WHERE AT ALL.
SOME-TIMES...
YOU NEED TO TAKE A DETOUR.

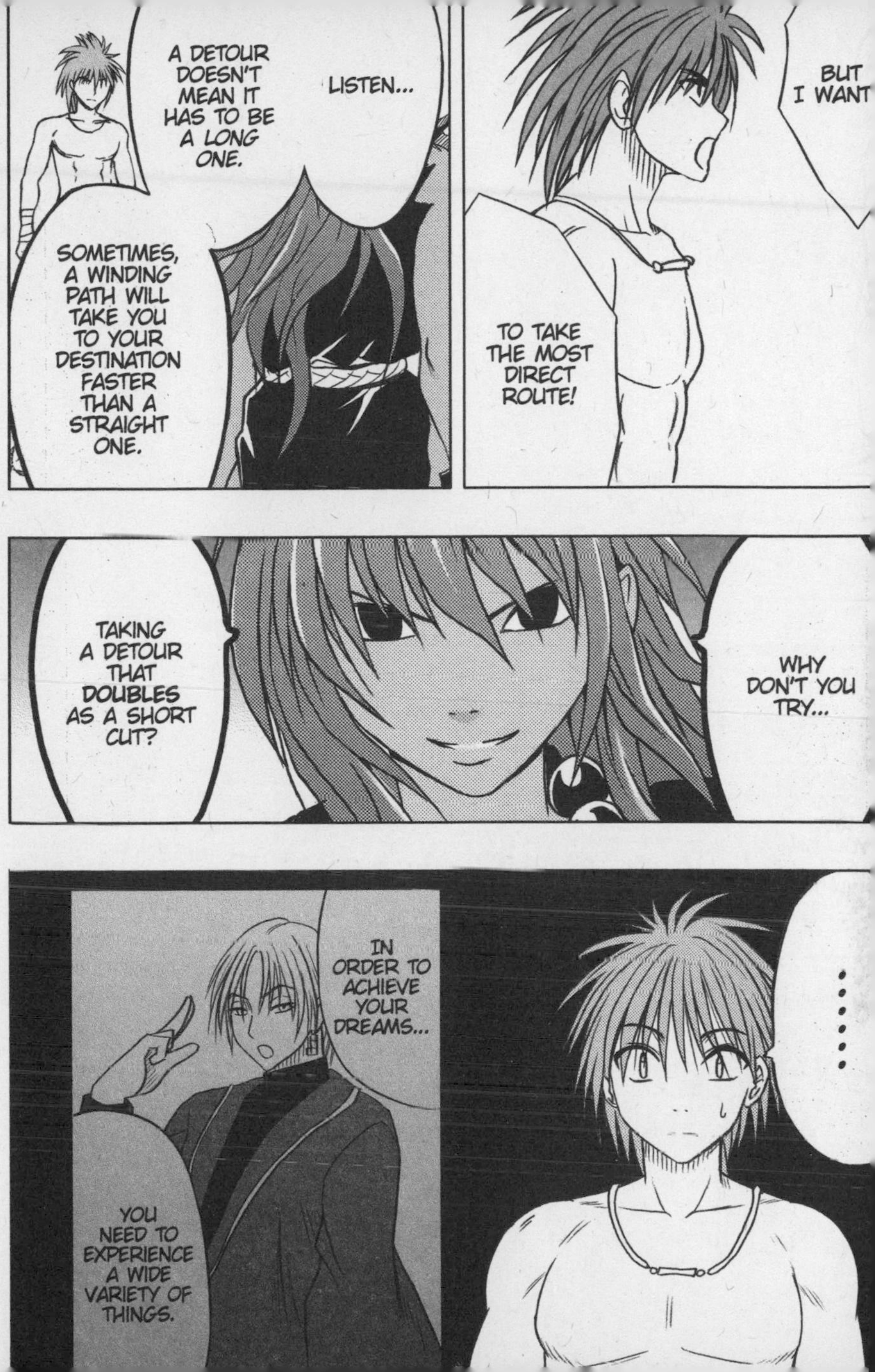
BUT I WANT
TO TAKE THE MOST DIRECT ROUTE!
LISTEN...
A DETOUR DOESN'T MEAN IT HAS TO BE A LONG ONE.
SOMETIMES, A WINDING PATH WILL TAKE YOU TO YOUR DESTINATION FASTER THAN A STRAIGHT ONE.
WHY DON'T YOU TRY...
TAKING A DETOUR THAT DOUBLES AS A SHORT CUT?
......
IN ORDER TO ACHIEVE YOUR DREAMS...
YOU NEED TO EXPERIENCE A WIDE VARIETY OF THINGS.

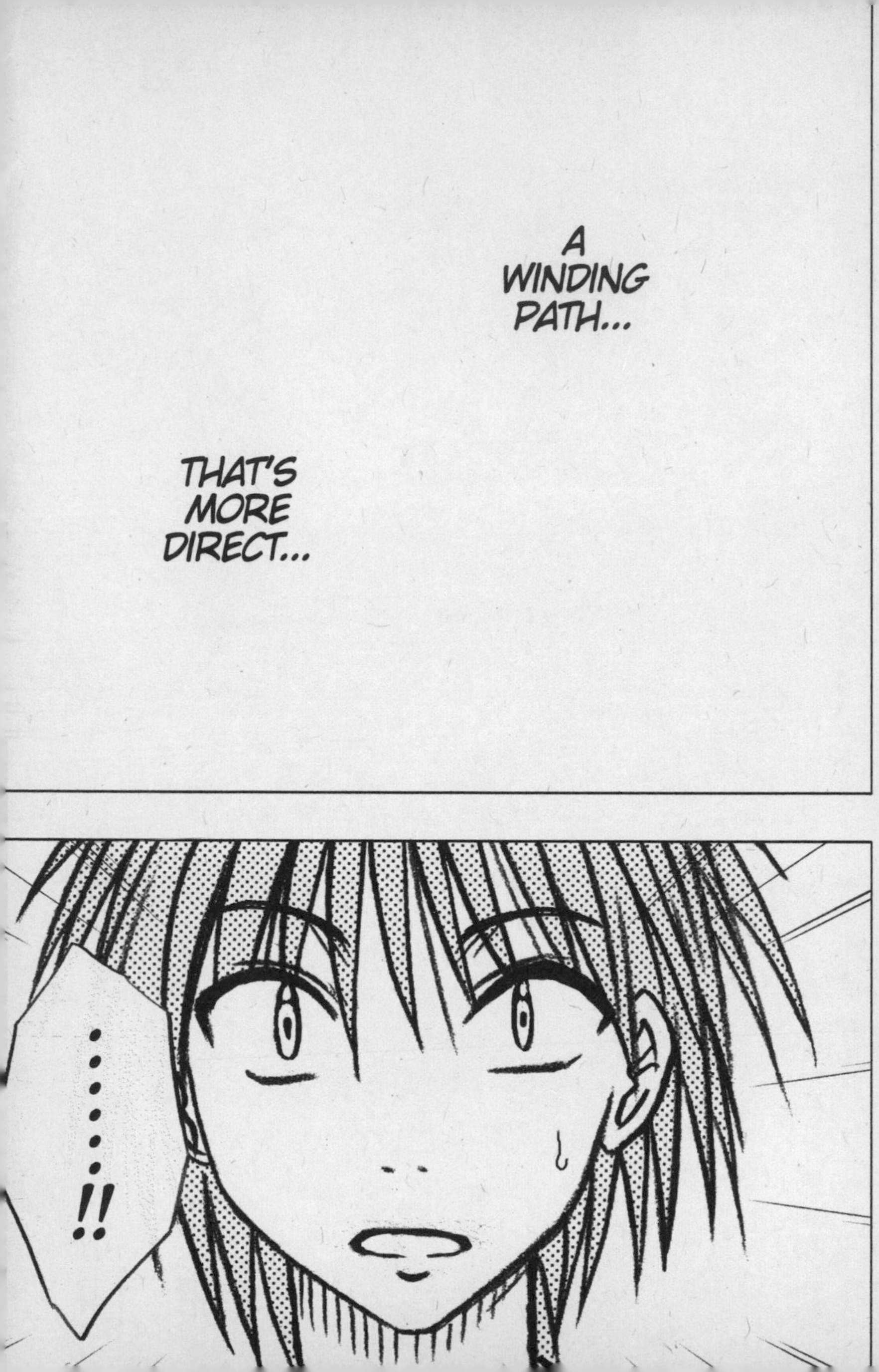
A WINDING PATH...
THAT'S MORE DIRECT...
......!!

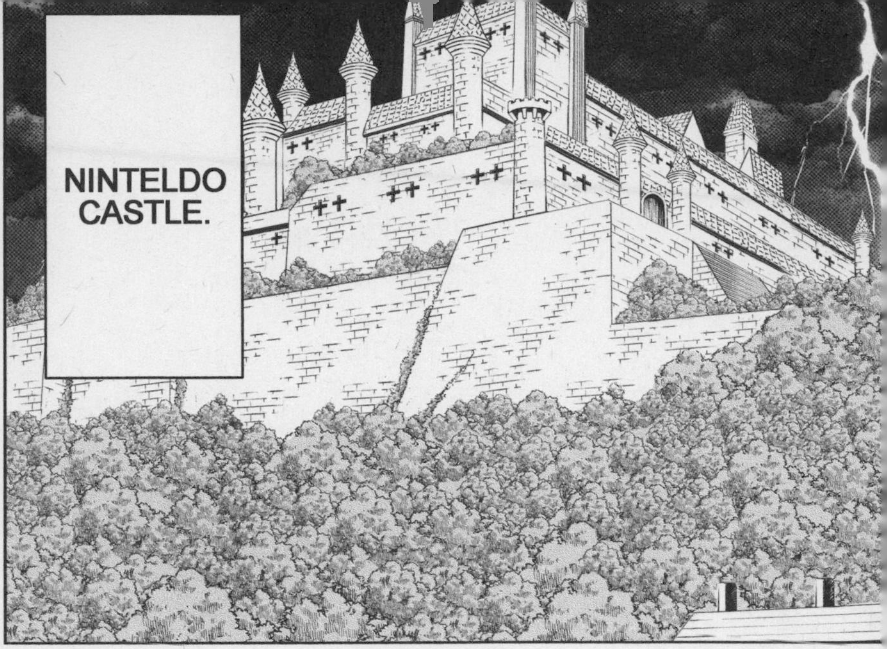
NINTELDO CASTLE.

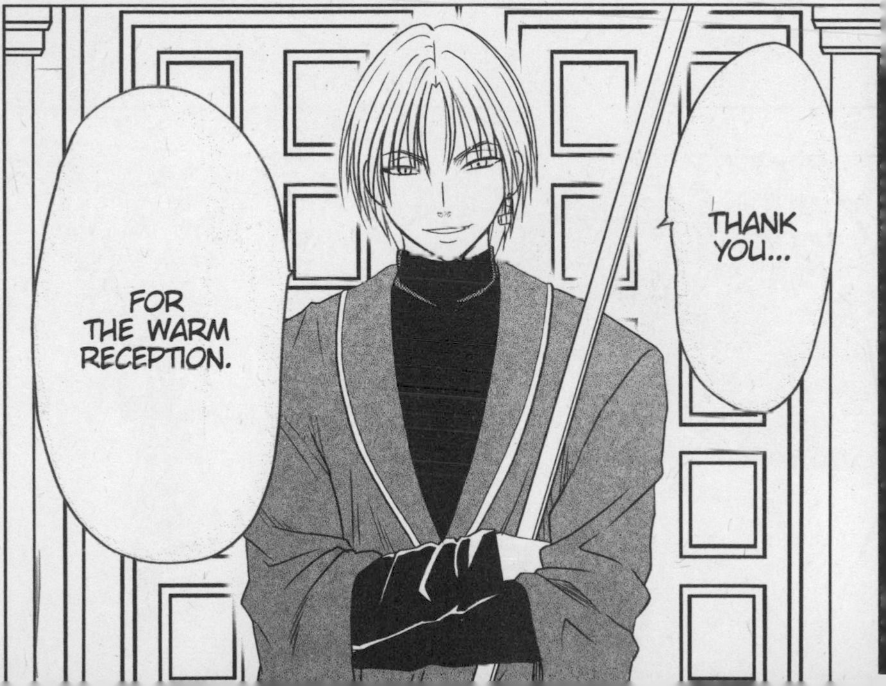
THANK YOU...
FOR THE WARM RECEPTION.

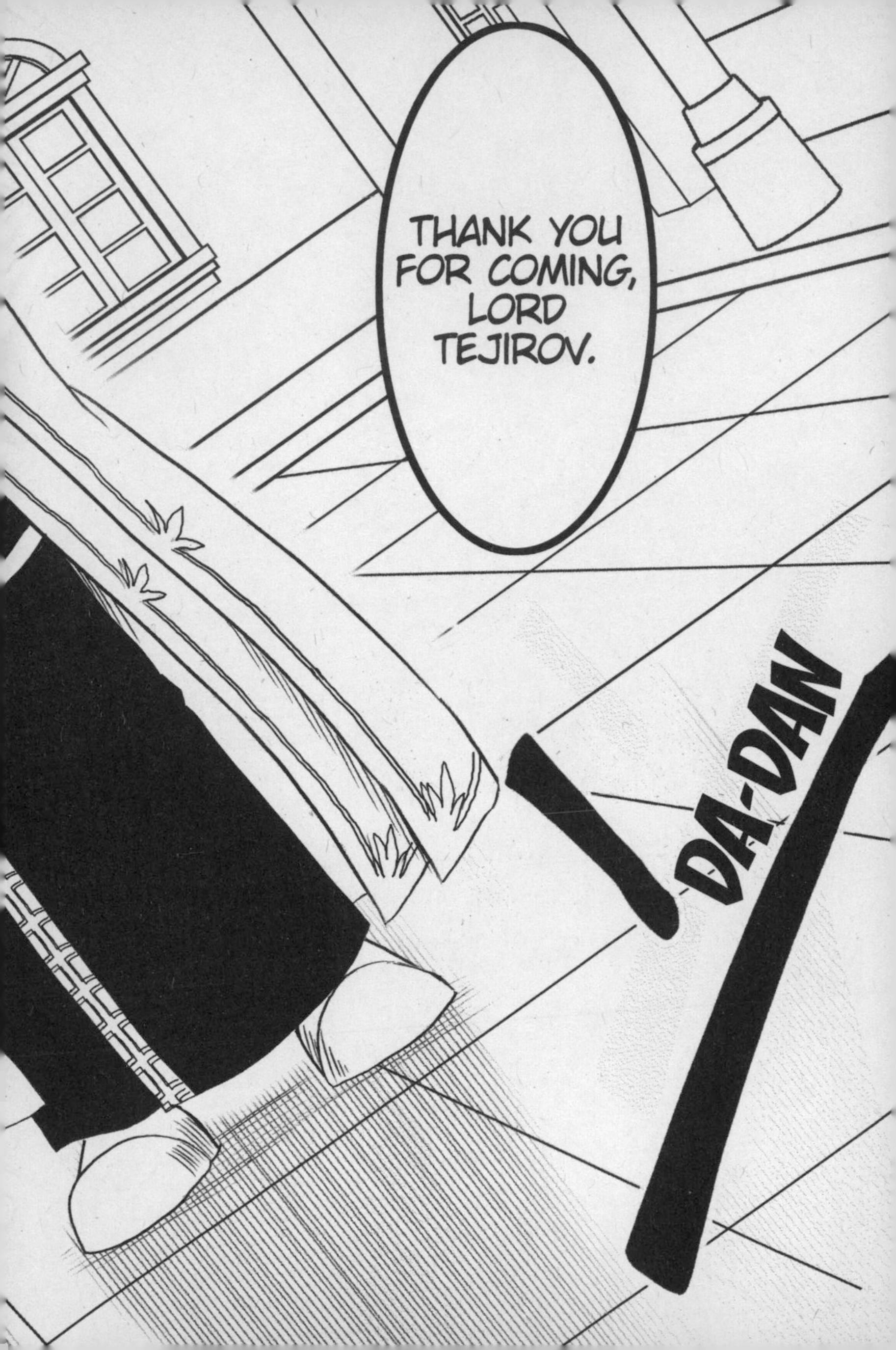
THANK YOU FOR COMING, LORD TEJIROV.
DA-DAN

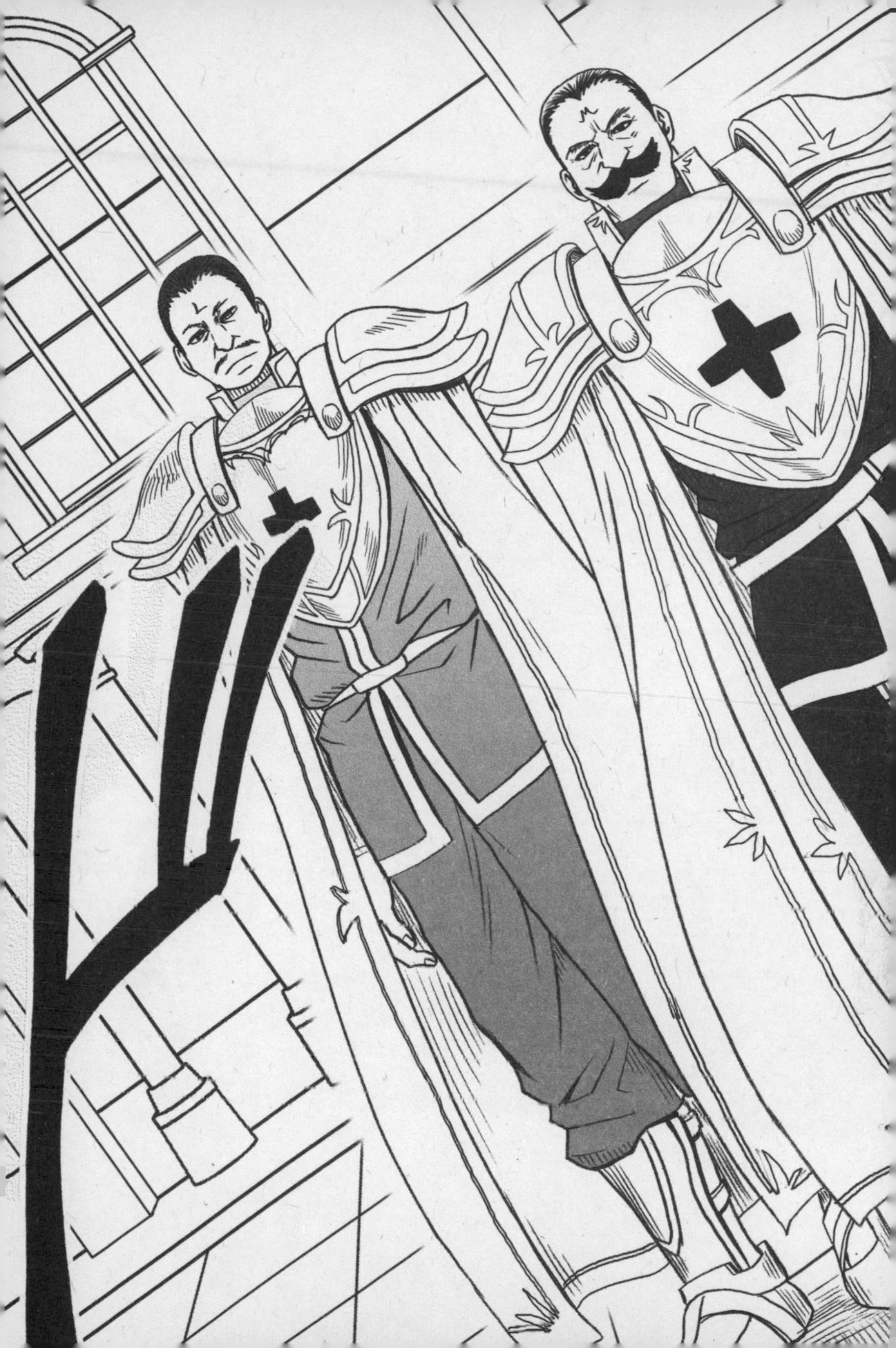

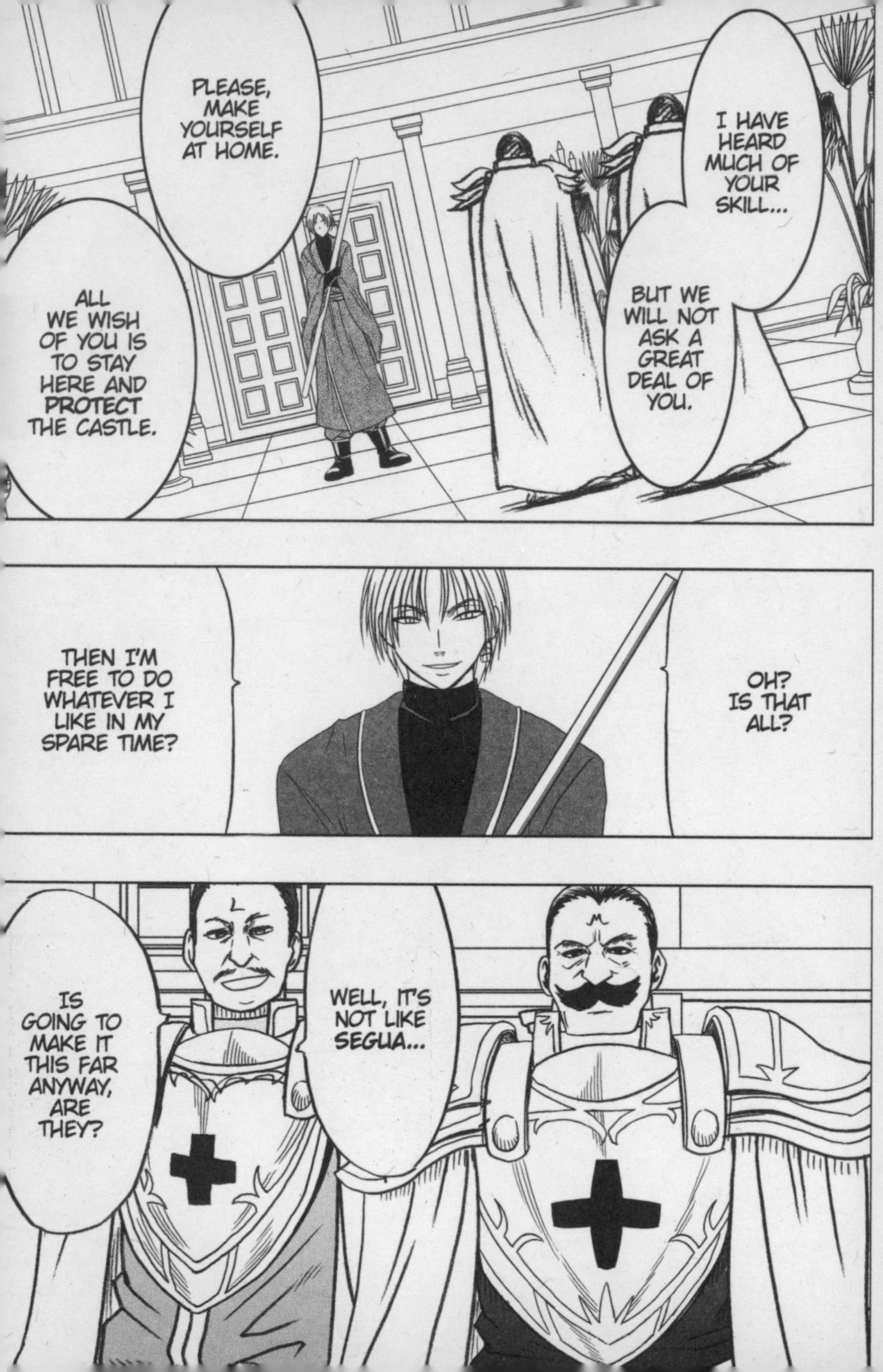
I HAVE HEARD MUCH OF YOUR SKILL...
BUT WE WILL NOT ASK A GREAT DEAL OF YOU.
PLEASE, MAKE YOURSELF AT HOME.
ALL WE WISH OF YOU IS TO STAY HERE AND PROTECT THE CASTLE.
OH? IS THAT ALL?
THEN I'M FREE TO DO WHATEVER I LIKE IN MY SPARE TIME?
WELL, IT'S NOT LIKE SEGUA...
IS GOING TO MAKE IT THIS FAR ANYWAY, ARE THEY?

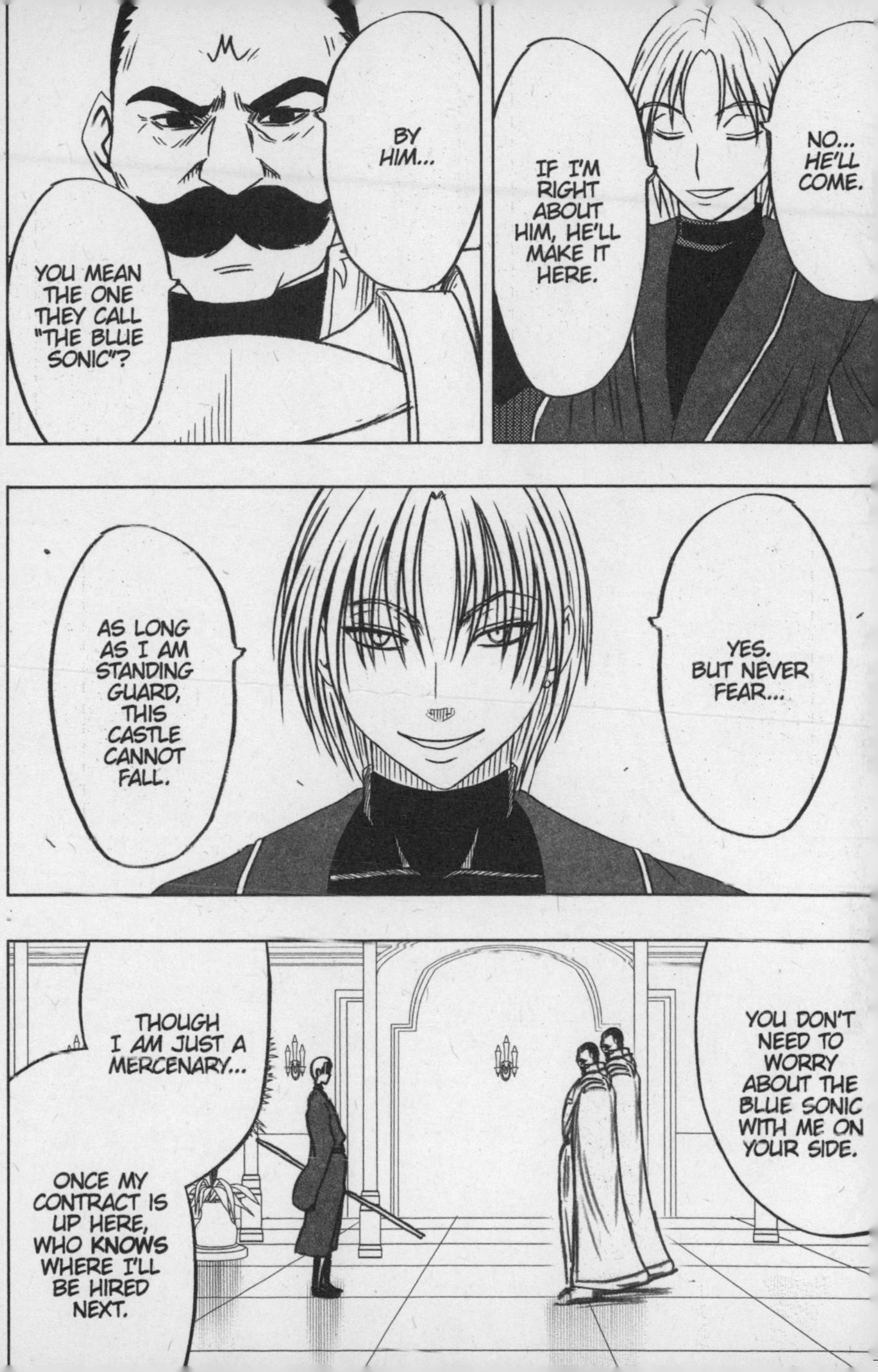
NO... HE'LL COME.
IF I'M RIGHT ABOUT HIM, HE'LL MAKE IT HERE.
BY HIM...
YOU MEAN THE ONE THEY CALL "THE BLUE SONIC"?
YES. BUT NEVER FEAR...
AS LONG AS I AM STANDING GUARD, THIS CASTLE CANNOT FALL.
YOU DON'T NEED TO WORRY ABOUT THE BLUE SONIC WITH ME ON YOUR SIDE.
THOUGH I AM JUST A MERCENARY...
ONCE MY CONTRACT IS UP HERE, WHO KNOWS WHERE I'LL BE HIRED NEXT.

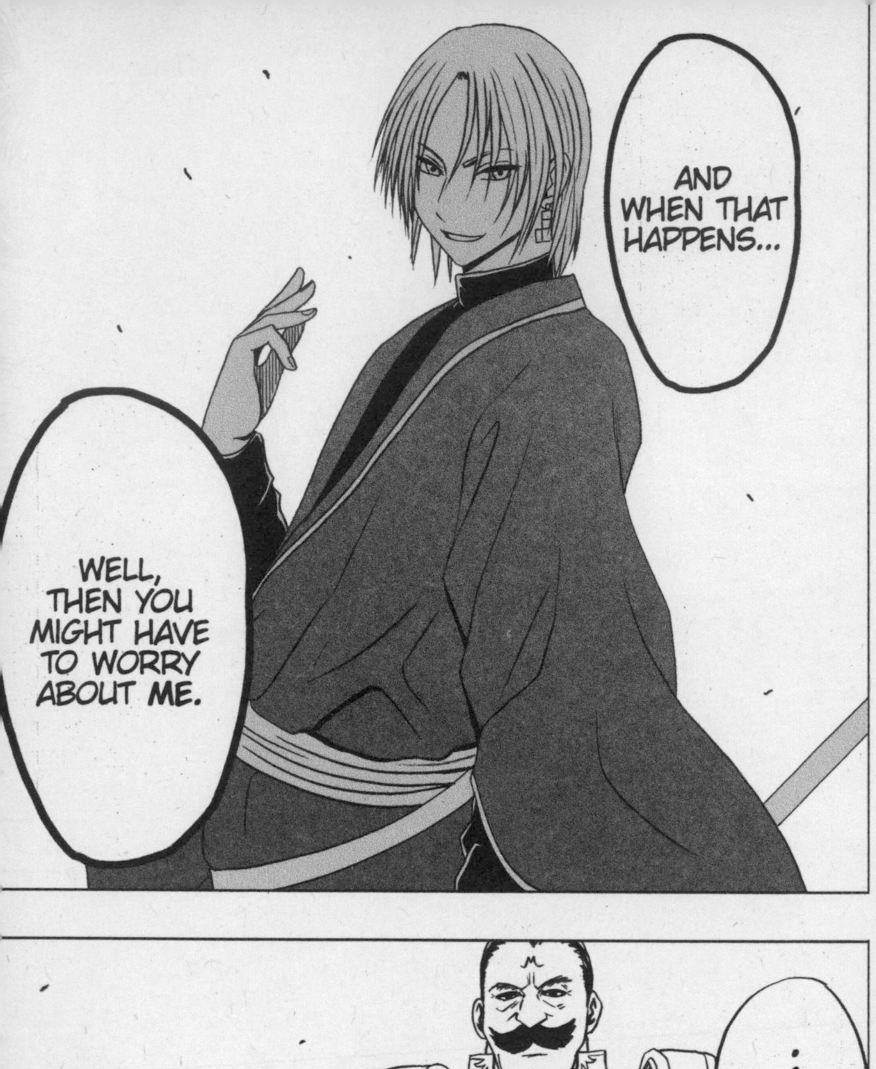
AND WHEN THAT HAPPENS...
WELL, THEN YOU MIGHT HAVE TO WORRY ABOUT ME.

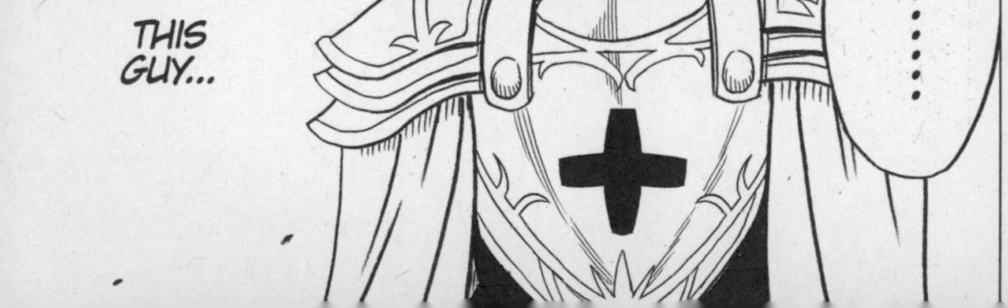
.........
THIS GUY...

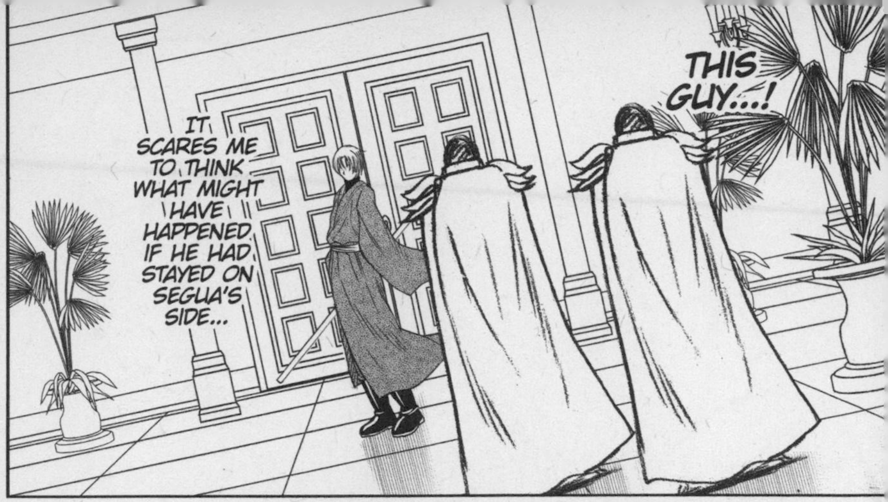
THIS GUY...!
IT SCARES ME TO THINK WHAT MIGHT HAVE HAPPENED IF HE HAD STAYED ON SEGUA'S SIDE...

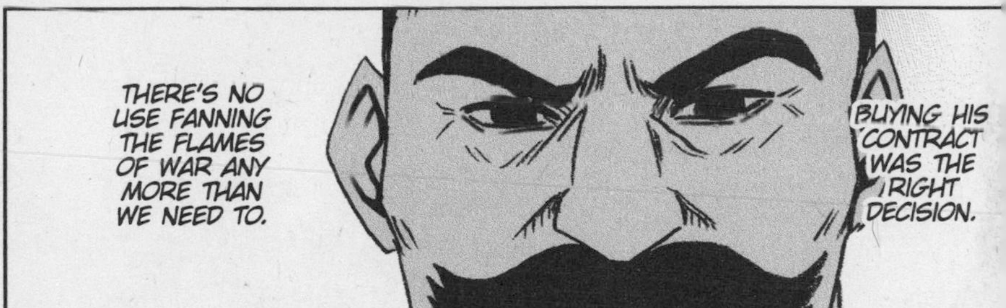
BUYING HIS CONTRACT WAS THE RIGHT DECISION.
THERE'S NO USE FANNING THE FLAMES OF WAR ANY MORE THAN WE NEED TO.

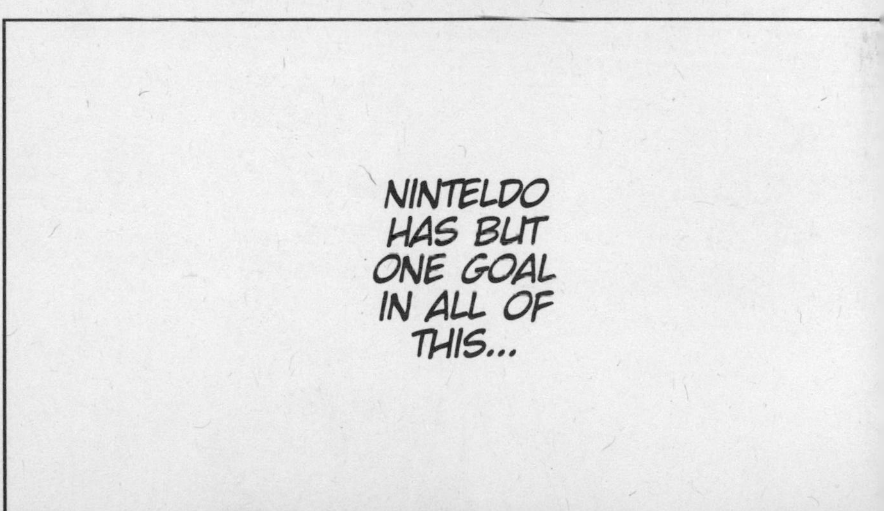
NINTELDO HAS BUT ONE GOAL IN ALL OF THIS...

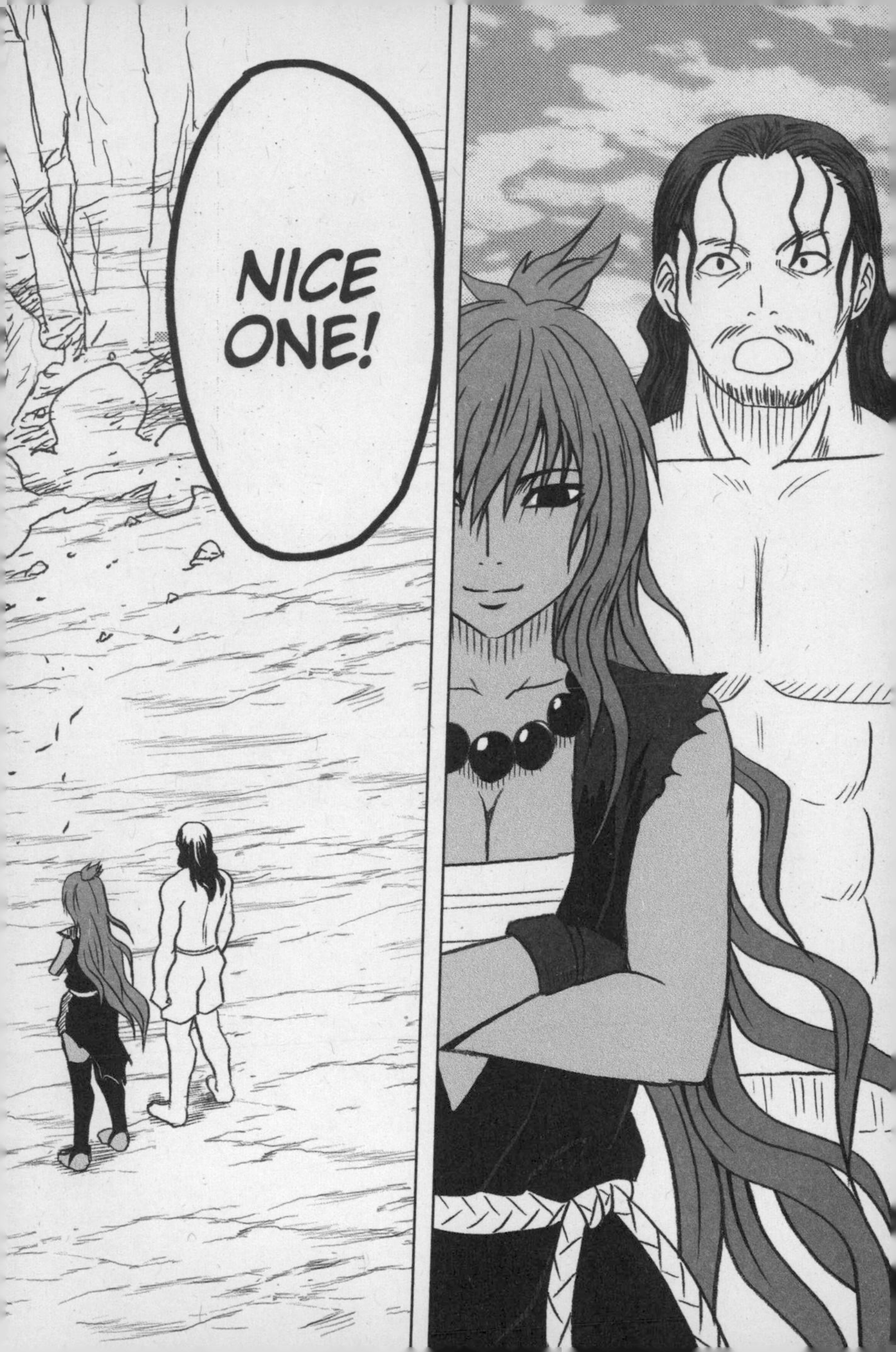
NICE ONE!

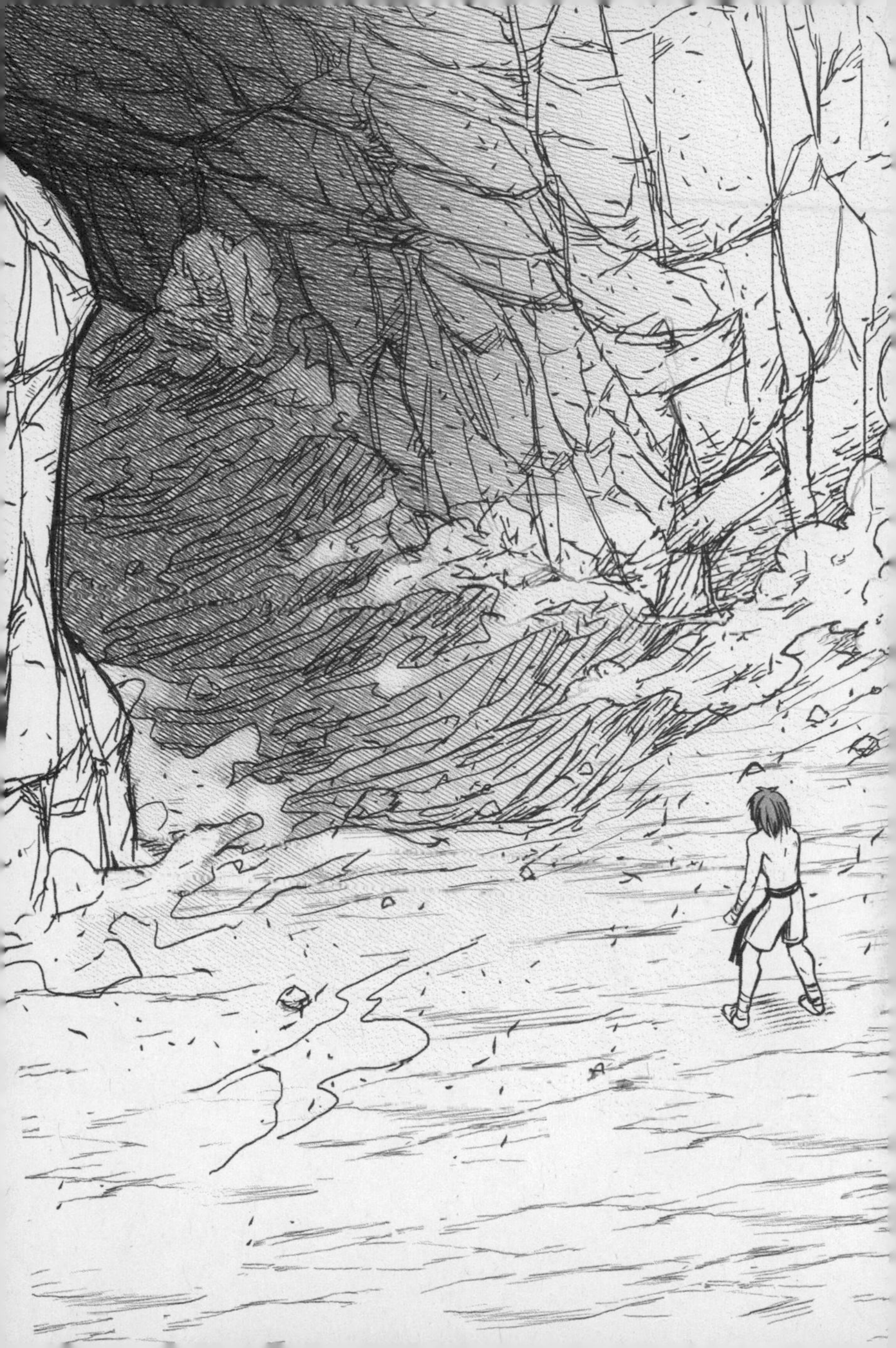

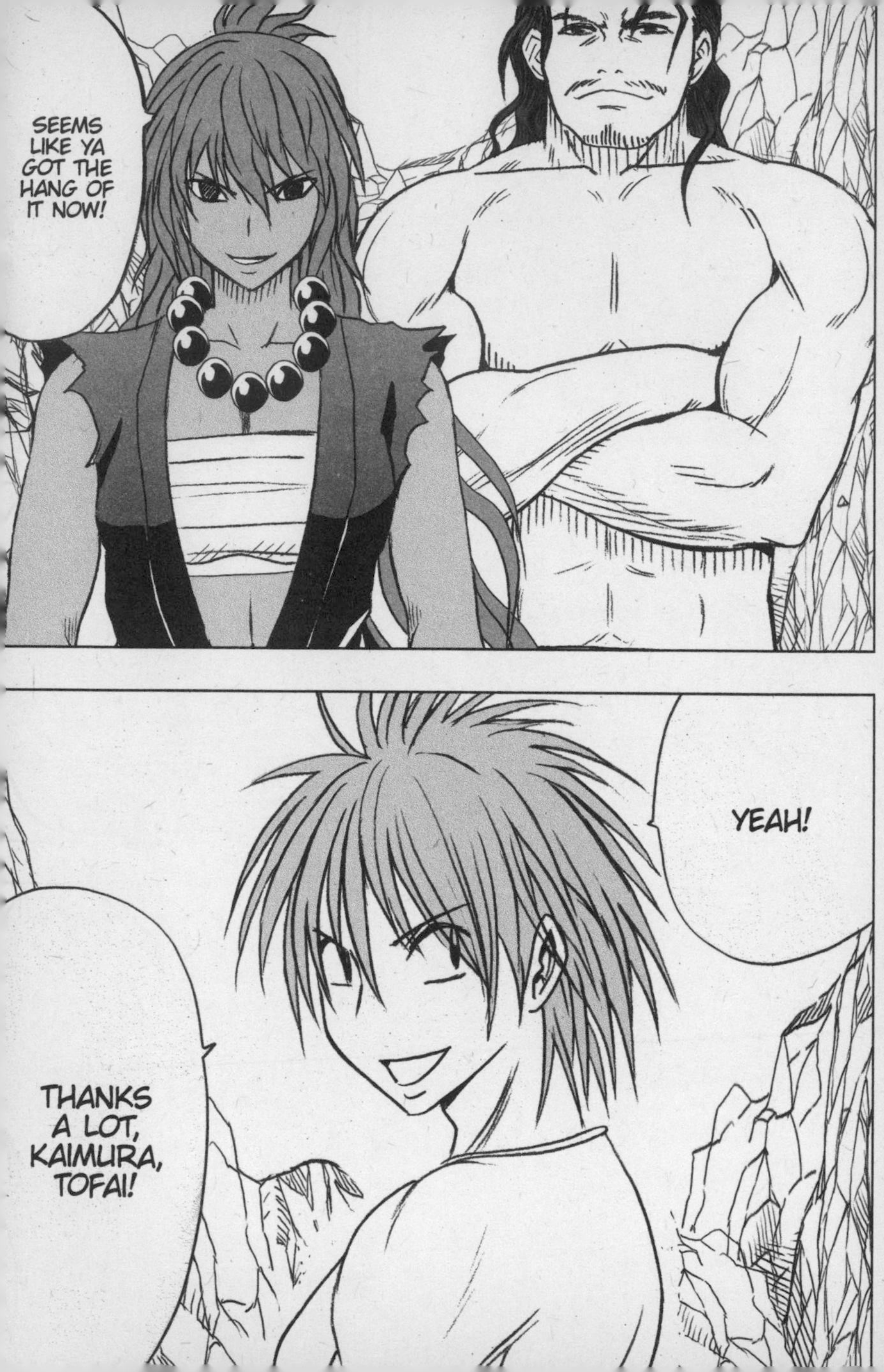
SEEMS LIKE YA GOT THE HANG OF IT NOW!
YEAH!
THANKS A LOT, KAIMURA, TOFAI!

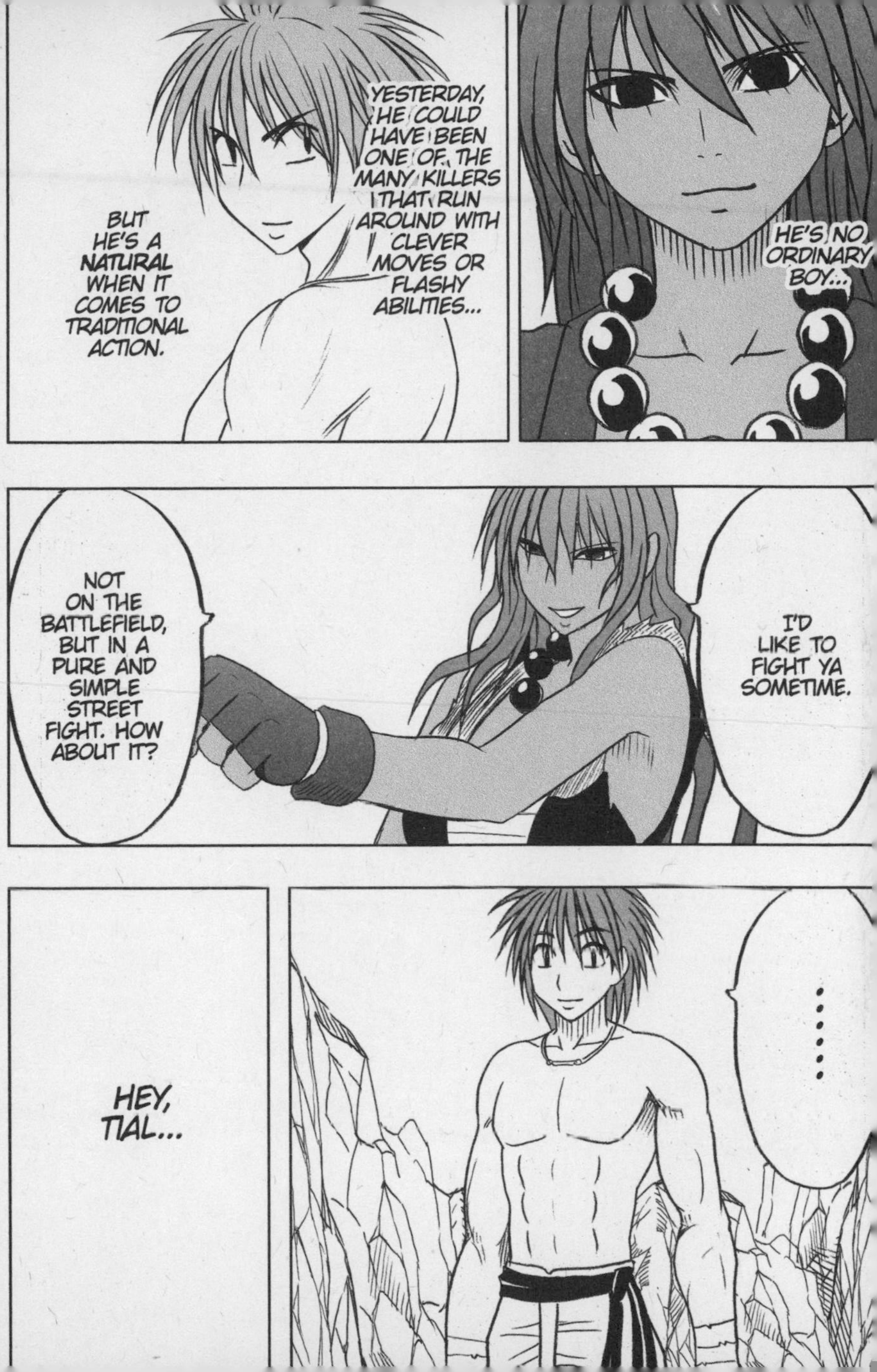
HE'S NO ORDINARY BOY...
YESTERDAY, HE COULD HAVE BEEN ONE OF THE MANY KILLERS THAT RUN AROUND WITH CLEVER MOVES OR FLASHY ABILITIES...
BUT HE'S A NATURAL WHEN IT COMES TO TRADITIONAL ACTION.
I'D LIKE TO FIGHT YA SOMETIME.
NOT ON THE BATTLEFIELD, BUT IN A PURE AND SIMPLE STREET FIGHT. HOW ABOUT IT?
......
HEY, TIAL...

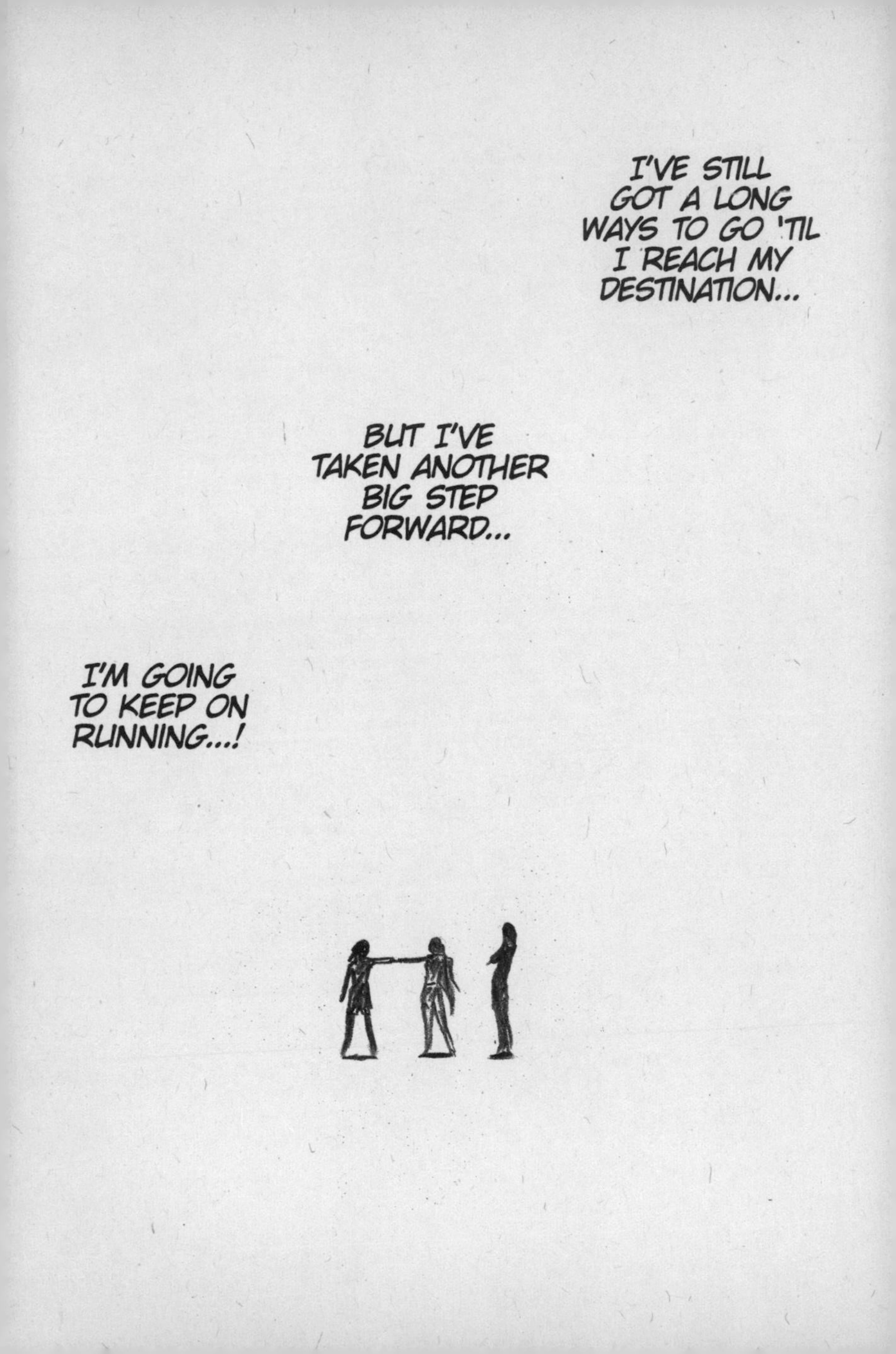
I'VE STILL GOT A LONG WAYS TO GO 'TIL I REACH MY DESTINATION...
BUT I'VE TAKEN ANOTHER BIG STEP FORWARD...
I'M GOING TO KEEP ON RUNNING...!

# WORLD WAR BLUE
## CHARACTER INTRODUCTION

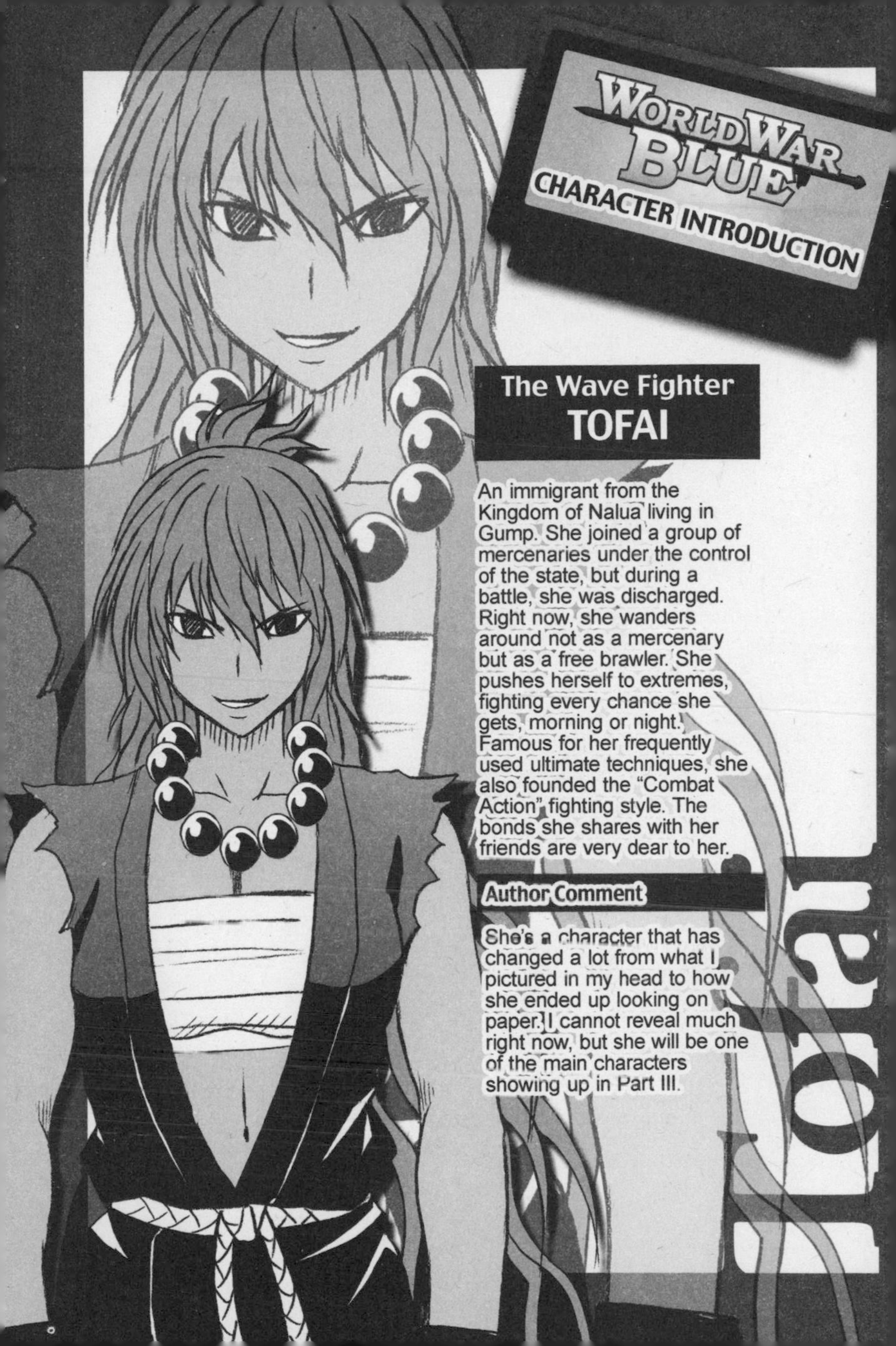

### The Wave Fighter
# TOFAI

An immigrant from the Kingdom of Nalua living in Gump. She joined a group of mercenaries under the control of the state, but during a battle, she was discharged. Right now, she wanders around not as a mercenary but as a free brawler. She pushes herself to extremes, fighting every chance she gets, morning or night. Famous for her frequently used ultimate techniques, she also founded the “Combat Action” fighting style. The bonds she shares with her friends are very dear to her.

**Author Comment**

She's a character that has changed a lot from what I pictured in my head to how she ended up looking on paper. I cannot reveal much right now, but she will be one of the main characters showing up in Part III.

Perusing Video Game History

# ON THE EDGE OF THE BLUE WORLD

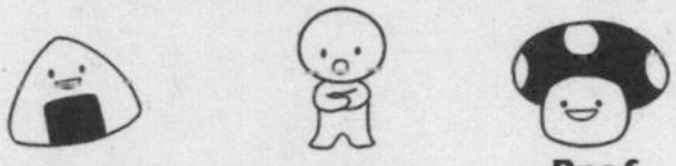

Dr. Onigiri
Mr. Why
Prof. Mushroom


Today's Topic

## CAPCOM

**Mr. Why:** While I'd love to talk more about Tetris, let's take some time to talk a little about Capcom first.

**Dr. Onigiri:** When you think of Capcom, you think of popular series such as *Monster Hunter, Biohazard* (released as *Resident Evil* in North America), *Phoenix Wright: Ace Attorney, Sengoku Basara,* etc. They're an exciting company that has produced numerous killer games.

**Prof. Mushroom:** And they have a history of producing great hits, dating back to the time of the original Famicom/Nintendo.

**Mr. Why:** What kinds of games were they famous for?

**Prof. Mushroom:** Well, let's see... A long time ago, they were pretty famous for shooting games. Even back then Capcom was synonymous with "action."

**Prof. Mushroom:** But they became really famous for their fighting games, a genre we were discussing back in volume 2.

**Mr. Why:** *SFII!*

**Dr. Onigiri:** Indeed. In *Street Fighter II,* you input the commands to throw out your ultimate attacks. One-on-one fighting games were all the rage in Japan, but those came a little later in the timeline (1991, to be precise).

**Prof. Mushroom:** In 1985, arcade game graphics were improving and 2D-style side-scrolling games of all kinds were beginning to have a huge presence in arcades.
It was during this time that Capcom released one of their masterpieces, *Ghosts 'n Goblins,* which received a popular home console port the following year.

**Mr. Why:** *Ghosts 'n Goblins...* that sounds like a scary name for a game.

**Prof. Mushroom:** You play the role of Arthur, a knight on a quest to save his princess. You fight zombies and other monsters, but if you get hit, your armor goes flying off and you're left running around in your underwear.

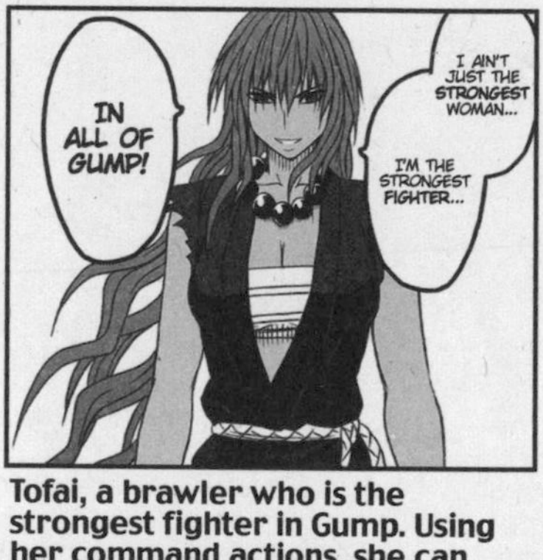

I AIN'T JUST THE STRONGEST WOMAN...
I'M THE STRONGEST FIGHTER...
IN ALL OF GUMP!


**Tofai, a brawler who is the strongest fighter in Gump. Using her command actions, she can launch various attacks.**

**Dr. Onigiri:** Right! Sega was the first one that had *Tetris*, but then...

**Prof. Mushroom:** Oops, we're out of time! We'll have to tell the rest of the story later!

To be continued...

KI-YAH!

**All of those who live in the Federation of Gump are fighters. They go through rigorous hand-to-hand combat training and many of them are well trained in the use of action.**

YOU MUST BE EAGER TO BEGIN YOUR TRAINING!

NOW THEN...

**Kaimura, master of action. A fighter skilled with the lance. He wears nothing under his armor and is quick to strip down to his underwear.**

The spookiness and humor in *Ghosts 'n Goblins* really made this traditional action game special. Using the lance as a weapon was also a fairly new idea.

**Dr. Onigiri:** It was even released by Sega...

**Dr. Onigiri:** The original 1988 sequel, *Ghouls 'n Ghosts,* was also released on the Sega Mega Drive/Genesis, but when Sega ported it to the Genesis, they used that game's technology and ideas to make *Sonic The Hedgehog.* You could even say that without *Ghouls 'n Ghosts,* Sonic wouldn't exist.

**Mr. Why:** Speaking of games released by Sega, why didn't they release *Tetris* on their home consoles?

**Prof. Mushroom:** Nintendo released *Tetris* for their home and portable consoles.

**Dr. Onigiri:** There is a very good reason for that...

**Mr. Why:** Oh, this sounds like a sad story.

**Prof. Mushroom:** We mentioned that *Tetris* is a Russian game last time, didn't we?

**Dr. Onigiri:** So, Sega purchased the rights to release the game in arcades...

**Mr. Why:** Oh, but I thought Nintendo released *Tetris* first. But that's not right, is it?

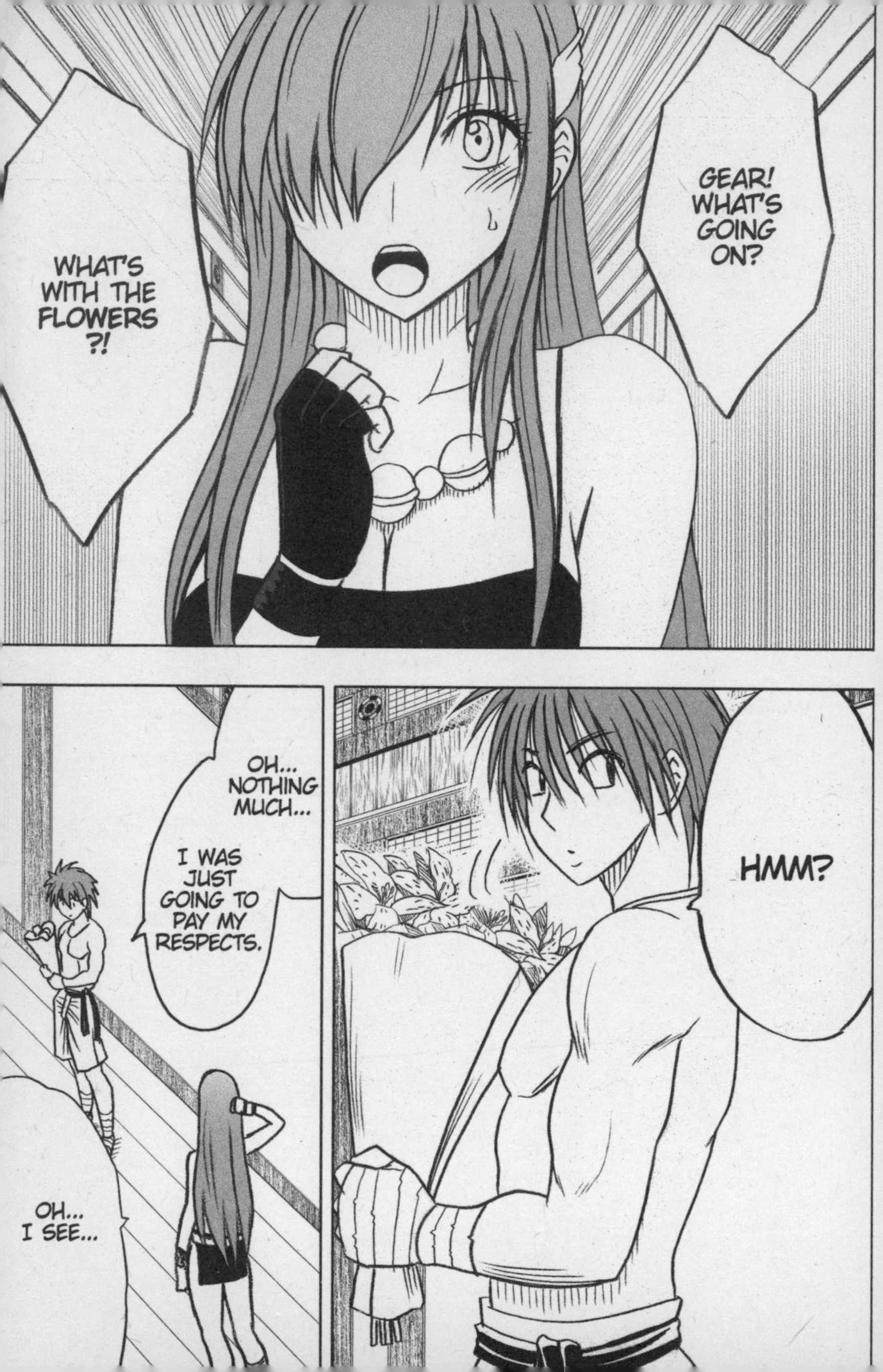
GEAR! WHAT'S GOING ON?
WHAT'S WITH THE FLOWERS ?!
HMM?
OH... NOTHING MUCH...
I WAS JUST GOING TO PAY MY RESPECTS.
OH... I SEE...

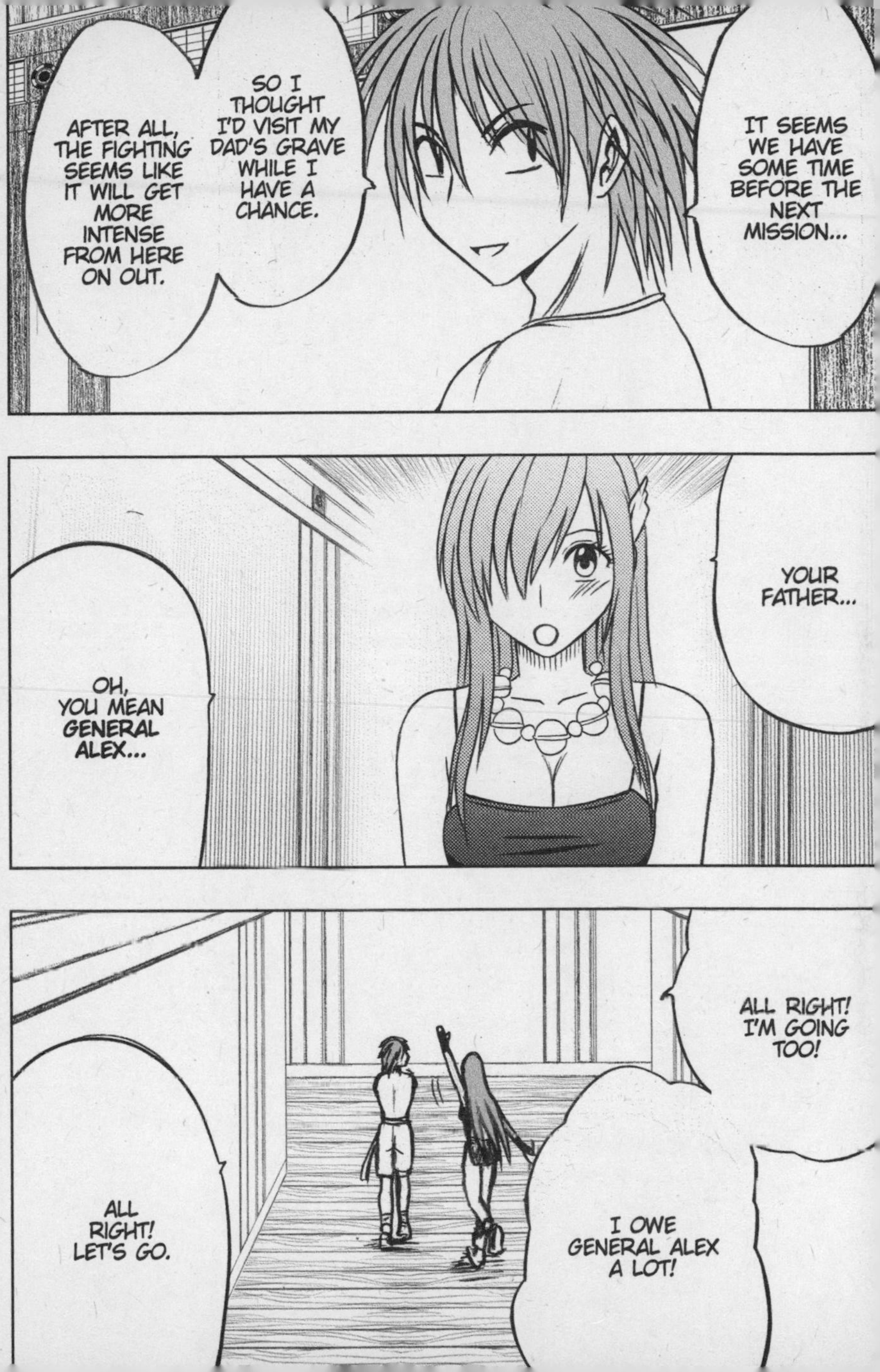
IT SEEMS WE HAVE SOME TIME BEFORE THE NEXT MISSION...
SO I THOUGHT I'D VISIT MY DAD'S GRAVE WHILE I HAVE A CHANCE.
AFTER ALL, THE FIGHTING SEEMS LIKE IT WILL GET MORE INTENSE FROM HERE ON OUT.
YOUR FATHER...
OH, YOU MEAN GENERAL ALEX...
ALL RIGHT! I'M GOING TOO!
I OWE GENERAL ALEX A LOT!
ALL RIGHT! LET'S GO.

Part 2

# CHAPTER 16

# NINTELDO'S TEJIROV

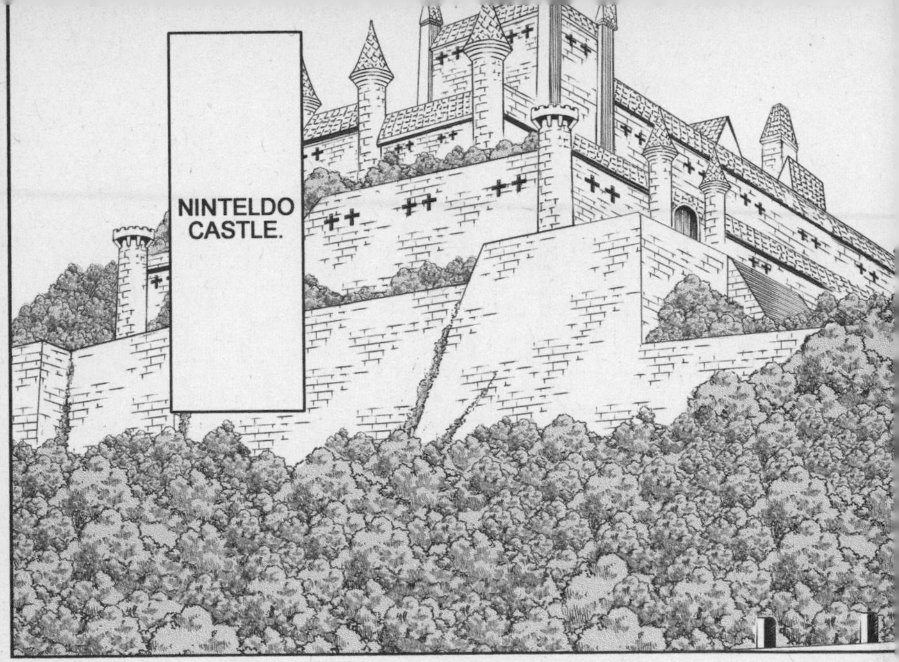
NINTELDO CASTLE.
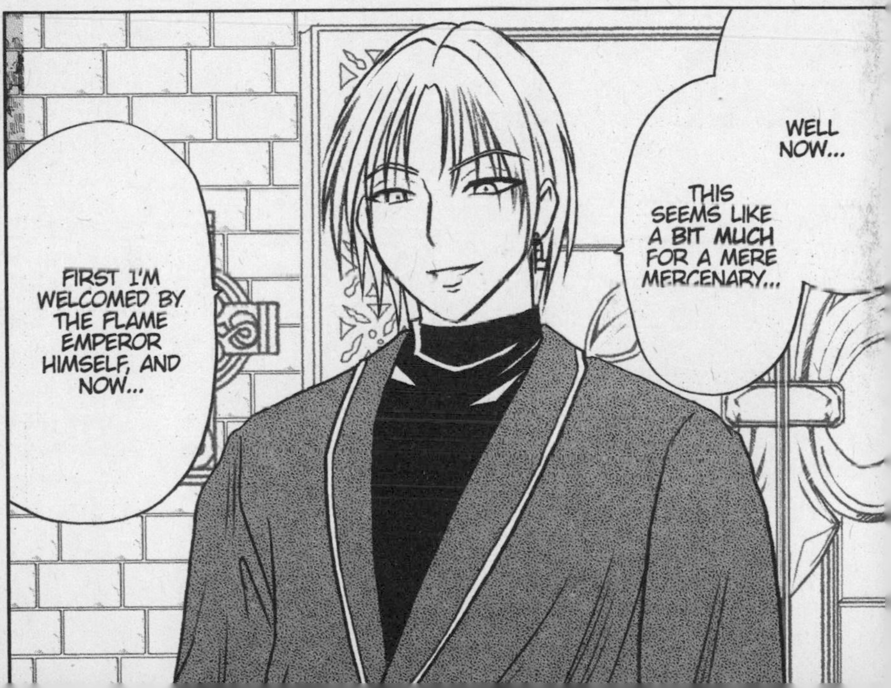
WELL NOW...
THIS SEEMS LIKE A BIT MUCH FOR A MERE MERCENARY...
FIRST I'M WELCOMED BY THE FLAME EMPEROR HIMSELF, AND NOW...

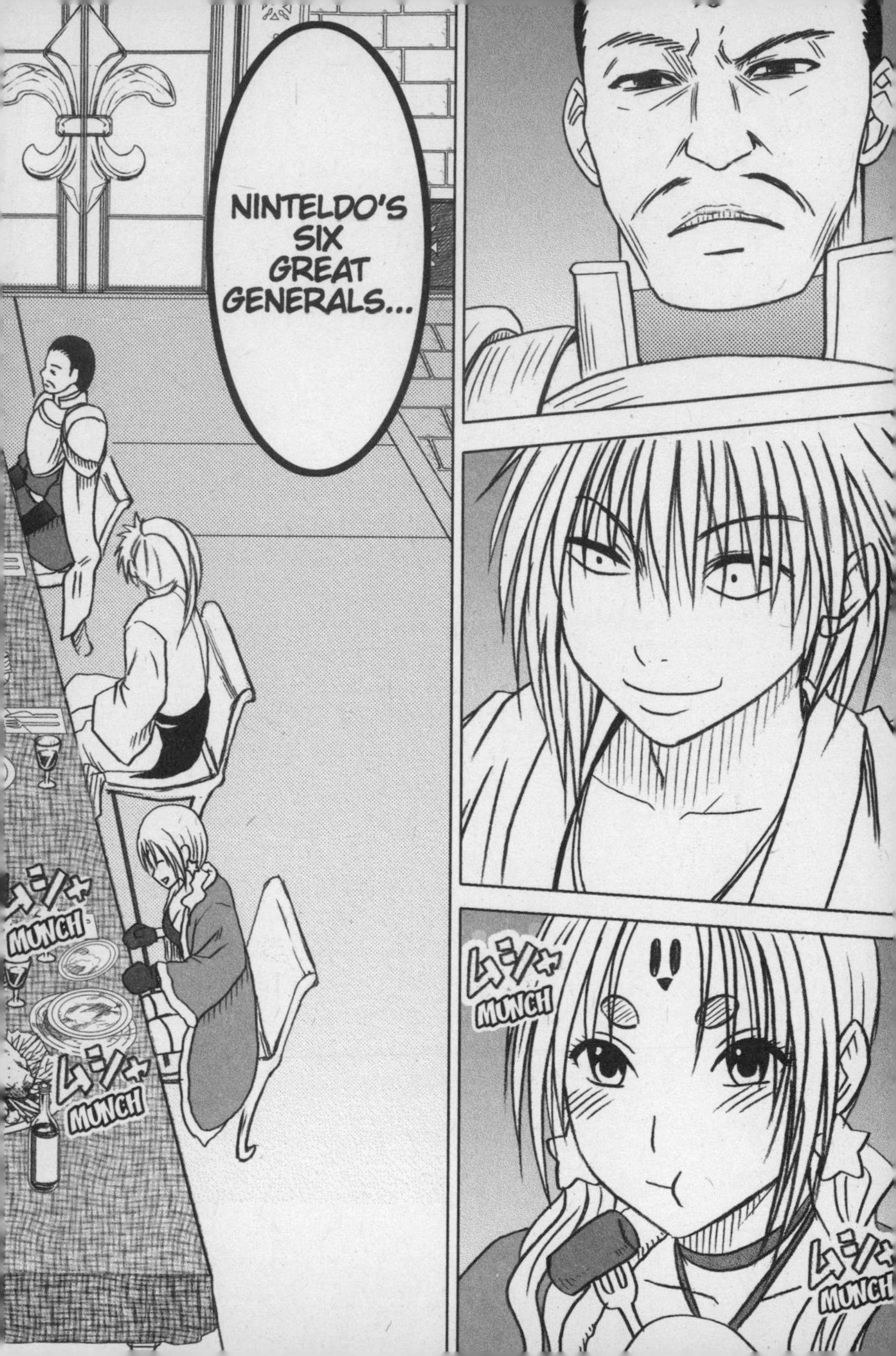
ムシャ
MUNCH
ムシャ
MUNCH
NINTELDO'S SIX GREAT GENERALS...
ムシャ
MUNCH
ムシャ
MUNCH

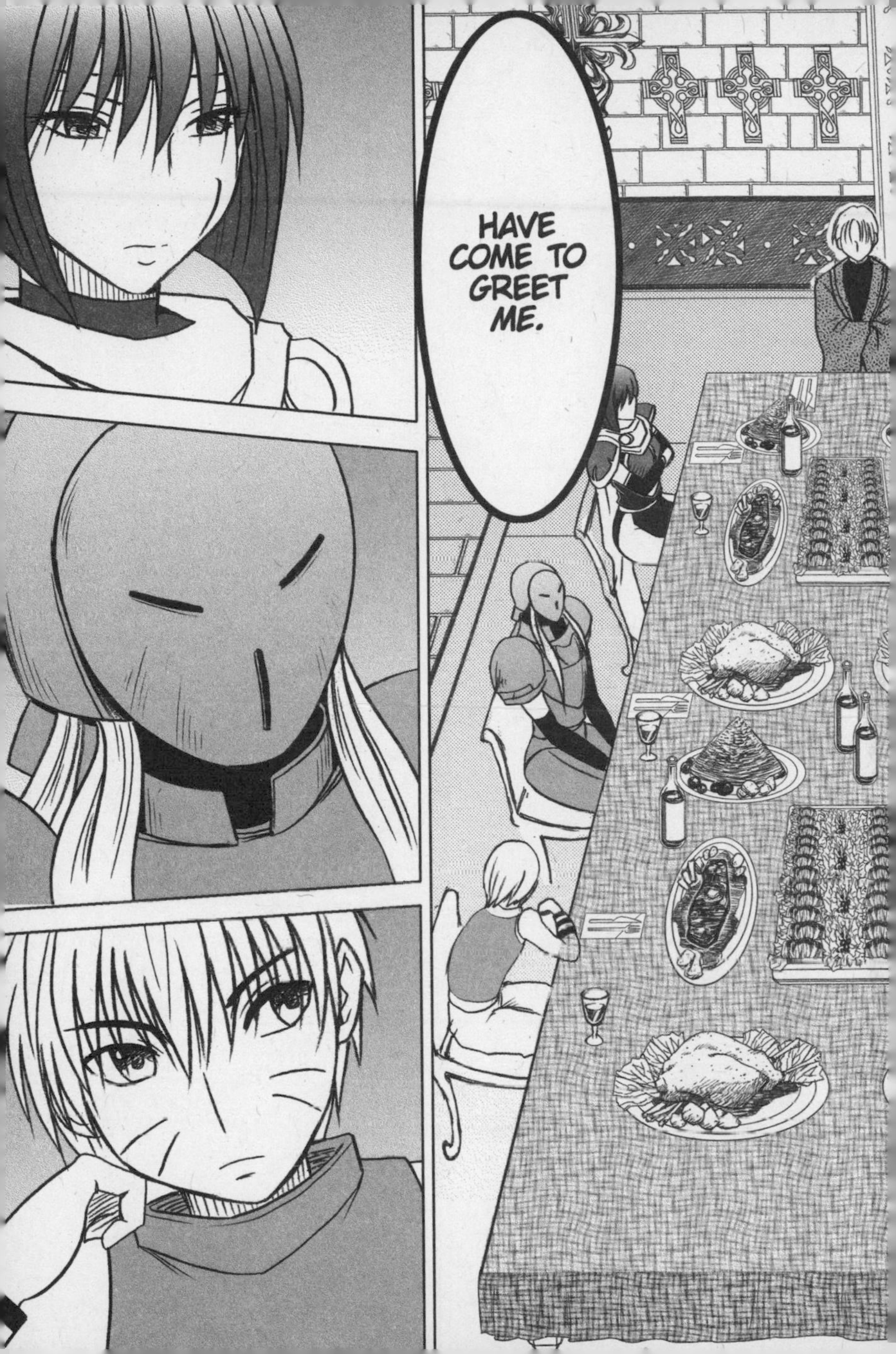
HAVE COME TO GREET ME.

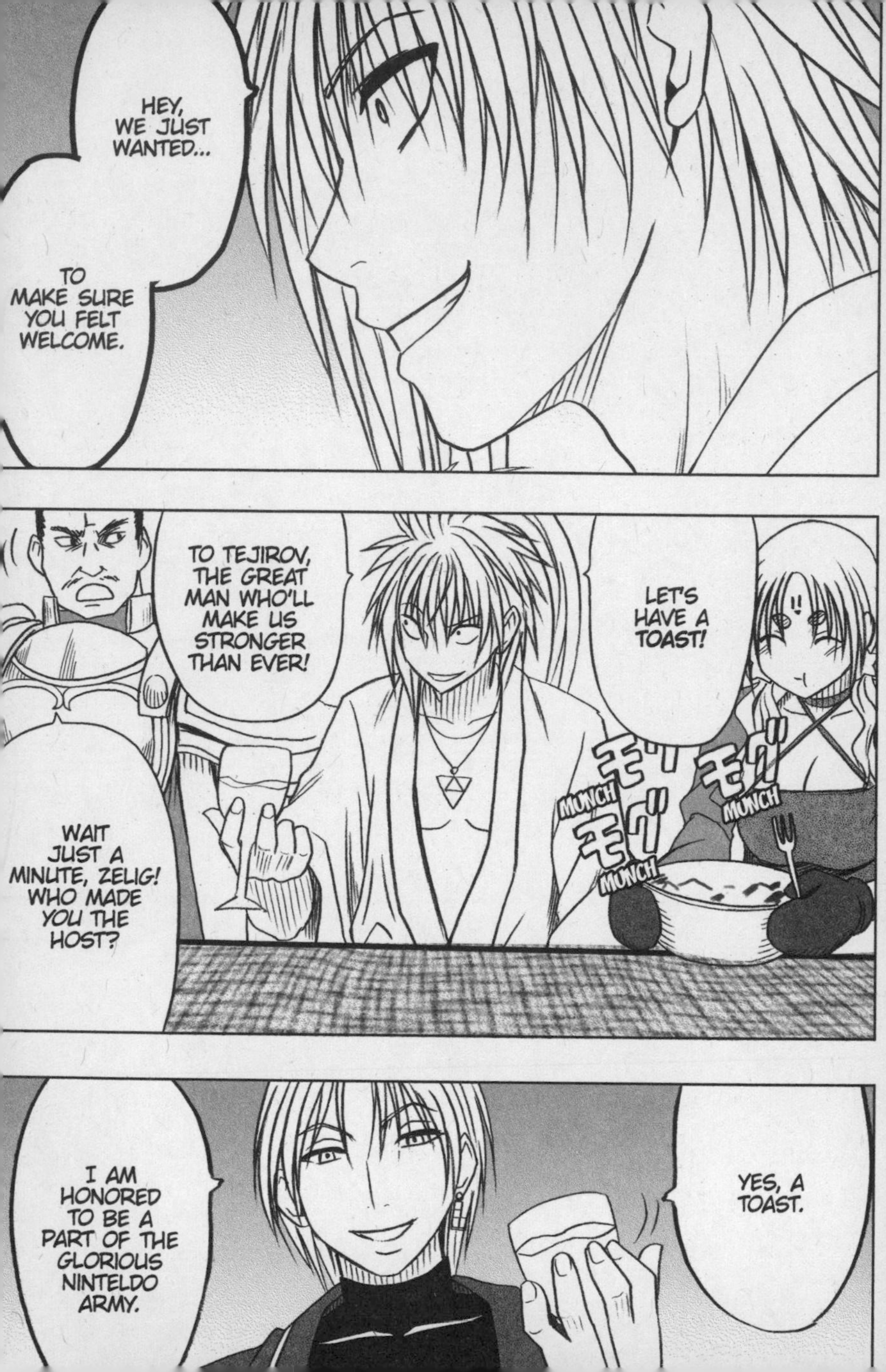
HEY, WE JUST WANTED...
TO MAKE SURE YOU FELT WELCOME.
LET'S HAVE A TOAST!
モグ
MUNCH
モッ
MUNCH
モグ
MUNCH
TO TEJIROV, THE GREAT MAN WHO'LL MAKE US STRONGER THAN EVER!
WAIT JUST A MINUTE, ZELIG! WHO MADE YOU THE HOST?
YES, A TOAST.
I AM HONORED TO BE A PART OF THE GLORIOUS NINTELDO ARMY.

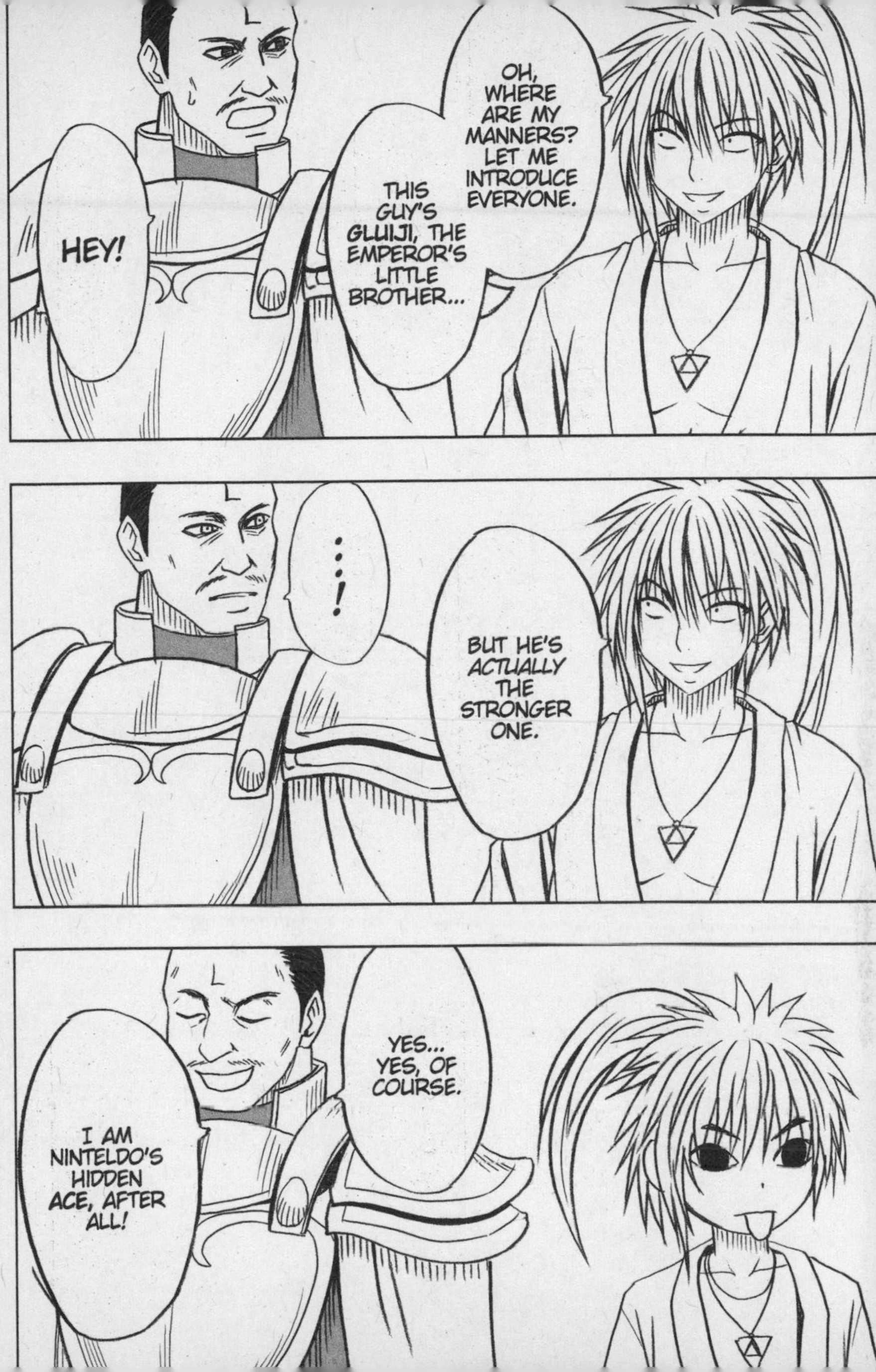
OH, WHERE ARE MY MANNERS? LET ME INTRODUCE EVERYONE.
THIS GUY'S GLUIJI, THE EMPEROR'S LITTLE BROTHER...
HEY!
BUT HE'S ACTUALLY THE STRONGER ONE.
...!
YES... YES, OF COURSE.
I AM NINTELDO'S HIDDEN ACE, AFTER ALL!

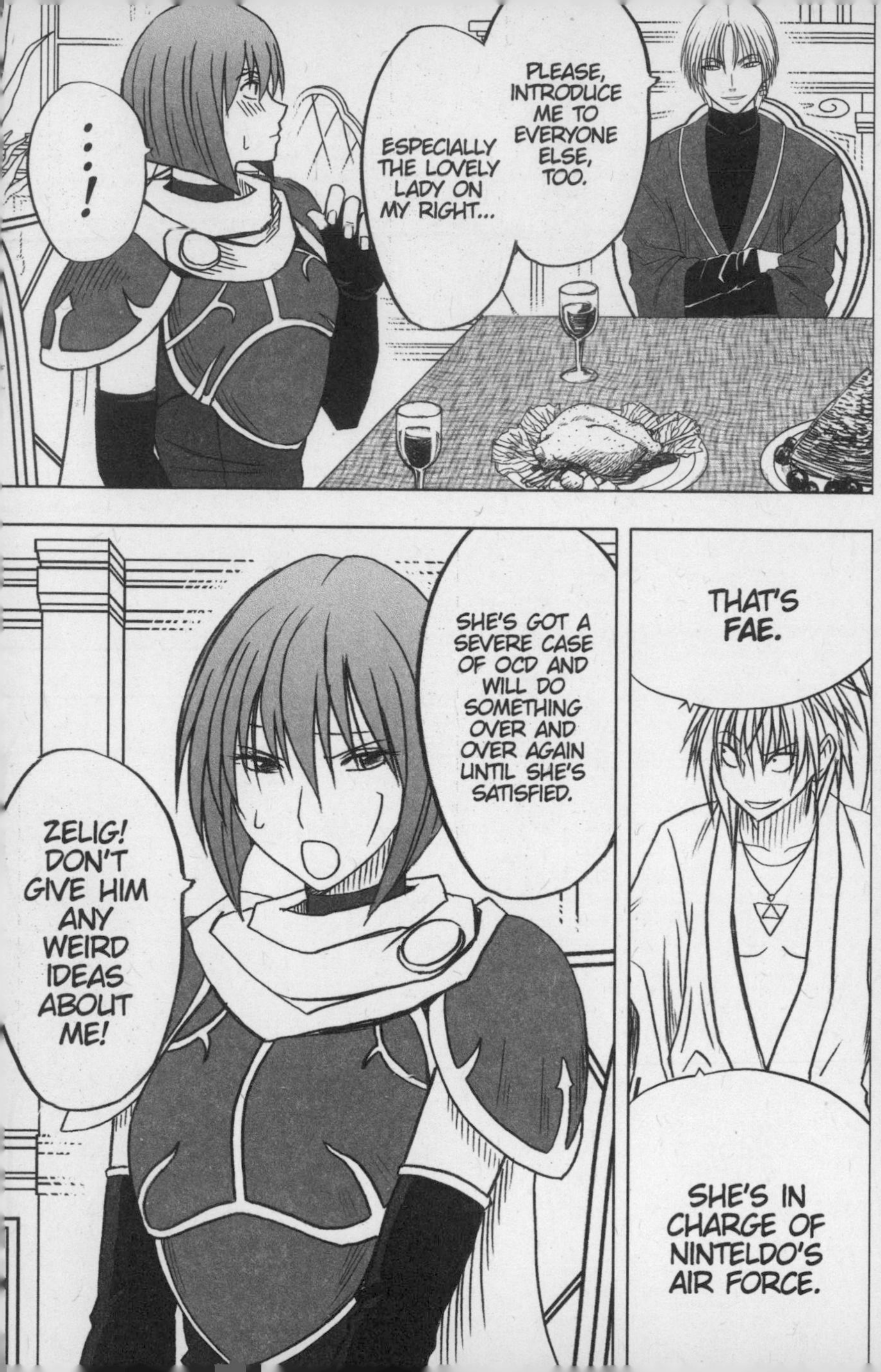
PLEASE, INTRODUCE ME TO EVERYONE ELSE, TOO.
ESPECIALLY THE LOVELY LADY ON MY RIGHT...
...!
THAT'S FAE.
SHE'S IN CHARGE OF NINTELDO'S AIR FORCE.
SHE'S GOT A SEVERE CASE OF OCD AND WILL DO SOMETHING OVER AND OVER AGAIN UNTIL SHE'S SATISFIED.
ZELIG! DON'T GIVE HIM ANY WEIRD IDEAS ABOUT ME!

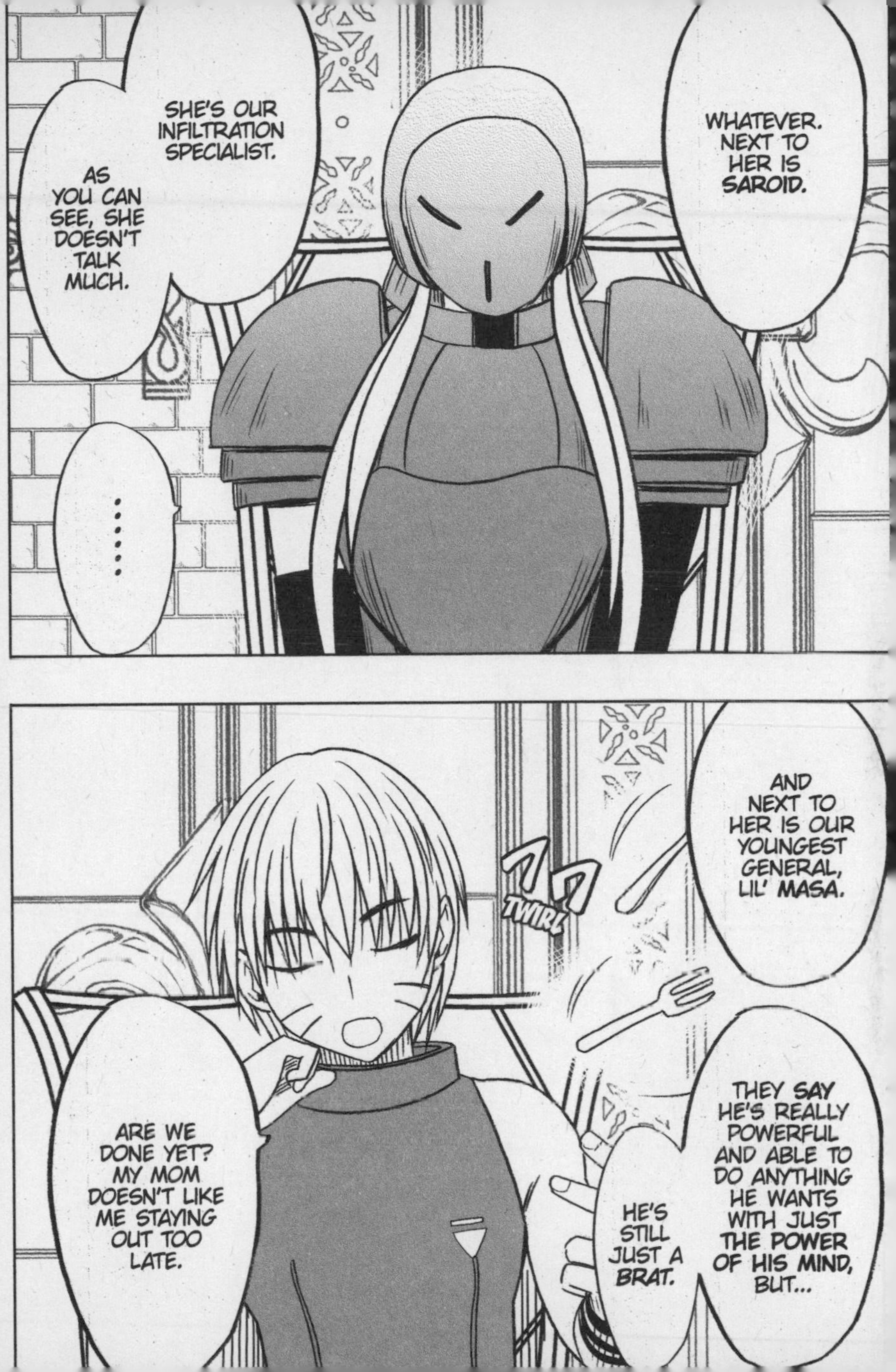
WHATEVER. NEXT TO HER IS SAROID.
SHE'S OUR INFILTRATION SPECIALIST.
AS YOU CAN SEE, SHE DOESN'T TALK MUCH.
......
AND NEXT TO HER IS OUR YOUNGEST GENERAL, LIL' MASA.
TWIRL
THEY SAY HE'S REALLY POWERFUL AND ABLE TO DO ANYTHING HE WANTS WITH JUST THE POWER OF HIS MIND, BUT...
HE'S STILL JUST A BRAT.
ARE WE DONE YET? MY MOM DOESN'T LIKE ME STAYING OUT TOO LATE.

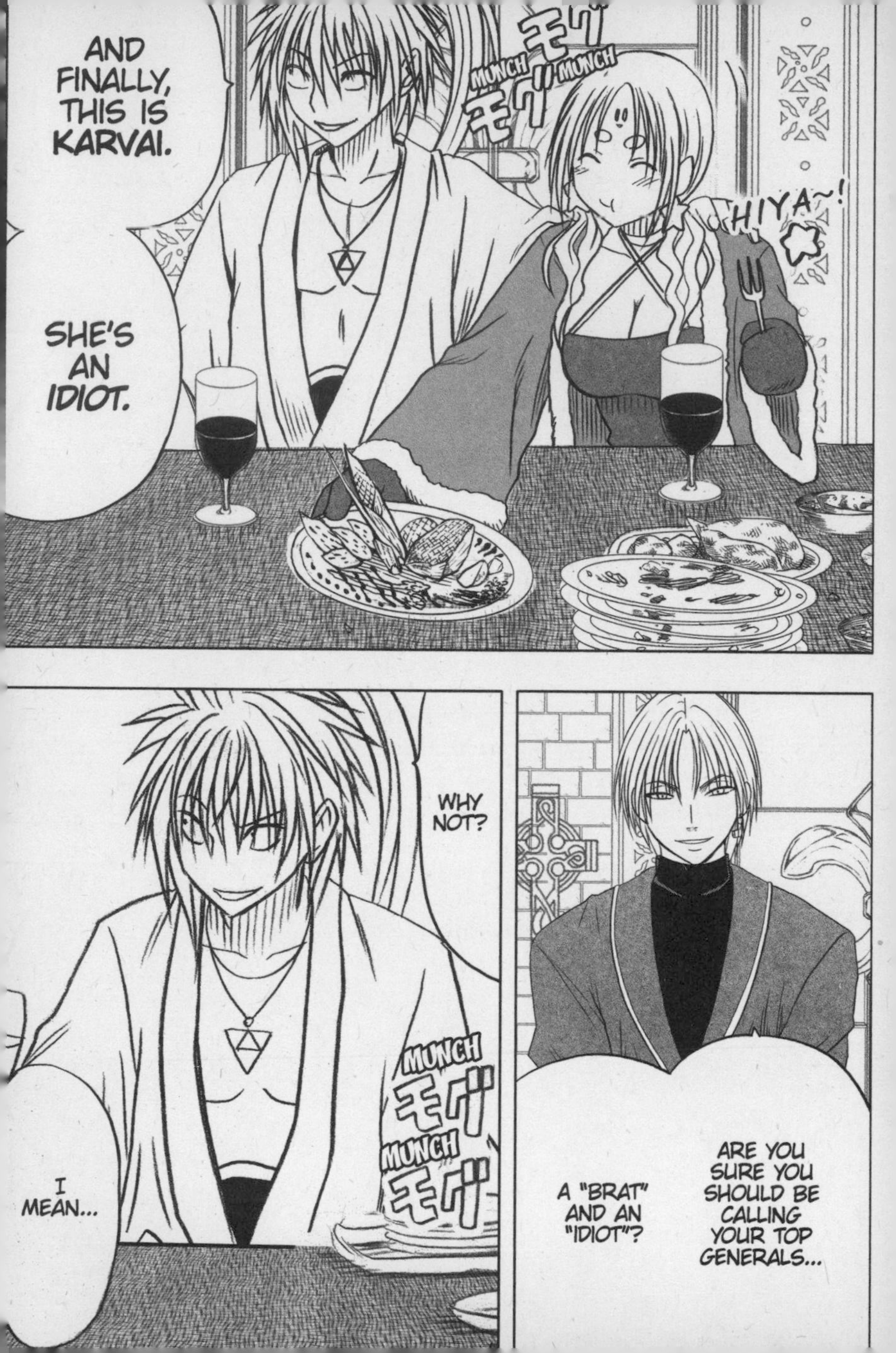
MUNCH モグ MUNCH モグ
HIYA~!
AND FINALLY, THIS IS KARVAI.
SHE'S AN IDIOT.
ARE YOU SURE YOU SHOULD BE CALLING YOUR TOP GENERALS...
A "BRAT" AND AN "IDIOT"?
WHY NOT?
MUNCH モグ MUNCH モグ
I MEAN...

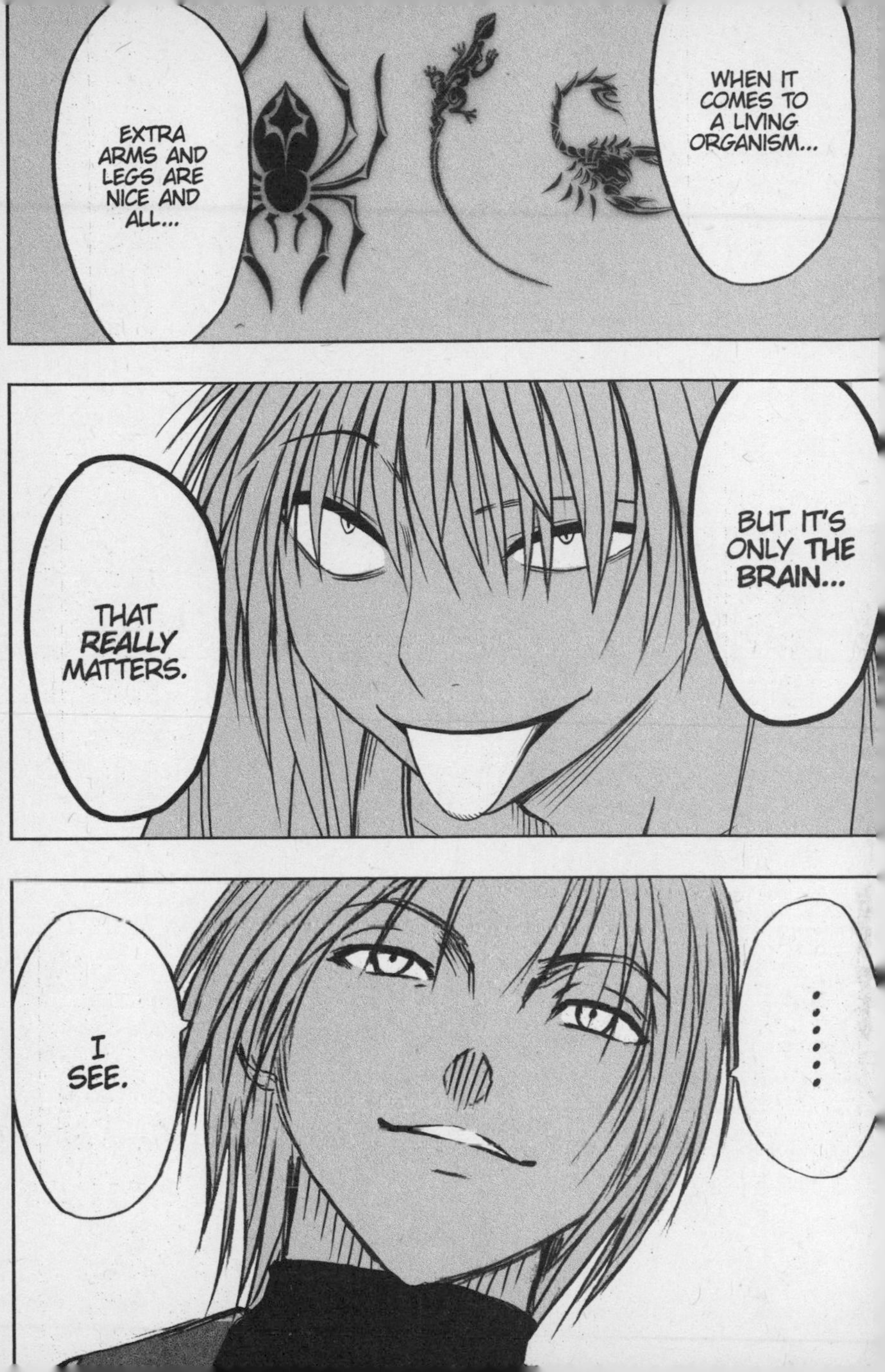
WHEN IT COMES TO A LIVING ORGANISM...
EXTRA ARMS AND LEGS ARE NICE AND ALL...
BUT IT'S ONLY THE BRAIN...
THAT REALLY MATTERS.
......
I SEE.

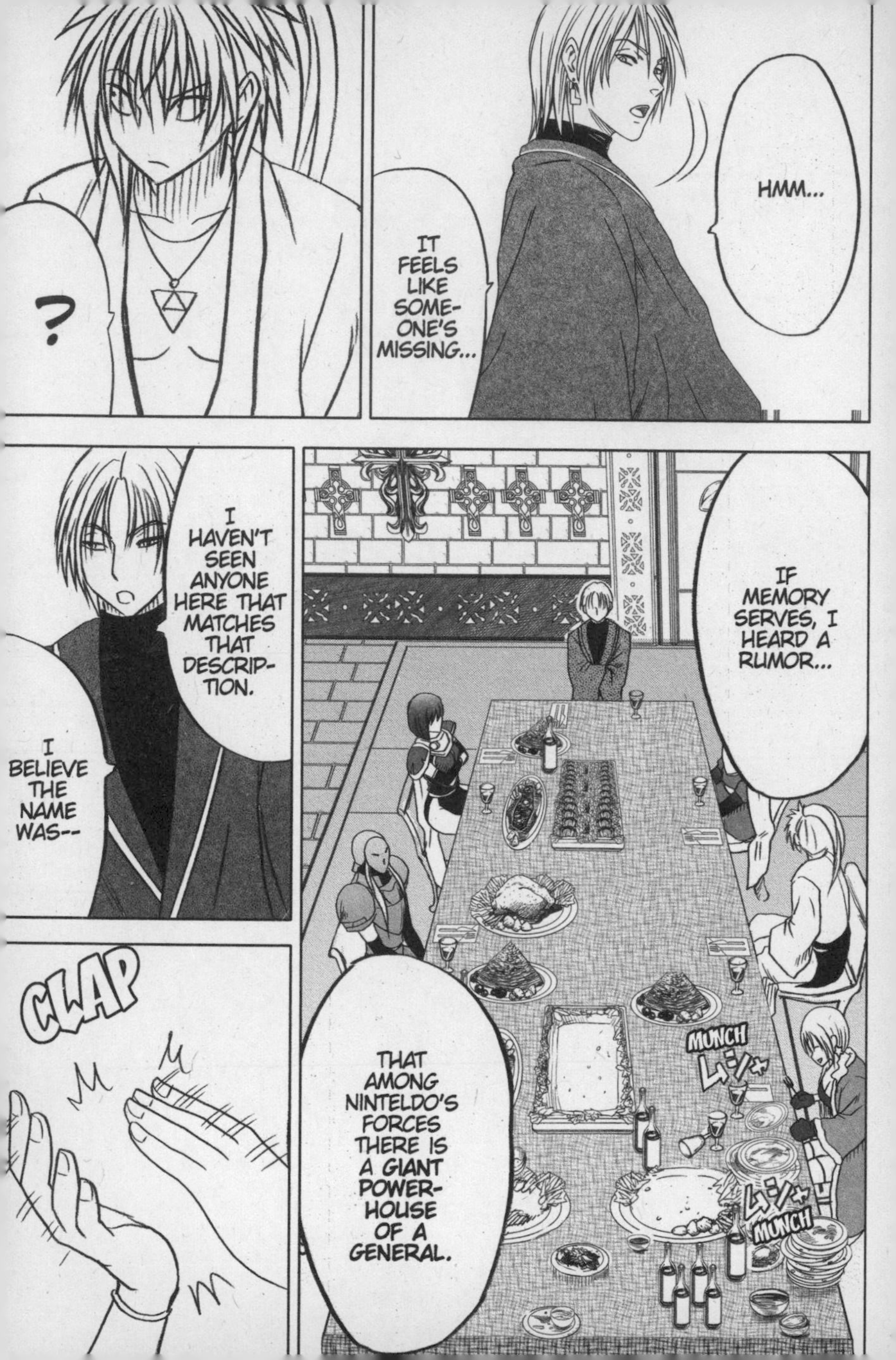
HMM...
IT FEELS LIKE SOME-ONE'S MISSING...
?
IF MEMORY SERVES, I HEARD A RUMOR...
MUNCH
MUNCH
THAT AMONG NINTELDO'S FORCES THERE IS A GIANT POWER-HOUSE OF A GENERAL.
I HAVEN'T SEEN ANYONE HERE THAT MATCHES THAT DESCRIP-TION.
I BELIEVE THE NAME WAS--
CLAP

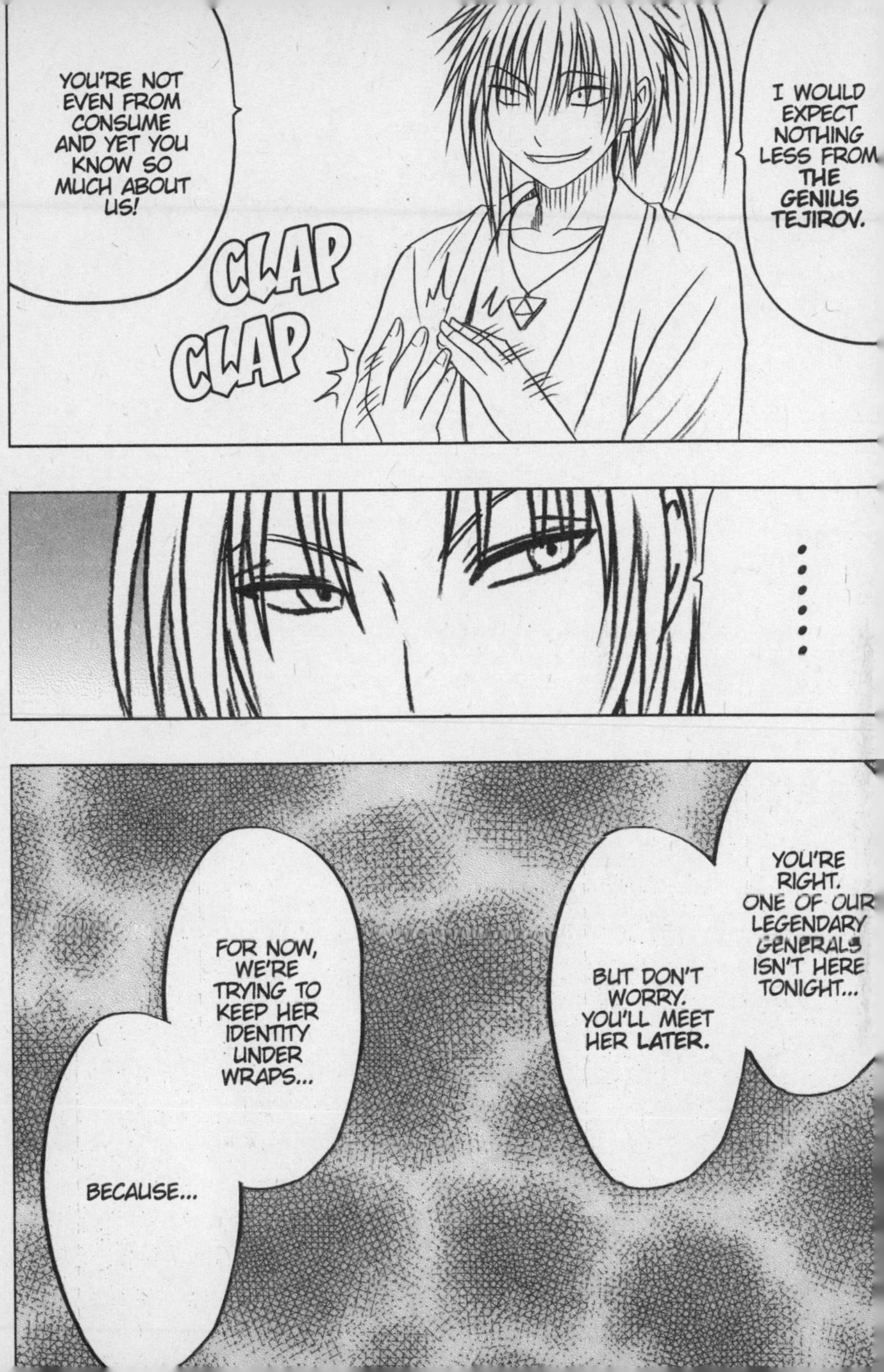
I WOULD EXPECT NOTHING LESS FROM THE GENIUS TEJIROV.
CLAP
CLAP
YOU'RE NOT EVEN FROM CONSUME AND YET YOU KNOW SO MUCH ABOUT US!
......
YOU'RE RIGHT. ONE OF OUR LEGENDARY GENERALS ISN'T HERE TONIGHT...
BUT DON'T WORRY. YOU'LL MEET HER LATER.
FOR NOW, WE'RE TRYING TO KEEP HER IDENTITY UNDER WRAPS...
BECAUSE...

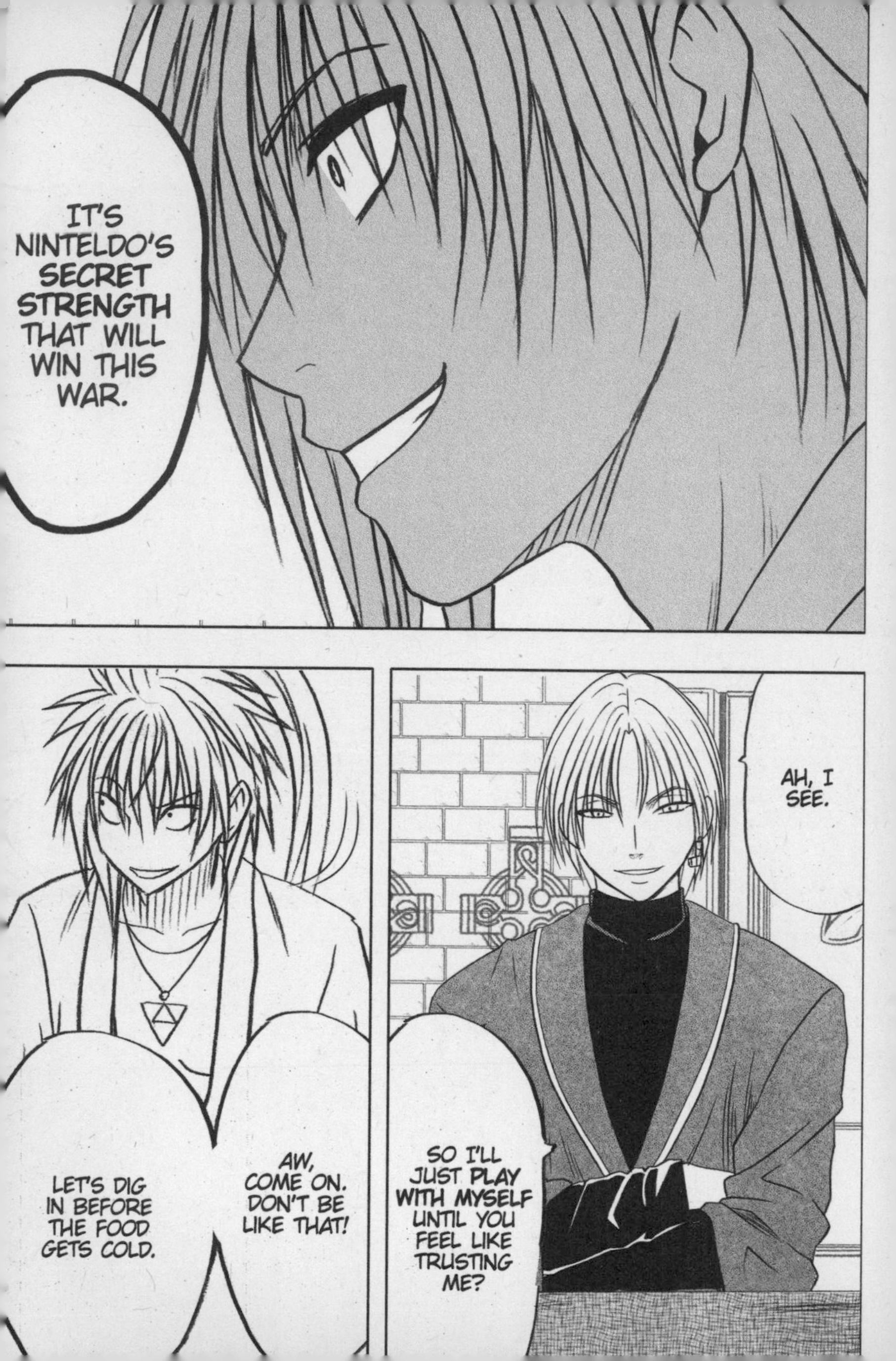
IT'S NINTELDO'S SECRET STRENGTH THAT WILL WIN THIS WAR.
AH, I SEE.
SO I'LL JUST PLAY WITH MYSELF UNTIL YOU FEEL LIKE TRUSTING ME?
AW, COME ON. DON'T BE LIKE THAT!
LET'S DIG IN BEFORE THE FOOD GETS COLD.

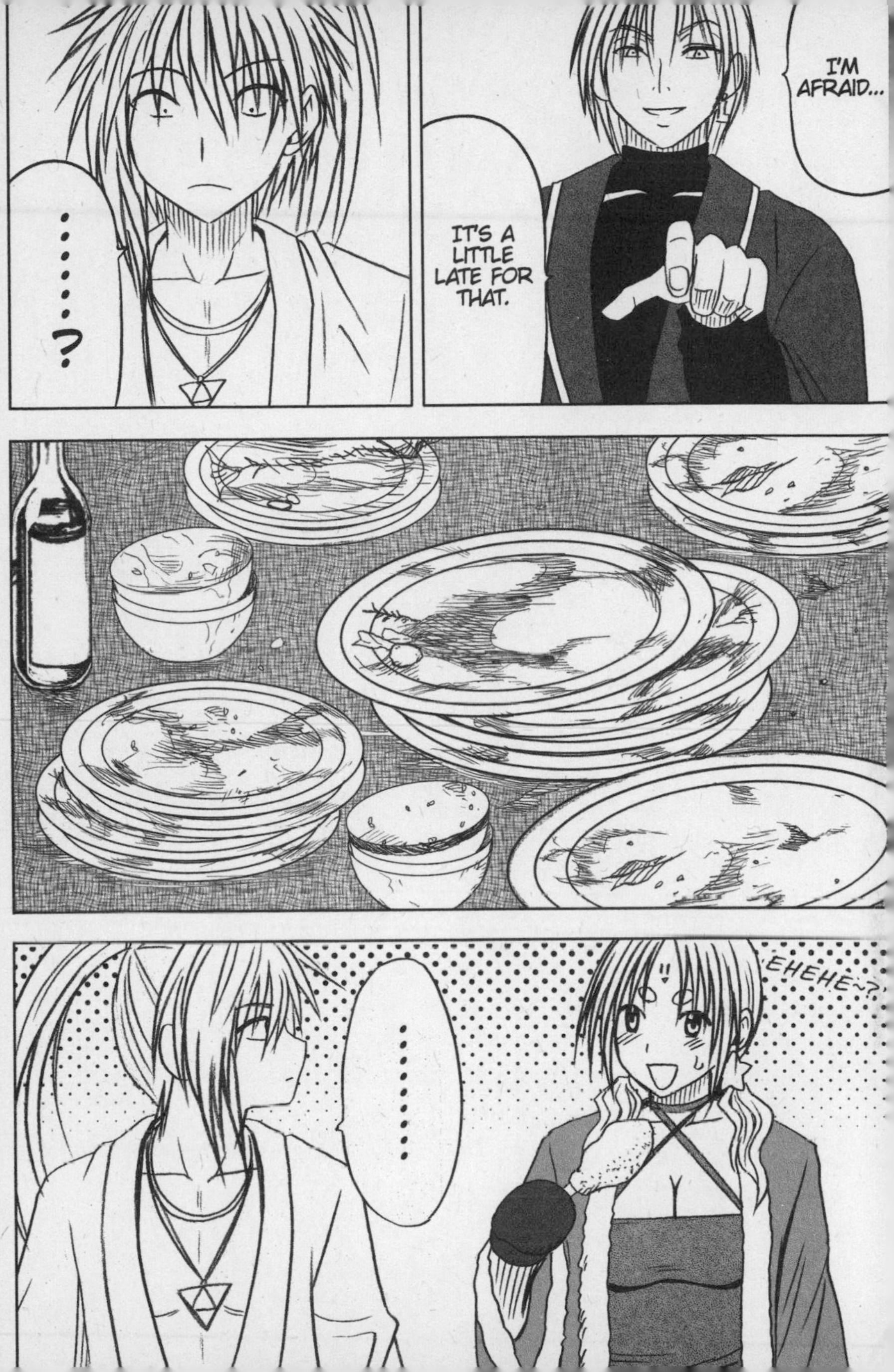
I'M AFRAID...
IT'S A LITTLE LATE FOR THAT.
......?
EHEHE~?
......

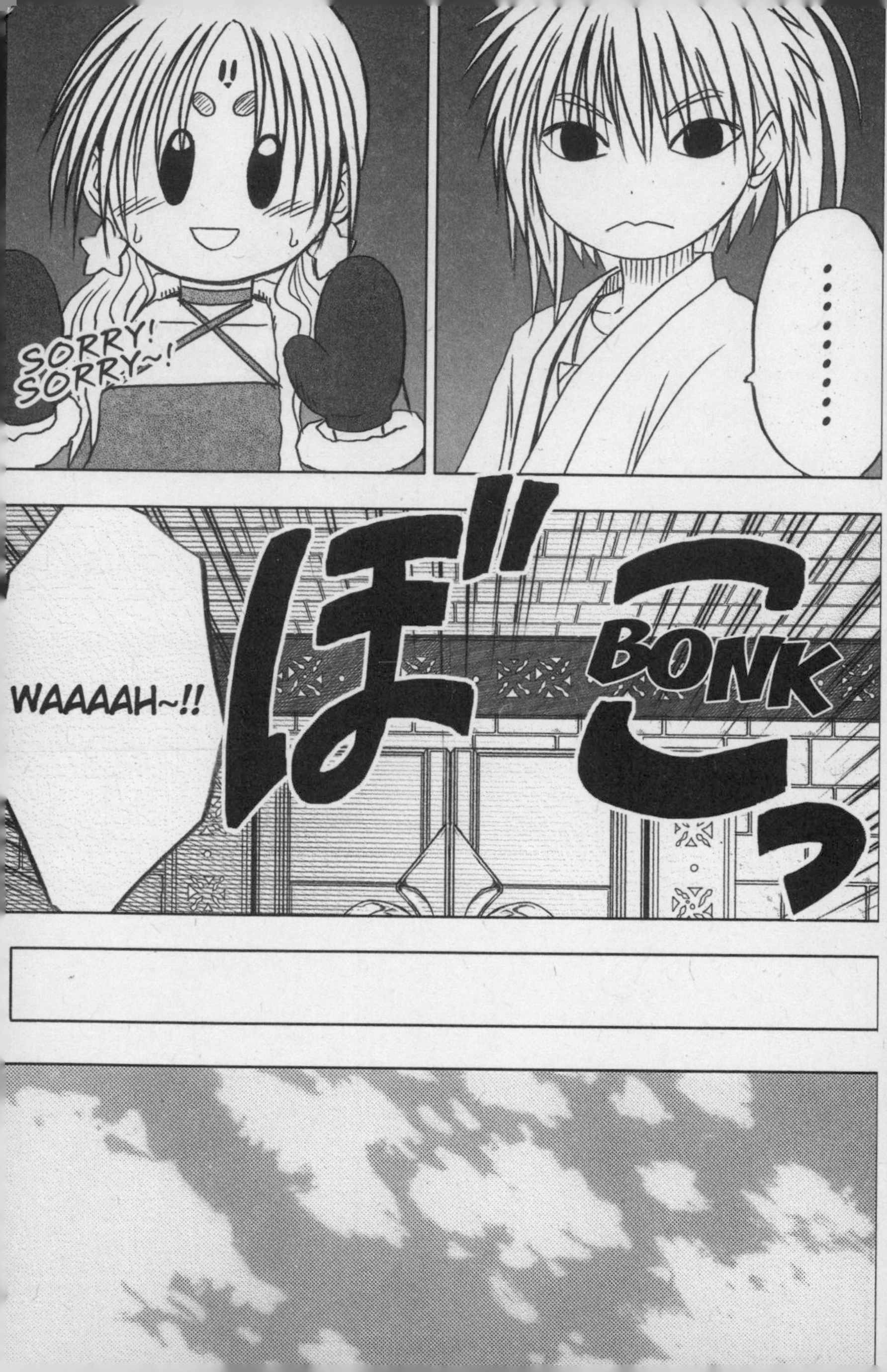

........
SORRY! SORRY~!
ぼこっ
BONK
WAAAAH~!!

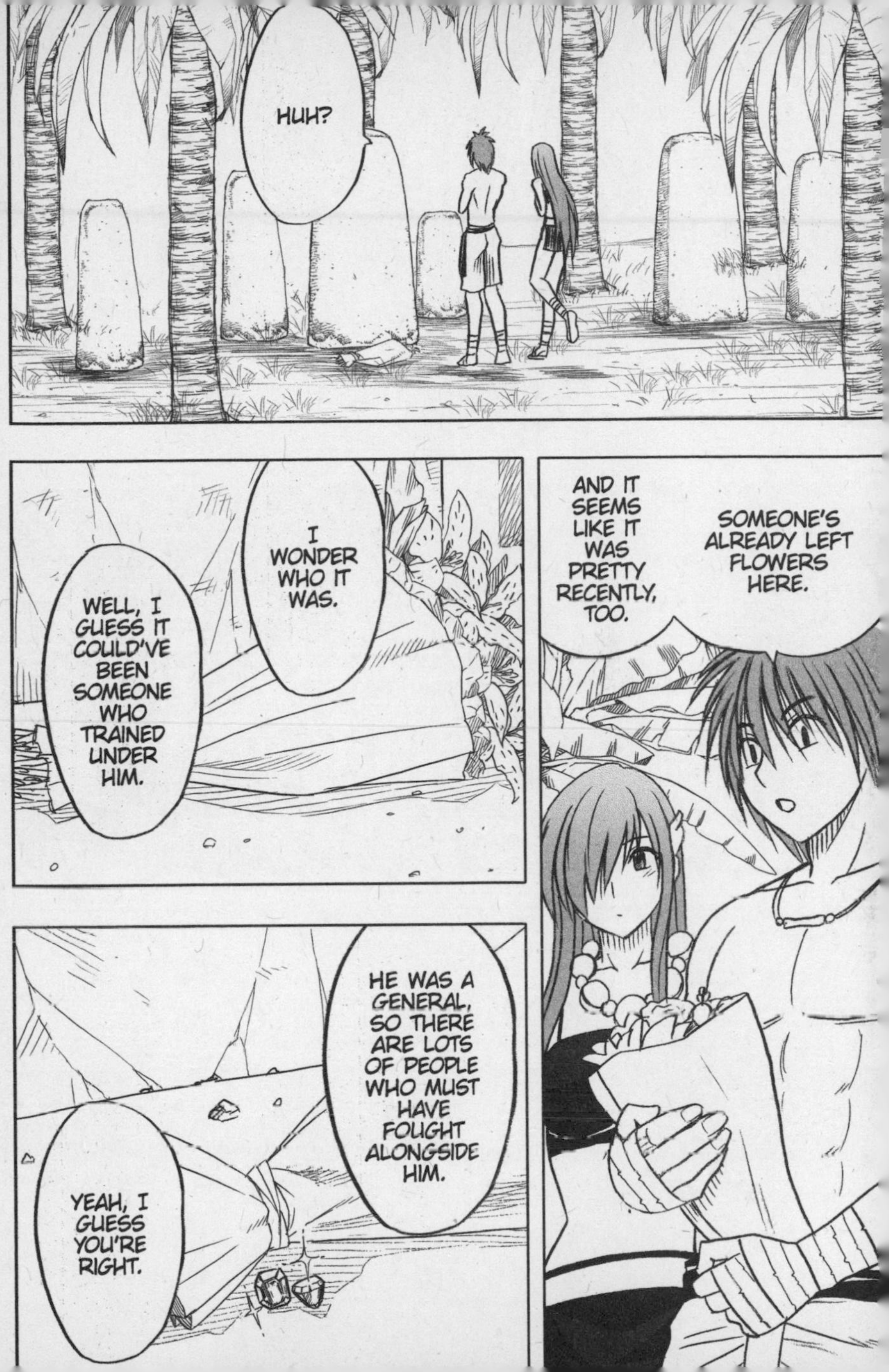
HUH?
SOMEONE'S ALREADY LEFT FLOWERS HERE.
AND IT SEEMS LIKE IT WAS PRETTY RECENTLY, TOO.
I WONDER WHO IT WAS.
WELL, I GUESS IT COULD'VE BEEN SOMEONE WHO TRAINED UNDER HIM.
HE WAS A GENERAL, SO THERE ARE LOTS OF PEOPLE WHO MUST HAVE FOUGHT ALONGSIDE HIM.
YEAH, I GUESS YOU'RE RIGHT.

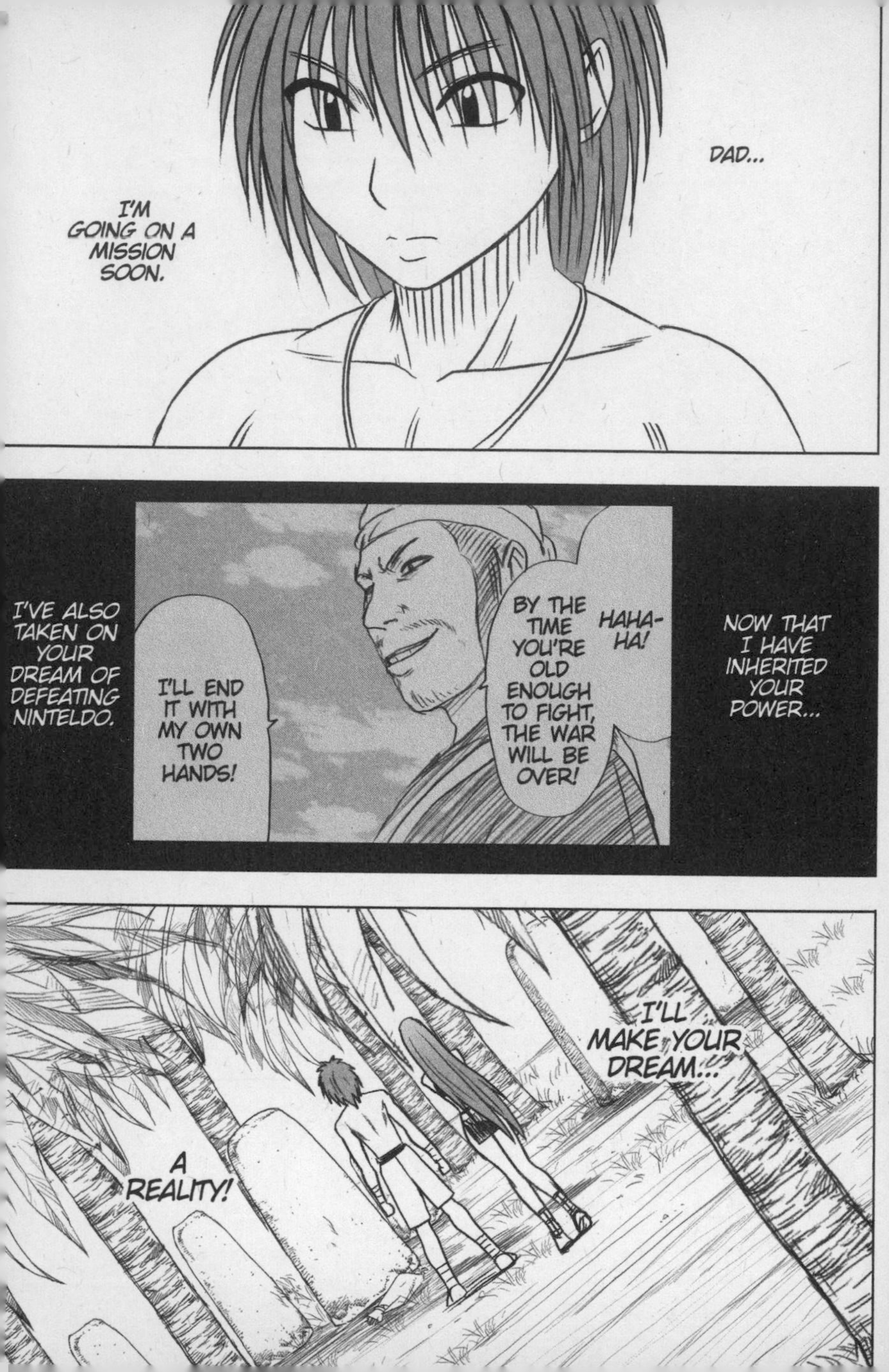
DAD...
I'M GOING ON A MISSION SOON.
NOW THAT I HAVE INHERITED YOUR POWER...
HAHA-HA!
BY THE TIME YOU'RE OLD ENOUGH TO FIGHT, THE WAR WILL BE OVER!
I'LL END IT WITH MY OWN TWO HANDS!
I'VE ALSO TAKEN ON YOUR DREAM OF DEFEATING NINTELDO.
I'LL MAKE YOUR DREAM...
A REALITY!

SINCE YOU ATE ALL THE FOOD, NO DINNER FOR YOU TONIGHT!
I'M SORRY...!☆

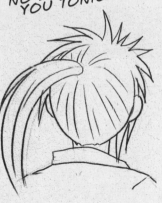

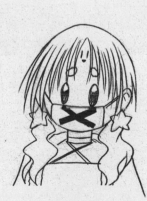

Perusing Video Game History

# ON THE EDGE OF THE BLUE WORLD

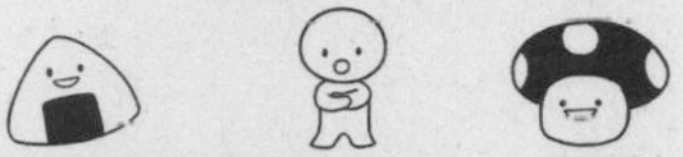

Dr. Onigiri Mr. Why Prof. Mushroom

Today's Topic

## NINTENDO AND TETRIS

**Mr. Why:** Last time we left off on the question of how Nintendo could release *Tetris* on their consoles, when Sega had already bought a license for the game, right?

**Dr. Onigiri:** Uhhh...

**Prof Mushroom:** Well, it is important to look back and study your history.

**Mr. Why:** Well, Sega was the first to license *Tetris*, right?

**Dr. Onigiri:** That's right. Sega bought the license from the game maker in 1988 and released the arcade version of *Tetris* and subsequently, the console version on the Sega Genesis. But... there was a loophole in the license.

**Mr. Why:** A loophole?

**Dr. Onigiri:** The license that Sega bought only covered versions compatible with the IBM computer. It didn't include home consoles. In truth, when Sega bought the license, several companies took advantage of that loophole and things got complicated from there.

**Prof. Mushroom:** Nintendo was the one that really benefited in the end. Once they realized the situation, they approached the parent company, ELORG, and bought the home gaming console license before Sega could.
They went on to make Tetris for the handheld Game Boy in 1989, which was included as a pack-in game in North America. They even added the popular Russian folk song,
Kalinka, in the background. It really fit the game well, improving it
greatly and causing the song to be become synonymous with the game.

**Mr. Why:** They really undermined Sega!

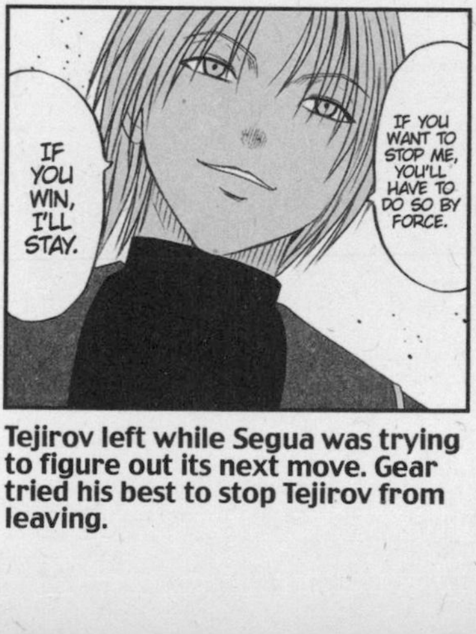
IF YOU WANT TO STOP ME, YOU'LL HAVE TO DO SO BY FORCE.
IF YOU WIN, I'LL STAY.

**Tejirov left while Segua was trying to figure out its next move. Gear tried his best to stop Tejirov from leaving.**

**Prof. Mushroom:** The Nintendo Game Boy sold over 4.2 million units and puzzle games were the biggest seller amongst Game Boy software.

**Dr. Onigiri:** Meanwhile, Sega tried to release their arcade port of *Tetris* on the Sega Mega Drive in Japan, but couldn't. The game wasn't allowed to make it to retail, creating a huge loss for them.

**Mr. Why:** That seems kind of unfair...

**Dr. Onigiri:** Doesn't it?

**Prof. Mushroom:** Foreign licensing can be a tricky beast, and sometimes things don't turn out so well for all the parties involved. Sega had tried to counter with their puzzle game *Columns*, but it could never hold a candle to *Tetris*.

**Dr. Onigiri:** That certainly had to make Sega stop and think.

**Mr. Why:** Nintendo is pretty smart.

**Dr. Onigiri:** Well, it's not that Sega is stupid.

**Prof. Mushroom:** But at least in the case of *Tetris*, Nintendo came out ahead and got themselves another killer title.

**Mr. Why:** Nintendo sure has a lot of killer games.

**Prof. Mushroom:** We've even talked about some of them such as the pinnacle of Puzzle Solving Action Games: *The Legend of Zelda*, the story of Mario and Luigi in *Super Mario Bros.*, and the cute little pink ball that can eat just about everything, *Kirby*. But those aren't Nintendo's only heavy hitters...

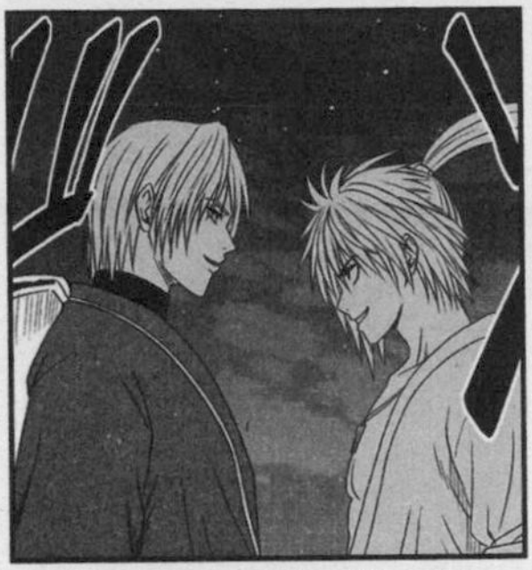

**Tejirov coming to Ninteldo from Segua. What are his true intentions?**

**Mr. Why:** Wow! They have even more?

**Prof. Mushroom:** Indeed they do. First off, they have the notoriously difficult RPG, *Fire Emblem*. I believe we've mentioned that in a previous volume, didn't we? It was a pioneer fantasy simulation game for home consoles.

**Mr. Why:** Simu...? Fire... Em...

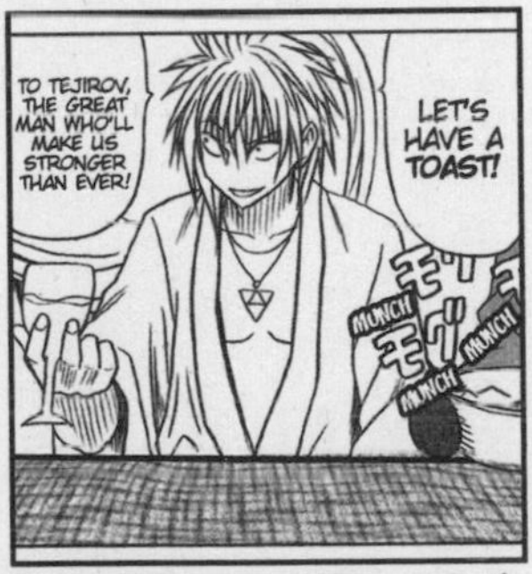
TO TEJIROV, THE GREAT MAN WHO'LL MAKE US STRONGER THAN EVER!
LET'S HAVE A TOAST!
MUNCH
MUNCH
MUNCH

**The genius swordsman, Zelig, known for his intelligence throughout Consume. He never loses when it comes to mind games.**

**Mr. Why:** What then?! *What then?!*

**Prof. Mushroom:** Well, um, let's see... in the game you could go around and kill enemies, which is always fun. Then, there was this...

**Dr. Onigiri:** Stop! That's all the time we have! Don't forget, Sega made games too! See you next time!

To be continued...

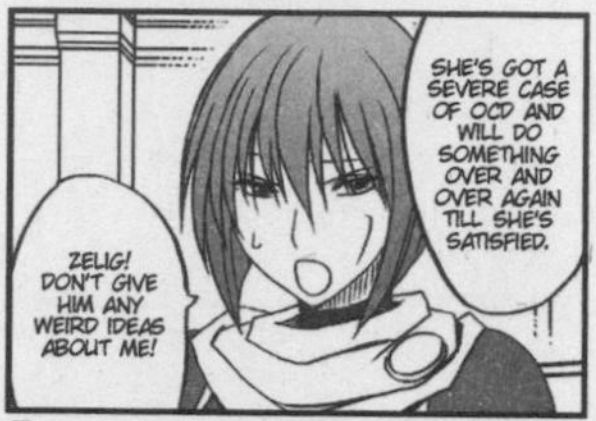

SHE'S GOT A SEVERE CASE OF OCD AND WILL DO SOMETHING OVER AND OVER AGAIN TILL SHE'S SATISFIED.
ZELIG! DON'T GIVE HIM ANY WEIRD IDEAS ABOUT ME!


**Fae, a very difficult person. She is also quite a capable dragon trainer.**

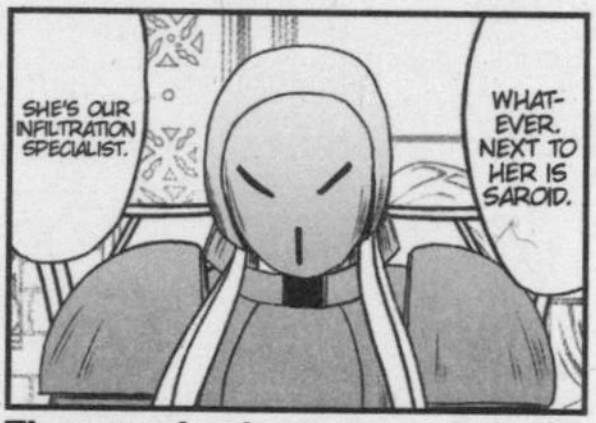

WHAT-EVER. NEXT TO HER IS SAROID.
SHE'S OUR INFILTRATION SPECIALIST.


**The masked woman, Saroid. You never really see her face, but rumor has it she's a blonde.**

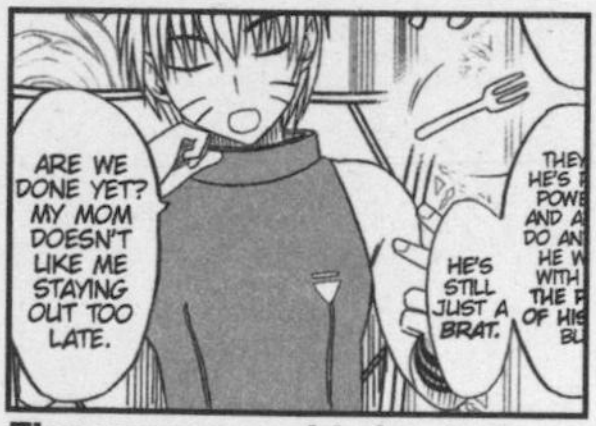

HE'S STILL JUST A BRAT.
ARE WE DONE YET? MY MOM DOESN'T LIKE ME STAYING OUT TOO LATE.


**The young and talented general Masa. He seems to be a mama's boy...**

Emooboolemoo? That's hard to read...

**Prof. Mushroom:** Emblem is pronounced "Em-blem." As for a simulation RPG... it's kind of like Shōgi (Japanese Chess) where all the pieces have hit points. There's money and you can have your units walk on the field. You can also exchange which units you want to use in battle. When you capture or defeat the enemy's leader, you clear the mission. Each piece represents a character or unit. There could be a dragon or a knight, or various other fantasy based characters, that's why it's called a fantasy simulation.

**Mr. Why:** Oh, okay. I get it.

**Prof. Mushroom:** *Fire Emblem* is quite difficult. I reset the game time and time again whenever a character died.

**Dr. Onigiri:** Expanding your knowledge of strategy and tactics is the fun part of those kinds of games. Sega even had their own fantasy simulation, *Bahamut Senki ("War Chronicles of Bahamut").*

**Prof. Mushroom:** Moving on! Nintendo also had the really popular 2D action-adventure game, *Metroid,* where you control a character named Samus Aran. Just an FYI, but Samus wore a full body suit, so you couldn't tell if you were playing a boy or a girl. Turns out Samus was actually a girl.

**Mr. Why:** And then?! What else?!

**Prof. Mushroom:** Then in 1989, Nintendo released another popular series on the Famicom called *Mother.* In this game, you controlled a young boy from the United States who had powerful psychic abilities. You would heal by eating your mom's home cooking and it was a game that centered heavily on a maternal figure. Its sequel, *Mother 2,* was released in North America as *Earthbound.*

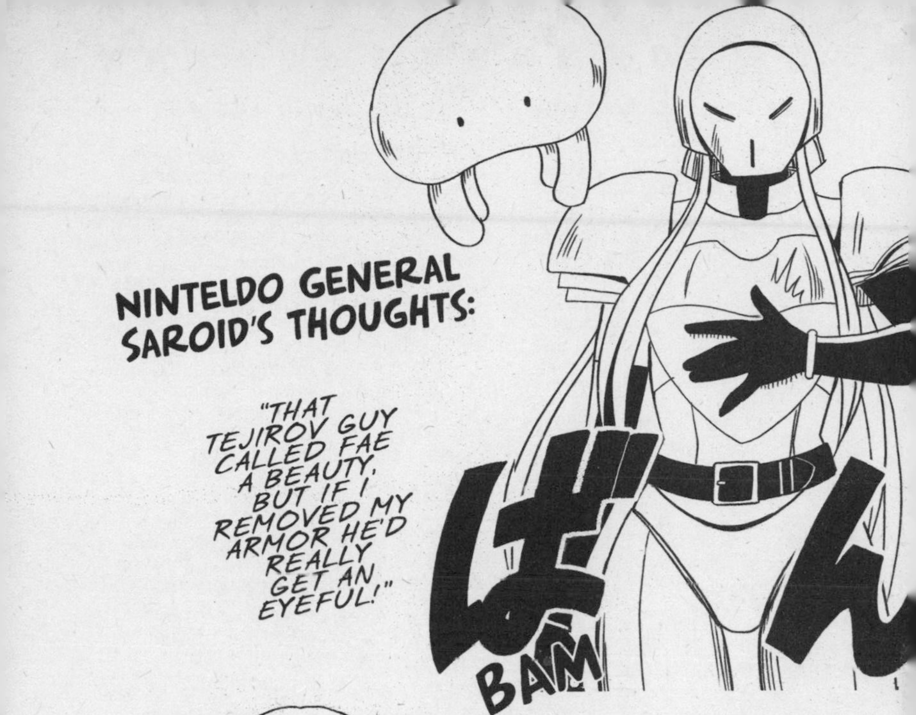
NINTELDO GENERAL SAROID'S THOUGHTS:
"THAT TEJIROV GUY CALLED FAE A BEAUTY, BUT IF I REMOVED MY ARMOR HE'D REALLY GET AN EYEFUL!"
ばん
BAM
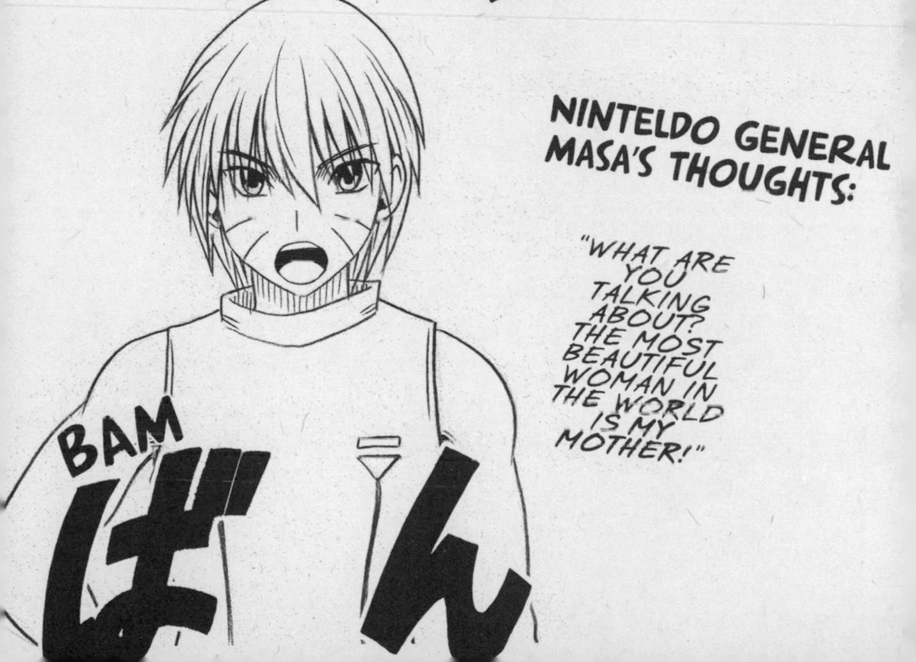
NINTELDO GENERAL MASA'S THOUGHTS:
"WHAT ARE YOU TALKING ABOUT? THE MOST BEAUTIFUL WOMAN IN THE WORLD IS MY MOTHER!"
BAM
ばん

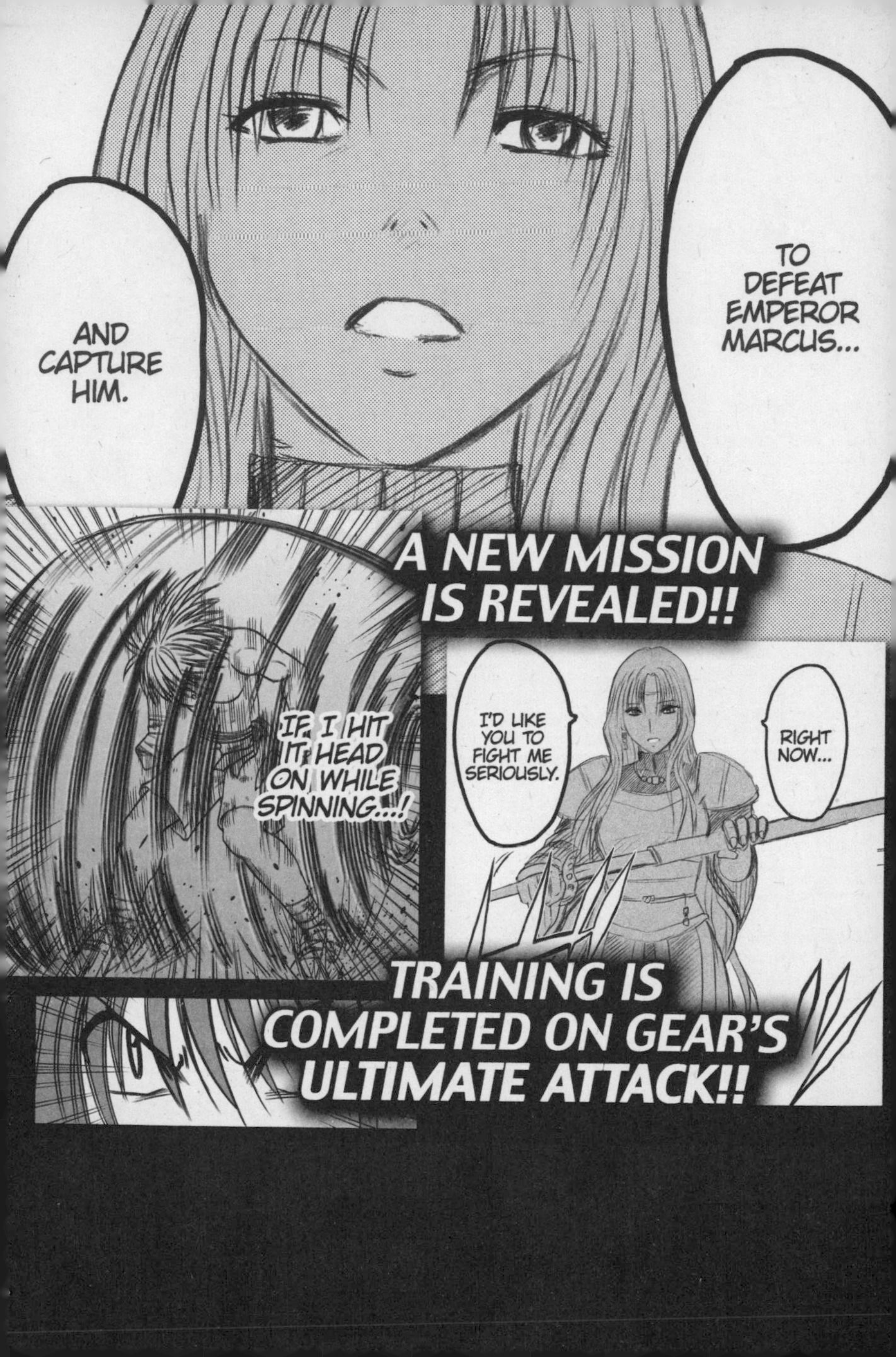
TO DEFEAT EMPEROR MARCUS...
AND CAPTURE HIM.
A NEW MISSION IS REVEALED!!
RIGHT NOW...
I'D LIKE YOU TO FIGHT ME SERIOUSLY.
IF I HIT IT HEAD ON WHILE SPINNING...!
TRAINING IS COMPLETED ON GEAR'S ULTIMATE ATTACK!!

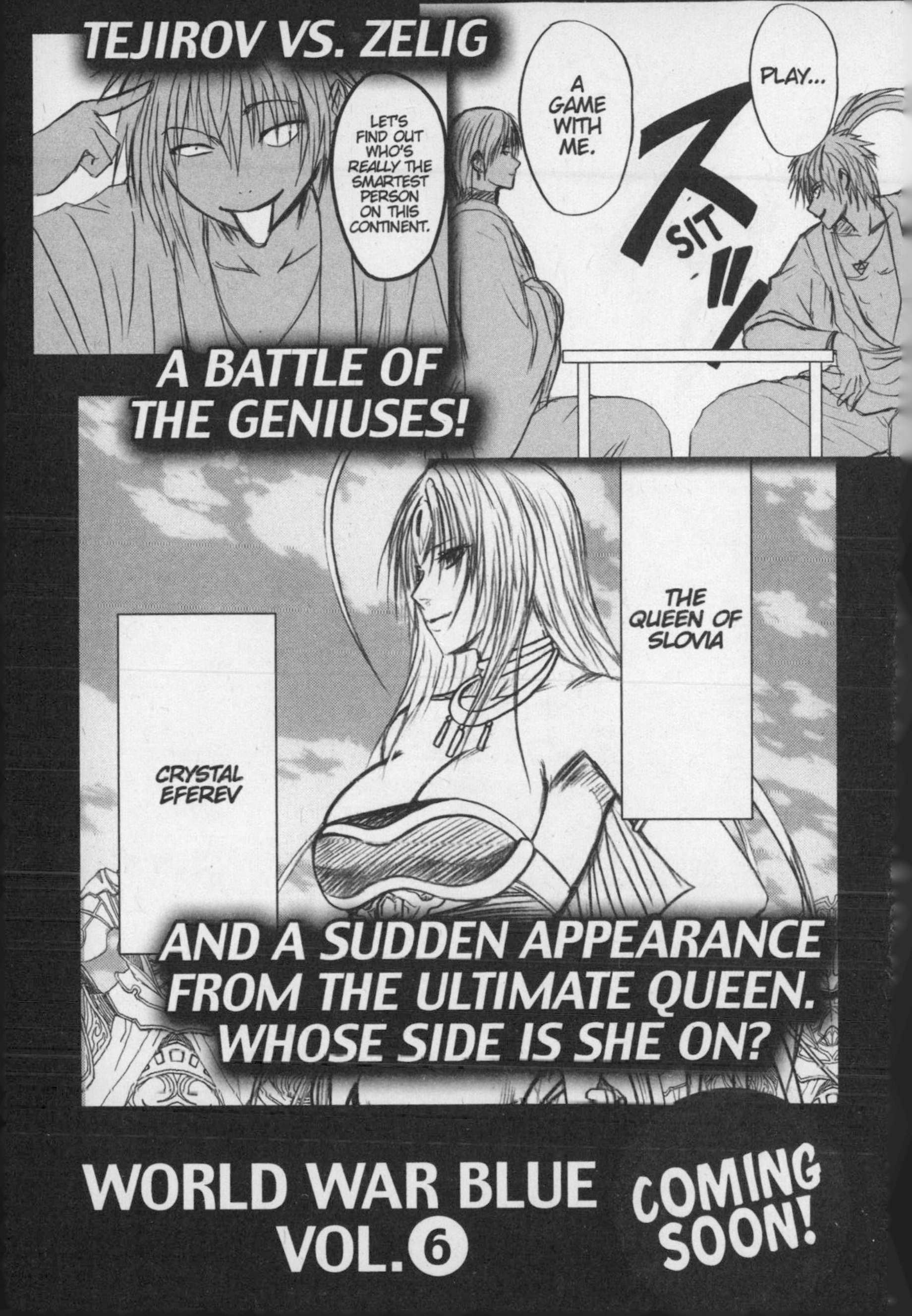
TEJIROV VS. ZELIG
PLAY...
A GAME WITH ME.
SIT
LET'S FIND OUT WHO'S REALLY THE SMARTEST PERSON ON THIS CONTINENT.
A BATTLE OF THE GENIUSES!
THE QUEEN OF SLOVIA
CRYSTAL EFEREV
AND A SUDDEN APPEARANCE FROM THE ULTIMATE QUEEN. WHOSE SIDE IS SHE ON?

WORLD WAR BLUE VOL. 6

COMING SOON!

SEVEN SEAS ENTERTAINMENT PRESENTS

# WORLD WAR BLUE

### art by CRIMSON / story by ANASTASIA SHESTAKOVA    VOLUME 5

TRANSLATION
**Wesley Bridges**

ADAPTATION
**Shannon Fay**

LETTERING AND LAYOUT
**Laura Scoville**

LOGO DESIGN
**Courtney Williams**

COVER DESIGN
**Nicky Lim**

PROOFREADER
**Janet Houck**
**Conner Crooks**

MANAGING EDITOR
**Adam Arnold**

PUBLISHER
**Jason DeAngelis**

AOI SEKAI NO CHUSINDE KANZENBAN VOL. 5
© 2011 ANASTASIA SHESTAKOVA / © 2011 CRIMSON
This edition originally published in Japan in 2011 by
MICROMAGAZINE PUBLISHING CO., Tokyo. English translation rights
arranged with MICROMAGAZINE PUBLISHING CO., Tokyo through
TOHAN CORPORATION, Tokyo.

Seven Seas books may be purchased in bulk for educational, business, or
promotional use. For information on bulk purchases, please contact Macmillan
Corporate & Premium Sales Department at 1-800-221-7945 (ext 5442)
or write specialmarkets@macmillan.com.

Seven Seas and the Seven Seas logo are trademarks of
Seven Seas Entertainment, LLC. All rights reserved.

ISBN: 978-1-626920-13-2

Printed in Canada

First Printing: April 2014

10 9 8 7 6 5 4 3 2 1

FOLLOW US ONLINE: **www.gomanga.com**

# READING DIRECTIONS

This book reads from *right to left*, Japanese style.
If this is your first time reading manga, you start
reading from the top right panel on each page and
take it from there. If you get lost, just follow the
numbered diagram here. It may seem backwards at
first, but you'll get the hang of it! Have fun!!

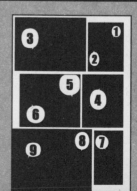